Blackness in Opera

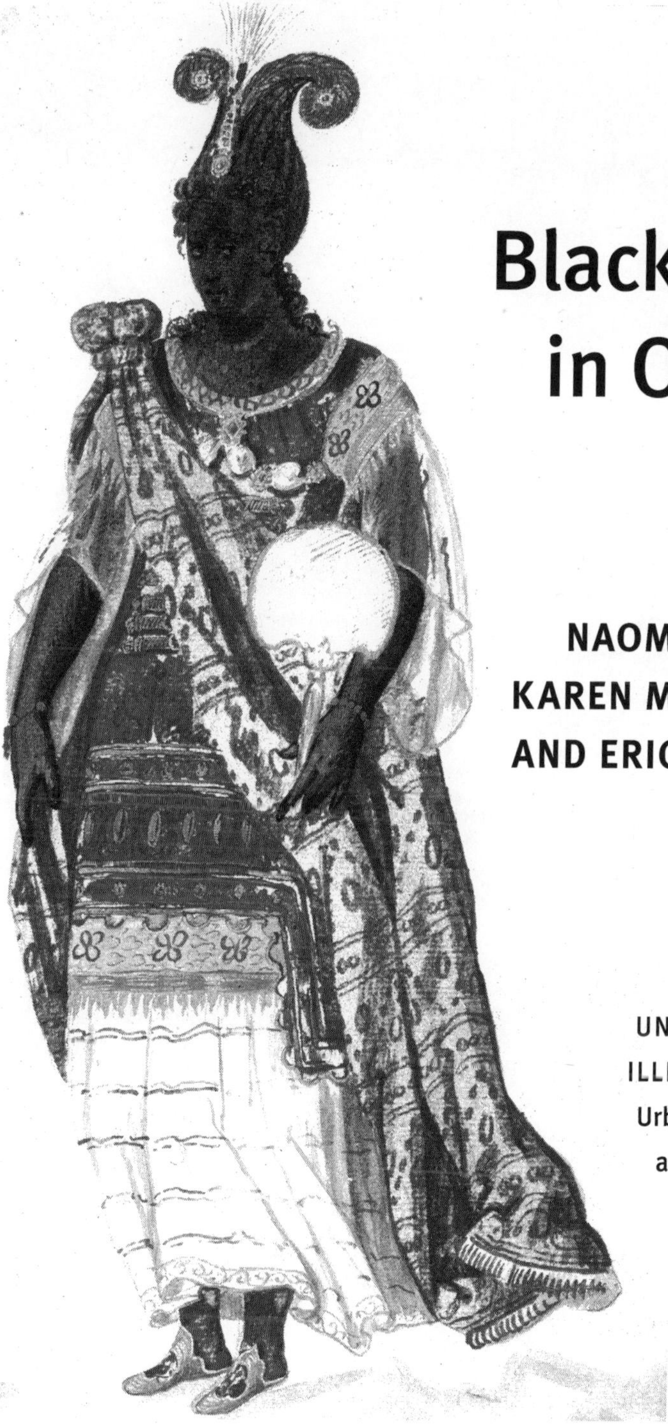

Blackness in Opera

Edited by
NAOMI ANDRÉ,
KAREN M. BRYAN,
AND ERIC SAYLOR

UNIVERSITY OF
ILLINOIS PRESS
Urbana, Chicago,
and Springfield

First Illinois paperback, 2014

♾ This book is printed on acid-free paper.

Publication of this book was supported by grants from the Henry and Edna Binkele Classical Music Fund; the Office of the Vice President for Research at the University of Michigan, Ann Arbor; the Publications Endowment of the American Musicological Society, supported through the National Endowment for the Humanities; and Friends of Drake Arts, Drake University.

Frontispiece: Inigo Jones, costume for daughters of Niger, *The Masque of Blackness.* © Devonshire Collection, Chatsworth. Reproduced by permission of Chatsworth Settlement Trustees.

The Library of Congress cataloged the cloth edition as follows:
Blackness in opera / edited by Naomi André, Karen M. Bryan, and Eric Saylor.
p. cm.
Includes bibliographical references and index.
ISBN 978-0-252-03678-1 (hardcover : alk. paper) —
ISBN 978-0-252-09389-0 (e-book)
1. Blacks in opera. 2. Opera.
I. André, Naomi Adele. II. Bryan, Karen M. (Karen McGaha).
III. Saylor, Eric.
ML1700.B53 2012
782.1089'96—dc23 2011027787

PAPERBACK ISBN 978-0-252-08043-2

This collection is dedicated
to the memory of
Catherine Parsons Smith

Contents

Foreword: Singing in the Dark ix
Guthrie P. Ramsey Jr.

Preface xi

Introduction: Representing Blackness on the Operatic Stage 1

1. From Otello to Porgy: Blackness, Masculinity, and Morality in Opera 11
Naomi André

2. Hearing the Other in *The Masque of Blackness* 32
Sarah Schmalenberger

3. Nationalism, Racial Difference, and "Egyptian" Meaning in Verdi's *Aida* 55
Christopher R. Gauthier and Jennifer McFarlane-Harris

4. Race, "Realism," and Fate in Frederick Delius's *Koanga* 78
Eric Saylor

5. Political Currents and Black Culture in Scott Joplin's *Treemonisha* 101
Ann Sears

6. Clarence Cameron White's *Ouanga!* in the World of the Harlem Renaissance 116
Karen M. Bryan

7. New Paradigms in William Grant Still's *Blue Steel* 141
Gayle Murchison

8. Performers in Catfish Row: *Porgy and Bess* as Collaboration 164
Gwynne Kuhner Brown

9. Searching for "Authenticity" in Paul Bowles's *Denmark Vesey* 187
Melissa J. de Graaf

10. The Politics of Color in Oscar Hammerstein's *Carmen Jones* 212
Melinda Boyd

11. Performing Race in Ernst Krenek's *Jonny spielt auf* 236
Jonathan O. Wipplinger

12. Il Rodolfo Nero, or The Masque of Blackness 260
George Shirley

Contributors 275

Index 279

FOREWORD

Singing in the Dark

GUTHRIE P. RAMSEY JR.

The present collection of essays attempts to identify and theorize the various ways in which the idea of blackness has worked as a practice—as a complex of representational strategies in the genre of opera. Taken as a single body of work, they do not present a unified theoretical voice, but like the practice of blackness itself, these essays forward complex ideas about race, humanity, and creativity, some familiar and others newly found and sharp around the edges. As the editors' introduction indicates, *Blackness in Opera* seeks to denaturalize some of the conventions that have governed blackness's presence in opera. What we learn from the diversity of approaches in this collection is that something called an "Africanist" presence represents an enduring and—judging from the historical sweep of this project—notoriously unstable set of assumptions, ploys, signs, and compositional strategies.

This collection is staged in a rich, interdisciplinary arena of study that contemplates race as a unit of analysis in expressive culture. Scholars of literature from all destinations in the African diaspora have provided us with powerful theories and ruminations, detailing rich ways to interpret issues of power, identity, and culture in the written word. Art historians of this same Africanist presence have given us new ways to "see" difference, myth, ritual, and all manner of structures of feeling in artworks whose categories range from representational to abstract, conceptual, and performance. And music scholars have attended to blackness with a particularly keen interest in what qualitative sensibilities may or may not have been passed along its often violent and certainly multifarious routes of dispersion, settlement, and stunning transformation and development.

My hope for this collection is that it will become a complementary treatise for Samuel A. Floyd's landmark study *The Power of Black Music* (1995). Floyd's perceptive study, as we know, provides a historical account of how "the presence" has informed the development of myriad genres, specifically in the American musical landscape. *The Power of Black Music* together with Ronald M. Radano's *Lying Up a Nation* (2003) form bookends to a critical space that defines the historical and material grounding of what might be called a black musical nationalism specific to the United States. *Blackness in Opera,* while casting a wider geographical net perhaps, fills in some of the blanks by taking into account the role that codes from opera might offer the conversation.

It has long been established that operatic conventions have reinforced our knowledge about the gendered dimensions of sound organization in Western art music. As this collection instructs, opera's gender-specific assignment of musical procedure can serve as an important model for understanding how race and other social meanings derived from and contextualized within musical practice. The focus on race and opera, then, particularly the essays on the New World, shows yet again how we—black, white, and others—have been conditioned, as Langston Hughes said, to "sing America" in the dark, in harmony and dissonance.

With the publication of *Blackness in Opera,* the cultural studies turn in black music scholarship expands into new sound worlds, ones previously understudied due to the force and richness of research on blues, jazz, rock and roll, hip-hop, and dance forms. Nevertheless, these essays provide further and powerful evidence of the historical processes of "naturalization" that have linked black social history to sound organization.

In an important departure from "vernacular" music studies, the composers under consideration here are treated as making conscious artistic decisions with their materials. This consideration lays out a desired avenue to examine constructions of musical blackness without the claptrap of biological essentialism—a wearisome perception that in the past has dogged the realm of vernacular music. What is presented here, rather, is a set of nuanced studies that value creative agency, center social meaning, and plunge headfirst into the sounds of art music, a world in which pool dark waters, vital, deep, and revealing.

Preface

When we decided to undertake the editing duties for this collection, it is fair to say that we did so with a combination of excitement and trepidation. Excitement, because we had all conducted research related to opera and blackness, and agreed that this was an area of compelling scholarly possibilities that had not yet been addressed in any major forum. Yet given our backgrounds and primary interests (a white southern woman specializing in Italian and American music, a biracial New Yorker known for her work on opera and gender, and a white male from the upper Midwest active in British musical studies), we felt an unlikely trio to spearhead such a project. But during the time we have worked on this collection, we have seen some rather unlikely events. Certainly, the election of the first black president of the United States stands near the top of such a list—all the more so when one considers that his early momentum came from winning the caucuses in Iowa, a state whose population is about 90 percent white. At the same time, however, affirmative action policies of the mid– to late twentieth century that came out of the civil rights era are being rethought and, in some cases, repealed, while anti-immigrant sentiments and legislation sweep the nation—showing that we are very far indeed from realizing the dream of a racially nondiscriminatory society. As Americans, we belong to a society inextricably bound to and shaped by racial politics and culture, and so we bear a certain responsibility to approach the topic in a thoughtful and considered manner—a goal that we and our fellow contributors to this volume hope that we have achieved.

On a more personal note, however, we are very fortunate that many of our collaborators have realized their own dreams over the course of this project: four tenure promotions, one Ph.D. completed, eight children who have entered our homes (including one adoption), two grandchildren (and one great-grandchild!), three marriages, and seven job changes, all of which have shaped the daily rhythms of our lives. We are grateful to all of those who signed on to this collection for their great efforts, their greater patience, and their estimable contributions.

Several people have encouraged and helped us along the way. Foremost among them is our editor at the press, Laurie Matheson; we are extremely grateful for her belief in this project from its inception and her thoughtful shepherding of us. The generous subventions provided by the Henry and Edna Binkele Classical Music Fund, the Office of the Vice President for Research at the University of Michigan, the American Musicological Society, and the Friends of Drake Arts have been invaluable, and we appreciate their faith in the value of our work. We would also like to recognize our anonymous reviewers who have given us very helpful advice at key points in the process, as well as one reviewer who chose to have her identity made known to us from the beginning: Catherine Parsons Smith. Her encouragement of many of us involved with this project individually as scholars (as well as with this essay collection specifically) has been a great treasure. It is from our deep appreciation of the example she set in her pioneering work and her many friendships that we miss her and why we wish to dedicate to her this collection of essays. Though she did not live to see its completion, she had a great hand in shaping this volume early on, and we cherish the memory of her vast goodwill.

Finally, we would like to thank our families and those closest to us who have seen us through the unglamorous process of writing, editing, and pulling things together. Your support, as always, gives us the incentive to keep forging ahead.

Blackness in Opera

INTRODUCTION

Representing Blackness on the Operatic Stage

Despite notable scholarly contributions over the past few decades, the issue of race still presents significant hurdles for many musicologists. This may be due in part to issues raised by the theoretical approach Toni Morrison advanced in *Playing in the Dark: Whiteness and the Literary Imagination* (1992). Much as Edward Said's *Orientalism* (1978) implored readers to examine how the West's view of the East is fraught with subordinating power relationships, Morrison analyzes what she calls the "Africanist" presence in American literature. This Africanist presence refers to, in her words, "the denotative and connotative blackness that African peoples have come to signify, as well as the entire range of views, assumptions, readings, and misreadings that accompany Eurocentric learning about these people."[1] In scholarly arenas like musicology that have long emphasized traditions and practices derived primarily from white or Western European cultures (or both), Morrison's "Africanist" paradigm obliges researchers to rethink established opinions on race in new and often challenging ways.

This is not to suggest that such approaches to the subject of race are absent from the scholarly musicological literature. Samuel Floyd, Guthrie Ramsey, Ronald Radano, and Philip Bohlman, among others, have helped establish a variety of methodologies and models for addressing the issue of race within musical scholarship, particularly regarding the African American diaspora in the United States.[2] Their array of case studies and theoretical frameworks for dealing with race and music led us to consider applying such perspectives within a single genre: opera. Opera's enduring and wide-ranging popularity, rich traditions of artistic collaboration and exchange, diversity of styles, and ability to blur the lines between cultivated and vernacular forms of art make questions about the intersections between race, ethnicity, and identity within that genre both trenchant and valuable.

The exploration of these topics forms the backdrop for most of the essays within this collection. Featuring a cross-section of scholars working in musicology, cultural studies, sociology, German literature, women's studies, and African American studies, this project brings a wide range of strategies and philosophies to the central theme of how "blackness" is constructed in opera. Our goal is to explore how blackness has been represented and perceived by presenting new readings of both canonical and lesser-known operas by black and nonblack composers alike—addressing what is at stake with such representations, exploring what meanings they had in their original contexts, and examining what kind of performative and cultural significance they have retained. Our focus on blackness does not, of course, preclude considering how other types of racial and ethnic differences are presented in opera generally. But the colonization of Africa and (especially for those operas that involve the United States) the repercussions of slavery provide a particular set of power relationships unique to defining a black experience, which in turn can manifest in arenas often deemed more entertaining than political, such as music.

Consider, for example, the simple act of "blacking up," the stage practice of applying dark makeup—often, though not exclusively, by white performers—in order to "pass" as a black or dark-skinned character (as often seen with the title characters in *Otello* or *Aida*, though several other operatic characters have traditionally received similar treatment).[3] The opera stage is perhaps the only space in American culture today where such overt racial imitation is routinely performed without comment or query. Such a practice is all the more unusual when one recalls that the other major historical forum for blackface portrayals in America—a nation where race occupies a uniquely problematic cultural position—was the minstrel show, a locus for the establishment and reinforcement of the many negative stereotypes aimed at African Americans (for example, as lazy, ignorant, violent, hypersexualized, conniving buffoons). While today it is tempting to dismiss these genres' shared use of blackface as coincidental and unrelated in terms of actual practice—perhaps based on grounds of high versus low art, or on changing attitudes about race and racism, or on distinctions between representing a character and playing to a stereotype—the vast scholarship on minstrelsy, which focuses on the genre's construction and negotiation of many complicated signs of racial and cultural difference (both in America and overseas), suggests otherwise.[4] The historical popularity of minstrelsy presents another formative factor for the reception of black performers by audiences and the fashioning of black characters and performers in opera, and even in the development of an operatic tradition in the United States.

In fact, as a dynamic nexus of popular and highbrow theater, minstrelsy provided diverse opportunities for black and white performers alike. For white performers, it provided a point of mimicry and domination, as well as a transgressive and socially uninhibited space for embodying the Other. The shows themselves appealed to white audiences by invoking elements of nostalgia for an imagined past (for example, benevolent slaveholders and peaceful plantations with happy workers). Minstrelsy did, of course, entail greater challenges for black performers who donned the burnt cork, obliged as they were to present horrendous stereotypes that systemically reinforced notions of white superiority and models for self-deprecation. Ironically, however, minstrelsy's grotesque imitations of black life also provided black performers with one of the earliest socially acceptable public spaces (and often the only one) for professional musicianship. Given the limited public performance venues deemed appropriate or suitable for African Americans prior to the latter half of the twentieth century, it is not surprising that many black performers who might have been involved with opera were funneled into minstrelsy.[5]

Indeed, minstrel companies, touring concert companies, and black opera companies became intertwined, as performers sang with all three groups as performing opportunities arose. (The close relationship among them is reflected by one of the nicknames for minstrelsy popularized during Reconstruction: "black opera.") Traveling minstrel troupes would often perform on the same stages where touring opera companies were featured, whether this was in a rented town hall, a schoolhouse, or the town's "opera house," which led to certain expectations on the part of audiences as to what performers (of either genre) should present onstage. As a result, there were frequently close connections between the songs, music, acting, and dancing of the minstrel tradition and the performance of opera scenes, with the latter sometimes adapted and inserted—usually with an eye toward parody or satire—within a minstrel show. Well into the early twentieth century, minstrel stereotypes provided a coded norm for how blackness was performed in a musico-dramatic setting and thus became potent models for depicting blackness on the operatic stage, whether in terms of story lines, characterization, or the simple application of dark makeup.

Hence, the division between minstrelsy and opera performances by black artists is not always easy to discern and reflects the tension that irresistibly follows black performers into the opera house. Even the seemingly progressive issue of color-blind casting raises certain practical concerns.[6] For instance, how should makeup be applied to light-skinned black people? Should the goal be to have lighter skin tones blend into a white or European hue (that is, to "pass" as white) for roles initially designated as "nonblack"? Conversely, should a light-skinned black singer be given darker makeup when he or she is singing a black character—actually to "black up" for the role? And if color-blind casting is appropriate for black performers in opening up opportunities for talented singers, we come full circle by asking what happens to this power dynamic if producers cast nonblack performers in specifically black roles.

The point is that getting a black opera singer onstage involves successfully negotiating many professional and cultural barriers, but achieving that aim can lead to new and equally limiting obstacles. Like Morrison's paradigm of the "Africanist" presence whose "shadow hovers in implication, in sign, in line of demarcation," what we are calling the "representation of blackness in opera" allows us to examine a multivalent system in ways that give meaning to questions about race and identity that are inextricably tied to questions of musical presentation.[7] The practice of blacking up represents only one aspect of a larger phenomenon that not only animated our initial interest in this collection, but undergirds most of the essays within it: the treatment of darker-skinned people as exotic or Other.

Such practices might be assumed to be most conspicuous in the essays dealing with operas set in the United States. As a phenotypically distinct group of people, many of whom are legatees of the Middle Passage and slavery, African Americans embody a specialized racial history that continues to have repercussions today. As one of the primary social challenges in American political culture—analogous to class status in Britain or religious affiliation in France—themes relating to racial conflict in the United States emerge in works written both by American composers and by European composers choosing to engage with the United States' distinctive cultural attitudes toward race. However, the treatment of black characters—as well as the attitudes of black and white composers and performers alike—often undermines or complicates intuitive assumptions about the presence of race in operas by Americans or set in the United States.

For example, can white composers or librettists ever create "authentic" black characters, or are they compromised from the outset by not having lived an "authentically black" experience? Does it make a difference if their creative approach is powerfully shaped by collaboration with black musicians (for example, George Gershwin in his preparation for *Porgy and Bess*) or by careful study and presentation of black culture (as with Paul Bowles and Charles Henri Ford's preparation for *Denmark Vesey*)? What if the composer is not directly implicated with America's racial struggles, but instead comes to it as an outsider, fascinated with and appreciative of a new culture (for example, Europeans like Frederick Delius or Ernst Krenek)? If none of these criteria suffices to bridge the racial divide, then does this imply that any black composer's operatic effort, regardless of how stylized or lacking in verisimilitude, is automatically a more "authentic" representation of blackness (or the black experience) simply by virtue of its creator's skin color?

That issue of skin color—intuitively, the most obvious marker of what constitutes blackness—is itself surprisingly challenging to parse, largely because its conceptual connotations have changed over time, ranging from now discredited theories on biological difference to signifying who has access to cultural or social power. (Notably, this last point is often divorced from skin color; throughout American history, ethnic groups such as Irish, Jews, and Italians have all at some time fit under the racial rubric of "black.") As such, this collection acknowledges that black taxonomy is unstable. However, we realize that a working outline for how we are thinking about blackness is necessary. In this collection, we use the terms *black* and *blackness* to refer to dark-skinned people from countries on the African continent, the islands of the Caribbean, and portions of Latin America, as well as diasporic communities of people from these locales living in the United States and Europe. This encompasses a broad spectrum of operatic characters, ranging from actual Africans (discussed by Eric Saylor and the team of Christopher Gauthier and Jennifer McFarlane-Harris), to slaves and citizens of the United States or Caribbean nations (discussed by Eric Saylor, Ann Sears, Gwynne Kuhner Brown, Karen Bryan, Gayle Murchison, Melissa de Graaf, and Melinda Boyd), to diasporic figures in European culture (as addressed by Jonathan Wipplinger, Sarah Schmalenberger, and Naomi André).

As noted previously, however, "blackness" is often applied as shorthand for "Otherness" and—as the previous discussion of "blacking up" clearly indicates—can function in contexts that transcend skin color. Thus, we complicate the conception of "blackness" when George Shirley reflects on his experience as a professional singer in the twentieth century (particularly in Europe), or when we observe how certain groups of white-skinned people can be considered "black" in the context of the seventeenth-century English imagination (as demonstrated by Sarah Schmalenberger), or when we consider how different groups of dark-skinned people established hierarchies of power within their race based on the specific shade of their skin, even if such distinctions were typically ignored by whites (as in Saylor's essay on Delius's *Koanga* or Gauthier and McFarlane-Harris's discussion of Verdi's *Aida*).

Of course, the demarcation of Otherness between blacks and nonblacks is not limited to skin color alone. Quite often, phenotypical distinctions are aligned, rightly or wrongly, with certain cultural ones as well, and few traditional aspects of African-derived culture have captured the imagination of white observers more effectively than religion, particularly as practiced in the African diaspora. This much is clear from the frequency with which the use of powers connected to the supernatural recurs over the course of this collection (notably in the essays by Bryan, de Graaf, Murchison, and Saylor). The most common vehicle for such powers is the religious tradition of voudon (our preferred spelling; it is also commonly known as voodoo or hoodoo), though it is also observable in *Candomblé* and *Santería* and discussions of Conjure and the use of Roots. While these practices vary in their geographical, cultural, and theological origins, all retain connections to the worship of spiritual ancestors, a belief system present in many African cultures that survived the Middle Passage to be reworked throughout the New World, specifically in the American South, Caribbean colonies, and the Brazilian coast. Several of the operas featuring characters from such locales emphasize the spiritual link between these diasporic peoples and their African ancestors; however, the dramatic rationale or application of these religious practices varies widely and reveals a great deal about the changing attitudes toward such beliefs over the better part of a century.

Somewhat paradoxically, this fascination with representing the irrational and supernatural in black culture reached its high point during the Harlem Renaissance, a movement dedicated to viewing black culture through the lens of the era's innovative cultural accomplishments, ranging from representations of the "New Negro" and the "Romantic savage" to the exoticism of Haitian voudon to the noble failure of Denmark Vesey's slave uprising of 1822 (discussed in Bryan, de Graaf, Murchison, Saylor, and Sears). Several of the essays also reveal the critical position Haiti had for the Harlem Renaissance. While Toussaint L'Ouverture's overthrow of Napoleon's French imperialist forces and the establishment of black indigenous rule in Haiti was undoubtedly inspiring for African Americans, the U.S. occupation of Haiti (1915–34) posed a challenge for Harlem Renaissance artists to grapple with, balancing the veneration of past black achievement with the uneasy—and often violent—imperialist aspirations of their home country.

As the first generations of African Americans born after the Civil War and the Emancipation Proclamation came of age, the years surrounding the Harlem Renaissance proved to be a fertile ground for black and nonblack composers to write operas with African American characters. Five essays (by Sears, Bryan, Murchison, Brown, and de Graaf) span the years 1911–38 and provide a cross-section of the subjects and characterizations allowed in portraying blackness onstage beyond minstrelsy. The first three essays focus on operas written by African Americans (Scott Joplin, Clarence Cameron White, and William Grant Still) and the last two by nonblack composers (Paul Bowles and George Gershwin).

The progressive attitudes of Bowles and Gershwin regarding race and class help demonstrate the increasingly significant impact black culture was having within American culture. Indeed, changes in racial attitudes were only one reflection of the new ethical and moral codes that began to emerge in the twentieth century, particularly in political arenas. Perhaps not coincidentally, conventions long taken for granted in the operatic world also began to give way. In the years immediately surrounding World War I, the heroism of the tenor, the innocence of the soprano, and the overriding sense of justice that governed most Romantic nineteenth-century opera plots were no longer guaranteed. Burgeoning voices in classical music, particularly in the United States and England, introduced new conceptions of national identity to a field long dominated by representatives from the Continent, creating opportunities for new and redefined conventions of opera. It is in this context that new types of racially diverse and unconventional protagonists were granted prominent roles within the genre, coinciding with similar expansions of forms, styles, and story types within opera as a whole. The essays by André, Brown, Boyd, Bryan, and de Graaf address such issues in detail, particularly from vantage points that examine the nature of the creative process itself—whether among composers, librettists, performers, or directors.

Opera's presentation of the world has always been filtered through the lens of its time. But despite changing ideals about representing "reality" onstage, and despite increasingly sophisticated and nuanced portrayals of black characters, there still exists the tacit assumption that the presence or portrayal of "blackness" inherently provides an alternative to traditional (that is, white, European, or both) power structures, even if a norm for blackness is established within the world of the opera. Yet the fact that black characters are typically employed as metaphors for difference should not mislead us into assuming those differences are exclusively racial. In the various approaches of these essays, we are constantly reminded of how "blackness" intersects with various social constructs (such as gender, nation, religion, and the aesthetics of popular taste) and the changing perceptions of the original performing context.

Finally, we are well aware that the scope of this collection is far from exhaustive. No doubt brilliant essays are still waiting to be written about the influence of black culture, artists, music, literature, or history in works like Virgil Thomson's *Four Saints in Three Acts* (1934), Kurt Weill's *Street Scene* (1946) and *Lost in the Stars* (1949), Anthony Davis's *X: The Life and Times of Malcolm X* (1986) and *Amistad* (1997), or Richard Danielpour's *Margaret Garner* (2005), to name only a few. But again, to take Toni Morrison's advice from the beginning of this chapter, to reconsider "the entire range of views, assumptions, readings, and misreadings" to which black people and cultures have been subjected is a daunting task indeed. No single work can accomplish such a goal, but we hope that the case studies presented in the current volume provide a first step in that direction.

Notes

1. Morrison, *Playing in the Dark*, 6.

2. See Floyd, *Power of Black Music;* Ramsey, *Race Music;* Radano, *Lying Up a Nation;* and Radano and Bohlman, *Music and the Racial Imagination.* The latter volume features a broader approach to race that goes beyond African American considerations; a similar model may be found in Born and Hesmondhalgh, *Western Music and Its Others.*

3. The "Moor" as a figure has traditionally been portrayed in blackface in opera, with examples ranging from Mozart's Monostatos (*Magic Flute*) and Osmin (*The Abduction from the Seraglio*) to Rossini's and Verdi's *Otello*s and to the Ethiopian characters in *Aida* (Aida herself, Amonasro, the enslaved Ethiopians, and the "little Moorish ballerinas" in act 2, scene 2, who dance for Amneris). Additional factors influencing whether blackface is used are the director's decisions relating to the larger operatic production.

4. A condensed (though far from comprehensive) list of helpful minstrelsy sources include Cockrell, *Demons of Disorder;* Mahar, *Behind the Burnt Cork Mask;* Lott, *Love and Theft;* and Bean, Hatch, and McNamara, *Inside the Minstrel Mask.*

5. Information in the preceding paragraphs about black musicians in the United States during the nineteenth century is primarily gleaned from Southern's *Music of Black Americans;* Graziano's "Images of African Americans"; and Story's *And So I Sing.*

6. For an excellent discussion of color-blind casting in Shakespeare and the issues surrounding this practice, see Thompson, *Colorblind Shakespeare,* especially Thompson's introduction, "Practicing a Theory/Theorizing a Practice."

7. Morrison, *Playing in the Dark,* 38.

Bibliography

Anderson, Jeffrey E. *Hoodoo, Voodoo, and Conjure: A Handbook.* Westport, Conn.: Greenwood Press, 2008.

Bean, Annemarie, James V. Hatch, and Brooks McNamara, eds. *Inside the Minstrel Mask: Readings in Nineteenth-Century Blackface Minstrelsy.* Hanover, N.H.: Wesleyan University Press, 1996.

Berger, Michele Tracy, and Kathleen Guidroz, eds. *The Intersectional Approach: Transforming the Academy through Race, Class, and Gender.* Chapel Hill: University of North Carolina Press, 2009.

Blier, Suzanne. *African Vodun: Art, Psychology, and Power.* Chicago: University of Chicago Press, 1995.

Born, Giorgina, and David Hesmondhalgh. *Western Music and Its Others: Difference, Representation, and Appropriation in Music.* Berkeley and Los Angeles: University of California Press, 2000.

Cockrell, Dale. *Demons of Disorder: Early Blackface Minstrels and Their World.* Cambridge: Cambridge University Press, 1997.

Crenshaw, Kimberle. "Mapping the Margins: Intersectionality, Identity Politics, and Violence against Women of Color." *Stanford Law Review* 43, no. 6 (1991): 1241–99.

Dilworth, Thomas, and Susan Holbrook, eds. *The Letters of Gertrude Stein and Virgil Thompson: Composition as Conversation.* New York: Oxford University Press, 2010.

Floyd, Samuel A. *The Power of Black Music: Interpreting Its History from Africa to the United States.* New York: Oxford University Press, 1995.

Graziano, John. "The Early Life and Career of the 'Black Patti': The Odyssey of an African-American Singer in the Late Nineteenth Century." *Journal of the American Musicological Society* 53, no. 3 (2000): 543–96.

———. "Images of African Americans: African-American Musical Theatre, *Show Boat,* and *Porgy and Bess.*" In *The Cambridge Companion to the Musical,* ed. William A. Everett and Paul R. Laird, 89–102. 2nd ed. Cambridge: Cambridge University Press, 2008.

Largey, Michael. *Vodou Nation: Haitian Art Music and Cultural Nationalism.* Chicago: University of Chicago Press, 2006.

Locke, Ralph P. *Musical Exoticism: Images and Reflections.* Cambridge: Cambridge University Press, 2009.

Lott, Eric. *Love and Theft: Blackface Minstrelsy and the American Working Class.* New York: Oxford University Press, 1993.

Mahar, William J. *Behind the Burnt Cork Mask: Early Blackface Minstrelsy and Antebellum American Popular Culture.* Urbana: University of Illinois Press, 1999.

Mitchell, Mozella G. *Crucial Issues in Caribbean Religions.* New York: Peter Lane, 2006.

Morrison, Toni. *Playing in the Dark: Whiteness and the Literary Imagination.* New York: Vintage Books, 1992.

Radano, Ronald. *Lying Up a Nation: Race and Black Music.* Chicago: University of Chicago Press, 2003.

Radano, Ronald, and Philip V. Bohlman. *Music and the Racial Imagination.* Chicago: University of Chicago Press, 2000.

Ramsey, Guthrie, Jr. *Race Music: Black Cultures from Bebop to Hip-Hop.* Berkeley and Los Angeles: University of California Press, 2003.

Said, Edward. *Orientalism.* New York: Pantheon Books, 1978.

Sheppard, Anthony. *Revealing Masks: Exotic Influences and Ritualized Performance in Modernist Music Theater.* Berkeley and Los Angeles: University of California Press, 2001.

Southern, Eileen. *The Music of Black Americans: A History.* 3rd ed. New York: W. W. Norton, 1997.

Story, Rosalyn M. *And So I Sing: African-American Divas of Opera and Concert.* New York: Amistad, 1990.

Taylor, Timothy D. *Beyond Exoticism: Western Music and the World.* Durham: Duke University Press, 2007.

Thompson, Ayanna, ed. *Colorblind Shakespeare: New Perspectives on Race and Performance.* New York: Routledge, 2006.

———. "Practicing a Theory/Theorizing a Practice: An Introduction to Shakespearean Colorblind Casting." In *Colorblind Shakespeare: New Perspectives on Race and Performance,* ed. Ayanna Thompson, 1–24. New York: Routledge, 2006.

1

From Otello to Porgy

Blackness, Masculinity, and Morality in Opera

NAOMI ANDRÉ

One of the most reliably predictable figures in the grand opera tradition is the male protagonist: the heroic tenor. Regardless of whether the final curtain finds him dying for his beliefs or saving the heroine from a fate worse than death, the lead tenor has traditionally set the standard for heroism and positive masculine behavior throughout an opera.[1] But around the beginning of the twentieth century, the codes for representing masculinity in opera began to change. Puccini's *Tosca* (1900) provides an apt example of this transformation, in which the lead tenor is never put in the typical masculine position of having to rescue the heroine. In fact, the opposite is true: Tosca spends most of the opera trying to save her lover (and lead tenor), Cavaradossi, and is ultimately unsuccessful. Moreover, the most dynamic male character is the villainous Scarpia, who tries to sexually conquer Tosca and assassinate Cavaradossi. This is not a new position for the bass or baritone antagonist, long distinguished as the unsuccessful suitor of the soprano and perpetrator of evil deeds. What is striking is that his actions are not balanced by the presence of an equally effective and noble male protagonist.

Concurrent with this transformation of character treatment was an increase in operas featuring nonwhite or non-European characters. The theme of exoticism was by that time a regular feature in opera and brought with it an added dynamic for representing the Other.[2] In this essay, I focus on how the changing codes of masculinity in leading male roles are calibrated differently for white European characters and nonwhite characters with non-European ancestry (for example, African American, Caribbean, Moorish, or African) and show how masculinity and heroism are brought together differently for black and nonblack characters.

In order to provide both a close reading of a specific musical moment and a larger overview of broader trends about the representation of blackness in opera, I have divided this essay into two sections. The first examines Giuseppe Verdi's *Otello* (1887) and focuses on a critical moment near the end of the opera that links orchestral developments in Italy at the end of the nineteenth century with the way Verdi dramatizes Otello's vicious murder of Desdemona. The broader overview considers four operas written in the first half of the twentieth century: Alban Berg's *Wozzeck* (1925), Ernst Krenek's *Jonny spielt auf* (1927), George Gershwin's *Porgy and Bess* (1935), and Benjamin Britten's *Peter Grimes* (1945). Two of these operas (*Wozzeck* and *Peter Grimes*) feature white European title characters, while the other two feature African American protagonists.[3]

The "Chocolate" Project

Though English literature has examined race and themes of darkness in Shakespeare's *Othello,* practically no attention has been given to the theme of blackness in the musical settings of *Othello.*[4] Even more striking by today's standards, several times in the correspondence between Verdi and those who were involved in the creation of *Otello* are references to getting the "chocolate" ready;[5] Giulio Ricordi even sent Verdi a holiday panettone (a traditional Milanese cake) around Christmas in 1881 and 1882, each topped with an unfinished figure of Otello in chocolate—not-so-subtle indications that he was looking forward to Verdi's completed opera.[6] Today, it is easy to look at this situation and think of it less as a deliberate racial slur and more like a convenience of shorthand. Referring to *Otello* as the "chocolate project" could easily have been a casual way to talk about the possibility of composing another opera without seeming to commit Verdi to another major work. After all, Verdi, now on the cusp of his seventies, was content to retire after *Aida* in 1871 and live the life of the gentleman farmer.

There are also other frameworks that surround these comments as they are contextualized in the nineteenth century. Chocolate was introduced to Europe from the New World of Central and South Americas in the sixteenth century.[7] On its own, the cocoa bean is quite bitter; while hot peppers, ginger, and other additives for cacao were sometimes used in the Americas, the need for additional sweeteners or spices became a standard requirement for the European palate. The reputation of chocolate was that it carried various powers that ranged from its being used as a therapeutic medicine, a place to hide poisons, or an aphrodisiac. Hence, this edible substance produced several different meanings. Originating from a foreign, exotic place (associated with the Mayans, Aztecs, and other Indian tribes), it was a food that could produce curative, dangerous, or erotic effects. Yet in order to be enjoyed, it needed to be tamed in taste by adding something to make it palatable.

Another related arena may be found in a whole collection of aphorisms born out of the craft of making chocolate that circulated in nineteenth-century French culture. As an avid traveler to France and someone who kept up with French culture, Verdi quite probably had knowledge of chocolate's various connotations. In a particularly poignant connection to Shakespeare's Othello, the following saying has an apt relevance: "To be like chocolate *(être chocolat)* was to be deceived or play the fool. As a substance surrounded by ambiguous moral and medical notions, chocolate evoked persistent anxieties in its early consumers." In another application to having an especially vulnerable nature subject to outside influences, "to act like chocolate (*faire le chocolat*) meant to be naïve or gullible and to court numerous social risks, from deception to death." Quite directly, relevant to a character such as Othello/Otello, "The noun *chocolat* has long signaled not only a tropical foodstuff but also men of African descent."[8] These expressions associate chocolate with things that extended beyond food, charging the word with a deeper resonance than we might expect today.

A final association of chocolate in the nineteenth century and Verdi's opera may be seen in imperial development. Though Italy's most well-known expansionist ventures in the twentieth century were under Mussolini, current scholarship traces colonialist energies as far back as the mid–nineteenth century. Patrizia Palumbo, a noted Italian historian, writes, "The nationalistic belief in Italy's civilizing mission that informed much of the later colonial discourse is deeply embedded in the Risorgimento." Verdi was aware of at least some of these activities when he refers to Italy's failed attempt against the French to appropriate Tunisia in 1881 in a letter to his friend Oppradino Arrivabene. Modern historians view an escalation in the more formal Italian attempts to act on their interests a few years later, in 1885, when "the Italian government initiated its colonial campaigns in Africa."[9] Such activities occurred two years before the premiere of *Otello* and during the time in which Verdi was most active in composing it. Behind the seemingly innocent use of "making chocolate" and the "chocolate project" are the deeper contexts in which Verdi lived. Moreover, the act of eating chocolate could be seen as a metaphor for the colonization process itself—transforming something bitter and exotic into a safe, desirable product for ravenous consumers.

Staging Otello's Base Deed

One of the chief figures behind nineteenth-century Italian conceptions of Shakespeare was August Wilhelm Schlegel. Schlegel's influential Viennese lectures, *Vorlesungen über dramatische Kunst und Literatur*, first appeared in Italian translation in 1817, shortly after their original presentation.[10] They were so popular that most Italian translations of Shakespeare in Verdi's lifetime included Schlegel's remarks. Verdi and Boito owned copies of such translations and would have had ample opportunity and motivation to familiarize themselves with Schlegel's ideas about the character of Othello himself. Schlegel described the Moorish general as

> covered with dark shadows. . . . One may see in Othello the savage nature of that burning zone which produces the most ferocious animals and the most poisonous plants. . . . One drop of this poison put into his blood gives rise to the most fearful effervescence. Othello shows himself to be noble, sincere, full of trust, fully aware of the love that he inspires; he is a hero who scorns danger, the worthy head of his soldiers, the solid supporter of the State. But the purely physical power of his passions demolishes his adopted virtues with one blow, and the savage supplants in him the civilized man. . . . He suffers double; he suffers in both of the spheres into which his existence is divided.[11]

By contrast, Verdi and Boito's Otello is no "savage" noble doomed to reveal his ferocious elemental nature. Rather than distinguish Otello by an exotic Saracen or Turkish outfit (as was suggested by Alfredo Edel, the costume designer at La Scala), Verdi wanted Otello to be dressed throughout as a Venetian nobleman.[12] However, there were other geographical and musical ways that *Otello* is marked with difference, highlighting the dual nature of his existence.

Unlike Shakespeare's *Othello,* which opens in Venice, Verdi's opera is entirely set in Cyprus—an exoticized locale outside mainland Europe. Both Venice and Cyprus have historically been "in between" sites where the West meets the East (in terms of economic trade and cross-cultural exchange). The exoticization of *Otello* is heightened by taking the action entirely off the European continent and placing it in Cyprus, an island that has connections both to Greece (with its European alliances) as well as to Turkey (considered part of Southwest Asia), and part of the Ottoman Empire.[13] Cyprus starts out as the localized norm where Otello is unquestionably in charge. From his opening "*Esultate!*" as he steps off the ship (victorious from his battle overseas with the Turks), to the quelling of the rowdy argument (instigated by Iago) between Cassio and Montano later in the act, to the intimate love duet at the end of act 1, Otello is shown to be a well-rounded and capable hero: a victor in battle, an effective military leader, and a tender lover to his wife. Moreover, his triumphant entrance into the opera signals his distance from the combative Other:

> Esultate! L'orgoglio musulmano
> Sepolto è in mar, nostra e del ciel è gloria!
> Dopo l'armi lo vines l'uragano.

> Exult! Muslim pride
> is buried in the sea. The glory is ours and heaven's!
> After our arms conquered them, so did the storm.

In act 1, Verdi's Otello is carefully drawn to be considered one of "us" rather than the aggressive Muslim Turks he has just defeated.

Musically, the dramatic moment that epitomizes the clash between Otello's love for Desdemona and the murderous rage he later feels for her at the end of the opera has been noted in the recurrence of the *bacio* (kiss) theme from their love duet in act 1 during the final moments of the opera.[14] In this recurrence, Otello's passionate love and unjustified jealousy are poignantly recalled when he looks at the murdered Desdemona as he lies dying. The return of the *bacio* theme from the climax of their duet reminds the audience of how far the two have fallen from the celestial joy they had once shared. Yet there exists another sonic signal augmenting the characterization of Otello at the end of the opera; rather than recalling the nobility of his love for Desdemona, however, this other musical gesture speaks to Otello's darker, baser instincts.

Musically, Otello is given a special aural cue when he enters Desdemona's bedroom in the fourth act to kill her. The directions for his entrance are noted in the *disposizione scenica* (production book) Giulio Ricordi wrote for the first production:

> As soon as Desdemona is asleep, and precisely on the first note of the solo of the double-basses, the secret door opens rapidly, and Otello appears at the threshold. He takes a small step forwards, then stands still, while he immediately closes the secret door behind him. He holds a scimitar in his right hand.
>
> The actor must memorize the solo of the double-basses well since all of the action must take place exactly as indicated by the composer on specific beats. Especially at the initial performances, it would be helpful if the same person who has prompted the "Ave Maria" were behind the closed secret door, where, with the score in hand, he could indicate to the actor *sotto voce* exactly which movements to make. For our part, we will indicate these movements briefly, since it is up to the actor alone, in such a highly dramatic moment, to integrate these movements into an effective scenic action. He should not forget that Desdemona is asleep and must not be awakened by any inopportune noise.[15]

A note on the development of the double bass is instructive here. Beginning in 1832, the Paris Conservatory used a four-string double bass tuned in fourths (E, A, d, g) that mirrors the tuning of the modern double bass. However, Italian performers were slower to make this change.[16] Following in the footsteps of the great Italian double bass virtuoso Domenico Dragonetti (1763–1846), for most of the nineteenth century, Italian tuning was for a three-string double bass in fourths (A, d, g). Verdi attended operas regularly in Paris from the mid-1840s through the 1860s and sporadically thereafter. During this time, he had plenty of opportunities to hear the French four-string double bass in the orchestra and wrote for them in his two operas for the Paris Opéra (*Les Vêpres siciliennes* of 1855 and *Don Carlos* of 1867). The four-string basses were hardly found in Italian orchestras until the Milan Congress of 1881, but even within the La Scala orchestra, then considered the most progressive orchestra in Italy, the switch was neither instantaneous nor consistent, resulting in a period during which bass sections comprised both four- and three-string instruments.[17]

In the score of *Otello,* Verdi indicates that he only wanted the four-stringed double basses ("*i soli contrabassi a quattro corde*") to play their open E string during Otello's entrance, with no octave doublings from above on the three-string basses. It is on this note, one of the lowest possible in the orchestra, that Otello enters from the secret door.[18] The note is marked *pianissimo,* and the double basses play with mutes, so it is barely audible. Anticipating this situation, Verdi has prepared the audience: Desdemona has just sung the "Willow Song" and her prayers ("Ave Maria"). The upper strings (violins and violas) play in their higher registers and sustain their last notes (spelling an A-flat major chord) with the expression marking *morendo* (dying). The scene is solemn and everything is quiet. As Desdemona's prayers ascend to heaven, her voice soars up to a sustained high A-flat before it whispers the "Amen" a twelfth lower on the E-flat above middle C. During the six-measure postlude, the accompanying strings stay high in their range as Desdemona rises from her prayers and goes to bed.

With the extensive pantomime movements outlined in the *disposizione scenica,* Otello emerges from the secret trapdoor. Timed precisely with the low E-natural in the double basses, he enters the room on this foreign sound, probably the first highlighted solo of this new low note in the Italian orchestra. In most live performances, the note is so low and quiet that it is almost felt more than heard.

This deep E-natural entrance is a striking contrast to the tonic A-flat major chord immediately preceding it. From Desdemona's "Ave Maria," the diminished fourth (formed with the high A-flat in the violin) along with the minor second (voiced in the viola's E-flat) against the E-natural for Otello's entrance in the double basses act as harmonic and registral representations of the diametrically opposed emotional worlds Desdemona and Otello now inhabit. The dignified, elegant Otello we first saw in the opening scene is now gone; he has been replaced with a murderous savage whose base intentions are heralded by the lowest and darkest bass sound possible. He is no longer the sympathetic figure we saw in the opening of the opera; his Otherness is now also marked sonically. Whatever goodness this tenor once possessed has been purged, his inner darkness now matching his external complexion.

Verdi, *Otello*, act 4 (end of Desdemona's "Ave Maria" and entrance of Otello).

Masculinity and Responsibility: Otello Juxtaposed with Wozzeck, Peter, Jonny, and Porgy

Otello's treatment could be written off as simply reflecting a typical Shakespearean plot; the Moor is a placeholder for any hero whose fatal flaw—in this case, his intense jealousy—is his undoing. In *Macbeth,* another Shakespearean comparison (which also happened to be Verdi's first Shakespearean opera), this jealousy is replaced by Macbeth's (and his wife's) unquenchable thirst for power.[19] However, in Verdi's famous operatic Otello, we uncover the roots of the corruptible tenor that came to fruition in the twentieth century. Intersecting with the nature of this corruption, and the responsibility for the actions that result from it, is the race of the protagonist. Though nonblack characters might act in dishonorable ways, it is the feature of difference articulated through race—and specifically blackness—that distorts the balance of what happens. At this point I will move from the single example of Verdi's *Otello* to its broader influence on the pairing of race and heroic masculinity in opera from the first half of the twentieth century. Wozzeck, Peter, Jonny, and Porgy reinforce the legacy of Otello, where racial difference mitigates the fate of each character.

Wozzeck and *Peter Grimes* have come to represent paradigmatic expressions of early-twentieth-century alienation. Their title characters belong to the fringes of society and are unable to sustain meaningful relationships with others. Frustrated by the indignity of their situations, each one resorts to violence, loses touch with reality, and ultimately takes his life by drowning. Perhaps most surprisingly (and paradoxically), since Wozzeck murders Marie (his girlfriend and the mother of his son) out of jealousy and Peter Grimes is responsible for the deaths of his two boy apprentices, both men emerge as sympathetic characters who are alienated and shunned by society, even before their heinous actions. Despite their intentions to become respectable members of their communities, their actions are misunderstood and acceptance eludes them. As they stand too low on the social ladder, their attempts to connect even with those closest to them fail.

Ultimately, both Wozzeck and Peter Grimes end up being punished for their actions, though that punishment—suicide—is self-imposed. Georg Büchner's unfinished nineteenth-century play *Woyzeck* was based on a real historical event that became the first court case where the insanity defense was used (though unsuccessfully). Berg's opera presents a man broken down by society who resorts to crime and pays the price with his own life. George Crabbe's nineteenth-century poem "The Borough" revealed the difficulty of life within a North Sea fishing village and presents Peter Grimes as a clear-cut villain who has murdered his father and three boy apprentices. Britten and his librettist, Montagu Slater, altered

Peter Grimes by limiting the death toll (Crabbe's poem has three boy apprentices, while Britten's opera has two) and plausibly suggesting that the deaths of the boy apprentices could be accidental. As in many of his other operas, Britten's characterization of Peter Grimes is open to various interpretations; nonetheless, like Wozzeck, Grimes does not fit into his community and is misunderstood.[20] Both of them break rules that make them Outsiders, and as a result, both of them pay for these actions with their deaths. Their fates allow the audience to sympathize for them while also believing that justice has been served.

Though perhaps less renowned than *Wozzeck* or *Peter Grimes,* Ernst Krenek's *Jonny spielt auf* (1927) and George Gershwin's *Porgy and Bess* (1935) are both pivotal twentieth-century operas. A signature work of the Weimar Republic, *Jonny* enjoyed phenomenal success in the years before the rise of the Nazi Party in the early 1930s, but since 1938—the year that Krenek was branded an *entartete* (degenerate) composer by the Third Reich—the opera has virtually disappeared from the repertory.[21] *Jonny spielt auf* makes broad statements about the future of German music and the role of nationalism in music through the juxtaposition of the two main characters, Jonny and Max. Max, the serious art music composer, represents the German Romantic tradition trying to adapt to the twentieth century; Jonny, by contrast, embodies the energy of modern music (specifically jazz). Max spends his time in the mountains monumentalizing the glaciers as he contemplates composing and musing on the direction his life should take. Jonny's character is more dynamic; he knows how to size up a situation, make decisions, and act. The contrasts within the opera reflect the contemporaneous cultural divide between the Old World (Europe) and the New (the United States), as well as the fragmentation of European classical art music and the rising popularity of jazz dance music. Max and Jonny embody the two poles set up in the opera, with the two female characters (Anita and Yvonne) circulating between them.

Unlike *Jonny spielt auf,* Gershwin's *Porgy and Bess* had a troubled beginning but has gradually gained widespread acceptance. *Porgy and Bess* is an African American story: all of the principal characters and large chorus are black, and the story revolves around their lives. Its position on the opera stage was not initially clear to critics of either opera or musical theater; issues surrounding the jazz-influenced score, the use of a nearly all-black cast, and a story about poverty among southern blacks in the United States were new concepts for both genres.

Gershwin's own personal and professional background complicated the situation even further: born in Brooklyn to Russian Jewish immigrant parents, Gershwin was a leader in the popular song tradition of Tin Pan Alley as well as in the emerging styles of jazz. Musically, he combined the Tin Pan Alley song tradition, jazz, and a classical art music sound (especially his writing in the 1920s with *Rhapsody in Blue, Concerto in F, An American in Paris,* and *Second*

Rhapsody); *Porgy and Bess* melds all three musical styles together. As a first-generation Russian Jew, Gershwin's ethnicity did not easily fit into what today is considered "white."[22] The strong anti-Semitic sentiment of that time linked many negative racial characteristics of blackness with being Jewish. Gershwin's identity as a Jewish person in the beginning of the twentieth century occupied a type of liminal position between whiteness and blackness.

Gershwin had firsthand experience with black music in Harlem, and he spent time with the black population on Folly Island (off the coast of South Carolina) with Dubose Heyward, one of the opera's librettists and the author of *Porgy* (1926), the novel on which the opera was based. Though Gershwin described the work as "an American folk opera," the United States was still defining itself in regards to art music; consequently, the plot stretched people's conception of opera as a genre. Nonetheless, this reticence has gradually dissipated, and *Porgy and Bess* has found its place on the opera stage as the Great American Opera.[23]

Porgy and Bess and *Jonny spielt auf* are very different operas; however, the male title characters share similar features and fulfill parallel roles. Both operas present the minstrel history of black characters as entertainers (though while Jonny is a jazz musician, Porgy's role as an entertainer, I will argue, comes at the end of the opera). Krenek's debt to the minstrel tradition is more overt than in Gershwin's opera, not least in the use of blackface characters (for Jonny as well as his jazz musicians). At points in the libretto Jonny's actions are characterized as being "im Ton eines Niggerliedes" (in the style of the "Nigger minstrel show").[24] Gershwin had seen Krenek's *Jonny spielt auf* in Vienna when traveling in Europe in 1928, and at a very early point in his letters to Heyward, Gershwin mentions the possibility of Al Jolson as a blackfaced Porgy, though the idea was soon abandoned.[25] Both operas also transcend typical minstrel stereotypes; for example, Krenek and Gershwin each employ musical scores with pronounced jazz influences while also requiring the singers to perform in an operatic style.

Additionally, and true to their *verismo* ancestry, we see the characters' weaknesses and flaws along with their aspirations and goals. While Wozzeck and Peter Grimes are tortured characters throughout the entirety of their respective operas, Jonny and Porgy are more socially integrated in their communities. As an African American musician, Jonny plays several instruments that are associated with jazz: the trombone, banjo, saxophone, and the jazz violin. His first appearance is in the third scene of part 1 and is situated in a Parisian hotel. We hear his jazz band before we see him; when he comes onstage, he is carrying his saxophone as a marker of his musicianship. He flirts with Yvonne, the hotel maid, and we learn that they are lovers. As she cleans the room of the virtuoso violinist Daniello (who plays a seventeenth-century Amati violin), Jonny expresses his desire to steal the violin so that he can play jazz on it. Though initially foiled by Daniello's sudden appearance, Jonny eventually steals the violin by hiding it in Anita's banjo case.

This image of the seventeenth-century Amati violin hidden in a banjo case becomes a trope for the opera. Jazz comes to represent the new modern music in the character of Jonny, an African American foreigner in Europe. The Old World traditions are not discarded, just transformed and repackaged. Jonny emerges as the most dynamic presence in the opera, both sexually and musically. He is the only man associated with two women (he is dating Yvonne and attempts to seduce Anita, Max's girlfriend), and musically, he is the most versatile performer: he plays multiple instruments, his music is widely popular, and he makes people dance.

Yet there is an unrefined element to Jonny, which comes to the fore with Anita. As he tries to seduce her, he says, "I know what you white women are like: first you resist . . . then you're ecstatic . . . and then goodbye! That's how you turn us into animals!"[26] When Daniello sees Jonny, his response references a savage element in Jonny's blackness:

> What a gorgeous woman!
> And in that beast's hands!
> What sensuality!
> I'll take her from him.
> (*grabbing Jonny by the scruff of his neck*)
> Ote toi, (*contemptuously*) négrillon![27]

Whereas Max represents the paralysis of the great German (and, by extension, classical) art music tradition, Daniello embodies its refinement.[28] However, Daniello forfeits his connection to a vital modern musical expression when he loses his violin. While Jonny can only attempt to seduce Anita, he does steal Daniello's violin and plays a significant role in the imbroglio that leads to Daniello's undoing. Jonny, in the marked body of a black foreigner, represents the energy of the "new and modern" performer: he travels to Paris and the Alps, he plays the saxophone and the Amati violin, and the jazz music he plays is loved across the world. Krenek's use of multiple musical idioms in the same score shapes Jonny as the only musician who is not afraid to bridge the traditional and contemporary, an attitude reinforced when in the wake of Daniello's accidental death, he finally recovers the violin that he had hidden in Anita's banjo case.

> Everything of value in the world is mine
> The old world created it
> But no longer knows what to do with it.
> So now the new world in all its splendour
> Arrives across the sea
> And conquers old Europe through dance.[29]

With these words, we see Jonny claim the traditions of the past on behalf of the new world that will shape the future. Jonny reinforces his position as the master entertainer in the opera's closing scene at the train station. The stage directions indicate: "The lighted globe [transformed from the train station clock] begins to rotate. Jonny stands on the North Pole, playing the violin; everybody dances in a circle round the globe."[30] The opera's epilogue sees Jonny literally on top of the world, playing his violin while the principal characters reunite onstage and sing, "Listen to the sound of his violin wherever you go! Behold he comes among you, and Jonny strikes up."[31] Even after this short epilogue, Jonny remains playing his violin until the final curtain falls.

In Gershwin and Heyward's Catfish Row, the African American characters form a tight-knit community, one similar to the worlds of Peter Grimes and Wozzeck in its existence on the margins of society, a society in which, as Wozzeck's Captain would state, people have no morality (though Catfish Row's inhabitants are generally more pleasant).[32] For Catfish Row, the respectable and "moral" society beyond the village borders is personified by the coroner, the detective, and the policemen. The white characters possess not only the moral superiority but also the hegemonic power in the opera—they are the ones who make and enforce the laws of the land. When there is a murder in Catfish Row, the white police and detective are called in to investigate, and the white coroner makes sure that the fees are paid for a legal burial.

But though the members of Catfish Row repeatedly call the white characters "Boss" when they respond to interrogation, they also resist the laws of white society. A different code of justice exists inside the gates of Catfish Row. This is demonstrated on multiple occasions: Crown kills Robbins in the first act and rapes Bess in the second act, but the police never find him; Sportin' Life peddles drugs and never gets caught; and even Porgy gets off lightly after he kills Crown, going to jail not because he is convicted as the murderer, but because he refuses to identify the killer and the police never suspect that a crippled beggar (such as Porgy) could kill Crown.

Yet the nobility of Porgy's love for Bess, distorted though it may be, is not repaid in kind. What is unusual about Bess's character is that she lets Porgy down at the end. Her rehabilitation from Crown's hard-drinking, drug-addicted girlfriend to Porgy's loving partner seems to evolve from moral bankruptcy to mature love. In their declaration of love to each other, the gorgeous act 2 duet "Bess, You Is My Woman Now" and "I Loves You, Porgy," the audience is convinced that their love is real and will last; in traditional opera, only people who are truly in love can sing that passionately to each other. Yet when Porgy temporarily goes to jail for not revealing Crown's killer, Bess capitulates to Sportin' Life the very first time he comes on to her, effortlessly slipping back into her drug addiction and running off with him to New York City. Bess's actions diminish both her status as an honorable heroine and the perception of Porgy's manliness for falling in love with her. Her behavior also provokes a devastating reaction from the audience.

Rather than believing in a hero whose love can save the leading lady, at the end of the opera Porgy is seen as being no better off than he was at the beginning. Tragically, he remains deficient in every way: his body is still crippled, he has learned to love only to be duped, and his heart is newly broken.

Judged by a Different Moral Compass

When Verdi's Otello dies, he is treated heroically in the opera. We watched in horror as he murdered the innocent Desdemona, but when Verdi brings back the *bacio* theme from their act 1 love duet in the final moments of the opera, we feel Otello's remorse and realization of his tragic mistake. He pays for his jealousy, even though it was Iago who led him to such dishonorable ruin. It is unjust that Iago gets away, but Otello is ennobled by his death and elevated to the level of a Shakespearean hero whose complexity and flaws lead to his undoing.

Yet there is another, racialized, way of looking at Otello: he is an exoticized Moor whose civilized demeanor might have been more of a shock when he does *not* fulfill the stereotype of the wild savage. Both Shakespeare's and Verdi's audiences did not have a wide range of black heroes to draw from. Shakespeare's Othello has many more racialized references, mostly negative, to Othello's blackness than Verdi's opera. The opera does a good job of making Otello heroic from his opening line in the opera, with the triumphant melody in his exclamation "*Esultate!*" that keeps leaping higher and higher in the tenor's range while ringing out in forte dynamics. Although late-nineteenth-century imperial Europe might have had more contact with colonized Others than Shakespeare's Elizabethan audiences, they still lacked a canon of well-respected dark-skinned protagonists in opera; the presence of a sophisticated black hero was quite novel to Verdi's audience.

Verdi's Otello goes far in establishing his heroic credentials, framing him as the tragic victim of Iago's poison. I venture that the anticipation for this Otello, the "ennobled savage," to show his expected "true" nature (that is, that of a violent, uncivilized beast) strongly shaped the initial reception of his character. Given the dearth of extant positive models for black operatic characters and the negative associations blackness had in connection to the Atlantic slave trade and colonialism, a black character in opera could easily fall victim to the beliefs the audience brought to the theater. While Otello might be initially seen as an innocent pawn of Iago, his ultimate fall at the end reinforces any negative suspicions the audience might possess; the sinister employment of the double basses in the murder scene provides further musical support for such a stance.

The devastating endings of *Wozzeck* and *Peter Grimes* are powerful because they speak to latent fears of alienation within viewers. Both Wozzeck and Peter Grimes die by suicide drownings, and no one seems to notice or care. Wozzeck is so crazed that he hardly realizes what he is doing. The "moral society" represented by the Doctor and the Captain threatens to break down when they think they hear someone drowning; rather than stop to investigate or help, they quickly walk by and do nothing. The final scene shows young children taunting Wozzeck and Marie's uncomprehending illegitimate child about Marie's dead body found near the pond. As the little boy pathetically hops around on his hobbyhorse, before running off to witness the scene himself, it seems that the present holds no hope for the future.

Peter Grimes goes mad toward the end of the opera as the angry mob of the Borough closes in to dispense their own vigilante justice. When Ellen and Balstrode, the only two people who have shown Grimes any kindness, encourage him to go out to sea and sink his boat, he complies. The final moments of the opera show dawn breaking and the Borough starting a new day. When Swallow, the town lawyer, mentions a coast guard report of a sinking boat (the audience figures out that it is Peter's), it is decided that the boat is beyond reach, and no one does anything about it. As in *Wozzeck*, the antihero protagonist dies in the midst of a morally self-righteous community that chooses to ignore him.

The audience feels the tragedy of these deaths, having witnessed the protagonists' struggle and inner pain as they unsuccessfully tried to fit into their surroundings. Though we watch Wozzeck murder Marie (act 3, scene 2), we know that the Doctor is conducting medical experiments on Wozzeck through starvation and a severely limited diet. We understand that Wozzeck is a victim himself: we see him suffer from hallucinations, and we understand that he is not in his right mind. When the second boy apprentice dies under Peter Grimes's care, we know it is not because of any direct action on Grimes's part (though we also know he is capable of violence, demonstrated when he strikes Ellen in act 2, scene 1). Despite our sympathy, both men pay for their actions. Though both operas' societies are operating with a broken moral compass, each antihero is ultimately held responsible for his deeds.

Gershwin's Porgy is also set up for a tragic finale. We see it in the chorus members' faces when they try to avoid telling him that Bess has run off to New York with Sportin' Life. Yet instead of singing the blues, Porgy leads the chorus in a rousing finale. When he asks where New York is, he is told it is "a thousand mile from here" and "way up North pas' de custom house." On hearing this, he calls for his goat cart and then begins the final number, "I'm on My Way to a Heav'nly Lan.'"

In this stirring final scene, the audience is led to believe that Porgy really is on his way to find Bess and that the Lawd is going to take his han' and lead him there. Yet if we stop to think for just half a moment, we know that there is no way that Porgy, a poor crippled black man from the Depression-era South, is ever going to find his way up to New York City and reunite with Bess. No stretching of logic can make this happen. The success of the final curtain is keeping the audience from making the connection between what we *want* to have happen and what lies within the realm of probability; the reality and Porgy's fantasy are two entirely different things.

To buy into the triumphant finale, the audience needs to believe that love can, in fact, conquer all, an operatic trope as old as the genre itself. And it is part of the work's brilliance that one can think that cliché is as applicable in Catfish Row as anywhere else in the world. Porgy is sympathetic as a crippled and poor black man who does not mind that he "has plenty o' nuttin.'" When Bess is on his arm, he has a song in his heart and feels that heaven is on his side.[33] Yet Porgy also occupies a world where he makes his living from begging and gambling. He has no trouble becoming a murderer when Crown comes back to claim her; indeed, the audience practically cheers when Porgy outsmarts Crown as he lies in wait and then brutally stabs him. When the white Detective and Coroner come to Catfish Row, we hold our breath because we do not want them to find out the truth about Porgy. We let out a sigh of relief when we realize that Porgy is going to jail only because he will not identify Crown's murderer and not because he is suspected of killing Crown himself. We also know perfectly well that Porgy is not going to make it to Harlem; he is too limited by his race, poverty, physical disability, and the realities of the Jim Crow South. But rather than viewing it as the futile gesture it is, we cheer his plucky obliviousness as he sings his final aria, "I'm on My Way." It is almost as if the artificially triumphant ending tells the audience that these poor black people should not suffer the consequences of their actions, because, after all, they can't really help themselves for not knowing better. If anything, we are willing to forgive them because they struggle against such devastating odds.

The final image in Krenek's *Jonny spielt auf* reinforces this logic even further. As the blackfaced jazz musician Jonny is literally on top of the world with the stolen violin, he plays his music as the European crowd below dances. As Porgy struggles offstage on his way to New York City, his voice is strong and his tune is riveting. The community of Catfish Row sings his song and cheers him on his journey. In fact, most performances of this number make us, in the audience, want to jump to our feet and join the chorus; we are willing to let Porgy lead us to the "Heav'nly Lan.'" As the final curtain comes down, we hum the tune, stomp our feet, and clap our hands in dancelike imitation of Jonny's European crowd. Porgy, like Jonny, is a masterful entertainer whose music makes us forget our cares as we leave the theater.

One of the things we forget is that, in the final tally, Jonny and Porgy have evaded responsibility for their actions. Admittedly, their offenses are quite different. Though Jonny could be seen as a womanizer in his failed seduction of Anita, his primary crime is stealing the violin. On the other hand, Porgy, a chronic gambler, has committed the premeditated murder of Crown. Though differing in severity, their crimes have the common link of being committed by black characters who seem to be held to a different moral standard than nonblack characters. Wozzeck and Peter Grimes might be unjustly misunderstood, but when each of them does bad things, he is ultimately punished. Their deaths at the end of their operas articulate the real tragedy of their situations. They are held responsible for their behavior, even though they are products of malevolent systems that did not give them a fair chance.

Though Verdi's Otello is the victim of the malicious Iago, he almost seems to fit into the category of Wozzeck and Peter Grimes, a tragic antihero. Otello murders Desdemona and pays with his life at the end. However, the theme of redemption for his ending is marred. Unlike Wozzeck or Peter Grimes, Otello's actions seem to confirm his "savage" nature. As in any great Shakespearean tragedy, the heroism he embodied at the beginning of the opera was undermined by his fall from grace, which reinforced the suspected baseness of his "true" character. Otello shows how black characters in opera, even when they seem to share a similar fate, are not on the same footing as nonblack characters. Judged by a different moral compass, their failings do not reinforce the complexity of their humanity, but rather support a reading that sustains their "inherently inferior" nature.

Jonny and Porgy show an evolution of the black operatic protagonist. In the age of the operatic antihero, the two do not get caught or suffer the consequences of their crimes. Each opera also ends with a pseudo-rousing finale, with Jonny and Porgy leading the crowd in a seemingly triumphant number. Such endings can be seen to provide each character with the sought-after hero status black characters have so poignantly lacked. Ultimately, they appear to conclude the opera on a triumphant note, leaving everything upbeat and better than before. Yet when black characters are given a "free pass," they conjure up stereotypes of brutish physical aggression and moral bankruptcy. What differentiates the black and white antiheroes are the conditions that surround their lost innocence. Both types of antiheroes are violent and sympathetic. Yet the white or European characters extend the *verismo* aesthetics when their "realistic" and "naturalistic" negative deeds are not preconceived expectations in the minds of the viewers, and the characters are punished for them. In this way, their behavior has been contextualized, and they are made more believable and humane. The black antiheroes lose their heroism and survive through deception and trickery as they elude a greater moral justice. Jonny and Porgy are antiheroic survivors who entertain us so we fail to remember that they have not paid the price of their actions. As the black characters divert us with song, dance, and negative stereotypes, we are shuffled away from opera and pushed closer into minstrelsy. By presenting aspects of minstrel caricature, they make us forget that opera aims to emulate truer-to-life emotions, feelings, and experiences.

Notes

1. The "grand opera tradition" referred to here is, primarily, Italian and French opera after 1830. Few studies focus on the general characterization of the tenor male hero past the generalization of his role as the soprano's love interest. A few sources that discuss masculinity in opera are Hamm's *Opera,* De Van's *Verdi's Theater,* and Gallo's *Opera.* Auner discusses masculinity in Krenek's *Jonny spielt auf* in his "'Souless Machines' and Steppenwolves." This paper challenges the evolution of the heroic tenor in the late-nineteenth and early twentieth centuries and leaves open the possibility of a reappraisal of this character type even earlier.

2. For one of the most recent in-depth discussions of exoticism in music, see Locke, *Musical Exoticism.*

3. Reynolds has written about connections between Berg's *Wozzeck* and Gershwin's *Porgy and Bess* in *"Porgy and Bess."* Reynolds's article takes as a starting point Gershwin's known admiration for Berg and explores structural similarities between the two operas (for example, the presence of a lullaby). My essay here focuses on the outsider status of the two male title characters and explores how race creates meaning in the opera.

4. The best-known operatic settings of Shakespeare's *Othello* are Rossini's *Otello* (1816) and Verdi's *Otello* (1887). Other musical settings on this theme include Salvatore Viganò's *Otello* (ballet, 1818), Dvorak's *Othello* Overture, Op. 93; Samuel Coleridge-Taylor's *Othello,* Op. 79 (incidental music to Shakespeare's play, 1910–11), and Manuel de Falla's *Otelo* (incidental music to an adaptation of Shakespeare's play, 1915, now lost).

5. Busch, *Verdi's "Otello,"* 1:3, 11–14. Several references are made to working on *Otello* as preparing chocolate, especially early on in 1879 before things had gotten very far. Verdi to Giulio Ricordi, Genoa, July 18, 1879; Ricordi to Verdi, Milan, July 23, 1879; Boito to Eugenio Tornaghi, July 1879; Ricordi to Giuseppina Verdi, Milan, November 4, 1879; Ricordi to Giuseppina Verdi, Milan, November 8, 1879; Ricordi to Verdi, Milan, November 13, 1879; Verdi to Ricordi, St. Agata, November 18, 1879; Ricordi to Verdi, Milan, January 6, 1880.

6. Ibid., 127 (Giuseppina Verdi to Ricordi, Genoa, January 1, 1882). There are three letters that mention it for 1883: Verdi to Ricordi, Genoa, December 25, 1882; Emanuele Muzio to Ricordi, Genoa, December [25?], 1882; and Giuseppina Verdi to Ricordi, Genoa, December [25?], 1882. Ibid., 137–38.

7. Coe and Coe, *True History of Chocolate.*

8. Terrio, *Crafting the Culture,* 237, 238.

9. Palumbo, *Place in the Sun,* 5–6; Busch, *Verdi's "Otello,"* 1:102; Verdi to Oppradino Arrivabene, St. Agata, May 27, 1881; Palumbo, *Place in the Sun,* 5–6.

10. Hepokoski, *Giuseppe Verdi: "Otello."*

11. From Schlegel's introduction to Carlo Rusconi's Italian edition of Shakespeare's *Othello,* reproduced in ibid., 165–66.

12. Ibid., 107–8, 171. There are early letters where it appears that Verdi initially wanted an exotic costume, but then he changed his mind.

13. This situation around Cyprus's political affiliations is complicated by events in the 1870s. After the Suez Canal opened in 1869, Cyprus became a more strategic access point in this geographical location. Between the Congress of Berlin (1878) and Great

Britain's interest in Cyprus, the pull between the West and the East in Cyprus was especially strong during the time of *Otello.*

14. For discussion on the *bacio* theme in acts 1 and 4, see David Lawton, "On the 'Bacio' Theme in *Otello*"; and Parker and Brown, "Ancora un bacio."

15. Production book written by Giulio Ricordi for the first performances. Busch, *Verdi's "Otello,"* 2:606.

16. Thanks to Dr. Anthony Stoops for bringing this information about the double bass to my attention.

17. Brun, *History of the Double Bass,* 130–40.

18. Like with the double bass, Italy was also slower to adapt developments in low brass instruments than its European neighbors. The cimbasso was in use much longer before the modern tubas in Germany and France.

19. In Verdi's *Macbeth* (1847), the title character is a baritone, and the tenor is Macduff, a much smaller role.

20. Though not explored here, a compelling reading of Britten's operas that includes a careful consideration of his homosexuality can be found in Brett's "Britten's Dream."

21. Krenek's *Jonny spielt auf* (1927) was produced at forty-two opera houses (including the Metropolitan Opera in New York) in its first season, with 421 performances in Germany alone. By 1929 the opera was translated into fourteen languages. The opera has been revived several times since the 1950s with black singers in the title role. Additionally, the opera was performed at Krenek's ninetieth birthday with the composer in the audience. In 2003 there was a performance in Vienna with a return to the original production with blackfaced singers.

22. There is a vast literature about the invention of "whiteness" as an identity and the time it took several immigrant groups (for example, people who were Irish, Jewish, or Catholic) to "become" (be considered) white. A helpful source is Jacobson's *Whiteness of a Different Color.*

23. The performance and subsequent recording of *Porgy and Bess* by the Houston Grand Opera in 1976 can be seen as a turning point that led other major opera houses to add *Porgy and Bess* to their repertoires. Fifty years after the opera's first performance, the Metropolitan Opera house did its first production of *Porgy.* Though the opera has seen performances in cities that tend to have large black populations (for example, Detroit and Washington, D.C.), the opera is still receiving first performances in major houses. The Chicago Lyric Opera gave its first production in November 2008.

24. Also translated as "nigger-minstrel fashion," according to stage direction in part 1. Krenek, *Jonny spielt auf,* liner notes, 63. Another instance is the stage direction in part 2, "Jonny nimmt das 'Banjo' und beginnt es wähend des Folgenden auszupacken, wobei er, wie eben ein Neger, herumtanzt" (Jonny picks up the "banjo" and begins to unpack it while dancing around nigger-minstrel fashion). Ibid., 94.

25. Letters in September 1932 between Gershwin and Heyward talk about Al Jolson for Porgy, but Gershwin abandons this idea early on. See Wyatt and Johnson, *The George Gershwin Reader,* 202–3.

26. "(Jonny hat sie bis zum Divan gedrängt, sie sinkt auf, diesem nieder er beugt sich über sie) 'Ich kenne ja euch Weißen: erst wehrt ihr euch—Dann seid ihr beglückt—und dann, adieu! So macht ihr wilde Tiere aus uns.'" Krenek, *Jonny spielt auf,* liner notes, 55.

27. Welch ein schönes Weib!
In den Händen dieser Bestie!
Welche Sinnlichkeit in ihr!
Die jag'ich ihm ab!
(packt Jonny am Kragen)
Ote toi (verächtlich) négrillon!
(Ibid., 55–56)

28. For a complementary reading of Daniello as an Italian foil to Jonny's character, see Jonathan O. Wipplinger's essay in this volume.

29. Mir gehört alles, was gut ist in der Welt.
Die alte Welt hat es erzeugt,
sie weiß damit nichts mehr zu tun.
Da Kommt die neue Welt
übers Meer gefahren mit Glanz
und erbt das alte Europa durch den Tanz.
(Ibid., 95)

30. "Der leuchtende Globus beginnt zu rotieren. Jonny steht auf dem Nordpol und spielt die Geige, alles tanzt im Kreis um die Kugel." Ibid., 125.

31. "Hört seiner Geige Ton, wohin ihr auch geht! Denn seht, er tritt unter euch, und Jonny spielt auf." Ibid., 126–27.

32. The Captain and Wozzeck talk of morality in the opening scene of the opera when Wozzeck is shaving him.

33. The last lines of Porgy's song "I Got Plenty o' Nuttin'" are "No use complainin' / Got my gal, got my Lawd, got my song."

Bibliography

Auner, Joseph Henry. "'Soulless Machines' and Steppenwolves: Renegotiating Masculinity in Krenek's *Jonny spielt auf.*" In *Siren Songs: Representations of Gender and Sexuality in Opera,* ed. Mary Ann Smart, 222–36. Princeton: Princeton University Press, 2000.

Brett, Philip. *Benjamin Britten: Peter Grimes.* Cambridge Opera Handbooks. Cambridge: Cambridge University Press, 1983.

———. "Britten's Dream." In *Musicology and Difference: Gender and Sexuality in Music Scholarship,* ed. Ruth A. Solie, 259–80. Berkeley and Los Angeles: University of California Press, 1993.

———. "'Grimes Is at His Exercise': Sex, Politics, and Violence in the Librettos of *Peter Grimes.*" In *Siren Songs: Representations of Gender and Sexuality in Opera,* ed. Mary Ann Smart, 237–49. Princeton: Princeton University Press, 2000.

Brun, Paul. *A History of the Double Bass.* Chemin de la Flanerie: Brun, 1989.

Busch, Hans, ed. and trans. *Verdi's "Otello" and "Simon Boccanegra" (Revised Version) in Letters and Documents.* Vol. 1, *Letters and Telegrams.* Vol. 2, *Documents.* Oxford: Oxford University Press, 1988.

Cheatham, Wallace McClain, ed. *Dialogues on Opera and the African-American Experience.* Lanham, Md.: Scarecrow Press, 1997.

Coe, Sophie D., and Michael D. Coe. *The True History of Chocolate.* New York: Thames and Hudson, 1996.

Daileader, Celia R. *Racism, Misogyny, and the Othello Myth: Inter-racial Couples from Shakespeare to Spike Lee.* Cambridge: Cambridge University Press, 2005.

De Van, Gilles. *Verdi's Theater: Creating Drama through Music.* Trans. Gilda Roberts. Chicago: University of Chicago Press, 1998.

Erickson, Peter, and Maurice Hunt. *Approaches to Teaching Shakespeare's "Othello."* New York: Modern Language Association of America, 2005.

Fisher, Neil. "The First Black Otello and Opera's Final Frontier." *London Times,* November 27, 2009. http://entertainment.timesonline.co.uk/tol/arts_and_entertainment/stage/opera/article6933828.ece.

Gallo, Denise. *Opera: The Basics.* New York: Routledge, 2006.

Greenberg, Michael. "The Double Bass Class at the Paris Conservatory, 1826–1832." *Bass World* 24, no. 3 (2001): 17–19.

Hall, Kim F. *Things of Darkness: Economies of Race and Gender in Early Modern England.* Ithaca: Cornell University Press, 1995.

Hamm, Charles. *Opera.* Boston: Allyn and Bacon, 1966.

Hepokoski, James A. *Giuseppe Verdi: Otello.* Cambridge Opera Handbooks. Cambridge: Cambridge University Press, 1987.

Jacobson, Matthew Frye. *Whiteness of a Different Color: European Immigrants and the Alchemy of Race.* Cambridge: Harvard University Press, 1998.

Krenek, Ernst. *Jonny spielt auf.* London: Decca, 1993. Conductor Lothar Zagrosek, Gewandhausorchester Leipzig. Liner notes: Claudia Maurer Zenck, "*Jonny spielt auf*: Between Jazz and New Music"; and Thomas Gayda, "Ernst Krenek: A Composer between Worlds." English translation of libretto by Gery Bramall, 1993.

Lawton, David. "On the 'Bacio' Theme in *Otello.*" *Nineteenth-Century Music* 1 (1978): 211–20.

Locke, Ralph P. *Musical Exoticism: Images and Reflections.* Cambridge: Cambridge University Press, 2009.

McClary, Susan. *Georges Bizet: "Carmen."* Cambridge: Cambridge University Press, 1992.

Palumbo, Patrizia, ed. *A Place in the Sun: Africa in Italian Colonial Culture from Postunification to the Present.* Berkeley and Los Angeles: University of California Press, 2003.

Parker, Roger, and Matthew Brown. "Ancora un bacio: Three Scenes from Verdi's *Otello.*" *Nineteenth-Century Music* 9, no. 1 (1985): 50–62.

Reynolds, Christopher. "*Porgy and Bess:* 'An American *Wozzeck.*'" *Journal of the Society for American Music* 1, no. 1 (2007): 1–28.

Smart, Mary Ann, ed. *Siren Songs: Representations of Gender and Sexuality in Opera.* Princeton: Princeton University Press, 2000.

Smith, David. "So Long Mammy: Opera Says Farewell to Blacking Up." *Observer,* November 20, 2005. http://www.guardian.co.uk/uk/2005/nov/20/race.arts.

Smith, Valerie, ed. *Representing Blackness: Issues in Film and Video.* New Brunswick: Rutgers University Press, 2003.

Solie, Ruth A., ed. *Musicology and Difference: Gender and Sexuality in Music Scholarship.* Berkeley and Los Angeles: University of California Press, 1993.

Steiner, Christian. *Opera People.* New York: Ventrome Press, 1982.

Terrio, Susan Jane. *Crafting the Culture and History of French Chocolate.* Berkeley and Los Angeles: University of California Press, 2000.

Thompson, Ayanna, ed. *Colorblind Shakespeare: New Perspectives on Race and Performance.* New York: Routledge, 2006.

Wyatt, Robert, and John Andrew Johnson. *The George Gershwin Reader.* New York: Oxford University Press, 2004.

FILM AND VIDEO

Aida's Brothers and Sisters: Black Voices in Opera. Directed by Jan Schmidt-Garre and Marieke Schroeder. PARS Media. West Long Branch, N.J.: Kultur (2139), 2000.

"Porgy and Bess": An American Voice. Producer James A. Standifer, Director Nigel Noble. Princeton, N.J.: Films for the Humanities & Sciences, 1999.

2

Hearing the Other in *The Masque of Blackness*

SARAH SCHMALENBERGER

On January 6, 1605, Queen Anne presented her husband, King James I of England (r. 1603–25), with *The Masque of Blackness,* a court entertainment of unusual scale and spectacle.[1] She had commissioned dramatist Ben Jonson and designer Inigo Jones to collaborate on the project, and Alfonso Ferrabosco II (c. 1575–1628) to compose its songs. Once the king had been seated in the Whitehall Banqueting House to watch the masque, an actor presented a prologue requesting those assembled to imagine a journey originating in Africa. The stage curtain then opened to reveal a mystical ocean scene. A parade of characters in sea-foam-blue costumes entered, followed by the featured masquers—none other than Queen Anne and her ladies-in-waiting—whose costumes caused quite a sensation. Seeming to cross a watery channel in a giant seashell-shaped boat, they arrived onstage disguised with blackened faces, hands, and legs.

Through recited and sung verse, pantomime and dance, Queen Anne and her ladies were presented as daughters of the African king Niger, "blackamoors" on a journey to the mystical island of Albion (the ancient name for Britain).[2] Legend told that the cool and superior northern rays of Albion's sun could transform their primitive beauty, borne naturally but imperfectly by a homeland sun that burned hot and darkened their skin. Rejoicing at the end of their long journey, the masquers danced onstage and then descended from it to choose partners for an extended period of dancing (the "revels"). The spectacle ended with the masquers returning to the stage, with the promise that the imminent reappearance of Niger's daughters at Albion—in the sequel *Masque of Beauty*—would see their dark visages miraculously replaced with gleaming white skin.

Sir Dudley Carleton's oft-quoted objection to the masquers has become an obligatory starting point for discussing the queen's apparent dalliance with blackface. In his letter criticizing the masque to Ralph Winwood, Carleton described Anne and her ladies as "ugly . . . lean-cheek'd Moors" and further registered concern that the Spanish ambassador, who partnered with the queen during the aforementioned revels, would get black makeup on his lips from kissing her hand.[3] Other accounts of the event confirm the masque's many entertaining novelties, yet only Carleton persisted in calling attention to themes of racialized difference.[4]

That so many scholars have proposed critical readings of *The Masque of Blackness* based on Carleton's comments attests to the work's importance in discourses exploring English historical perspectives through drama, especially in how its dramatic spectacle articulated social identities and power relationships in monarchical regimes. Such perspectives posit the role of music in masques generally (and this one in particular) as a metaphor for the drama's larger didactic function: to preserve the social order of the monarchy and its conventions of cultural expression.[5] The social framing of race in *The Masque of Blackness* thus raises several questions about its genesis and reception, particularly regarding Queen Anne's intent in commissioning the work.[6] This essay explores the role that the music for the masque may have played in constructing a "black Other," questioning existing interpretations about that concept's meaning and framing historical perspectives of musical affect with regard to Otherness.

At the turn of the seventeenth century, as England's foreign policy grew increasingly aggressive, the Jacobean monarchy spent considerable resources on the arts to promote their ideology.[7] Propagandist by design, masques and other dramatic spectacles were potent political tools in regimes that embraced the philosophy of the divine right of kings (a subject upon which James I penned a well-known thesis).[8] Pageantry and dramatic spectacles like the masque were carefully planned public events that articulated and reinscribed notions of a ruler's natural right and ability to govern.[9] This belief was perpetuated by a diffuse application of Neoplatonist philosophy in the dramatic arts that linked ideologies of ordered universal humanism to the ordered hierarchy of the sovereign's rule. Masques were allegorical dramatizations of this link, persuading spectators through metaphor and mythology of their ruler's earthly and divine competencies.[10]

Implicit in a masque's theme (or "conceit") was the expectation of a gift or generous act from a powerful mythological character who signified the extraordinary powers of a mortal ruler (in this case, a king). The gift or act was typically dramatized as a miraculous transformation or a restoration of social order that no ordinary human being could accomplish. As such, the masque did not narrate a developing plot as much as affirm a situational premise requiring the intervention of a divinely empowered monarch, a conceit that foreshadows opera seria's use of the magnanimous tyrant (not coincidentally, another genre that depended on the patronage of the ruling classes for its cultivation).

Stephen Orgel indicates that the miraculous act in the masque, as performed by a deity, was connected to reality through the physical act of dancing between masquers and audience: "The key moment of the masque occurs when the body showing the device of the miracle offers its hand to the court, literally symbolizing in revels [the dancing between masquers and audience] the acceptance of reality of the conceit."[11] Spectators recognized the masque's characterization of their ruler as divine, and they expected, if not demanded, a display of fantastical scenarios rich with allusion and referential meaning. Thus, each masque was designed to "argue" the hierarchical social order of its particular conceit through a combination of rhetoric, symbol, music, and dance.[12]

As previously noted, the argument presented in *The Masque of Blackness* was originally meant to be resolved through a complementary masque, *Masque of Beauty*, within a year.[13] Ben Jonson wrote the pair of masques for Queen Anne in celebration of the new Jacobean monarchy, so named for her spouse James VI, former king of Scotland. Soon after ascending to the English throne as King James I in 1603, he announced his intention to govern Scotland and Ireland as part of his expanded kingdom of Great Britain. Thus, it is not surprising to discern in these masques both an underlying imperialist rhetoric and evidence that the queen's obligation as the sovereign's cultural ambassador led her to dramatize one of her husband's primary political objectives at the outset of his reign.[14]

The sequence of events in a masque was loosely organized around points dramatizing the relationship between the masquers (that is, the commonwealth) and their benefactor (the king) in a miraculous transformational situation.[15] The masque was preceded by a stately procession during which the ruler or patron arrived in the hall. An actor then introduced the masque's allegorical conceit in a short speech. The ensuing spectacle alternated between songs, choreographed dances, and recitations designed as a self-referential loop of commentary on the masque's theme. An extended period of revels bridged the onstage fantasy to the spectators' reality, until a final song called the masquers back to the stage to end the drama. The entire entertainment could last up to five hours, and a banquet afterward (with informal dancing) often extended the event late into the evening.

The Masque of Blackness adheres to this loose model. Its prologue recalls the accounts of Pliny, Solinus, Ptolemy, and Leo the African, who traveled the Niger River and encountered people of the "blackest nation of the world."[16] Following this, a song of praise to Oceanus ("Sound, sound aloud, the welcome of the orient flood into the west") accompanies the parade of characters arriving onstage. Jonson's description of this opening scene referred to their costumes, from the blue-skinned god Oceanus and the accompanying Tritons playing instruments shaped like seashells to various sea monsters, torchbearers, singing sea-maids, and finally the queen and her ladies. A dialogue initiated by Oceanus to Niger (who, it is revealed, is a mortal son of Oceanus) describes his long journey with his daughters to seek a miracle: the transformation of their skin color. Niger breaks into song ("O see, our silver star!") at seeing the moon Aethiopia, who confirms that Niger has found the place where its ruler can "blanch an Ethiop and revive a cor's" (that is, course of action). Aethiopia calls forth Niger's daughters to dance before the "Britain men," and the Tritons play a signal on their instruments to announce a dance to display the masquers' skill.

As required, the blackamoor queen and ladies come forth and execute paired dances before the audience. Jonson had names and symbols imprinted on their shell-shaped fans, noting that the pairings intentionally designated complementary meanings, or "mixed names" and "mixed qualities."[17]

Emblems and other impresa were common features in dramatic spectacles like the masque, and the pairing of names and symbols would have invited audience members to speculate upon their related meanings. The preceding qualities and symbols suggest the world of the sovereign as encompassing abstract, divine, and earthly matters. On a more personal level, the queen's quality of grace was an appropriate designation of her position, and the symbol of the tree laden with fruit likely referred to the fact that she was pregnant.

At the end of the paired dance, the masquers are poised to initiate the revels when singers onstage attempt to stop them from dancing with the audience ("Come Away, come away, we grow jealous of your stay"), a common tactic of building suspense. The masquers proceed nevertheless, dancing several "measures and corantos" with their selected partners, before a song announcing the end of the revels ("Daughters of the subtle flood, do not let earth longer entertain you") beckons the masquers back to the stage. Another dance guides the masquers back to their seashell boat, and a final tune ("Now Dian' with her burning face") ends the masque in celebratory joy of finding the land of Albion.[18] Festivities following the masque proper included more dancing and a banquet.

Table 1. Guide to emblems and impresa

Masquer	Name (Meaning)	Symbol
Queen Anne	Euphoris (grace)	Golden tree laden with fruit
Countess of Bedford	Agalaia (grace)	
Lady Herbert	Diaphane (transparency)	The figure isocahedron of crystal
Countess of Derby	Eucampse (flexibility)	
Lady Rich	Ocyte (swiftness)	A pair of naked feet in a river
Countess of Suffolk	Kathare (spotless)	
Lady Bevill	Notis (moisture)	The salamander simple
Lady Effingham	Psychrote (coldness)	
Lady Elizabeth Howard	Glycyte (sweetness)	A cloud full of rain, dropping
Lady Susan de Vere	Malacia (delicacy)	
Lady Wroth	Baryte (weight)	An urn, sphered with wine
Lady Walsingham	Periphere (revolving, circular)	

Jonson's song lyrics and "textual marginalia" provide valuable clues to what the audience witnessed at the Whitehall Banqueting House in 1605. He printed a quarto containing *The Masque of Blackness* and *Masque of Beauty,* ostensibly to preserve the spirit (if not his own literary creation) of an entertainment intended for a single performance; as was the customary practice of masque festivities, spectators destroyed the scenery after the revels.[19] The passage of time between *The Masque of Blackness* and its sequel allowed him to amend his original manuscript with detailed descriptions of the costumes and sequence of events that had occurred three years prior.[20]

A cursory sketch of the masque's activities underscores the important role of music, if only to clarify the sequence of events. Music for the songs and dances of the English masque reflected a diversity of styles largely derived from national practices. The lute song repertoire was extensive, as were adaptations of part-song and consort repertoires. Music from other countries was not unknown at the English courts, of course, and composers of Ferrabosco's generation were keen to learn all the contemporary idioms of musical expression.[21] Nevertheless, England's history of political and religious conflicts with continental Europe often led to periods of cultural schisms with other countries; such inward-looking times often encouraged the development of distinct national traditions, as seen in the music for the Anglican rite.[22] The English court masque, by virtue of its function to magnify and promote its patrons' ideologies, favored themes of distinctly national provenance both in subject and in music.[23] Projecting a distinctly English cultural face was important for the Scottish-born King James, whose deficiency of birthright could potentially be ameliorated through the procession of dances, songs, and recitations describing his powers—or at least, we assume so, since very little of the actual music for the masque has survived to the present day.

The absence of a fully notated musical score for the masque should not suggest that the music was inconsequential in realizing the masque's conceit. On the contrary, music was crucial in conveying the meaning of the masque's spectacle; the fact that much of it was not written down simply reflects the strong oral tradition of music making at the time. Understanding this blend of oral and written musical practices is crucial in exploring whether the masque projected an audible sense of Otherness.[24] Whether Ferrabosco's music for this masque contributed to its connotations about difference, racial or otherwise, is a question scholars have not yet considered, most likely because the small quantity of extant music for this masque has deterred such inquiry.

Only one song ("Come Away"; see example 1) has survived from this masque, composed by Ferrabosco and published in 1609 within a compendium of his compositions available only as a modern edition.[25] There is no other notated music for the masque; however, all song lyrics are included as part of Jonson's

Example 1. "Come Away" *ayre* from *The Masque of Blackness,* by Ferrabosco.

text (the recited words, as well as stage directions and commentary). Tunes for masque dances were generally not preserved as discrete compositions associated with a specific drama, although it is possible to infer from contemporaneous instrumental music books the kinds of styles musicians favored for initiating and accompanying the dances. It would be foolhardy for anyone to examine extant songs from any dramatic spectacle of this time with an eye toward discerning racial qualities embedded in specific notes or harmonies, given the realm of interpretative realization that defined the performance practices of the Renaissance and early Baroque. Yet Ferrabosco's compositional style demonstrates a level of musical sophistication that could have intimated the English monarchy's response to cultural differences.

Music's dramatic equality to text and dance in the court masque has been documented and discussed extensively by Peter Walls. Walls delineates distinct functions and types of songs in the masque tradition, describing the settings in which they were used. Songs are essential in the absence of a teleological plot, as they punctuate the sections of a masque as a series of tableaux; the type of song employed indicated a specific type of dance or section of dancing, such as the revels. Much of what survives from Jacobean masques are solo songs called *ayres,* some of which were derived from older polyphonic consort music, but also from newer accompanied declamatory solo songs. Walls further distinguishes the song repertories from the music composed to accompany dances in the masque, which were governed more by choreography than by text.[26]

Dance and music were inextricably linked in the masque, insofar as composers were bound by choreographic conventions to provide audible cues for the dance steps. Courtly behavior linked dance with markers of social standing; an individual's dancing skills could seal that person's fate at court. Political decorum in a masque demanded evidence of strict organization and social control, governed by conspicuous displays of dancing in manners delineating codes of proper social conduct.[27] Music set the tone of the dance, supporting this vital social ritual so thoroughly that Tom Bishop has described "dancing as social singing."[28]

Regrettably, none of the choreography for the masque survives, nor does the music with which the dances were associated appear in printed editions.[29] Moreover, we cannot say with any certainty who would have written the music for those dances, as Ferrabosco would have been only one of several composers employed to provide music for *The Masque of Blackness.*[30] This collaborative model of composition reveals not only an absence of a musical urtext but also a problem of authorship. Jonson's masques are filled with musical indications, from descriptions of sounds and dance types to song lyrics he penned himself. Walls thus cautions against "assuming too readily that the music and the other elements of the entertainment shared the kind of unity of purpose found in the libretto and score of an opera."[31]

Nevertheless, both masque and opera share a common goal of employing a musical style intended to clarify the declamation of text. Indeed, the flexibility of the masque's structure in setting words and inserting ad hoc musical numbers allowed composers like Ferrabosco to incorporate the new Italian monody without having to rely on audiences' recognition of monodic style. For example, the song "Come Away" (example 1), which precedes the revels in *The Masque of Blackness,* points toward new compositional conventions. The regularity of the song's formal, metric, and phrase structures, its emphasis on a composed solo melody, and the sequence of precise chordal harmonies all point to the new declamatory style of the Baroque era (though the absence of monody would preclude its classification as operatic). Vestiges of the Renaissance polyphonic practice appear in the accompanying voices that move independently or obliquely, but they are much less florid than earlier styles of continuous polyphony. The vocal melody's rhythm is close enough to the accompaniment that it could almost be joined with the other three parts and performed like a madrigal.[32]

Ferrabosco also likely provided clever musical effects for some of the lyrics in Jonson's text. For example, in "Daughters of the Subtle Flood," Jonson formatted the words as lines with echoes in the first verses. The echoes contradict the meaning of their preceding derivative phrases:

> Daughters of the subtle flood, Do not let earth longer entertain you
> [echo 1] Let earth longer entertain you
> [echo 2] Longer entertain you
> 'Tis to them enough of good, That you give this little hope to gain you
> [echo 1] Give this little hope to gain you
> [echo 2] Little hope to gain you

The auditory concept of echoing is simple enough to imagine Ferrabosco crafting the melodies for this song into a repeated phrase structure.

Word painting and madrigalisms notwithstanding, the mechanics of forging a new relationship between music and text proved a difficult task. Notated music at the turn of the seventeenth century was commonplace, but it was not altogether standardized. This explains in part why no complete musical score for *The Masque of Blackness* exists. Songs such as "Come Away" were "fixed" compositions suitable for repeated performances and publication; in fact, Ferrabosco included this song in a later collection, *Solo Ayres* (1609). Music performed extemporaneously, however, was left unnotated. This included musical effects created specifically for points in the drama, or lyrical gestures, and implied meanings that are embedded in Jonson's scripts.[33] Even published songs from the English masque repertory did not imply a cohesive, predetermined, and completely notated "composition" in the sense that we understand it today.

To be sure, Ferrabosco's extant works, even in their modern editions, display consistent stylistic traits of complex chordal structures and progressions, lyrical yet declamatory text setting, and a sophisticated knowledge of writing for solo and consort instruments.[34] But whether he or anyone else could have conceived of an audibly distinct "Other" in conjunction with the rhetoric of Jonson's prose, the iconography in Jones's sets and costumes, or the stylized dances is a problem involving myriad perspectives beyond the music itself.

Regardless of nationality or style, composers at the turn of the seventeenth century struggled to connect sounds with sights, words, and symbols, hoping to create frames of reference to enclose the rich synthesis of interwoven dramatic elements on the stage. This process is difficult to describe precisely, because the performance practices that achieved this synthesis were more rhetorical than reified. Musicians today might assume that music found in manuscripts and published compilations represents sovereign and fully realized "works" to be performed exactly as written, but the musician of the sixteenth and seventeenth centuries would not have treated most notated music as immutable. In fact, the credibility of a musician from that period often rested on their capacity to realize the most "appropriate" performance based on a simple "gloss" of the written music; even music that contained complete parts for four voices was understood as a blueprint to be interpreted by its performers.[35]

In light of these considerations, it seems quite plausible that the cultural meaning of *The Masque of Blackness* comes less from its ostensible creators than its central performer—Queen Anne herself—whose political ambitions in commissioning the masque may be more significant than previously believed. Jonson's complex web of political and cultural references to the Jacobean court, Jones's incorporation of intricate and esoteric symbols into the costumes and sets, and Ferrabosco's adaptation of continental musical practices within a distinctly English genre all confirm the work as overtly imperialistic, if not also clearly racialist and perhaps gendered aggressively feminine. Thus, in a single masque, the queen (via Jonson) united several themes in English cultural, historical, and political topics, all viewed through the prism of the racial Other.

The recognition and exploitation of racial difference by the English court was not new. The sixteenth-century Tudor court was familiar with the sight of dark-skinned people, although their presence at court was rare. However, contemporaneous dramatic works from England and continental Europe contained notable references to skin color. Actors in the Italian commedia dell'arte tradition wore masks and improvised stories around stock characters, some of whom were black or Moorish. Perhaps the most familiar Moorish characters in English drama are those in Shakespeare's plays *Othello, The Merchant of Venice* (Prince of Morocco), and *Titus Andronicus* (Aaron), but many other English dramas from the sixteenth century delineated the character and qualities of dark-skinned people, as shown in Anthony Gerard Barthelemy's study of black characters on the English stage from 1589 to 1695.[36] After his examination of dramas ranging from plays and masques and Lord Mayor's pageants, Barthelemy notes that they promoted a consistently negative image of dark-skinned people. He argues persuasively that dramatic spectacle reflected, if not propagated, hostile English attitudes toward people of African descent. Moreover, he points out several instances in these dramas where the designation of "Moor" was applied in reference to any character deviating from European Christian values, customs, or appearances.

Virginia Mason Vaughan also confirms the presence of Moorish characters in court masques during the reigns of Henry VIII, Edward VI, and Elizabeth I. Some of these court pageants and urban processions, she notes, contained a transformation scene wherein characters blackfaced as Moors were suddenly turned white. Vaughan argues that the black-white transformation "symbolically enacted the colonizing myth through which King and merchants could control and transform the darkened aliens beyond England's shores."[37] More direct control could take place within England's own borders. In 1596, Queen Elizabeth issued expulsion orders for all blacks in England to stem the tide of illegal foreign labor, with the exception of those blacks whom the monarchy held in esteem (such as the Moroccan ambassador).[38] Interestingly, the same expulsion order included Irish laborers, a class of people also deemed "black," although they were not sold as chattel labor.[39] This unlikely combination of ethnic groups under a single designation suggests that "blackness" in English nomenclature could refer to qualities other than (or in addition to) skin color.

When added to Barthelemy's documentation of the overgeneralized designation of "Moor," the interpretive possibilities of the blackened masquers in *The Masque of Blackness* could extend to designating people as "dark" in ways other than the purely physical. One of the most notable traits associated with black characters in drama was their consistently negative connotation, which rendered the designations "black" or "dark" as powerful value signifiers. These values, when attached to new concepts or objects, could influence perceptions about people beyond the criterion of skin pigmentation. For example, in the English political mind-set at the time of James I's reign, Scotland and Ireland represented "dark" territories as unfamiliar and foreboding as Africa.[40] Taming these "black" northerners required advanced diplomatic techniques, if not assurances that the king had the best interests of England in mind. Opponents to the king's vision of an expanded Great Britain feared that it revealed his true nature: a quintessentially barbaric Scotsman seeking to conquer England (with the assistance of Irish thugs).

But on hand to promote the king's vision for a unified Britain was the queen, performing her duties as his cultural ambassador. The conceit of blackness would seem in this light a thinly veiled apologetic for James's maneuvers to subsume Ireland and Scotland under his rule, and the masque itself would act as a conciliatory gesture to the political conflict he caused in pressuring his Parliament to support an unpopular venture. Perhaps in an attempt to woo English adversaries to consider the benefits of a new Great Britain, the mixed names and qualities on the masquers' fans suggested a melding of diverse sources. More obvious perhaps are the lines in Jonson's text that iterate several times the suffix *-tania*—found in Niger's account of traveling to Mauritania (Northwest Africa),

Lusitania (Spain and Portugal), and Aquitania (France) before finding Britannia, evoking the name for James's visionary kingdom.[41]

Using the broadened contexts suggested by Orgel, Barthelemy, and Vaughan, spectators at the masque could have interpreted the blackness of King Niger and his daughters as representing any number of foreigners. This would suggest that the miracle of transformation in the masque had more to do with changing ideas and temperaments than appearances.[42] Orgel's argument—that blackness symbolized a generally negative quality—is significant for his reading of Queen Elizabeth's expulsion of blacks as a type of spiritual deficiency, which was argued on a deeper level in *The Masque of Blackness*: "The option of a royal miracle was not offered to the blacks at whom Elizabeth aimed her expulsion order, but even the rhetoric of that document suggests that their essential defect is not the colour of their skin or any racial infection, but simply—like the daughters of Niger before their enlightenment—a failure of comprehension and conversion."[43] An English court audience knowledgeable about current issues would have understood the burden of negotiating or absorbing foreign "humours" within English cultural identity.[44] Changing Irish and Scottish personality traits, perceived as drastically foreign, thus would have seemed as futile as trying to change black skin into white. Similarly, English expatriates felt keenly the difference in cultural values in foreign lands where they were charged with asserting their "English" identity and culture over local practice.[45]

If the new Jacobean court aimed to reign supreme over peoples from foreign lands (African and elsewhere), then all aspects of dramatic spectacle would have been deployed to confirm this agenda, regardless of their verisimilitude. The masque was never intended to depict a realistic society, but rather an ideal world under the benevolent rule of a monarch. Because they were safely insulated from the institution of slavery that European nations (and by the latter part of the century, the English monarchy itself) propagated abroad, Queen Anne and her court artists could only guess at how to dramatize a black Other.[46] The costumes for the masquers, for example, did not reproduce the dress of indigenous Africans. Rather, their design arrived from a composite of styles that Inigo Jones and the queen determined would be most effective in appearing fashionably exotic (figure 1). Orgel traces the sources for Jones's ideas to a book, published by Venetian merchant Cesare Vecellio, of various contemporary national costumes—specifically, the headpiece for the masquers derived from that of a Thessalonian (Turkish) bride and the gown from an Ethiopian virgin (figure 2).[47]

Any established facts about foreign lands were subject to reinterpretation (or deliberate misinterpretation) so long as they all projected an ideology of the sovereign as having extraordinary or supernatural powers to bring order to the world. This enabled a liberal juxtaposition of symbols, images, and references in

Figure 1. Inigo Jones, costume for daughters of Niger, *The Masque of Blackness*. © Devonshire Collection, Chatsworth. Reproduced by permission of Chatsworth Settlement Trustees.

the court masque that allowed its patrons to decipher both obvious and subtle layers of meaning.[48]

The most obviously exotic aspects of *The Masque of Blackness* were visual, beginning with the masquers themselves. There were the queen and her ladies, smeared with black makeup on their faces, arms, and legs (and in the process breaking court etiquette by baring their legs and arms in public). The queen further challenged convention by eschewing the use of a vizard—a leather, cloth, or hard mask that was customary to wear when playing the role of a foreigner,

Figure 2. Inspiration for Jones's masque costumes: Thessalonian bride and Ethiopian virgin. *Source:* Cesare Vecellio, *Clothing, Ancient and Modern, of Various Parts of the World,* translated by Ann Rosalind Jones and Margaret F. Rosenthal (London: Thames and Hudson, 2008).

regardless of ethnicity—choosing instead to apply black makeup directly to her skin. Not even male masquers had done this so extensively, and her decision furthered her reputation as an independent and willful woman. The novelties of Jones's costume design were reinforced by his equally novel set, which dispensed with the conventional static stage blocking and introduced a new style of movement onstage that gave audiences the illusion of motion across large expanses of space. Jones also employed moving scenery in dramatic spectacle: for example, constructing a wheel-machinery mechanism underneath turquoise cloth on the floor that created the effect of moving water upon which the masquers' seashell boat "moved" across the ocean.

Such exotic sights would presumably warrant equally exotic music. Evoking the sound of the Other would have necessitated a series of audible cues that the audience would perceive as not only "different," but distinctive enough to identify its foreign provenance. This poses several problems. If the masquers' black makeup alluded not specifically to Africans but to any culture deemed inferior or hostile to English rule (that is, the Irish), then Ferrabosco might have been at a loss to select which ethnic music would best represent the intended foreign culture. Moreover, even if we assume that Ferrabosco had read about or heard indigenous music from Africa, he probably would have been at a loss to adequately notate it or explain the performance of such an unfamiliar practice to the musicians at court. The possibilities seem endless when imagining the kinds of music that could possibly reinforce the multiple layers of Otherness suggested in this masque—or, more important, whether such music ever existed.

Music was undoubtedly a crucial element in promoting the meaning of Jonson's drama, but perhaps not in the manner of evoking chaos or disorder; indeed, the opposite seems to have been the case. There is no evidence in any of the surviving documentation of any exotic or aberrant musical effects included in the work. The extant song, along with edited collections of music from dramas and other entertainments from this time, suggests that music's corroborative role in *The Masque of Blackness* was to allude to its own potentially stabilizing power. Ferrabosco's music seems to provide the one "conventional" component in an otherwise unconventional spectacle. As such, the music for the masque's songs and dances preserved its rhetorical paradigm of articulating the sovereign's power over social and political order through the allegorical story of Niger's travels to Albion. The lone surviving song for *The Masque of Blackness,* as well as the substantial consort and dance music, can symbolize an effective method to contain, control, and even silence Otherness.

When melded to the rich mythological symbolism of Jonson's prose, the hieroglyphic symbols on costumes and sets, and the stylized dance, music added the ultimately divine representation of the monarchy in *The Masque of Blackness.* In both *The Masque of Blackness* and *Masque of Beauty,* the mystical properties of Albion-Britain derive from the powers of Neptune and Oceanus, deities appropriately assigned to a nation surrounded by the sea. King James is therefore linked to classical gods reigning over sea and land, and the masques effectively use mythological allusions to amplify his attributes. The ancient and universal harmonic logic of music bestowed a resolution of divine and mortal proportions upon a situation presented by characters black and white, foreign and native.[49] Thus, English music, constructed upon a harmony of rationally derived and ordered sounds, emerges as the lingua franca of absolutist rule, the apex of the sophisticated and modern expressive style.

Jonson's marginalia describe the opening song of the masque as a hymn to Oceanus (the godly analogue to King James), who addressed the weary travelers (the masquers) at the shores of Albion. Had Niger and his daughters attempted to communicate with Oceanus using the musical and spoken languages of their homeland, no one would have understood them, much less welcomed them onto shore. To approach a king as powerful as James I—as Niger and his daughters most certainly did by landing on Albion—required displays of great humility, beginning with observing the host's codes of conduct. Jonson's masque does not speak of Oceanus-James visiting Africa, nor do the foreigners extol the virtues of their native culture. This masque is not a diplomatic visit but a request to become part of Albion's world, and the prospective "immigrants" have already decided, by the time they arrive, that they wish to relinquish that which makes them citizens of a foreign land: their skin color.

Acclimatization to English social values thus began prior to the masque's beginning. Indeed, the account of Niger and his daughters journeying to other lands before arriving at Albion's shores implies their rejection of other nations populated by ethnicities other than the Anglo-Saxon peoples. Their efforts garner credibility for them as worthy recipients of the king's favor, as does their flattery of him as the only being capable of transforming their pigmentation. At a court where conspicuous displays of etiquette were paramount to maintaining social order, it bode well for Niger's daughters to demonstrate their knowledge of the dancing customs of Albion, as evidenced by their dance before "Britain men." By acting in accordance with a crucial ritual of masquing, rather than misbehaving in a manner characteristic of a comedy or antimasque (that is, an introductory section of a masque that presented unruly characters who engaged in disorderly behavior), they proffered their worthiness to "be white."[50]

Finally, it is significant that the exotic appearance of the queen and her ladies-in-waiting did not necessarily imply that they were "savage" and incapable of temperamental or spiritual enlightenment. As daughters of an African king, they belonged to a social class higher than those relegated to slave status. By all standards other than skin color, Niger's daughters appeared to be readily assimilative into English (that is, white) society. Race was therefore not necessarily a fixed distinction within the British construction of social hierarchy but potentially negotiable when combined with other considerations such as class. Like the "mixed qualities" on the fans the queen and her ladies carried, Niger's daughters may have been valued for their exotic beauty, providing the ornamental decorations for what David Cannadine describes as vital to building the notion of a globally dominant British Empire. Olivia Bloechel develops this idea with regards to English court masques that portrayed Native Americans as exotic new features of colonial expansion, masques mounted just a few years after this one.[51]

To be sure, the music for *The Masque of Blackness* illustrates the extent to which the absence of firsthand contact with non-European cultures would support assumptions of an English supremacy that privileged whiteness as a cultural hallmark. Yet the music's highly ordered structures projected a model of rational response that symbolized an effective containment of various forms of social dissonance. In a country perpetually vulnerable to invasion from all shores, people's faith in their sovereign depended on his or her ability to neutralize the discord caused by "others" and to cultivate harmonious relationships at home and abroad.[52] What better way to signify the king's actions in this regard than with music?[53] English music does not merge with "black" music, and so the musical affect is nonrepresentative in terms of sounding any singular or localized gesture in contrast with established conventions. Musical "Otherness" can only be implied (if at all) because of its conspicuous absence. *The Masque of Blackness* therefore reflects an ethos of privilege by which members of the ruling classes could define others without accounting for themselves, using a disguise to engage in free play of liberally interpreting symbols without substantiating those claims.

The power of drama to inculcate social values by means of constructing associations between the physical and ideological cannot be underestimated in a highly mediated spectacle such as the masque. While the English court composer of the seventeenth century may have been wholly ignorant of African musical idioms, the close proximity of blacks and whites on English colonies inevitably produced an exchange of cultural knowledge, distorted though it may have been. Negative valuations of blackness, as articulated through English dramas such as the masque, were thus reified through successive generations of dramatic works.

Such distorted exchange came to fruition centuries later in the United States, where the minstrel show denigrated black Americans through its songs, dances, and recitations. This is not to center *The Masque of Blackness* as the taproot of American blackface minstrelsy, but rather to consider the trajectory of deepening signification of blackness through dramatic elements. The novelty of the minstrel show derived largely from its "exotic" elements of sight and sound (that is, dialects, timbres, dances), stylistic features that eluded Ferrabosco and his peers. Yet the damaging effects of minstrelsy in the United States would seem to challenge the simplistic notion that composers would naturally portray different social groups with equanimity if only they experienced their musical traditions firsthand.[54] An empirical survey of music that sounds different (or has been marketed as different) does not necessarily cultivate thoughtful dialogue, especially when dominant social groups—then and now—belittle such styles in order to validate their own cultural preferences.

Where the masquing traditions of England and Europe afforded actors a measure of personal liberty to project an alternate identity onstage and then return to their "authentic" selves once they relinquished their mask, such freedoms were generally not extended to black minstrel performers.[55] Blackness seems subject to be forever defined in relation to whiteness. When empowered with the agency to represent themselves, black performers reveal the points of slippage or cultural dissonance within dramatic conventions that have imposed social Othering as a matter of course.

We may proclaim an understanding of world cultures far more extensive than that of Queen Anne and King James, yet, when we consider what previous generations assumed about their own world (and their place in it), we might be well advised to challenge the kinds of boundaries we currently perceive between self and Other.[56] With the ensuing decades' worth of growth and change in mass entertainment, the ubiquitous dichotomy between black and white has often become simplified to the point of caricature. *The Masque of Blackness* would have us explore carefully the roots of a culture's assumptions about what blackness represents, what kinds of qualities make people and societies different from one another, and whether the differences we perceive are only skin deep.

Notes

1. Herford, Simpson, and Simpson, *Ben Jonson: Complete Works,* vol. 7.

2. Ibid.

3. Dudley Carleton to Ralph Winwood, January 1604/5, in ibid., 10:448–49.

4. Vaughan, *Performing Blackness,* 69. See also Ravelhofer, *Early Stuart Masque,* 176.

5. For a helpful overview of metaphor and allegory in early Baroque dramatic spectacle, see "Prelude: The View from Above" and the introductory chapter, "Feasts, Allegories, and Politics," of Aercke's *Gods of Play.* See also Strong, *Art and Power,* which includes a chapter ("Illusions of Absolutism") on dramatic spectacles during the reign of Charles I, James's successor. Hart provides a thorough overview of the Socratic and Platonic precedents in all the arts serving the Stuart monarchy from James I to Charles I in *Art and Magic.*

6. Anne of Denmark (1574–1619), who married James VI of Scotland in 1589, commanded a considerable budget for her personal court's retinue of entertainers and other artists. Although many aristocratic women were known for their generous patronage of the arts, Anne's patronage at the English Court was particularly remarkable for its lavish expenses on elaborate costumes and staging. For an extensive discussion of Anne and her contribution to the arts in England, see McManus, *Women on the Renaissance Stage;* and Barroll, *Anna of Denmark.*

7. A thorough reference work on the cultural and political contexts for the performing arts during the early Jacobean era is Spink, *Blackwell History of Music.*

8. James's apologist essay on absolutism and monarchy, "The Trew Law of Free Monarchies (1597–98)," provides scriptural references to support his thesis elevating kings above ordinary humans. His supplement to the essay, "Basilkion Doron," was the practical application of these principles for his son Prince Henry, age four and the firstborn heir to the throne.

9. Orgel has written extensively on the Jonsonian masque. See *Illusion of Power, The Jonsonian Masque,* and, with Roy Strong, *Theater of the Stuart Court.* See also his "Marginal Jonson."

10. Lindley, "Stuart Masque and Its Makers."

11. Orgel, *The Jonsonian Masque,* 117.

12. Bishop, "Gingerbread Host," 96.

13. In reality, cutbacks in the queen's discretionary budget postponed the sequel's performance until 1608.

14. The contributions of Queen Anne's court in promoting the Jacobean monarchy have been discussed extensively in Barroll, *Anna of Denmark.*

15. An overview of the sequence of the events in the court masque can be found in Styan, *English Stage,* 187–98. See also *Cambridge History of British Theatre.*

16. All quotes in this summary of the work are taken from Jonson, *The Masque of Blackness,* 660–63. Also available as an e-text by Luminarium Editions, ed. Anniina Jokinen, http://www.luminarium.org/editions/maskblack.htm.

17. Gordon, "Imagery of Jonson's *Masque of Blacknesse* [*sic*]." Hagerman provides the meaning of the names for each of the fans in "'But Worth pretends,'" n. 7.

18. This summary of the events from the masque is derived from the text as it appears in Herford, Simpson, and Simpson, *Ben Jonson: Complete Works,* vol. 7.

19. This quarto is the primary source used to prepare the critical edition of Jonson's *Complete Works.*

20. As a sequel to Jonson's first masque for the queen, *Masque of Beauty* begins with a reference to its precedent by querying the whereabouts of Albion (Neptune's son). The new masque recounts the transformational miracle of *The Masque of Blackness* before proceeding with its own conceit, the description of how grateful Niger's daughters are to have been the recipients of Albion's gift.

21. Lindley notes that recitative styles and elaborate improvisatory skills were considered the most sophisticated musical competencies at the time. "Politics of Music," 286. Ferrabosco was a renowned viol player and teacher (he tutored Prince Henry) who published several arrangements of songs for viol consort. Jonson wrote an effusive introduction to Ferrabosco's 1609 publication of courtly *ayres* and dances, wherein he extolled the composer's versatility to perform and write in any idiom with ease.

22. Of course, the Anglican rite displays stylistic characteristics clearly traceable to continental practices; moreover, English music was influenced by a prodigious amount of imported music (for example, *Musica Transalpina* of 1588). Be that as it may, the self-conscious rhetoric of a "national" expressive identity in England at this time (and especially at court) rendered foreign genres malleable to adaptations that aimed to show English mastery over them in interpretation and innovation.

23. Contrasting with the early Jacobean court's self-conscious cultivation of English music during the early seventeenth century, the Restoration era (post-1660) saw the cultivation of foreign music styles at the court of Charles II, who wished to promote an image of international cosmopolitanism.

24. The meeting of oral and written traditions in early opera is discussed extensively in Hansen, "From Invention to Interpretation."

25. The extant song from the masque is included in Alfonso Ferrabosco's collection *Ayres,* originally scored for voice and lute and published in London by John Browne in 1609. David Greer prepared a critical edition of *Ayres* from a copy in the British Museum (Menston, UK: Scolar Press, 1970). The song also appears in Sabol, *Four Hundred Songs.*

Sabol has also published performing editions of music for two later masques: *Score for "Lovers Made Men"* and *Score for "The Lords' Masque."*

26. Walls, *Music in the English Courtly Masque,* 46–68, 104–7, 123–26.

27. McManus, "'Defacing the Carcass,'" 100. The most detailed accounts of the choreography and extensive rehearsal schedules preceding a masque performance can be found in Ravelhofer, *Early Stuart Masque.*

28. Bishop, "Gingerbread Host," 97.

29. Walls, *Music in the English Courtly Masque,* 123–27.

30. Walls confirms this by examining a roster of services for a later masque (*Love Freed from Ignorance and Folly* [1611]) for which Ferrabosco provided songs. Ibid., 36. Additional composers, assigned to the task of "setting the songs" and arranging the instrumental dance music, are listed under Ferrabosco's name.

31. Ibid., 33.

32. In character, it resembles a later madrigal of Monteverdi, whose collected books of madrigals show a clear progression from Renaissance part-writing derived from polyphony to a new practice of homophony conceived as a solo melody with accompaniment.

33. See Lindley, "Politics of Music," 285.

34. Walls reproduces Jonson's epigram for Ferrabosco's collection. *Music in the English Courtly Masque,* 9. Jonson clearly held the composer in high esteem, especially for his knowledge of many contemporary continental styles.

35. This was especially the case if the text underlay did not visually line up with the corresponding melodic pitches or indicate rhythmic organizing principles.

36. Barthelemy, *Black Face, Maligned Race.*

37. Vaughan, *Performing Blackness,* 65, 33.

38. Exemptions also apparently included black entertainers at court, whose presence is evident in artworks depicting lavish spectacles and descriptions of such events. See, for example, a memorial painting of Sir Henry Unton's life by an unknown painter (ca. 1596) showing several black masquers carrying torches as part of the opening procession (along with a discussion of such processionals and their characters) in Daye, "Torchbearers in the English Masque."

39. Orgel, "Marginal Jonson," 161. Designations of Irish people as "black" stems from a long (and misguided) tradition of characterizing black-haired Caucasians of Irish descent as evincing African, Spanish-Iberian, Italian, even Jewish lineages. English caricatures of "black Irish" portray them with dark skin, jutting jaws, and so on to suggest their subhuman intelligence and social status.

40. The negative connotation of Irish people as "black" is also found in popularly oriented Irish ethnic music scores from the late nineteenth and early twentieth centuries, the cover art of which often includes cartoonish Paddies with dark skin and (often) protruding lips and noses.

41. Dudley Carleton, who had written so disdainfully about the ugliness of the masquers, opposed the idea of absorbing these other regions into the whole of England. His criticism may therefore have stemmed from his recognizing the masque's true political message.

42. Several additional readings of *The Masque of Blackness* suggest that Queen Anne's

concept of blackness encompassed multiple types of difference. Murray, for example, claims that the queen and Ben Jonson's collaboration served to validate their secret Catholic identities in the face of James's Protestantism. "Performing Devotion," 427. See also Norbrook, "Reformation of the Masque." Similarly, Hall, McManus, and others have used a gendered lens to interpret Queen Anne's flaunting her embodied self, exposed and six months pregnant, as transgressing the sexually oppressive moral codes imposed on women in an overly mannered English society. See Hall, *Things of Darkness;* and McManus, "'Defacing the Carcass.'"

43. Orgel, "Marginal Jonson," 164.

44. The concept of "humours" refers to theories of geoclimatic temperament used (among other purposes) to explain and justify social constructions for dealing with ethnicity and race. See Floyd-Wilson, *English Ethnicity and Race.*

45. Hall, "Sexual Politics and Cultural Power," 15.

46. For further information about British contact with dark-skinned peoples of Africa and the Caribbean, see Earle and Lowe, *Black Africans in Renaissance Europe;* Foster, *Out of Slavery;* and Thomas, *History of the Atlantic Slave Trade.*

47. The *Ethiopian Virgin* in Cesare Vecellio, *Degli habiti antichi et moderni di diverse parti del mondo* (Venice, 1590, plate 427), shows draping and horizontal striping similar to the costume in figure 2, and a color engraving by Jean Jacques Boissard, *Jeune mariée Thessalonique* (1581), strikingly resembles the turquoise color and headpiece of Jones's costume.

48. The choice of a specific dance to signify character and social status may lead some to query whether the "Moresca" or the popular English "Morris" dance would have appeared in this spectacle to reinforce the masquers' ethnicity as "blackamoor." In the case of the Border Morris dances among the Welsh border counties in England, performers blacken their faces. It is tempting to envision the queen and ladies-in-waiting dancing in a manner that would have reinforced the exoticism of their appearance, but to do so would have been interpreted as an incredible and likely unforgivable breach of etiquette, given the importance of dancing to delineate social status. If someone as outspoken as Sir Dudley Carleton noted the masquers' blackened faces, he and others would have certainly reported gross manners in dancing. An extensive study on these dances may be found in Forrest, *History of Morris Dancing.*

49. Both Lindley and Walls discuss the architectural principles of proportion that Jones brought to his designs for buildings and masque collaborations that derived from or were commensurate with proportional principles of music theory. See Lindley, "Stuart Masque and Its Makers," 395; and Walls, *Music in the English Courtly Masque,* 47.

50. Lindley describes antimasques that call for disruptive sounds, although these spectacles were performed at least a decade later than *The Masque of Blackness.* "Politics of Music," 275.

51. Cannadine, *Ornamentalism;* Bloechel, *Native American Song,* specifically the chapter "Musicking Indians in the Stuart Court Masque."

52. Lindley describes the use of loud, disruptive music in the masque *Triumph of Peace* (1634) to signify "bad" northerners and the use of courtly music to contain their disruptiveness. "Politics of Music," 275–76, 283.

53. Indeed, Lindley grounds the success of the masque's argument as dependent on its music, that the "translation of music into an emblem of the harmony engendered by the monarch was a familiar trope." "Stuart Masque and Its Makers," 397. As such, music could be used to imply that a ruler like James I was godly enough to harness musical powers to his liking.

54. See, for instance, Pickering, *Blackface Minstrelsy in Britain*. American music scholars often assume that the minstrel show was indigenous to the United States, but in fact Pickering shows that England's history of racial oppression was equally suited to support the cultivation of music dramas that depicted non-Anglo whites as superior. By the 1830s in both countries, the close proximity of blacks and whites—even with the former in a subservient role—generated substantial exchanges (unwittingly perhaps) of each group's musical customs.

55. The masking makeup worn by African American minstrels may have emboldened them to dispense social critique and double entendres under the guise of "entertainment." Yet the mask was nevertheless imposed upon these performers, designed to exaggerate their features and depict them as fundamentally flawed or grotesque.

56. An exemplary set of essays exploring this issue can be found in Biddle and Knights, *Music, National Identity, and the Politics of Location*.

Bibliography

Aercke, Kristiaan. *Gods of Play: Baroque Festive Performances as Rhetorical Discourse*. New York: State University of New York Press, 1994.

Barroll, J. Leeds. *Anna of Denmark, Queen of England: A Cultural Biography*. Philadelphia: University of Pennsylvania Press, 2001.

Barthelemy, Anthony Gerard. *Black Face, Maligned Race*. St. Louis: St. Louis University Press, 1987.

Biddle, Ian, and Jessica Knights, eds. *Music, National Identity, and the Politics of Location: Between the Global and the Local*. Aldershot, Hampshire: Ashgate, 2007.

Bishop, Tom. "The Gingerbread Host: Tradition and Novelty in the Jacobean Masque." In *Politics of the Stuart Court Masque*, ed. David Bevington and Peter Holbrook. Cambridge: Cambridge University Press, 1998.

Bloechel, Olivia. *Native American Song at the Frontiers of Early Modern Music*. Cambridge: Cambridge University Press, 2008.

Cambridge History of British Theatre. Vol. 1. Cambridge: Cambridge University Press, 2004.

Cannadine, David. *Ornamentalism: How the British Saw Their Empire*. Oxford: Oxford University Press, 2002.

Daye, Anne. "Torchbearers in the English Masque." *Early Music* 26, no. 2 (1998): 246–62.

Earle, Thomas Foster, and Kate Lowe, eds. *Black Africans in Renaissance Europe*. Cambridge: Cambridge University Press, 2005.

Ferrabosco, Alfonso. *Ayres* [1609]. Ed. David Greer. Menston, UK: Scolar Press, 1970.

Floyd-Wilson, Mary. *English Ethnicity and Race in Early Modern Drama*. Cambridge: Cambridge University Press, 2003.

Forrest, John. *History of Morris Dancing, 1458–1750*. Cambridge: John C. Clarke, 2000.

Foster, Nardia. *Out of Slavery: African-Caribbean History from a British Perspective; An Educator's Resource.* Bristol: Redcliffe, 2004.

Gordon, D. A. "The Imagery of Ben Jonson's *Masque of Blacknesse* [*sic*]." *West Virginia Studies in Language and Literature* 10 (Spring 1985): 49–61.

Hagerman, Anita. "'But Worth pretends': Discovering Jonsonian Masque in Lady Mary Wroth's *Pamphilia to Amphilanthus.*" *Early Modern Literary Studies* 6, no. 3 (2001): 1–17.

Hall, Kim. "Sexual Politics and Cultural Power in *Masque of Blackness.*" In *The Performance of Power: Theatrical Discourse and Politics,* ed. Sue-Ellen Case and Janelle Reinelt, 3–18. Iowa City: University of Iowa Press, 1991.

———. *Things of Darkness: Economies of Race and Gender in Early Modern England.* Ithaca: Cornell University Press, 1995.

Hansen, Jett Barnholdt. "From Invention to Interpretation: The Prologues of the First Court Operas Where Oral and Written Cultures Meet." *Journal of Musicology* 20, no. 4 (2003): 556–96.

Hart, Vaughan. *Art and Magic in the Court of the Stuarts.* London: Routledge, 1994.

Herford, C. H., Percy Simpson, and Evelyn Simpson, eds. *Ben Jonson: Complete Works.* 7 vols. Oxford: Clarendon Press, 1925–63.

Jonson, Ben. *The Masque of Blackness.* In *The Works of Ben Jonson.* Boston: Phillips, Sampson, 1853.

Lindley, David. "The Politics of Music in the Masque." In *The Politics of the Stuart Court Masque,* ed. David Bevington and Peter Holbrook. Cambridge: Cambridge University Press, 1999.

———. "The Stuart Masque and Its Makers." In *The Cambridge History of British Theatre,* ed. Jane Milling and Peter Thomson, 1:383–406. Cambridge: Cambridge University Press, 2004.

McManus, Clare. "'Defacing the Carcass': Anne of Denmark and Jonson's *The Masque of Blackness.*" In *Refashioning Ben Jonson: Gender, Politics, and the Jonsonian Canon,* ed. Julie Sanders, Susan Wiseman, and Kate Chedgzoy, 93–113. New York: St. Martin's Press, 1998.

———. *Women on the Renaissance Stage: Anna of Denmark and Female Masquing in the Stuart Court, 1590–1619.* Manchester: Manchester University Press, 2002.

Muller, Frans, and Julie Muller. "Completing the Picture: The Importance of Reconstructing Early Opera." *Early Music* 33, no. 4 (2005): 667–81.

Murray, Molly. "Performing Devotion in the *Masque of Blackness.*" *Studies in English Literature, 1500–1900* 47, no. 2 (2007): 427–49.

Norbrook, David. "The Reformation of the Masque." In *The Court Masque,* ed. David Lindley, 94–110. Revels Plays Companion Library. Manchester: Manchester University Press, 1984.

Orgel, Stephen. *The Illusion of Power: Political Theater in the English Renaissance.* Berkeley and Los Angeles: University of California Press, 1973.

———. *The Jonsonian Masque.* 2nd ed. New York: Columbia University Press, 1981.

———. "Marginal Jonson." In *Politics of the Stuart Court Masque,* ed. David Bevington and Peter Holbrook, 144–75. Cambridge: Cambridge University Press, 1998.

Orgel, Stephen, and Roy Strong. *The Theater of the Stuart Court.* Berkeley and Los Angeles: University of California Press, 1973.

Pickering, Michael. *Blackface Minstrelsy in Britain.* Aldershot, Hampshire: Ashgate, 2008.

Ravelhofer, Barbara. *Early Stuart Masque: Dance, Costume, and Music.* Oxford: Oxford University Press, 2006.

Sabol, Andrew, ed. *Four Hundred Songs and Dances from the Stuart Masque.* Providence: Brown University Press, 1982.

———, ed. *Score for "Lovers Made Men," a Masque by Ben Jonson: The Music Adapted and Arranged for Dramatic Performance from Compositions by Nicholas Lanier, Alphonso Ferrabosco, and Their Contemporaries.* Providence: Brown University Press, 1963.

———, ed. *A Score for "The Lords' Masque" by Thomas Campion: Performed 14 February 1613.* Hanover, N.H.: University Press of New England, 1993.

Spink, Ian. *The Blackwell History of Music in Britain.* Vol. 3, *The Seventeenth Century.* Oxford: Blackwell, 1991.

Strong, Roy. *Art and Power: Renaissance Festivals, 1450–1650.* Rev. ed. Woodbridge, Suffolk: Boydell Press, 1999.

Styan, J. L. *The English Stage: A History of Drama and Performance.* Cambridge: Cambridge University Press, 1996.

Thomas, Hugh. *The History of the Atlantic Slave Trade, 1440–1870.* New York: Simon and Schuster, 1997.

Vaughan, Virginia Mason. *Performing Blackness on English Stages, 1500–1800.* Cambridge: Cambridge University Press, 2005.

Walls, Peter. *Music in the English Courtly Masque, 1604–1640.* Oxford: Clarendon Press, 1996.

3

Nationalism, Racial Difference, and "Egyptian" Meaning in Verdi's *Aida*

CHRISTOPHER R. GAUTHIER AND JENNIFER MCFARLANE-HARRIS

In a July 16, 1870, letter to Giuseppe Piroli, a good friend in Rome, Giuseppe Verdi writes, "I am busy. Guess! . . . Writing an opera for Cairo!!! *Oof.* I shall not go to stage it because I would be afraid of being mummified. . . . If anyone had told me two years ago, *You will write for Cairo,* I would have considered him a fool; but now I see that I am the fool."[1] Verdi's humor reveals his attitude toward Egypt; like many Westerners of the period, Verdi regarded Egypt and its "civilization" as a curiosity. In fact, as the above letter indicates, Verdi did not go to Cairo for the world premiere of *Aida* at the Cairo Opera House on December 24, 1871. Instead, he put monumental effort into preparing the singers and staging for *Aida*'s European debut at La Scala in Milan.[2] Critics and commentators ever since seem to have followed Verdi's lead; effectively, the history of the performance of *Aida* does not begin until 1872.[3] Perhaps a lack of information on the first performance in Cairo has led to a certain silence about *Aida* as it was first staged in Egypt. Indeed, other than the oft-quoted article by Filippo Filippi, an Italian critic who attended the Egyptian premiere, there seems to be little information available on the first production of *Aida* in Cairo.[4] Despite a lack of evidence regarding the Egyptian reaction to this first performance, however, we should no longer ignore the Egyptian context. Instead, we must return to Cairo circa 1871 to answer one of the most intriguing questions suggested by this opera: how do we make sense of the dynamics of race in *Aida*?

Race Relations

Race matters in *Aida,* but how it matters hinges on multiple factors. Although race has been discredited as a valid scientific means of human classification, it is still tempting to view race as a biological concept based on correlations between heredity and physiology. This temptation likely arises from a "commonsense" understanding of race as a taxonomic system based on "a set of physical categories that can be used consistently and informatively to describe, explain, and make predictions about groups of human beings and individual members of those groups."[5] The fact that the physical characteristics employed to differentiate racial categories (such as complexion, hair texture, facial features, and so on) vary across cultures and throughout history makes biological explanations of racial difference dubious. The very idea of race is a product of human endeavor rather than "natural" forces. Furthermore, because racial signifiers and their meanings are articulated differently according to time, place, and social context, the content of racial categories is highly unstable.[6] Ian F. Haney López maintains that this instability stems from the fact that racial categories are constructed in order to perform the ideological function of justifying or explaining the relative positions of subjugated and elevated groups.[7] Simply put, race is a signifier that justifies and explains social difference. Therefore, any meaningful analysis of race must bypass the compulsion to treat race as a universal concept in favor of an approach that is sensitive to history, contingency, and local meaning.

In this chapter we will focus on *Aida* as a European cultural artifact that, when considered in the context of nineteenth-century Egypt, generates Egyptian meaning as a by-product. The 1871 Cairo premiere of *Aida* is a fruitful historical locality to examine when trying to understand the workings of racial difference, particularly because such differences lie uncomfortably on the surface of the opera. Our interpretation locates *Aida* at the nexus of race and nationalism in Egypt. We argue that, for Egyptians, *Aida* may have spoken to a sense of emergent Egyptian identity, an identity at least partially forged in relation to darker-skinned Africans living to the south. By analyzing the libretto and music of *Aida* and demonstrating how these elements connect to discourses of light-skinned Egyptian superiority and dark-skinned African inferiority, we will show that racial dynamics in the opera are revealed through aural, visual, and textual dynamics.[8] The specificities of Egypt's relations with its racial-national Others are manifested through the relationships between characters in the opera, illuminating a larger project of Egyptian identity formation through "racial fabrication."[9]

Aida and the Orientalist Critique

In order to understand how identity categories such as Ethiopian-Egyptian and dark-skinned–lighter-skinned are constructed relationally in *Aida*, we must add another set of terms to our analysis: *Orient-Occident* or *East-West*. The late Edward Said was a preeminent authority on this topic, and it is within his own analysis of *Aida* that we find both the importance and limitations of his influential work on power, discourse, and positional superiority. *Aida,* according to Said, is undeniably about European domination, a fact that he claims is not so much inherent in the opera itself as in its manufacture.[10] Verdi had never visited Egypt and therefore had no "real" relation to the country he sought to represent, though he familiarized himself with the work of Belgian musicologist François-Joseph Fétis (who claimed to have outlined the structure of ancient Egyptian tonality) and fabricated the existence of priestesses for which there was no actual Egyptian analogue.[11] Furthermore, Said points to French Egyptologist Auguste Mariette's dependence on that Orientalist document *par excellence,* the *Description de l'Égypte,* when designing the set and costumes, and takes this as evidence that *Aida*'s aspirations of visual authenticity were themselves spawned from Western representations (in this case, French) of the Orient.[12] As he writes in *Orientalism,* "Every writer on the Orient . . . assumes some Oriental precedent, some previous knowledge of the Orient to which he refers and on which he relies. Additionally, each work on the Orient *affiliates* itself with other works, with audiences, with institutions, with the Orient itself."[13] Conceptions of the Orient, then, are built on other Western ideas about the Orient, which may have little relation to the material realities of the countries and peoples that make up this "Orient."[14]

Said also finds it significant that Verdi viewed the opportunity to compose an opera about Egypt as a chance to exert control over the creative process. Said contends that this opportunity inspired in Verdi a conviction common to those in a position of imperial power: namely, that he was free to do as he pleased when it came to constructing an opera about a non-European entity to which he did not feel accountable. In other words, Orientalism in *Aida* manifests in Verdi's *attitude* toward the composition of the opera. For Said, the infusion of Orientalism in *Aida* is as evident in Verdi's unrestrained enthusiasm for creating his vision of Egypt as it is in the music, libretto, or stage production.

Compelling as this interpretation is, Said takes us no further. His analysis contains within it the logic of his larger project of describing the origins and mechanics of European presumptions of superiority over the East. However, Said is unable to pull himself away from the binary on which his formulation depends. As much as Said criticizes the West's project of homogenizing and essentializing cultures within the East, he, too, implicitly treats the East as one-dimensional. In Said's setup, the West alone possesses agency, while the East passively languishes, subject to the discourse of inferiority and its attendant colonial intervention.[15]

It is no wonder, then, that Said chose to ignore the actual story line of *Aida* in favor of examining the opera's creation.[16] The opera itself, if Said had chosen to look, is a complicated place to find representations that go beyond the East-West binary. There is no European presence in *Aida;* if taken literally, *Aida* is about the imperial designs of one African country on another. Moreover, as Paul Robinson has pointed out, it is the Ethiopians who are most frequently rendered musically exotic in *Aida,* more so than the Egyptians (who are the Oriental focus in Said's reading).[17] Indeed, Said fails to consider *Aida*'s place in Egyptian society, stating simply that "Verdi must have had opportunities to wonder what modern Egyptians thought of his work, how individual listeners responded to his music, what would become of the opera after the premiere."[18] Rather than continuing to overlook the Egyptian perspective, we must pick up where Said's musings leave off, establishing an "Egyptian" meaning that does not presume that *Aida* is singularly about European domination.

For a specific instance of this contrast in potential meaning, consider two distinct performances of *Aida.* To an Italian viewing the European opening of *Aida* at La Scala in 1872, the opera may have evoked notions of the Risorgimento as much as it might have served to reinforce or invent Orientalist conceptions of Egyptians and Africa.[19] But we cannot assume that the opera would function this way for an Egyptian audience, nor in the description, recounting, rumor, and discussion of the opera among Egyptians not in attendance at the 1871 Cairo premiere. As Hans Busch suggests, the khedive himself may have commissioned the production of *Aida* because the story related to contemporary Egyptian conflicts. "In 1861, [Ismail] led an army of 14,000 men to suppress an insurgence of slaves in the Sudan. This recurring hostility with the Ethiopians may have contributed to his decision to have the story of *Aida* made into an opera."[20] In this case, dark-skinned Ethiopians represented an archetypal racial Other from dangerous conquered lands to the southeast of Egypt.

Therefore, in considering who constitutes the Other, we can no longer focus exclusively on the Western imperial gaze from a Western vantage point. Instead, we must contemplate Egypt's racial Others in order to see how *Aida* may have been viewed given the sociohistorical zeitgeist in nineteenth-century Egypt. As we shall see, interpreting an opera that is, on the surface, about an ordered and efficient Egyptian military and a dark-skinned slave from Ethiopia takes on an entirely different meaning when viewed in light of the nineteenth-century transformation of Egyptian society and the rise of nationalism in Egypt that depended on notions of racial difference and intra-African imperialism.

A Step Closer: Egypt as Agent

If Said's work presents Egypt as an object of European intervention, Timothy Mitchell's analysis in *Colonising Egypt* seeks to complicate this narrative. Mitchell points to the ways in which Egyptian elites remade the military, schools, and economy, relentlessly bringing life in Egypt into line with European blueprints of order and rationality.[21] This process, Mitchell argues, marked a transition from repressive discipline—a form not effective or pervasive enough to ensure obedience in an emerging modern order—to more subtle and effective mechanisms of continuous surveillance. Drawing on Michel Foucault's theory of discipline, Mitchell observes that Egyptians gained compliance from their soldiers, schoolchildren, and farmers by imposing precise order on their regiments, drills, dress, classrooms, curricula, houses, and agricultural methods.[22] Continuous surveillance, when combined with standardized laws and rules and seemingly inescapable punishments, coerced Egyptians to discipline themselves, therefore ensuring self-regulating military, agricultural, and bureaucratic productive forces for Egypt as it emerged as a modern regional power.

Khaled Fahmy, whose work on transformations in the Egyptian military builds on Mitchell's Foucauldian analysis of power, contends, "The most powerful tool in controlling men, their activities and their bodies appeared to be no more than a piece of paper: the roll call or inventory list."[23] With the ability to order bodies and register their positions in space, the military was able to address the problem of desertion through simple and seemingly passive means. Soldiers knew that they would be counted and that any movement outside their prearranged orbit had to be processed and approved. As a result, soldiers no longer had to be forced to stay, but instead forced themselves, knowing that any illicit movement would be recorded and summarily addressed. For Mitchell and Fahmy, Egypt was remade in accordance with the principles of control, assent, and domination through containment, visibility, and the seemingly dispassionate accrual of knowledge.

Mitchell's work takes us further than Said's in restoring agency to Egypt, even if this agency is expressed largely through remaking the country along Western lines of order and rationality—a process fashioned by Egyptian elites but dependent on the self-discipline of Egyptians at large. Indeed, given this process, *Aida* can be understood as an opera about the emergence of new technologies of power that took hold of Egypt starting in the early nineteenth century: technologies that enforced self-discipline through surveillance.[24] Radames is, after all, a soldier who desires to flee to a foreign land but ultimately turns himself in to his superiors, impassive and resigned.[25] We are thus able to go beyond Mitchell's colonization-from-within approach in our analysis of *Aida* by appreciating the emergence of Egyptian imperial designs on the Sudan and the Nile Valley, as well as the ways in which this imperialism was racialized. Only then can we assess the ways in which racial tensions direct the narrative arc of *Aida*.

Miscegenation Impossible: The Politics of Race and Nation

The crisis of *Aida* involves the politics of nationhood writ large through the vehicle of a romantic triangle: Radames, a young Egyptian warrior, is in love with Aida, a former princess from Ethiopia who is now the slave of Amneris, daughter of the king of Egypt (who also happens to be in love with Radames and is determined to keep Aida away from him). The conflict between Egypt and Ethiopia outlined by Ramfis, the high priest of Egypt, in act 1, scene 1, remains largely abstract until the more personal romantic scenario is superimposed on it. Indeed, the trumpets of war that sound just before the first aria ("Celeste Aida"), stirring Radames's heart in a desire to be chosen to lead the Egyptian armies to victory against the Ethiopian invaders, are juxtaposed in the aria proper with woodwinds that will later be associated with Aida and her homeland as Radames sings, "Il tuo bel cielo vorrei ridarti, / Le dolci brezze del patrio suol" (I would like to give you back your lovely sky, / The gentle breezes of your native land).[26] In the space of a single recitative and aria, Radames brings together two impossible aspirations: he longs to lead the Egyptians to victory over the Ethiopians—Aida's own people—and somehow, paradoxically, dedicate this victory to Aida, his love, the queen of his thoughts ("Del mio pensiero tu sei regina").[27] For Radames, martial victory means little without the promise of a marital one.

The incompatibility of Radames's dreams for Egypt and Aida demonstrates how *Aida* embodies the complexities of representing and enacting nationhood. As Benedict Anderson's landmark work *Imagined Communities* reminds us, the concept of "nation" is challenging, defying simplistic definition. How much more difficult, then, does it become when bound up with questions of race? "Race" is often taken for granted, viewed as primordial and natural. It connotes heritage and lineage, nation and origin, phenotype and internal qualities, a specific type (classification) and a kind of universality ("human race"). As these connotations imply, the concept of "race" may be grafted onto that of "nation," resulting in a symbiotic relationship. Again turning to Anderson, we find that "race" and "nation" are two sides of the same coin; in "cultural products" that display "political love" (nationalism), we find "either . . . the vocabulary of kinship (motherland, *Vaterland, patria*) or that of home. . . . Both idioms denote something to which one is naturally tied." However, there is danger lurking in such discourse: "In everything 'natural' there is always something unchosen. In this way, nation-ness is assimilated to skin-colour, gender, parentage and birth-era—all those things one can not help."[28]

When Aida sings alone onstage at the end of act 1, scene 1, about the absurdity of telling Radames to "Ritorna vincitor!" (Return victorious!) when such victory would mean the defeat of her own brothers and Radames "Tinto del sangue amato" (Stained with their beloved blood), she invokes this very problem of the unchosenness of race and blood that binds her to her brothers and homeland, but not to Radames.[29] Musically, a thrice-repeated figure builds the drama of "Ritorna vincitor!" at the crucial moment when Aida reflects on the irony of wishing her lover success in a war against her brothers and father, a figure featuring the oboe and bassoon. This seven-note chromatic figure, punctuating Aida's lines with increasing tension, culminates in the return of Aida's theme in the clarinet as she sings, "Ah! sventurata! che dissi?" (Ah! Hapless me! What have I said?).[30] As Aida herself admits, the "sacri nomi" (sacred names) of *father* and *lover* cannot be uttered in the same sentence.[31] The woodwinds that intensify the absurdity of Radames's words in "Celeste Aida" also appear when Aida's desire to be devoted to both "father" and "lover" becomes a literal contradiction in terms.

In truth, the internal struggle for Aida and Radames is essentially the same: both recognize the practical impossibility of their love in light of their divergent national and racial allegiances. However, in terms of the logic of the opera, their situations are quite different. As a male Egyptian subject, Radames can choose whether to continue leading the Egyptian armies against Ethiopia or give up his sword and wed his fate to Aida's. On the other hand, Aida is a dark-skinned slave whose fate is tied to the whims of Amneris and the outcome of the war between Radames-Egypt and Amonasro-Ethiopia. And in fact, as Camille Du Locle's notes for act 2, scene 1, demonstrate, the physical differences between conquering Egypt and a conquered Ethiopia are made obvious onstage: "Joyful chorus. The princess [Amneris] is being adorned for the festivities about to take place. Her slaves add finishing touches to her attire. They burn perfume at her feet, they wave large fans in the air around her. Day blessed by the Gods. Day of feast! The sons of Osiris have won! Their enemies, the black Ethiopians, are dispersed and annihilated."[32] It is not just Aida's status as "enemy" that divides her from Radames but her status as an enemy from a *black* nation that threatens her love.

Egypt's Racial Others

In her book *A Different Shade of Colonialism: Egypt, Great Britain, and the Mastery of the Sudan,* Eve M. Troutt Powell demonstrates that blackness matters a great deal in terms of both material realities and the production of nationalist discourses, particularly when analyzing the position of Egypt in the Sudan and East Africa during the nineteenth century. Powell explains, "The Sudan remained under Egyptian authority from 1821 until 1884. These six decades (almost the length of the British occupation of Egypt) affected the lives of many Egyptians—differently than their encounter with western Europe but in ways just as profound and complicated." She does not claim we can equate European colonial power with what Egypt had at its disposal, but she does challenge Said's notion that "Egyptians suffered in silence, the idea that many in Egypt did not themselves engage in a discourse of stereotypes and fantasies about the Sudan specifically and Africa in general, a discourse that paralleled Orientalist imagery."[33]

What Powell unearths in her analysis of the literature generated about the Sudan by elite Egyptians during the *nahda,* the late-nineteenth-century Egyptian cultural and scientific renaissance, is that the emergence of Egyptian nationalism depended in no small part on racialized notions and caricatures of the Sudanese and dark-skinned Africans from Nubia and Abyssinia.[34] For example, she points to Egyptian educator, administrator, and engineer ʿAlî Mubârak, whose writing conveyed an impression of the Sudan and Africa "as a landscape of savagery, but one whose immaturity represented a past only recently shared by Egypt." Incidentally, it was upon seeing a manumitted and educated black-skinned Abyssinian in a position of power and prestige that Mubârak decided to pursue the schooling that led to his career in government and education. He reasoned, "If this school . . . could enable a former slave to achieve so much, then it was the path for him too." According to Powell, Mubârak's fictional work *ʿAlam al-Dīn* (1857, published 1882) asserted that Egypt's status in world affairs depended on exploring, generating knowledge about, and colonizing regions of Africa. Black-skinned Africans are portrayed in the book as primitive, with cultures and languages easily decoded by Western interlopers. At one point, James, an explorer who had been shipwrecked among black Africans, has a conversation with a fellow Englishman about how the slave trade in Africa resulted from general African backwardness, and "they debate the relative benefits of slavery to the generalized savagery of an entire continent, uniformly benighted and blackened." Powell intimates that, for Mubârak, adopting Western notions of colonization and control and applying them to Africa could prevent Egypt from being subsumed into a "benighted and blackened" continent.[35] By representing Africa as a blackened land of barbarism (even through the guise of European characters), Mubârak could participate in the crystallization of Egyptian nationalism by differentiating Egypt from the rest of Africa.

Rifa'ah Rafi' al-Tahtawî, a contemporary of Mubârak, had a starker view of racial Others in Africa and the Sudan specifically. He believed that Egyptian control of the Sudan was essential for the development of Egyptian national identity. Educated in Europe, al-Tahtawî was a teacher, administrator, and translator, perhaps best known for reforming Egypt's educational system in accord with Western pedagogical techniques that emphasized "precise methods of inspection, coordination and control." While exiled in the Sudan—a region that Egypt viewed as both rich in natural resources and an outpost from which Egypt could seek control of the Red Sea coast—al-Tahtawî was miserable. In his translation of Fenelon's *Aventures de Télémaque,* al-Tahtawî represents this land "only as the anathema to Egypt, the darkness against which Egypt is better drawn in contrast."[36]

But it was al-Tahtawî's subsequent work, Powell contends, that fully objectified the Sudan within the context of Egyptian nationalism: "In its passivity as the object of Egyptian imperialism, the Sudan played a crucial role in helping

Egyptians define and maintain their cultural, historical, political, economic, and geographic integrity [in relation to Europe]." Al-Tahtawî also portrays the Sudanese in racialized terms, describing them as "beasts" and "stones" and stating that the men "forced their women into prostitution" and "taught the women to fornicate like beasts," concluding that "if it had not been for the white Arabs . . . [the Sudanese] would have been blacker and blacker and blacker, nothing but blackness." According to Powell, al-Tahtawî's negative valuation of the Sudanese ascribed to them "no tribe, no religion, no language, no identity except that of slave or 'a blackness in a blackness in a blackness.'"[37] Just as Egypt sought to know itself through self-imposed Western order and rationality, it also constructed a sense of self that derived from the writings of elites like al-Tahtawî who drew a stark line between cultured, civilized Egypt and the uncivilized black Sudanese.

Like al-Tahtawî's uncivilized Sudanese and Mubârak's "benighted and blackened" Africans, the Ethiopians in *Aida* are clearly distinguished from their Egyptian counterparts. According to the cast notes in Giulio Ricordi's production book for La Scala, the actors playing Aida and Amonasro should be blackened with makeup; they should have "olive, dark reddish skin" onstage.[38] Rendered darker than the Egyptian characters, Ethiopians in *Aida* become the visual representatives of what Egypt is not, or what al-Tahtawî thought of as "the darkness against which Egypt is better drawn in contrast."[39]

In addition to phenotypic distinctions, the Ethiopians are also labeled "uncivilized" by the Egyptians, thus adding a further level of differentiation. In act 1, scene 1, the Ethiopians are referred to as invading "barbari" (barbarians) led by "Un guerriero indomabile, feroce" (A fierce, unconquerable warrior)—Amonasro, Aida's father. In this scene, the Egyptians contrast the savagery of their invading enemies with their own charge to defend the "sacro suolo dell'Egitto" (sacred soil of Egypt) from those who would destroy its crops and land.[40] This sense of sacred duty is reinforced by the proclamations of the Egyptian king and Ramfis, the high priest, as Radames is told to go forth to the Temple of Vulcan, where the aptly named "Consecration Scene" takes place (act 1, scene 2). The following hymnlike march is initiated by the king in act 1, scene 1:

> Su! del Nilo al sacro lido
> Accorrete, Egizii eroi;
> Da ogni cor prorompa il grido:
> Guerra e morte,
> Morte allo stranier!
>
> (On! Hasten to the Nile's
> Sacred shore, Egyptian heroes;
> Let this cry burst from every heart:
> War and death,
> Death to the foreigner!)[41]

The music of this march also returns for a brief moment in Amneris's apartments (act 2, scene 1) as a precursor to the Triumphal March (act 2, scene 2).[42] In this way, the sacrosanct duty of the Egyptians to triumph over the Ethiopians operates on both the public stage (through the consecration of Radames as leader of the Egyptian armies, who later parades Ethiopian idols, treasures, animals, and bodies past the king in the Triumphal Scene) and a private one (as Amneris reminds Aida that neither Aida's body nor fate is her own). Nationalism and racism entwine as Egyptian characters stereotype Ethiopians as barbarous, foreign savages marked by blackness (in contrast to the Egyptians—arbiters of civilization, organization, and sacred duty). As a result, captive Ethiopians (like Aida) are rendered knowable and controllable, minor threats to be dispassionately observed. Egyptians may show mercy, as the king does when he chooses to spare the lives of the Ethiopian prisoners, or they may persecute their enemies, as Amneris does when Aida is tricked into revealing her love for Radames. In either case, the Egyptians are the only ones who regulate what it means to be Egyptian, and they control the bodies and identities of Others in relation to their own.

Dangerous Associations

Such disparaging views of Ethiopia in *Aida* coexisted with a more complex set of understandings about Egyptian identity. By the time *Aida* was staged, many nationalist writers had grown critical of the khedive, his Ottoman administrators, and his imperial conquests—including a costly campaign in Ethiopia beginning in 1869—which often involved employing European administrators and necessitated the overextension of the Egyptian army.[43] At the same time, however, these writers beheld "the Sudan as wild territory that needed to be conquered according to Isma'îl's wishes." The stereotypes of the Sudan and Nile Valley that fostered support for their conquest coexisted with Egyptian awareness that dark-skinned Africans served as slaves for much of the nineteenth century. Egyptian notions of "foreignness" took multiple forms: "foreigners" could be agents of the Ottoman empire, Europeans, or simply dark-skinned Africans assigned a blanket identity, "that of *al-barbarī*, or the Nubian, whose color, customs, and accent Egyptian writers sketched out in numerous essays, dialogues, and stories."[44] The emergence of Egyptian national identity in the nineteenth century hinged (in part) on contradictory notions of black Africans constructed both as primitive, uncivilized Others hailing from lands deep in the Nile Valley and as familiar, acquiescent domestic servants or slaves. Both constructions imply that dark-skinned Africans would benefit from their association with Egypt; furthermore, they indicate that the construction of Egyptian identity depended to a large degree on a discourse of race that placed Egypt in "flexible positional superiority" over those with dark skin.[45]

This phenomenon is demonstrated in act 2, scene 1, of *Aida,* where Amneris asserts her relational superiority over her dark-skinned slaves, including Aida. The scene opens in Amneris's apartments to the sound of a harp accompanying the singing of a slave-girl chorus. The harp is immediately reminiscent of the offstage otherworldly incantations sung by the priestesses in the Consecration Scene, and the chorus of slave girls invokes their hero (Radames) using words similar to those used by the priestesses to invoke God (Fthà). Two forms of exoticization are thus linked; the priestesses call for the "Fuoco increato, eterno, / Onde ebbe luce il sol . . ." (Uncreated, eternal fire, / From whence the sun had light . . .) through flattened melodic intervals punctuated by grace notes, while the slave girls are accompanied by the oboe and clarinet as they reflect on the magnificence of Radames:

Chi mai fra gl'inni e i plausi
Erge alla gloria il vol,
Al par d'un Dio terribile,
Fulgente al par del sol?

(Who amid anthems and cheers
Is taking flight toward glory,
Terrible as a God,
Radiant as the sun?)[46]

The previous musical dialogue between the priestesses and the priests now becomes an encounter between the slave girls and Amneris. Much like the priests in the Consecration Scene, Amneris—whose solo lines are not accompanied by the harp and have no trace of the flattened supertonic—provides a solemn counterpoint that neutralizes the exoticized song of the slave girls. Here, the dichotomy between the exotic, dark-skinned slaves and the disciplined Egyptian is once again reinforced. Amneris is a representative of sober Egyptian nationality, while Aida and the other slaves must surrender their bodies and bend their wills to her. Truly, Amneris's slaves are rendered both Other (via their association with stereotypically exotic music) and acquiescent (their musical themes and outbursts cannot overtake Amneris).[47]

Additionally, the dance of the little Moorish slaves, which occurs after Amneris finishes singing about her longing for Radames, represents a moment where even foreign, undisciplined black slaves can be controlled. The fast tempo of the music, coupled with amateurish dancing, supplies nonthreatening entertainment for a reserved Amneris, as well as for the larger audience of the opera.[48] According to Giulio Ricordi's notes in the production book for La Scala, "The dance of the little Moorish slaves (ballerinas) must be very lively and rather grotesque, without many complicated steps which could not be executed considering the speed of the music."[49] Unsurprisingly, Amneris is content to observe, but not join, the dance.

Aida, however, is not just a figure of entertainment for Amneris. Because Radames loves her, Aida is a threat that Amneris must address more directly. Amneris must try to win Aida's trust, pretending to be her friend in the wake of her people's defeat. Of course, Amneris has an ulterior motive: to deceive Aida into revealing her true feelings for Radames by telling her that he is dead. Realizing how much she has accidentally conveyed by her reaction, Aida begins to stand up to Amneris, almost mentioning her status as an Ethiopian princess, the implicit equal to a pharaoh's daughter:

> Mia rivale! . . . ebben sia pure . . .
> Anch'io . . . son tal . . .
> Ah! che dissi mai?
>
> (My rival! . . . so be it then . . .
> I too . . . am . . .
> Ah! What have I said?)[50]

It is too late, however; the damage has been done. Amneris is affronted by Aida's audacity, thundering, "Trema, vil schiava!" (Tremble, base slave!). Amneris reminds Aida that she is her master and that such love for Radames could mean Aida's death.[51] In short, Ethiopians and Egyptians (or dark-skinned and lighter-skinned) are *not* equal, and slaves like Aida would do well to remember it.

Realizing that she is in a fight (or duet) she cannot win, Aida begins to abase herself before Amneris. Musically, the triplets of a plaintive bassoon are Aida's only ally as she sings,

> Pietà ti prenda del mio dolor . . .
> É vero . . . io l'amo d'immenso amor . . .
> Tu se felice, tu sei possente . . .
> Io vivo solo per questo amor!
>
> (Have pity on my grief . . .
> It's true . . . I love him with immense love . . .
> You are happy, you are powerful . . .
> I live only for this love!)[52]

However, Amneris continues her threats and is soon bolstered by the chorus outside, repeating the hymn "Su! del Nilo" that signals the ensuing Triumphal March. Amneris's voice complements the choral melody (first sung by the ministers and captains in the opening scene of act 1); she is a true Egyptian, and Aida is left only with her own suffering and wretchedness. Once again, Amneris asserts the control that is her birthright by dominating the conversation with Aida in their increasingly combative duet.

Unfortunately for Amneris, clinging to her Egyptian nationality later causes her pain. At the end of act 3, Amneris and Ramfis discover Radames's plan to flee to Ethiopia with Aida and Amonasro; although Aida and Amonasro attempt to escape, Radames turns himself over to Ramfis without a struggle, singing the resolute line, "Sacerdote, io resto a te" (Priest, I remain here, in your hands). Amneris proclaims Radames a traitor and, at the beginning of act 4, tells him that he must choose between her and Aida if he wants to avoid the terrible fate that awaits him when the priests sit in judgment of his treachery: "A lei rinunzia per sempre . . . / E tu vivrai!" (Give her up forever . . . / And you will live!). In essence, Amneris demands that Radames validate his own Egyptian identity by marrying her, forsaking his love for the dark-skinned Ethiopian slave. Yet Radames will not renounce Aida; even when interrogated by Ramfis and the Egyptian priests, he remains silent. Radames's choice causes Amneris great anguish because she knows her decision to turn Radames over to the Egyptian authorities has condemned him.[53] In an interesting twist, Aida's lamentations from act 1 become Amneris's in act 4; like Aida, she wishes for the victory of her beloved over her "brothers" (in this case, the Egyptian priests), but she cannot have it both ways. Having chosen to remain faithful to her Egyptian identity and forcing Radames to choose between his own Egyptian identity and Aida, Amneris has caused her own suffering.

Yet Amneris is doing more than telling Radames to remember the importance of his Egyptian identity in asking him to choose her over Aida. In fact, Amneris is reminding Radames that she and Aida have very different relationships to power. By offering herself to Radames, Amneris offers a union that her father, the king of Egypt, implicitly sanctioned in the Triumphal Scene (act 2, scene 2), saying, "Vieni, e mia figlia di sua man / Ti porga il serto trionfale" (Come, let my daughter give you / The triumphal crown with her own hands).[54] If Radames chooses his Egyptian identity, Amneris will be his reward, a key link to patriarchal power. As a dark-skinned Ethiopian, Aida cannot offer Radames a place in the power structure of his *patria,* nor can she offer him the light-skinned Egyptian offspring that Amneris could.[55] On these points, the power differential between Amneris and Aida is similar to the often unacknowledged power disparities between white women and women of color described by poet and essayist Audre Lorde in the early 1980s: "White women face the pitfall of being seduced into joining the oppressor under the pretense of sharing power. This possibility does not exist in the same way for women of Color. The tokenism that is sometimes extended to us is not an invitation to join power: our racial 'otherness' is a visible reality that makes that quite clear. For white women there is a wider range of pretended choices and rewards for identifying with patriarchal power and its tools."[56]

As Lorde makes clear, in a patriarchal power structure ruled by white men (or, in the Egyptian context of *Aida,* ruled by Egyptian elite males), white women and women of color are both at a disadvantage. However, their subordination is enacted through different means, leading to different outcomes.[57] Although Amneris's power can never equal her father's, her relationship to him allows her to exert her authority over Aida (who is visibly marked as racially and nationally inferior) and give Radames an ultimatum: choose me, or death.

Of course, this ultimatum does not ultimately serve Amneris well; by the close of the opera, she is thwarted and miserable. In terms of Western operatic conventions, when it comes to the trajectory of the love plot, the tenor (Radames) must end up with the soprano (Aida), despite the machinations of a mezzo (Amneris). Not even different *patrias* and racial disparities can keep Radames and Aida apart. Nevertheless, the price of their union is death. The harsh realities of racism and nationalism will ultimately triumph over their bodies, if not their spirits.

Interring Love, Liberating Meaning

The culmination of act 4, scene 2, finds Radames back in the Temple of Vulcan, this time doomed to die for treason against Egypt. In this famous split-level scene, Radames is shown encased below the floor of the temple in a shadowy stone vault. Above, standing on the stone that has literally sealed Radames's fate, appears Amneris. As the scene begins, a despairing Radames is startled by what he believes to be a ghost emerging from the darkness. It is Aida. Upon hearing her intentions to die with him in the burial chamber, Radames, formerly resigned to his own death, now vows to liberate Aida from the vault:

> T'avea il ciel per l'amor creata,
> Ed io t'uccido per averti amata!
> No, non morrai!
>
> (Heaven had created you for love,
> And I kill you because I loved you!
> No, you shall not die!)[58]

But Aida seems already focused on the afterlife, singing (*vaneggiando,* "delirious," as if in a trance):

> Già veggo il ciel dischiudersi,
> Ivi ogni affanno cessa . . .
> Ivi comincia l'estasi
> D'un immortale amor.
>
> (I see heaven opening already,
> There all pain ceases . . .
> There begins the ecstasy
> Of immortal love.)[59]

Aida's melody, notated by Verdi to be sung sweetly (*dolcissimo)* with a flowing tempo (*andantino*), rises and falls ethereally as she sings, reaching as high as a B-flat that seems directed skyward, beyond the walls of the tomb.[60]

As Aida's melody returns to earth, culminating in the tonic D-flat, the familiar chromatic incantation of the priestesses (beginning on D-flat, one octave above where Aida resolved) is once again heard from offstage.[61] As in the Consecration Scene, the priestesses' song is accompanied by the harp, leading Aida to tell Radames that the priestesses are singing their funeral hymn. In doing so, she acknowledges the danger implicit in pursuing the exotic Other, the only outcome of a love between a lighter-skinned Egyptian soldier and a darker-skinned Ethiopian slave. From the very first moments in the opera, Aida seems to understand that her love for Radames and her love for her *patria* can never be reconciled; by contrast, it has taken Radames the entire opera to realize that his martial and marital desires are incompatible. In the end, Radames is enveloped by Aida's exoticism, signified in the tomb by the subtly insistent chromatic melody of sinuous flutes accompanying Aida as she implores Radames to accept their shared fate, singing, "Invan! . . . / Tutto è finito sulla terra per noi . . . (In vain! . . . / All is finished on earth for us . . .).[62] Even though their voices soar out of the tomb in this final scene, death is imminent. All that is left for Radames and Aida is a darkness that is both chosen (Radames will not renounce Aida, no matter what the consequences, and Aida chooses to join Radames in the tomb rather than flee to her homeland) and inevitable (Aida did not choose her race or national origin, but anyone who chooses her shares her fate)—in other words, "a blackness in a blackness in a blackness."[63]

Audience members at the Cairo premiere who witnessed Amneris's final prayers and heard the soaring voices of Aida and Radames in the last moments of the opera would probably have understood the racial and national ideological formations in Egypt at the time, making the deaths of Aida and Radames poignant on both personal and political levels. Indeed, the close proximity of a darker-skinned Ethiopian heroine and lighter-skinned Egyptian hero may have reminded those in attendance of Egyptian circumstances and discourses that Verdi almost certainly would not have been aware of, let alone intended. But that is the advantage of placing *Aida* in an Egyptian context. By acknowledging that Egyptian nationalism depended on the simultaneous denigration and administration of the Sudan, and by recognizing nineteenth-century Egyptians' use of complex discourses of racial difference, we call into question the binary thinking often featured in analyses of Egypt, Europe, and *Aida*.

When considering *Aida* as part of an Egyptian discourse of nationalism, the operations of racial difference in the opera can be seen as part of a process that was unfolding within Egypt and Africa—a process that was influenced by, but ultimately unfolded outside of, the imagination of Europeans. Coming to terms with race in *Aida* requires that we move beyond viewing imperialism as an exclusively European phenomenon. Said may view *Aida* as Verdi's imperial composition, but the opera and its racial representations function in different ways and take on multiple meanings depending on the context of its deployment and the interpretive work of the audience.[64] Following Ralph Locke, who argues that representations in *Aida* are both invested with stereotypical meaning *and* function as signifiers that "[allow] audience members to make implicit connections to social structures and traits of character of their own time and place, or of any time and place," we advocate a flexible reading of *Aida* that takes seriously not only the position of the observer, but also the work that observers inevitably do in connecting the opera to their milieu.[65]

Throughout this chapter, we have tried to understand *Aida* as it might have been perceived by some Egyptians at a specific moment in the past. We do not aspire to put words or ideas in the mouths of Egyptians, pretending to "really" know how they would have made sense of *Aida;* such a task would be impossible, given the lack of historical record when it comes to Egyptian reactions to the opera. Instead, we have engaged a distinct and historically contingent approach to Egyptian subjectivity. In doing so, we ask a variant of Locke's question: "how does *Aida* portray the advantages, challenges, morality and price of imperial Egypt's rule over Ethiopia?"[66] If we fail to ask such questions, we may find ourselves inadvertently participating in another form of exoticization: neglecting the distinct circumstances of Egypt's politico-historical landscape at the time of *Aida*'s Cairo premiere.

Notes

The names of the coauthors are listed alphabetically.

1. Busch, *Verdi's "Aida,"* 34.

2. Verdi never intended to go to Cairo. In a handwritten copy of his terms for the contract with Cairo, Verdi included the following clause: "Maestro Verdi will not be obligated to go to Cairo for the rehearsals, but he will send a person he trusts so that the opera will be performed according to his intentions." Doc. 4, "Giuseppe Verdi's Terms for the Contract with Cairo," in ibid., 472; see also doc. 5, "Auguste Mariette's Contract with Giuseppe Verdi," in ibid., 473. Put simply, "Verdi regarded the first European production of *Aida* at La Scala, Milan, as of greater significance than the Cairo premiere." Osborne, *Verdi,* 224; see also 225–26 and Phillips-Matz, *Verdi: A Biography,* 587, 589.

3. Wechsberg implies that the difference between the Egyptian premiere and the European premiere was a qualitative musical one, as "the Cairo premiere was more a social than a musical event although the leading European music critics had been invited. They knew that the *real* premiere was being prepared by Verdi himself at La Scala." *Verdi,* 148 (emphasis in the original).

4. Filippi's article appeared in *La Perseveranza,* a Milan journal, on December 27, 1871. See Osborne, *Verdi,* 222ff.

5. Zack, *Philosophy of Science and Race,* 1. For an excellent discussion of "an ordinary or common sense idea of race" as inextricably linked to biology and a brief overview of the reasons why contemporary biological anthropologists, population geneticists, and evolutionary theorists find no scientific basis for racial categorization, see Zack, "Ethnicity, Race, and the Importance of Gender," 103–10.

6. Drawing on Michel Foucault, anthropologist and cultural historian Ann Laura Stoler notes that racisms and racial discourses are given "dynamic motility" precisely because race is a concept that cannot be easily pinned down. "Racial Histories," 376, 385. For Stoler, "Racial essences are not made up of a fixed and finite set of features but rather an interchanging and malleable range of them. . . . [R]acial systems combine elements of fixity and fluidity in ways that make them both resilient and impervious to empirical, experiential counterclaims." "Reflections on 'Racial Histories,'" 420. For more on the social construction of race, see López, "Social Construction of Race"; Gossett, *Race;* and Omi and Winant, *Racial Formation in the United States.*

7. López, "Social Construction of Race," 56.

8. McClary makes a similar point in her introduction to *Feminine Endings*: "Music is always dependent on the conferring of social meaning—as ethnomusicologists have long recognized, the study of signification in music cannot be undertaken in isolation from the human contexts that create, transmit, and respond to it" (21). For more on the dynamic process of language and the importance of context in meaning making, see Bakhtin, *Dialogic Imagination,* 282, 294; and Tambling, *Opera and the Culture of Fascism,* 75.

9. Following López, we use the phrase *racial fabrication* to highlight the human element necessary for Egyptian identity formation as a social process requiring individual actors (and, onstage, operatic actors) who possess distinct and individually subjective motivations for their behavior. See López, "Social Construction," 56.

10. "I shall put before the reader material that paradoxically cannot be overlooked but systematically has been. This is mostly because the embarrassment of *Aida* is finally that it is not so much *about* but *of* imperial domination." Said, *Culture and Imperialism,* 114 (emphasis in the original).

11. According to Said, "Fétis's value for Verdi was that he could read examples in his work of 'Oriental' music—the harmonic clichés, much used in carnival hoochy-kooch, are based on a flattening of the hypertonic—and instances of Oriental instruments." Ibid., 122. Said also writes that Fétis "seems to have irritated and fascinated [Verdi] in equal measure." Ibid., 121. See also Busch, *Verdi's "Aida,"* 40, 408–9; and Cruz, "*Aida*'s Flutes," 181. Additionally, and despite documented evidence to the contrary, Verdi decided to employ priestesses in *Aida*'s religious scenes, "following the conventional European practice of making Oriental women central to any exotic practice." Said, *Culture and Imperialism,* 121.

12. According to Said, Fétis most likely consulted the *Description de l'Égypte* when generating his work on the characteristics of "exotic" music. *Culture and Imperialism,* 121–22. Robert Irwin explains that the *Description* was one-dimensional in more than one sense: not only was it researched and written from a French perspective, but it also focused heavily on "Egypt's Pharaonic legacy," often to the exclusion of "Egypt's Islamic heritage." *For Lust of Knowing,* 140.

13. Said, *Orientalism,* 20 (emphasis in original).

14. Critics have pointed out that Said does not place much emphasis on lived realities in any case; rather, Said overemphasizes the textual aspects of Orientalism: "Said's presentation of the history of Orientalism as a canon of great but wicked books, almost all by dead white males, was that of a literary critic who wildly overvalued the importance of high literature in intellectual history. . . . As he saw it, it was discourse and textual strategies that drove the imperial project and set up the rubber plantations, dug out the Suez Canal and established garrisons of legionnaires in the Sahara." Irwin, *For Lust of Knowing,* 286.

15. See Powell, *Different Shade of Colonialism,* 9–10.

16. For Said, *Aida* is basically another Verdi opera "about a tenor and a soprano who want to make love but are prevented by a baritone and a mezzo." *Culture and Imperialism,* 114.

17. See Robinson, "Is *Aida* an Orientalist Opera?" 135–39. Ultimately, in Robinson's assessment, "it is not precisely Egypt that is orientalised by Verdi's exotic music but rather Egypt's imperial victims (the Moors and the Ethiopians), and, among the Egyptians themselves, state functionaries and entertainers, almost all of whom turn out to be women (and thus, presumably, not full-fledged members of Egyptian society)" (139).

18. Said, *Culture and Imperialism,* 122.

19. The Risorgimento, which lasted from the 1820s to the 1860s, refers to the movement to unify Italy into a single nation. Robert Viscusi views *Aida* as fundamentally about nationalism and therefore a part of Verdi's Risorgimento canon, reading the racial difference in *Aida* and the Egyptians' imperial designs on Ethiopia as analogous to the merging of disparate regional identities deemed necessary in the pursuit of a unified Italian identity. "Son of Italy," 46–47.

20. Busch, *Verdi's "Aida,"* 6.

21. Egyptian villages and cities were to be reorganized (and reconstructed) to reflect European models, so such "blueprints" could be quite literal, as demonstrated by Mitchell's discussion of "enframing," which he defines as "a method of dividing up and containing, as in the construction of barracks or the rebuilding of villages. . . . The plans and dimensions introduce space as something apparently abstract and neutral, a series of inert frames or containers." *Colonising Egypt,* 44–45.

22. According to Pfohl, Foucault believed that "the penitentiary enabled the state to isolate, observe, and then, based upon observation, manipulate and change the offender into a person whose calculated rationality and improved 'self-control' would better fit with the inner-discipline demanded by . . . modern society." *Images of Deviance and Social Control,* 15. See also Foucault, *Discipline and Punish.*

23. Fahmy, *All the Pasha's Men,* 146.

24. For more on the intricacies of power and its mechanisms as well as an articulation of the relationships between discourse, technologies of power, and the production of knowledge, see Foucault, *The History of Sexuality,* esp. 92–102.

25. Bergeron, "Verdi's Egyptian Spectacle." Making use of Mitchell's discussion of the Egyptian concept of *siyasa,* an Arabic word meaning "government" that, by the 1860s, came to have two meanings—to govern a group and to command or discipline the self—Bergeron seeks to understand Radames's decision to submit to Ramfis in act 3 of *Aida*

upon divulging Egypt's battle plans. Mitchell, *Colonising Egypt,* 102; Bergeron, "Verdi's Egyptian Spectacle," 152. She notes that Radames's actions are a personal equivalent to the public reordering of Egypt in accord with Western notions of rationality and control: "Accepting the moral consequences, Radames becomes the perfect representation of the colonial subject." "Verdi's Egyptian Spectacle," 153. See also Gauthier and McFarlane-Harris, "Verdi's Disciplined Subjects."

26. Weaver, *Seven Verdi Librettos,* 354–55. Budden suggests that the melody Radames starts to sing when "dwelling on Aida's 'native skies'" clearly references her homeland: "It is one of several themes to be found in the minor throughout the opera which begin with a descent from the fifth to the first degree; and their connotation . . . is always 'Ethiopia.'" *Operas of Verdi,* 203. For the woodwinds associated with Aida, see, for example, the reiteration of Aida's theme upon her first entrance, voiced by the clarinet. Verdi, *"Aïda": In Full Score,* 24. The lithe, supple music of the flute, clarinet, and bassoon in act 3 that limn "O patria mia" and later bolster the duet between Aida and Radames in which they discuss where they might live together is a good example of the association of woodwinds with Aida and her homeland.

27. Weaver, *Seven Verdi Librettos,* 352–53. For another critic who comments on the impossible desires of Radames, see Della Seta: "Radames remains unaware of the incompatibility of these two universes, of being simultaneously Aida's lover-redeemer and the king's commander-in-chief." "'O cieli azzurri,'" 59.

28. Anderson, *Imagined Communities,* 3, 143.

29. Weaver, *Seven Verdi Librettos,* 360–63.

30. Ibid., 362–63; Verdi, *"Aïda": In Full Score,* 64–65, 68.

31. Weaver, *Seven Verdi Librettos,* 362–63.

32. Busch, *Verdi's "Aida,"* 453–54. "This scenario, on which Verdi collaborated during Du Locle's visit to St. Agata (presumably 19 to 25 June 1870), is based on Auguste Mariette's French outline and the Verdis' translation of it." Ibid., 448.

33. Powell, *Different Shade of Colonialism,* 12, 10.

34. For more on the *nahda,* see Makdisi, "'Postcolonial' Literature in a Neocolonial World," 90. The term *Abyssinia* is generally accepted to refer to Ethiopia, although the term's etymology is a source of debate among some anthropologists. See Bender, "Two Notes on Terminology"; and Ater, "Making History," 21.

35. Powell, *Different Shade of Colonialism,* 56, 58, 59, 61. Powell is not convinced that Mubârak's thinking about race was as calcified as his prose suggests. She concludes, "Alî Mubârak was not so dismissive of Africans. There is a stronger identification with Africans within the text, and the narrative finds interesting links between Africans and Egyptians. For example, after many pages of excoriation, 'Alam al-Dīn himself notes that the 'ugly practices' of the Africans were once practiced also by Arabs in the pre-Islamic era." Ibid., 62.

36. Mitchell, *Colonising Egypt,* 74; Powell, *Different Shade of Colonialism,* 52.

37. Powell, *Different Shade of Colonialism,* 53, 54.

38. The production book includes a brief outline of both the physical characteristics and the personal dispositions of the principals. See doc. 12 in Busch, *Verdi's "Aida,"* 558–59.

39. Robinson has noted that Aida and Amonasro are also set apart from the Egyptians musically: "Much of the time, to be sure, Amonasro and Aida sing in an idiom that is not markedly different from the high European style that Verdi uses for all his major characters in the opera. But on a number of significant occasions Aida in particular is allowed to speak of her native land—whose luxurious beauty she contrasts with the aridity of Egypt—and on these occasions Verdi sets her utterances at the polar opposite of the sort of music he writes for his massed Egyptians." "Is *Aida* an Orientalist Opera?" 136.

40. Weaver, *Seven Verdi Librettos,* 358–59.

41. Ibid., 358–61.

42. Verdi, *"Aïda": In Full Score,* 46–47, 136–38.

43. For instance, Powell notes that "nationalist writers like [Ya'qûb] Sanû'a helped create Khedive Isma'îl's reputation for deceit and greed, and held him culpable for bankrupting Egypt and eventually causing it to be occupied by the British." *Different Shade of Colonialism,* 76.

44. Ibid., 77, 69–70.

45. Said, *Orientalism,* 7. For a typical example of this phenomenon in a dramatic context, see Powell's discussion of Ya'qūb Sanū'a's play *Abū Rida wa Ka'b al-Khayr,* in *Different Shade of Colonialism,* 82–85.

46. Weaver, *Seven Verdi Librettos,* 364–65, 368–69.

47. For more on stereotypical elements that connote exoticism in Western music, see Locke, *Musical Exoticism,* 50–54.

48. Naomi André has demonstrated that this undisciplined dance is a moment of high exoticism: "As a condensed microcosm of the exotic elements embedded in the opera, here we have Amneris, in all her imperial splendor, being entertained by the conquests of earlier territories." "Veiled Messages," 17.

49. Busch, *Verdi's "Aida,"* 574. Verdi refers to this scene as "a little ballet of little Ethiopian Moors at the beginning of the second act while Amneris conducts her toilette." Letter to Camille Du Locle, August 12, 1871, in ibid., 201.

50. Weaver, *Seven Verdi Librettos,* 372–73.

51. Ibid., 374–75.

52. Ibid., 372–75; Verdi, *"Aïda": In Full Score,* 133.

53. Weaver, *Seven Verdi Librettos,* 400–401, 404–5, 406–7. Amneris cries, "E in poter di costoro / Io stessa lo gettai!" (And I myself cast him / Into the power of those men!).

54. Ibid., 378–79.

55. Aida and Amneris's struggle for the love of Radames highlights two of the "five major ways in which women have been implicated in nationalism" posited by Nira Yuval-Davis and Floya Anthias and summarized by McClintock in *Imperial Leather*: "as reproducers of the boundaries of national groups (through restrictions on sexual or marital relations)" and "as biological reproducers of the members of national collectivities" (355). See also Hurtado, "Relating to Privilege," 843–44.

56. Lorde, "Age, Race, Class, and Sex," 118–19.

57. See Hurtado, "Relating to Privilege," 845.

58. Weaver, *Seven Verdi Librettos,* 412–13.

59. Ibid., 412–13; Verdi, *"Aïda": In Full Score,* 420.

60. Verdi, *"Aïda": In Full Score,* 420–23.

61. Ibid., 424.

62. Ibid., 426; Weaver, *Seven Verdi Librettos,* 414–15.

63. Al-Tahtawî, quoted in Powell, *Different Shade of Colonialism,* 54.

64. Consider the Zurich Opera House's 2006 production of *Aida* set in nineteenth-century colonial Egypt, which featured intentionally problematic allusions to Orientalist representations and themes of imperialism and control. Charles Friedman's 1952 musical *My Darlin' Aida* also offers an interesting context-specific interpretation. Relocated from Memphis, Egypt, to Memphis, Tennessee, at the time of the American Civil War, this version engages with Aida's race and slave status according to unequal conditions and Jim Crow ideologies extant in the United States during the first half of the twentieth century. See Woll, *Black Musical Theatre,* 190.

65. Locke, "Beyond the Exotic," 131.

66. Ibid., 106.

Bibliography

Anderson, Benedict. *Imagined Communities: Reflections on the Origin and Spread of Nationalism.* Rev. ed. New York: Verso, 1991.

André, Naomi. "Veiled Messages and Encoded Meanings: Exoticism, Verdi, and Women's Lower Voices." *Ars Lyrica* 11 (2000): 1–22.

Ater, Renée. "Making History: Meta Warrick Fuller's *Ethiopia.*" *American Art* 17, no. 3 (2003): 13–31.

Bakhtin, M. M. *The Dialogic Imagination.* Ed. Michael Holquist. Trans. Caryl Emerson and Michael Holquist. Austin: University of Texas Press, 1981.

Bender, M. Lionel. "Two Notes on Terminology: Reviews by Gamst and Austin." *American Anthropologist* 79, no. 4 (1977): 901–2.

Bergeron, Katherine. "Verdi's Egyptian Spectacle: On the Colonial Subject of *Aida.*" *Cambridge Opera Journal* 14, nos. 1–2 (2002): 149–59.

Budden, Julian. *The Operas of Verdi.* Vol. 3, *From Don Carlos to Falstaff.* London: Cassell, 1981.

Busch, Hans, ed. and trans. *Verdi's "Aida": The History of an Opera in Letters and Documents.* Minneapolis: University of Minnesota Press, 1978.

Cruz, Gabriela. "*Aida*'s Flutes." *Cambridge Opera Journal* 14, nos. 1–2 (2002): 177–200.

Della Seta, Fabrizio. "'O cieli azzurri': Exoticism and Dramatic Discourse in *Aida.*" Trans. Arthur Groos. *Cambridge Opera Journal* 3, no. 1 (1991): 49–62.

Fahmy, Khaled. *All the Pasha's Men: Mehmed Ali, His Army, and the Making of Modern Egypt.* New York: Cambridge University Press, 1997.

Foucault, Michel. *Discipline and Punish: The Birth of the Prison.* Trans. Alan Sheridan. New York: Vintage Books, 1977.

———. *The History of Sexuality.* Vol. 1, *An Introduction.* Trans. Robert Hurley. New York: Vintage Books, 1990.

Gauthier, Christopher R., and Jennifer McFarlane-Harris. "Verdi's Disciplined Subjects: Radamès, Amneris, and the Power of the Panopticon." *Discourse of Sociological Practice* 7, nos. 1–2 (2005): 103–17.

Gossett, Thomas F. *Race: The History of an Idea in America.* New York: Shocken Books, 1965.

Hurtado, Aída. "Relating to Privilege: Seduction and Rejection in the Subordination of White Women and Women of Color." *Signs: Journal of Women in Culture and Society* 14, no. 4 (1989): 833–55.

Irwin, Robert. *For Lust of Knowing: The Orientalists and Their Enemies.* New York: Allen Lane, 2006.

Locke, Ralph P. "Beyond the Exotic: How 'Eastern' Is *Aida*?" *Cambridge Opera Journal* 17, no. 2 (2005): 105–39.

———. *Musical Exoticism: Images and Reflections.* New York: Cambridge University Press, 2009.

López, Ian F. Haney. "The Social Construction of Race." In *An Introduction to Women's Studies: Gender in a Transnational World,* ed. Inderpal Grewal and Caren Kaplan, 54–58. Boston: McGraw-Hill, 2002.

Lorde, Audre. "Age, Race, Class, and Sex: Women Redefining Difference." In *Sister Outsider,* 114–23. Freedom, Calif.: Crossing Press, 1984.

Makdisi, Saree. "'Postcolonial' Literature in a Neocolonial World: Modern Arabic Culture and the End of Modernity." *Boundary 2* 22, no. 1 (1995): 85–115.

McClary, Susan. Introduction to *Feminine Endings: Music, Gender, and Sexuality.* Minneapolis: University of Minnesota Press, 1991.

McClintock, Anne. *Imperial Leather: Race, Gender, and Sexuality in the Colonial Contest.* New York: Routledge, 1995.

Mitchell, Timothy. *Colonising Egypt.* New York: Cambridge University Press, 1988.

Omi, Michael, and Howard Winant. *Racial Formation in the United States: From the 1960s to the 1990s.* New York: Routledge, 1994.

Osborne, Charles. *Verdi: A Life in the Theatre.* New York: Fromm International, 1987.

Pfohl, Stephen. *Images of Deviance and Social Control: A Sociological History.* New York: McGraw-Hill, 1994.

Phillips-Matz, Mary Jane. *Verdi: A Biography.* New York: Oxford University Press, 1993.

Powell, Eve M. Troutt. *A Different Shade of Colonialism: Egypt, Great Britain, and the Mastery of the Sudan.* Berkeley and Los Angeles: University of California Press, 2003.

Robinson, Paul. "Is *Aida* an Orientalist Opera?" *Cambridge Opera Journal* 5, no. 2 (1993): 133–40.

Said, Edward W. *Culture and Imperialism.* New York: Vintage Books, 1994.

———. *Orientalism.* New York: Vintage Books, 1978.

Stoler, Ann Laura. "Racial Histories and Their Regimes of Truth." In *Race Critical Theories: Text and Context,* ed. Philomena Essed and David Theo Goldberg, 369–91. Malden, Mass.: Wiley-Blackwell, 2001.

———. "Reflections on 'Racial Histories and Their Regimes of Truth.'" In *Race Critical Theories: Text and Context,* ed. Philomena Essed and David Theo Goldberg, 417–21. Malden, Mass.: Wiley-Blackwell, 2001.

Tambling, Jeremy. *Opera and the Culture of Fascism.* Oxford: Clarendon Press, 1996.

Verdi, Giuseppe. *"Aïda": In Full Score.* New York: Dover, 1989.

Viscusi, Robert. "Son of Italy: Immigrant Ambitions and American Literature." *Melus* 28, no. 3 (2003): 41–54.

Weaver, William. *Seven Verdi Librettos.* New York: W. W. Norton, 1975.

Wechsberg, Joseph. *Verdi.* New York: G. P. Putnam's Sons, 1974.

Woll, Allen L. *Black Musical Theatre: From Coontown to Dreamgirls.* Baton Rouge: Louisiana State University Press, 1989.

Zack, Naomi. "Ethnicity, Race, and the Importance of Gender." In *Race or Ethnicity? On Black and Latino Identity,* ed. Jorge J. E. Gracia, 101–22. Ithaca: Cornell University Press, 2007.

———. *Philosophy of Science and Race.* New York: Routledge, 2002.

4

Race, "Realism," and Fate in Frederick Delius's *Koanga*

ERIC SAYLOR

On May 30, 1899, London concertgoers had the opportunity to witness Frederick Delius's professional compositional debut. The performance, held at St. James Hall in Piccadilly, was notable for being entirely dedicated to his own works, a rare event for English composers of the day.[1] The first half of the concert featured several different pieces (symphonic poems, choral works, and an orchestral song cycle, among others), but the second half was devoted to excerpts from a single work: his new opera, *Koanga*.[2] *Koanga* must have seemed extraordinarily unusual to an English audience more familiar with Covent Garden's Italianate repertory, not least because of its twofold novelty: it was one of the first serious European operas to feature black characters as its protagonists and the first to prominently showcase examples of African American folk music.[3] Based on an episode from George Washington Cable's novel *The Grandissimes*, *Koanga*'s antebellum Louisiana setting tapped into the late Romantic fascination with the exotic, allowed for attractive local color in the form of African American work songs and folk tunes, yet avoided the clichés of those vernacular styles in the musical depiction of the opera's protagonists—Koanga, an enslaved West African prince and voudon priest, and Palmyra, a quadroon maidservant.

Yet despite the presence of black protagonists and African American folk music, *Koanga*'s characters, plot, and musical language are less reminiscent of Louisiana than Louisiana as Leipzig might imagine it; in fact, *Koanga* is a typical nineteenth-century story of love, jealousy, and betrayal enriched with local color. However, this otherwise familiar approach to late Romantic opera is complicated by the way Delius and his librettist, Charles Keary, imagined their African American subjects—in Delius's case, from his experience living among blacks in Florida during the 1880s, and Keary from his study of African culture and religion. Although their creative intent does not seem to have been maliciously racist, the dramatic portrayal of Koanga and Palmyra reflects period beliefs about the Otherness of blacks generally. At the same time, the compositional team treats the exoticism of "blackness," both physical and musical, as an attractive quality integral to achieving their dramatic and musical aims. It is this contradiction that makes *Koanga* such a problematic work, manifested most clearly in the disjunction between Keary's racially formulaic libretto and Delius's musical treatment of the protagonists, but also in Delius's struggle to resolve the demands of then contemporary operatic conventions—especially in the Wagnerian tradition—with his own interest in African American music.

Koanga: Genesis and Text

Delius began working on *Koanga* in 1895, completing it two years later. Unsurprisingly, his approach to opera was strongly influenced by the works of Wagner and Verdi, particularly the former. By the time he started writing *Koanga,* Delius had attended performances of *Lohengrin, Tristan und Isolde, Tannhauser, Die Meistersinger von Nürnberg,* the full *Ring* cycle, and *Parsifal;* he saw most of these multiple times, including several performances at Bayreuth. His admiration for the German master was also revealed in a letter he wrote to his American colleague Jutta Bell in 1894: "I should . . . like to give all my works a deeper meaning. I want to say something to the world very serious & music & poetry are my only means. . . . I want to tread in Wagner's footsteps and even give something more in the right direction. For me dramatic art is almost taking the place of religion. People are sick of being preached to. But by being played to, they may be worked upon."[4]

For Delius, the "right direction" that Wagner pioneered was the dramatically effective unification of music and poetry. Done correctly, he believed this could elicit a level of emotional expressivity so intense that it bordered on the spiritual. Wagner's influence is discernible in much of Delius's music, vocal and instrumental alike, and *Koanga* is no exception: it features highly chromatic musical language, rapidly shifting key areas, flexible arioso delivery (that is, "endless melody"), enormous vocal and instrumental ensembles, and long symphonic interludes that evoked atmospheric effects separate from the singers' text and actions. Yet Delius did not uncritically appropriate all of Wagner's techniques. Although it appears that he was trying to replicate the expressive effect of works like *Tristan* or *Parsifal* (describing the latter as "magnificent: the finest work of Wagner"), he clearly wanted to do so within his own musical idiom. For instance, he broke with Wagner's conception of composer as librettist, saying "my literature is not on a level with my music—And I believe in Colaboration [*sic*] a greater effect may be attained."[5] Other deviations included the absence of leitmotivs and the composition of conspicuous "numbers" for chorus and soloists alike; furthermore, Delius's extensive use of stacked ninths and elevenths, pentatonicism, and chordal planing recalls impressionist techniques more than Wagner's ultrachromaticism.[6]

Despite his Wagnerian tendencies, Delius was also willing to borrow from Italian operatic models. Sir Thomas Beecham believed that the composer "envied a little, I think, some of the rousing effects and unerringly dramatic strokes of *Aida*. Throughout the first two years of his residence in and around Paris [1888–90] he was obsessed with the ambition to write an opera on some grand historical subject, involving the employment of large resources such as processions, pageants, and dancers." But Beecham also claimed that while Delius "appreciated the musicianly workmanship of *Falstaff*, he regretted its lack of true melodic invention and genuine humour."[7] Beecham thus implies that Delius was less impressed by Verdi's music than by his dramatically effective reinterpretation of French Grand Opera, a goal that matched Delius's own.[8] In short, *Koanga* melds a broadly Wagnerian approach to tonality and text with the human drama and spectacle of Verdian opera, all of which was enriched by the exoticism of Cable's story.

The Grandissimes: A Story of Creole Life was originally serialized in *Scribner's Monthly* beginning in 1879 and published in full by 1880, a time when Cable, a lifelong New Orleanian, was at the height of his popularity. A forerunner of the "southern realist" style later associated with William Faulkner and Thomas Wolfe, Cable tended to emphasize veristic settings and characterization, particularly in his use of dialects and speech patterns. He was also notable, as a white man and Confederate army veteran, for his portrayal of postwar southern culture generally (and Louisiana's in particular) as that of a society in decline, thanks in no small part to slavery's legacy: legally codified racism, known in Louisiana as the *Code Noir.* Cable's reformist tendencies began to emerge around 1870, fired by a combination of Christian ethics and what today might be described as "white guilt"—the awareness of historical injustice by whites against blacks—resulting in his staunch desire to atone for the sins of his fathers by championing the rights of free blacks. This took a variety of forms: polemical articles and columns for the *New Orleans Picayune;* scholarly essays on administrative policies within southern governments, schools, and prisons; and, most important for posterity, several extended works of fiction that dealt with racial injustice, of which *The Grandissimes* is the most celebrated.[9] Aside from its implicit critique of Louisiana's racial politics, *The Grandissimes* was also distinguished by its inclusion of notated music for a pair of African American tunes within the body of the text, an indication of Cable's deep interest in Creole music and culture.[10] Cable became quite active in collecting Negro songs following the publication of his novel, writing two articles for *Century Magazine* detailing his firsthand observation of Creole songs and dances. His contributions to the field were acknowledged by his former field collaborator Henry Krehbiel in the latter's *Afro-American Folksongs* of 1914.[11]

Koanga is based on an episode within *The Grandissimes* titled "The Story of Bras-Coupé," a short story that Cable had first submitted to *Scribner's* in 1873, although it was rejected for publication. The tale was not his own, but rather a retelling of a Creole story that he had heard from the "old French-speaking Negroes" he knew in New Orleans.[12] In Cable's version of the story, Agricola Fusilier, manager of the Grandissime estate, purchases a cargo of West African slaves in New Orleans; he sells one of them, the giant Mioko-Koanga (in French, Bras-Coupé, or "Arm-Cut-Off," referring to the impact his absence will have on his people), to the overseer for local planter Don José Martinez. After Bras-Coupé injures several slaves when told to work, Martinez persuades Palmyre, the personal slave of his fiancée (referred to only as Mademoiselle), to talk Bras-Coupé into submission. He instantly falls in love with Palmyre; despite her initial objections, the two are immediately betrothed, to be married the same day as Martinez and Mademoiselle.

On the night of the wedding, Bras-Coupé becomes drunk (having tasted alcohol for the first time) and brutally assaults Martinez. Under the *Code Noir*, Bras-Coupé's life is now forfeit; he curses Don José and escapes into the swamps. The curse quickly takes effect, sickening first the land, then the slaves, then Don José himself, who soon dies. Three days later, Bras-Coupé returns, demanding Palmyre; when she is not brought forth, he utters a curse on the household and departs. He is later captured by police after joining the revels in Congo Square and, despite Palmyre's pleas for clemency, is flogged and hamstrung, and his ears are cut off. Only when Mademoiselle brings her infant son to him, who smiles at Bras-Coupé and touches his cheek, does his resistance break; his humanity touched, he lifts the curse, and dies transfixed by a vision of Africa.

The actual libretto for *Koanga* differed significantly from Cable's original text, both in language and plot, though it was similarly atmospheric. Delius briefly consulted Jutta Bell for assistance in adapting Cable's story for the stage, but later engaged English writer and museum curator Charles Keary to complete the libretto. Although Keary had authored monographs on a wide range of topics (including Norwegian geography and culture, archaic and non-Western religious practices, and numismatic holdings at the British Museum), as well as several novels, he was an unusual choice for a librettist. Not only had he never written for the stage, but he was also "unfamiliar with American literature and negro speech" and had been charged by critics with the crimes of "writing too fast, inadequate revising, and never rising above the commonplace."[13] Despite these handicaps, Delius's enthusiasm for his librettist was unwavering, and they evidently worked congenially throughout the compositional process.

Delius and Keary's version of the story takes place in flashback, framed by a prologue and epilogue in which a black servant ("Uncle Joe") relates a "story of grief and love" to a group of young white women. Koanga, a tribal chief and voudon priest recently abducted from West Africa, is brought as a slave to Don José Martinez's plantation, but refuses to work. In an attempt to win him over, Martinez offers him the hand of Palmyra, his wife Clotilde's quadroon maid (who, it later transpires, is also her half sister). Clotilde objects to this pairing on moral and familial grounds and conspires with the overseer Simon Perez—himself in love with Palmyra—to prevent the marriage; accordingly, he abducts Palmyra just before the ceremony is to take place. Enraged, Koanga strikes down Martinez and escapes into the swamps, where he calls upon voudon spirits to blight the plantation. He returns to rescue Palmyra from Perez, killing him in the process, but his attempt to escape again is foiled by his white pursuers; mortally injured, he is returned to the plantation, where he dies in Palmyra's arms. Grief-stricken, Palmyra renounces Christianity for voudon and then kills herself.

The veristic style of its source material notwithstanding, *Koanga* is far from a realistic portrayal of black life in the United States, and was almost certainly not meant to be. More likely, Delius was inspired by the story's exoticism, as he had been with other operatic subjects, and was more concerned with capturing a mood than faithfully re-creating a culture.[14] Delius's own comments bear this out; early on, he told Bell that when it came to revising the text, she should "not fear not being realistic—I dont [*sic*] believe in realism in opera—Fantasy and poetry."[15] Many of the changes Keary and Delius made to Cable's story were done in an attempt to bestow a more Wagnerian atmosphere on the drama. The most obvious homage lies in the closing *Liebestod,* where Koanga expires in Palmyra's arms, leading her to commit suicide rather than face the world without him.[16] The subtext of religious conflict also became more prominent, perhaps as a Nietzschean critique of Christianity (of which Delius, a great admirer of Nietzsche's writing and philosophy, would have approved) that would have furthered his desire to show religion's inadequate engagement with spiritual issues he felt were more suitable to the purview of art.

The most sweeping changes came to Cable's original dialogue, which was replaced with overblown, poetic language (mostly by Keary, though with Delius's approval) that undercut its original naturalistic sound and flow, but bestowed the portentousness of a Wagnerian libretto. This fulsome tone pervades Keary's writing, even in simple exchanges of dialogue, resulting in convoluted sentences forced into rigid rhyme schemes.[17] At best, this represents the sort of "verbal banality and artificiality" often associated with French Grand Opera;[18] at worst, it is a "crude" and "fatuous" treatment of the source material that dilutes much of Cable's initial veracity.[19]

These criticisms are, however, somewhat beside the point, since aside from the excerpts of *Koanga* presented at Delius's debut concert of 1899, there has never been a performance of the opera featuring the original libretto in English. The first complete performance took place in Elberfeld, Germany, in 1904, featuring a German translation of Keary's text made by the composer's wife, Jelka, herself a native German. The opera finally received a complete performance in England in 1935—one year after Delius's death—but not using Keary's original libretto. Instead, Jelka Delius retranslated her German-language version back to English with the assistance of Sir Thomas Beecham and Edward Agate.[20] (To make matters even more confusing, a fresh copy of the score was prepared by Delius's amanuensis, Eric Fenby, near the end of the composer's life that incorporated changes made to the original score for the German performance of 1904; it was with this new copy of the score that Jelka Delius, Beecham, and Agate worked.) Comparisons of the original text with the 1935 revision reveal substantial changes to at least three-quarters of the words, if not more (although the plot underwent relatively few alterations, and the textual revisions did not result in any significant changes to the dialogue's meaning). This translation by committee not only distorted the original libretto, but also made some significant—and not always desirable—alterations to Delius's music:

> Great fistfuls of words were pushed into musical phrases with little or no regard for the flow of the vocal line, nor for the vowels that the singer would have to cope with. Poetic idea followed inverted poetic idea, often with no connecting link and nearly always out of character and/or context. What foreman on getting the slaves up and off to work is going to tell them that "The dawn begins to gild the East"? . . . One particularly dramatic moment in Act II where Palmyra and Perez had a tremendous confrontation of lust and loathing was reduced to a discussion of Christian ethics! The general effect of all these "poetics" was to cast a blur over the entire opera, imbuing it with an almost claustrophobic sameness.[21]

As Jelka Delius was not a native English speaker, let alone familiar with American dialects, it is unsurprising that the German-to-English translation might display some awkward passages. Still, her disinclination to consult the original text, or of Beecham and Agate to suggest alternatives for the more unwieldy translations, made the problems inherent in the 1935 edition all the more frustrating.

In 1972, Douglas Craig and Andrew Page were enlisted to revise the libretto yet again, with the assistance of Eric Fenby, for a performance of the opera at Sadler's Wells. Most significantly, they reset many passages of dialogue to make them either more linguistically natural or dramatically appropriate and made more extensive use of vernacular speech. A section of dialogue between Perez and Palmyra from act 3 of the 1899, 1935, and 1972 versions of the opera (see table 1) serves as a representative example of the tones of each ("Honoré," in the 1899 version, is Honoré Grandissime, a character from Cable's story reimagined as Palmyre's departed lover, but who never appears in the opera; references to him were eliminated in later revisions).[22]

Some of Craig and Page's other changes made the work's exoticism seem more "authentic": the names of actual voudon orishas were substituted for made-up gods, and lyrics from preexisting spirituals were used rather than Keary's own for the slaves' choruses. (The latter change had the secondary effect of eliminating the "happy darky" stereotype that Keary's lyrics facilitated.)[23] Finally, certain extraneous plot elements were minimized, such as the underlying religious conflict and references to Palmyra's previous betrothal.

All of these revisions point to significant problems with Keary's original libretto. While many of the linguistic eccentricities have been attended to, the tropes of racial Othering informing the opera's plot and characterization have not. Keary portrays Koanga and Palmyra as figures of fear and disruption, Koanga through his frightening curses and unpredictable behavior, Palmyra through her seemingly irresistible powers of seduction (which direct her relationships with both Koanga and Perez). But the potential power these abilities provide remains unrealized because Koanga and Palmyra are constantly forced to submit to authorities—both seen and unseen—that exceed their own. They never seriously challenge the power structures already in place because their

Table 1. Textual variation in the three versions of *Koanga*

1899

PEREZ: O aye, call out for Honoré! He's but three thousand leagues away.
PALMYRE [*sic*]: It is a lie; liar, begone!
PEREZ: Not yet, until Palmyre I've won! Tis foolish thus to moan and sigh! We'll be happy, you and I! You with me and I with you!
PALMYRE: Do you dare? You would not with Koanga here!

1935

PEREZ: In vain to call Koanga; he is a thousand miles away.
PALMYRA: Nay, it is false; a shameless lie!
PEREZ: And yet, I will not leave your side! 'Tis foolish thus to moan and grieve! Let us be merry, while we may! You and I, Palmyra sweet!
PALMYRA: Oh coward! To face him you would never dare!

1972

PEREZ: Koanga will never hear you; he is a thousand miles away!
PALMYRA: No, it's not true, you're lying to me!
PEREZ: I'm not, so you'll have to face the truth! Why make yourself so ill with pining? Come, let's be happy while we may! You and I, Palmyra sweet!
PALMYRA: Oh coward! If he were here, you'd never dare!

ability for self-determination is suppressed.[24] Parallel situations can be found in many Romantic operas: the princess Aida is manipulated by Amneris, the talented Walther is frustrated by Beckmesser and the rules of the Meistersingers' guild, and destiny pulls the strings for the casts of the *Ring* cycle, *Rigoletto,* and *La Forza del Destino,* to name only a few. Yet a perusal of Keary's other writings reveals that Orientalism (in Said's sense of ethnocentric hierarchical relationships established by Westerners viewing non-Westerners or nonwhites) was integral to his conception of nonwhite cultures and must have affected his approach to *Koanga*'s libretto.

For example, when describing black Africans in his *Outlines of Primitive Belief among the Indo-European Races* (1882), Keary claimed that "the memories of savages are short; their emotions are very transitory, and are almost always under the immediate influence of outward sensations." In other words, not only were self-determination and self-control beyond the understanding of "savages," but their true motivations were shaped by forces they were inherently incapable of controlling. Keary alludes to this point in another passage from the same text: "We pass by the doings of African savages or of Red Indians without heed, because these races are of such a nature that their experience of life has never reacted in any effective way upon their national character. . . . [T]heir tides of fortune have left them where they found them, because they have not the power of profiting by the past, or of carrying its teachings forward to form part of a new present."[25] Black Africans, in Keary's view, are hostages to fate because their natural state is one of innocent ignorance. They cannot learn from the past, and so have no hope of changing their future; their present is perpetual and guided almost entirely by external events.[26] Even setting the opera as a flashback reinforces the idea that the story has already been told and that the protagonists cannot—indeed, will not be able to—resist the events that fate has in store.

Keary's reliance on supernatural plot devices further dilutes any sense that either Koanga or Palmyra possesses free will. For instance, Palmyra's love for Koanga is originally not her own; Martinez demands that she placate the rebellious slave when his own threats fail. Though initially reluctant, she soon finds herself irresistibly compelled to persuade him to stay ("What charm enfolds my mind, what spell of madness?" she asks herself).[27] It is as though she is powerless to resist the machinations of fate that require her to act. Likewise, Koanga immediately responds to Palmyra's charms, and inexplicably so, considering that only minutes before he swore never to submit to his captors. By irrationally responding to her entreaties (which Martinez describes as "magical"), Koanga sets a chain of events in motion that will seal his doom.

Even when the characters appear to be acting in their own interests, there are larger, unseen, forces working against them. Perhaps the best illustration of this phenomenon is Koanga's invocation of voudon spirits throughout the opera: he asks for strength in the face of captivity, assistance in blighting the plantation, forgiveness as he lies dying for renouncing them in the face of overpowering love, and so on. He relies so heavily upon them, in fact, that he cannot seem to do anything on his own. His authority comes only because he is willing to suborn himself to powers greater than his own; he is not a self-made man and, as such, cannot directly control his own destiny. Moreover, he cannot control the forces he wields. When he calls on spirits to blight the plantation, the curse manifests by sickening all of the slaves, including Palmyra, rather than striking down the white planters and overseers who are actually responsible for Koanga's situation.[28] This result can be explained in two ways. First, while incapacitating the slaves is apparently meant to strike at the planters' economic power, it is a frankly misguided manifestation of divine vengeance. In this scenario, Koanga either has not been specific enough in his request to the spirits or is paying the penalty for relying on pagan gods for deliverance. Either way, his renunciation of Christian ethics comes at a terrible moral price: it is he, not the white planters, who is responsible for the anguished slaves who lie "prostrate and almost dying on the ground."[29] The other scenario is hardly more appealing: if Koanga was in control of the spirits, then his apparent willingness to use Palmyra and the other slaves as pawns in his quest for vengeance further dehumanizes him. He is saddened by Palmyra's state, which he sees in a vision, but not enough to lift the curse. The cruelty he visits upon the plantation—notably, upon those who bear no blame for his condition—is more savage than noble. Instead of delivering the slaves from bondage, the actions of this charismatic black leader have left them far worse off than they were at the beginning of the opera.

The fact that Koanga bears the responsibility for the slaves' incapacitation is even more striking when comparing Keary's setting to Cable's original. In *The Grandissimes*, Bras-Coupé's curse also initially strikes the slaves, but Martinez himself is soon gripped by a terrible fever, which ultimately kills him. This leads directly to Mademoiselle's confrontation with Bras-Coupé at the novel's close and creates a satisfying (if tragic) sense of closure when he dies after lifting the curse on the plantation. Yet Keary eschewed this subtle and quiet conclusion for the more sensational *Liebestod* already described. It is odd that a reference to the curse's effect on Martinez was not included in the libretto, as it would have helped underscore the threat that Koanga posed to the plantation. Yet attacking the whites directly, while more sensible from a tactical point of view, apparently was not a viable dramatic option for Keary; to suggest that a pagan African could successfully harm white Christians would have implied an intelligence and agency for Koanga that Keary did not believe existed.

Delius's Music

Despite the problems one encounters with *Koanga*'s libretto, the opera's music is enormously compelling, uniting Romantic lyricism with elements of African American vernacular music. Cable's Louisiana setting gave Delius the chance to indulge his interest in the latter idiom, which had fascinated him for much of the previous decade. In early 1884, aged twenty-two, Delius left his home in Bradford, Yorkshire, for Solano Grove, Florida, a plantation about twenty-five miles south of Jacksonville on the St. John's River. Ostensibly, his reason for moving was to manage an orange grove—a commercial alternative to the family wool business—but it was just as much to get away from his domineering father. Upon arriving at the isolated and overgrown property, Delius was informed by the black caretakers (Albert Anderson; his wife, Eliza; and her sister, Julia) that the growing season for oranges was over and that he would have to find some other way to pass the time until the following winter. He did so by engaging the tutorial services of Thomas Ward, a Brooklyn organist, who taught him counterpoint and composition. During this period, Delius was also surrounded by the music of the Anderson family and their visitors, who would sing and play the banjo in the evenings. He was moved by the "truly wonderful sense of musicianship and harmonic resource" they demonstrated in performing spirituals and folk songs and claimed that upon "hearing their singing in such Romantic surroundings, it was then and there that I first felt the urge to express myself in music."[30] There is little reason to doubt his enthusiasm for the Andersons' music, particularly as he referred to the impression it left on him on several occasions throughout his life.

One should not, however, mistake Delius's professional interest for racial enlightenment. Delius, as Christopher Palmer notes, "was a confirmed egocentric; any problem which lay outside his immediate orbit of reference was of negligible interest to him . . . [s]o the suffering of the Negroes under the white man's yoke would have left him totally unaffected unless it had for him a symbolic value in relation to some deeply-felt emotional experience of his own."[31] As a member of the Victorian upper middle class, Delius was a product of the institutionalized racism and classism of imperial England[32] (he once told Eric Fenby that Ward made him "work like a nigger" on his counterpoint lessons),[33] and there is no evidence to suggest that he was conscious of or concerned with questions of racial representation during the composition or production of *Koanga*. This assumption is reinforced by the German premiere (1904), which featured a white American singer, Clarence Whitehill, in the title role, who performed in full black body makeup and a leopard-skin tunic. Even as late as the first full English performance in 1935—a year after the debut of Virgil Thomson's all-black cast in *Four Saints in Three Acts* and the same year as the premiere of *Porgy and Bess*—Koanga was still performed by a white man in blackface.[34]

Racial insensitivities aside, the presence of African American musical idioms is one of the most striking aspects of the opera. Delius made several arrangements of spirituals and work songs, many based on tunes collected and published by Cable himself, but their authenticity (in terms of their function) is questionable. For example, the melody for "John Say You Got to Reap What You Sow," set as a work song for the slaves, is actually based on a Creole dance tune, modified from a piece of music Cable included in *The Grandissimes*.[35] Other "folk" songs were of Delius's own creation, presumably aligning with his early intent to keep "the whole [work] in the character of the negro melody," and are difficult to distinguish from the genuine article.[36] All of the slaves' choruses (whether traditional or newly composed) feature a rhythmically regular 4/4 or 6/8 meter, are arranged in four- or six-part homophony, and are generally diatonic or pentatonic; the texts refer to subjects typically associated with Negro folk music (for example, biblical stories, or narratives about working in the fields). Delius also added a banjo to the orchestra for some of the songs, which, in combination with the chorus's distinctive sound and the exotic scenic backdrop, would instantly connote Otherness to audiences.

Yet Delius assigned an African American folk style only to the anonymous choruses of slaves, usually as a decorative or spectacular element, and contradistinctive to the post-Wagnerian idiom used by all the major white characters throughout the work. Moreover, the music for Koanga and Palmyra avoids the stereotypical hallmarks of African American folk music assigned to the other slaves, such as modal scales, syncopated rhythms, and simple antecedent-consequent phrases. Koanga's and Palmyra's parts instead feature long-breathed melodies, wide ranges, and extensive chromaticism, making them all but indistinguishable from those of the white characters. Avoiding race-based musical segregation for soloists (that is, in terms of conspicuously "exotic" idioms) is not without precedent, of course, as evinced by *Aida* and *Otello*.[37] Just as audiences do not listen to Aida sing a traditional Ethiopian lament in captivity, or hear Otello serenade Desdemona with a Moorish folk tune, so Delius does not make Koanga or Palmyra sing spirituals; to couple musical difference with already obvious racial distinctions would belabor the point. Palmyra's entrance aria (example 1) demonstrates the musical treatment that typifies her character later in the opera; note the long-breathed melodic line and the subtle yet persistent chromatic inflections.[38]

The dialogue between Palmyra and Perez in the first scene is also worth mentioning, as Perez's attempt to woo Palmyra takes place in counterpoint with the chorus of slaves. This suggests a subtle link between Perez and the slaves: although Perez controls them, he is himself obliged to submit to the control of

Example 1. *Koanga,* opening of act 1.

Martinez, the plantation owner, an analogous (albeit less crude) form of "enslavement." Palmyra, on the other hand, is the maid to Clotilde, Martinez's wife, and thus enjoys special status on the plantation. When Perez states that she is a slave while he is free, she responds by saying, "I am not a slave, but much more free than you. I have nothing to do with you or your master."[39] This is why she can turn down his proposal of marriage without fear of retribution: she enjoys a level of trust and intimacy with the upper classes that Perez does not, and this familiarity is reflected in the elevated quality of her music.[40]

Koanga's music, like Palmyra's, eschews clichéd exoticism for a more complex chromatic idiom. His first entrance follows a restatement of the folk tune "John Say You Got to Reap What You Sow" by the chorus and sets up an immediate contrast in timbre, texture, and harmony. The string-dominated folk tune gives way to a processional for winds and trumpet, underscored by syncopated timpani and horns, setting a grave and majestic atmosphere as Koanga enters in chains. His Straussian opening melody, nominally in C minor, quickly obscures a clear tonal center with its wide leaps, extensive chromaticism, and rapid tonicizations of distant keys. This entrance sets the tone for Koanga's musical idiom; it, like his personality, is unpredictable yet dignified, suggesting a parallel with the then popular literary figure of the "noble savage" (example 2).[41]

Example 2. *Koanga,* act 1, seven measures after [15].

Like Palmyra, Koanga is defiant from the start, vowing that although "now a captive, never, tho' my flesh be torn away with whip, will I be slave to those that bought me."[42] His confidence in this claim stems from his position as a voudon priest, allowing him spiritual access to forces beyond the understanding or control of the whites. This separates him not only from the white planters, but also from the other slaves who do not have the same spiritual connection. Delius's musical characterization reinforces this distinction, presenting an unusually nuanced approach to different social strata often absent in operas featuring nonwhite characters.

Modeling Blackness in *Koanga*

Koanga and Palmyra occupy unique positions among both blacks and whites (Koanga because of his royal rank and mystical power, Palmyra because of her mixed race and relationship to Clotilde), but ironically, their privileged status secures them few privileges. They are not allowed access to the social rank and power of the white gentry, but their abilities and their relationships with the white characters clearly set them apart from the anonymous slaves who labor in the fields. As a result, Koanga and Palmyra occupy a social no-man's-land, a sphere separate from everyone else on the plantation. Palmyra herself comments on this in her very first entrance in the 1934 edition: "How far remote my spirit seems from tyrant's hand or humble slave."[43] It is this ambiguity that needs to be addressed: the protagonists' inability to take power and their unwillingness to submit to it.

This conflict is heightened by the apparent contradiction between the libretto and the music. Delius's score portrays Koanga and Palmyra as heroic figures capable of transcending their racial and social stations; musically, they are utterly unself-conscious about inhabiting the world of the whites. A parallel may be drawn with Delius himself, the Yorkshire-born son of German immigrants and an unlikely example of a fin-de-siècle English musician. Beginning in the 1880s, many British musicians (initially led by prominent figures at the Royal College of Music) began working to professionalize and reform England's musical culture in performance, composition, teaching, and education; this movement (often referred to as the "English Musical Renaissance") had a profound impact on almost every serious musician in the nation.[44] Delius, however, was largely unconcerned about the state of English musical life or his place within it. His own style was more indebted to Grieg and Wagner than to any of his British contemporaries, and he was far more concerned with pursuing his own artistic interests than gaining acceptance within the English musical establishment. His typical remarks about English music were unflattering, whether made to fellow composer Granville Bantock ("I am afraid artistic undertakings are impossible in England—the country is not yet artistically civilised") or Eric Fenby ("English music? . . . Well—I've never heard of any!"). Lionel Carley suggests that even the simple association of Delius's music with that of his native country was taboo, attributing to him the comment "I don't claim to be a British composer."[45] Delius's ease in abandoning British musical culture resonates strongly with Koanga's and Palmyra's ability to transcend a stereotypically "black" idiom in favor of the style used by those in power and suggests that they have the potential to encroach upon the planters' power in other ways as well.

Keary's text, by contrast, literally dehumanizes both Koanga and Palmyra by eliminating consistent motivation and behavior in favor of stereotypical portrayals (if not necessarily crudely racist ones) of how blacks were expected to behave. Yet the Orientalist tropes that Keary engages suggest that he is doing so primarily not to argue for the inherent superiority of whites, but rather to create a convenient Other. The racial tendencies Keary describes in *Outlines of Primitive Belief* are enormously broad stereotypes that eliminate the potential for individuality within the populations he describes. Koanga and Palmyra are clearly not backward savages, but they are underdeveloped characters who, despite their superficial exoticism, have to act in particular (if implausible) ways in order to adhere to the conventions of late Romantic opera. They are generically tragic figures whose story could have been set in ancient Rome, feudal Japan, or any number of other slave societies without losing any of its poignancy. The emphasis is not on the characters' blackness per se, but on what they represent: a couple alienated from the society in which they live and whose love cannot be fully realized. To quote Ernest Newman, the two are "not simply a chance pair of lovers but the symbol and the essence of a love so overpowering that it is impossible for the human victims of it to achieve their heart's desire except in death."[46] Newman was not describing Koanga and Palmyra when he wrote that passage, however, but another pair of star-crossed lovers: Tristan and Isolde.

Given Delius's admiration for and knowledge of Wagner's works, one can reasonably speculate that he might have turned to *die Meister* for dramatic guidance as well as musical inspiration. As noted, the closing *Liebestod* in Delius's work is clearly based on the one from *Tristan,* but Delius goes beyond simple imitation: he attempts to capture something of the nobility and motivations of Tristan and Isolde themselves. Writing about *Tristan,* Newman claims that "from the very beginning the threads of Tristan's life are spun with slow inexorable intent by the Fates"; so too are Koanga's.[47] The situation he finds himself in strongly recalls Tristan's: a man of noble birth constantly aware of his allegiance to a greater authority (King Mark and voudon orishas, respectively), but enslaved by "magic" to a woman and doomed to die for choosing her over those to whom he owes allegiance. Palmyra faces similar challenges. Although half white, and despite her special status on the plantation, she is still a slave and is subjected to all the indignities this entails—more, in fact, because her potential power is exploited by others. She, like Koanga, has no control over this state of affairs, her race and rank determined long ago by the indiscretions of Clotilde's father. In her, we see Isoldean characteristics: the highest-ranking female member of her society offered as a token of peace from one ruler to another, a reluctant pairing that magically turns to passion so powerful as to transcend death itself.

Fate's role in controlling the destinies of both protagonists is communicated not only in the libretto but also in the music. Here again we see the influence of Wagner: immediately following the dramatic high point of Koanga's death, a motive combining the "Tristan" chord with the modulatory character of the "Fate" motif from the *Ring* is stated twice (examples 3–5).

Wagner's original "Tristan" chord was F—G-sharp—B—D-sharp, but Delius transposed and revoiced it to B-flat—D-flat—E[=F-flat]—A-flat, retaining the critical half-diminished sonority. The "Fate" motif has also been modified: its opening minor triad is preserved in the upper voices of Delius's transposed "Tristan" chord (D—F—A to D-flat—E—A-flat, reinforced with the B-flat in the bass) and is followed by a half-step descending appoggiatura in the soprano

Example 3. "Tristan" chord.

Example 4. "Fate" motif (from *Die Walküre*).

Example 5. *Koanga*, act 3, scene 2, twelve measures before [37].

(A-flat to G, rather than the original A to G-sharp), but instead of moving to an applied dominant seventh like Wagner does, Delius confirms his home key of F minor by resolving to the tonic. (The second statement of the Tristan-Fate motif, however, finds Delius moving from simple homage to a chromatically saturated reinterpretation of Wagner's original.)

The presence of the combined Tristan-Fate motive suggests that Koanga, the Tristan analogue, was destined to die for his rebellion; all the events leading to this point were preordained. His death elicits a profound spiritual transformation in Palmyra, awakening her bile for the "hated whites" and finally galvanizing her to take control of her own destiny. This is a new side of Palmyra: in general, she is a reactive character, more akin to a plot device than a protagonist (that is, things happen to her, or others use her to make things happen, but she lacks the agency to make things happen). But ironically, upon seizing her new spiritual freedom, she decides that the best way to strike against the whites is to kill herself. Ultimately, fate still conspires against her because the Isoldean model she follows does not allow her to actively resist the whites; as such, the passive resistance of death is the only option allowed to her.[48]

Conclusion

Koanga, then, is not necessarily what it appears to be. Despite its serious treatment of African American protagonists and folk music, the opera also revisits many familiar tropes of racial exoticism, subtly applied though they may be. It is also clear that any concerns that Delius and Keary might have had about the opera's representation of "blackness" were eclipsed by their shared desire to follow the broader musico-dramatic conventions of late Romantic (and particularly Wagnerian) opera. Viewed in this context, *Koanga* could uncharitably be described as little more than *Tristan und Isolde* in blackface—a reasonable conclusion, given the composer's Wagnerian tendencies and the striking dramatic parallels between the two works.

Still, Delius's willingness to showcase African American folk music in a serious opera—while also acknowledging its social and dramatic impropriety for certain black characters—reveals an unexpectedly shrewd take on musical representations of race at the end of the nineteenth century and suggests that *Koanga* is more than mere pastiche. Delius's adoption of a Wagnerian model for his own opera is hardly surprising; after all, such borrowing has been a time-honored tradition among fledgling composers for countless generations, particularly among those (like Delius) still trying to find their own distinctive expressive voices. But the deviations he made from Wagner were not just musical or dramatic; to a certain degree, they were also tied to questions of racial representation. For instance, Delius was not a musical purist in the sense that Wagner was; there is no equivalent to the praises of *heilige deutsche Kunst,* as the wide array of musical styles present throughout *Koanga*—cultivated and vernacular alike, and from racially diverse sources—clearly demonstrates. This marks an important step in the development of Delius's own musical idiom. By deviating from Wagner's model in such an idiosyncratic manner, Delius demonstrated that he was capable not just of stylistic imitation, but also of synthesizing other unrelated styles and extending a familiar tradition in a new way. Moreover, as previously noted, Delius genuinely admired African American vernacular music and saw Koanga and Palmyra as noble figures that deserved serious musical and dramatic treatment. By placing these black characters within an operatic idiom widely considered to be among the most transcendent and powerful of all time, Delius ennobles them, implicitly elevating them to a level typically reserved for white characters only.

Yet questions of destiny and free will, which function primarily as overarching dramatic forces in Wagner's music, take on troubling new resonances in Delius's opera. The tragedy of Tristan and Isolde's love comes (in part) from the manipulation of their feelings for each other via their consumption of the love potion; in other words, we assume that drinking the potion denies them the free will they would have otherwise possessed, causing them to act in ways that ultimately destroy them. By contrast, Keary (and, by extension, Delius) assumes that Koanga and Palmyra intrinsically lack the ability to determine their own destinies. Since they are already slaves to Fate by virtue of their race, then the tragedy of their story is greatly diminished—after all, according to this interpretation, they would not have been capable of resisting in the first place. They have no independence that can be taken away or free will that can be undermined.

Ultimately, these conflicts cannot be resolved. *Koanga* is both racially enlightened and racially limited, a product of its creators' fascination with black culture that was fixed within fin-de-siècle attitudes and stereotypes about racial hierarchies. For these reasons, *Koanga* will always be a problematic work; however, for all of its flaws, it marked an important—if tentative—first step in rehabilitating and redefining the portrayal of black characters on the operatic stage for the century to follow.

Notes

I am grateful to Drake University's Center for the Humanities, the Friends of Drake Arts, and Drake University's College of Arts and Sciences for their support of this research.

1. Delius made this possible by parlaying an inheritance into a public recital under the auspices of the Concorde Concert Control, a London performing arts agency. For an overview of the CCC's publicity campaign and critical commentary surrounding the concert, see Carley, *Frederick Delius,* 2–7.

2. The concert included the prelude to act 3, the quintet and finale from act 1, and act 2 in its entirety. See ibid., 3.

3. The performance of 1899 preceded the completion of Scott Joplin's *Treemonisha* by twelve years and *Porgy and Bess* by three and a half decades. As an aside, British attitudes toward race in the concert hall were somewhat in advance of America's; the year 1898 marked the London debut of *Hiawatha's Wedding Feast,* a choral-orchestral work by the Afro-British composer Samuel Coleridge-Taylor (1875–1912) that went on to become a staple at English choral festivals for the next several decades.

4. Carley, *Delius: Life in Letters,* 86.

5. Ibid., 90, 99.

6. Palmer makes similar assertions regarding a connection between Debussy and Delius in *Delius,* 16–19.

7. Beecham, *Frederick Delius,* 51, 195–96. Beecham's assessment is a bit more severe than Delius's own opinion about *Falstaff,* which he felt (at least as a young man) was a first-rate work.

8. He applied these Verdian models in *Koanga,* notably in the wedding party that opens act 2 and the voudon rite at the beginning of act 3, both of which recall similar crowd scenes in *Aida* and *Don Carlos* (although the supernatural atmosphere of the voudon rite in act 3 also evokes the Wolf's Glen Scene from *Der Freischütz*).

9. More on Cable the reformer can be found in *The Negro Question,* especially Turner's introduction (xi–xx) and Cable's essay "My Politics" (1–26).

10. See Cable, *Grandissimes,* 168, 188. The brief excerpts Cable included (two work songs) helped establish a sense of atmosphere but were incidental to the story; presumably, he included them simply because he saw an opportunity to display some of his fieldwork in a nonacademic venue.

11. Cable and Krehbiel had at one point planned to coauthor a book on African American folk music at the behest of Lafcadio Hearn, though Krehbiel later withdrew from the project. See Krehbiel, *Afro-American Folksongs,* x, 38–41.

12. Turner, *Creoles and Cajuns,* 20. Cable also claimed that his interest in the story was fired by the "sheer indignation" he felt when he came across descriptions of the *Code Noir* during his research into the history of New Orleans. See Cable, "My Politics," in *Negro Question,* 11.

13. Randel, "*Koanga* and Its Libretto," 143.

14. As early as 1894, Delius wrote that he had "a vague idea of writing 3 works: One on the Indians, one on the Gypsies and one on the Negroes & quadroons." Carley, *Delius: Life in Letters,* 88. The first two groups were prominently featured in *The Magic Fountain* (1895) and *A Village Romeo and Juliet* (1907).

15. Ibid., 99.

16. Delius had this in mind from the very beginning, confirmed in a letter from February 1896 to Jutta Bell: "Palmyre & Bras-Coupé are the two chief characters—I am not yet certain about the end—I must change the real end. Make Bras-Coupé kill himself & Palmyre or something of that sort—." Ibid., 98.

17. William Randel effectively illustrates Keary's literary pretensions in his article "*Koanga* and Its Libretto"; see, for example, 144–45. However, his quotation of Koanga's curse comes from the 1935 revision of the libretto made by Edward Agate and Sir Thomas Beecham. Keary's original version of the curse ran as follows:

> Hear me, god Voudou; I have been false to you,
> False to my home and race. Yea, false to all.
> Now bowing in the dust, upon thy name August [*sic*],
> Thy secret name and thy great might I call!
> Teach the white man the power of the mystic word;
> The charm I now rehearse that brings the threefold curse,
> The triple curse on land, on air and flood;
> Of water horrid death, white hunger on the earth,

And dreadful fevers that corrupt the blood!
These then send forth, O Lord, thy messenger
And let thy thunder sound accord!
(Delius, *Koanga,* autograph score, 2:72–78)

18. Randel, "*Koanga* and Its Libretto," 145.

19. Hutchings, *Delius: A Critical Biography,* 132.

20. Oddly, it seems that none of them bothered to consult either Keary's or Cable's version of the story for guidance in setting the text, though this is perhaps understandable given the quality of Keary's writing.

21. Douglas Craig and Andrew Page, "Preface to the Revised Libretto of *Koanga,*" in *Koanga,* rev. Page and Craig, v. However, in "The Early History of *Koanga,*" Threlfall contends that Delius's music and scoring "remained unchanged as Delius had left it after 1904" with the exception of Beecham's addition of Delius's *Irmelin Prelude* as a connecting passage in act 3 (9).

22. Quoted in part from Delius, *Koanga,* autograph score, 3:99–103; Delius, libretto to *Koanga,* rev. Beecham and Agate, 21; and Delius, *Koanga,* vocal score, 138–40.

23. Many of the slave choruses originally had embarrassingly condescending and racist lyrics. For instance, the tune in the 1972 version called "John Say You Got To Reap What You Sow" originally featured the following lyrics:

Work, niggers, work, with sickle in hand
We live by our labour and worship the land
For many a bundle of cane must be bound
In the meadows a'waving ere master comes round.
(Quoted in Randel, "*Koanga,*" 150)

24. See also Redwood, "Delius as a Composer of Opera," 236–37.

25. Keary, *Outlines of Primitive Belief,* 43, 18.

26. Cable's opinion, of course, had historical precedents both in anthropological and in musical literature. See Zon, *Representing Non-Western Music,* 27–29; and Saxton, "Blackface Minstrelsy," 78.

27. Delius, libretto to *Koanga,* rev. Beecham and Agate, 8. Keary's original also features this allusion, "What charm came o'er me now, what charm or curse?" and the revised version of 1974 is even more explicit about the supernatural overtones: "What strange magic power has overtaken me? It fills my heart with painful longing . . ." See Delius, *Koanga,* autograph score, 1:52–53; and Delius, *Koanga,* rev. Page and Craig, 80–82.

28. This recalls the Passover story from Exodus, where God kills the firstborn of Egypt as a means of punishing Pharaoh. Interestingly, Keary's original libretto took the trouble to specify that "white hunger" should result from Koanga's curse, but the slaves were sickened in that version as well.

29. Delius, *Koanga,* rev. Page and Craig, 298.

30. Fenby, *Delius as I Knew Him,* 25. Further information on Delius's time in Florida can be found in the chapter "The Music-Maker of Solano Grove," in *The Other Florida,* by Jahoda, 244–69.

31. Palmer, *Delius,* 4.

32. For background on English attitudes toward race in the mid– to late nineteenth

century, see Lorimer, *Colour, Class, and the Victorians,* esp. 92–107, and "Reconstructing Victorian Racial Discourse"; and Paul Rich, *Race and Empire in British Politics,* 1–26.

33. Fenby, *Delius as I Knew Him,* 168.

34. Frank Corsaro, "*Koanga* in America," included on the jacket notes for Frederick Delius, *Koanga,* starring Eugene Holmes, Claudia Lindsey, Raimund Herincx, Keith Erwen, Jean Allister, and Simon Estes.

35. The song Cable included in his text was a 6/8 dance tune at a relatively quick tempo, too fast to accompany long-term repetitive labor; see also Cable, *Grandissimes,* 168. A similar stylistic contradiction occurs with the "Calinda" dance in act 2, taken directly from Delius's *Florida Suite* of 1888. Cable describes the Calinda as a wild, overtly erotic dance, while Delius created a medium-tempo, graceful dance with mild syncopation. See Randel, "*Koanga* and Its Libretto," 148–51, for more.

36. Carley, *Delius: Life in Letters,* 98.

37. Ralph Locke also notes that most exotic or Orientalist operas of the nineteenth and early twentieth centuries, particularly those from France, have a "tendency to restrict the most overtly exotic music to the chorus and to numbers without singing," such as ballets or orchestral preludes, and rarely involve solo singers adopting the trappings of the exotic. "Cutthroats and Casbah Dancers," 125–27.

38. All musical excerpts feature text from the 1974 edition. The text from the 1935 edition reads, "Ah! Grief is mine! How sad and lonely all around! My country lost! My native land a stranger grown!" (Frederick Delius, *Koanga,* rev. Beecham and Agate, 10), while the original is set as "Woe! Woe is me! Never before so far away my Honoré" (Delius, *Koanga,* autograph score, 1:10).

39. Delius, *Koanga,* rev. Page and Craig, 35–36. The 1899 version uses very similar phrasing ("I am not a slave, but much more than you free; I have nothing to do with thy master or you"), although the 1935 revision is somewhat different ("Though you call me slave, a secret still I prize: Am I not from Jaloff race descended!").

40. Of course, this brings up the complicated question of racial distinctions that take place within class lines. Not only is Palmyra half white, but she is also (by extension) halfway between the lower and upper classes—the former because she is a quadroon maid, the latter because she is stepsister to the lady of the manor. The fact that the antagonists both sport surnames of Spanish derivation ("Perez" and "Martinez") only muddies the water further.

41. Delius greatly admired the works of authors James Fenimore Cooper and François-René de Chateaubriand (see Carley, *Delius: Life in Letters,* 88), who were both well known for their evocative North American settings and their use of heroic indigenous people.

42. Delius, *Koanga,* rev. Page and Craig, 59. The text is nearly identical in all three versions.

43. Craig and Page's 1974 revision makes Palmyra's complaint even clearer: "How far removed my spirit seems from that of master or of slave." Delius, *Koanga,* rev. Page and Craig, 20–21. The 1899 version makes no allusion to this, instead recalling Honoré Grandissime, Palmyra's lost love, who never actually appears in the opera. Delius, *Koanga,* autograph score, 1:10–12.

44. For more background on this period, see Stephen Banfield, "The Artist and Society," in *Music in Britain,* ed. Temperley, 11–28; Howes, *The English Musical Renaissance,* 17–162; Hughes and Stradling, *English Musical Renaissance,* 3–51; Kennedy, *Works of Ralph Vaughan Williams,* 1–10; and Trend, *The Music Makers,* 1–18.

45. Palmer, *Delius,* 144–45; Fenby, *Delius as I Knew Him,* 16; Carley, *Frederick Delius,* 4. See also Palmer, *Delius,* 143–44, 189–91.

46. Newman, *The Wagner Operas,* 186.

47. Ibid.

48. Palmyra does show some awareness of Fate's presence in act 1 after her pacification of Koanga. The 1899 libretto has her state, "It is fate, fate, fate that leads me to my doom" (Delius, *Koanga,* autograph score, 1:61), and the revision of 1935 reads, "My fate approaching leads me to my doom" (Delius, libretto to *Koanga,* rev. Beecham and Agate, 10). There is no allusion to Fate at this point in Craig and Page's revision, though Clotilde does claim to "feel a strange forboding in my heart; this Voodoo Prince will bring me to my grave" (Delius, *Koanga,* rev. Page and Craig, 92), which achieves much the same effect.

Bibliography

Beecham, Thomas. *Frederick Delius.* Rev. ed. London: Severn House, 1975.

Cable, George Washington. *The Grandissimes: A Story of Creole Life.* American Century Series. New York: Hill and Wang, 1957.

———. *The Negro Question: A Selection of Writings on Civil Rights in the South.* Ed. Arlin Turner. New York: W. W. Norton, 1968.

Carley, Lionel, ed. *Delius: A Life in Letters.* Vol. 1, *1862–1908.* Cambridge: Harvard University Press, 1983.

———. *Frederick Delius: Music, Art, and Literature.* Aldershot, UK: Ashgate, 1998.

Carley, Lionel, and Robert Threlfall, eds. *Delius: A Life in Pictures.* Oxford: Oxford University Press, 1977.

Corsaro, Frank. "*Koanga* in America." In *Koanga,* by Frederick Delius. Eugene Holmes and Claudia Lindsey, London Symphony Orchestra, and the John Alldis Choir. Charles Groves, conductor. Angel/EMI SBLX-3808, 1974. LP recording.

Delius, Clare. *Frederick Delius: Memories of My Brother.* London: Ivor Nicholson and Watson, 1935.

Delius, Frederick. *Frederick Delius: Complete Works.* Ed. Thomas Beecham and Robert Threlfall. Vol. 3, *Koanga: Opera in Three Acts.* Libretto by C. F. Keary. Rev. Douglas Page and Andrew Craig. London: Boosey & Hawkes, 1991.

———. *Koanga: Opera in Three Acts.* Autograph score. 3 vols. 1899. Delius Collection, Swisher Library, Jacksonville University, Jacksonville, Fla.

———. *Koanga: Opera in Three Acts.* Vocal score. Ed. Eric Fenby. Libretto by C. F. Keary. Rev. Douglas Page and Andrew Craig. London: Boosey & Hawkes, 1974.

———. *Koanga: An Opera in Three Acts with Prologue and Epilogue.* Rev. Thomas Beecham and Edward Agate. Vocal score. Ed. Eric Fenby. London: Winthrop Rogers, 1935.

———. Libretto to *Koanga: Opera in Three Acts.* Libretto by C. F. Keary. Rev. Thomas Beecham and Edward Agate. London: Boosey & Hawkes, 1935.

Fenby, Eric. *Delius as I Knew Him.* Rev. ed. London: Faber and Faber, 1981.

Green, Jeffrey. *Black Edwardians: Black People in Britain, 1901–1914.* London: Frank Cass, 1998.

Howes, Frank. *The English Musical Renaissance.* New York: Stein and Day, 1966.

Hughes, Meirion, and Robert Stradling. *The English Musical Renaissance, 1840–1940: Constructing a National Music.* 2nd ed. Music and Society Series, ed. Peter Martin and Tia DeNora. Manchester: Manchester University Press, 2001.

Hutchings, Arthur. *Delius: A Critical Biography.* London: Macmillan, 1948.

Jahoda, Gloria. *The Other Florida.* New York: Charles Scribner's Sons, 1967.

Jefferson, Alan. *Delius.* Master Musicians Series, ed. Jack Westrup. London: J. M. Dent and Sons, 1972.

Keary, Charles Francis. *Outlines of Primitive Belief among the Indo-European Races.* New York: Charles Scribner's Sons, 1882.

Kennedy, Michael. *The Works of Ralph Vaughan Williams.* 2nd ed. 1980. Reprint, Oxford: Clarendon Press, 1992.

Krehbiel, Henry. *Afro-American Folksongs: A Study in Racial and National Music.* 3rd ed. New York: G. Schirmer, 1914.

Locke, Ralph. "Cutthroats and Casbah Dancers, Muezzins and Timeless Sands: Musical Images of the Middle East." In *The Exotic in Western Music,* ed. Jonathan Bellman, 104–36. Boston: Northeastern University Press, 1998.

Lorimer, Douglas. *Colour, Class, and the Victorians.* Leicester: Leicester University Press; New York: Holmes & Meier, 1978.

———. "Reconstructing Victorian Racial Discourse: Images of Race, the Language of Race Relations, and the Context of Black Resistance." In *Black Victorians/Black Victoriana,* ed. Gretchen Holbrook Gerzina, 187–207. New Brunswick: Rutgers University Press, 2003.

Newman, Ernest. *The Wagner Operas.* New York: Alfred A. Knopf, 1963.

Palmer, Christopher. *Delius: Portrait of a Cosmopolitan.* London: Duckworth, 1976.

Randel, William. "*Koanga* and Its Libretto." *Music and Letters* 52, no. 2 (1971): 141–56.

Redwood, Christopher. "Delius as a Composer of Opera." In *A Delius Companion,* ed. Christopher Redwood. New York: Da Capo Press, 1977.

Rich, Paul. *Race and Empire in British Politics.* Comparative Ethnic and Race Relations Series, ed. John Rex. Cambridge: Cambridge University Press, 1986.

Saxton, Alexander. "Blackface Minstrelsy." In *Inside the Minstrel Mask: Readings in Nineteenth-Century Blackface Minstrelsy,* ed. Annemarie Bean, James V. Hatch, and Brooks McNamara, 67–85. Hanover, N.H.: University Press of New England, 1996.

Temperley, Nicholas, ed. *Music in Britain: The Romantic Age, 1800–1914.* Athlone History of Music in Britain, ed. Ian Spink, no. 5. London: Athlone Press, 1981.

Threlfall, Robert. "The Early History of *Koanga.*" *Tempo* 110 (September 1974): 8–11.

Trend, Michael. *The Music Makers.* New York: Schirmer, 1985.

Turner, Arlin, ed. *Creoles and Cajuns: Stories of Old Louisiana by George W. Cable.* Gloucester, Mass.: Peter Smith, 1965.

Zon, Bennett. *Representing Non-Western Music in Nineteenth-Century Britain.* Rochester: University of Rochester Press, 2007.

5

Political Currents and Black Culture in Scott Joplin's *Treemonisha*

ANN SEARS

What are these songs and what do they mean?
—W. E. B. Du Bois, *The Souls of Black Folk* (1903)

The life journey of Scott Joplin (1868–1917) has become an iconic part of black history, for it is representative of many African Americans of the post–Civil War generation. Freed from oppressive fears of slavery and hoping for a bright new future, African Americans, including Joplin, pursued education ambitiously, believing that "fortune favors the well-prepared mind" and that opportunities were open to those who worked hard to find their place in American society.[1] Joplin was particularly fortunate to meet music publisher John Stark, who gave Joplin a contract and royalties from "Maple Leaf Rag" in 1899 rather than buying the rights to the piece, thus providing Joplin a more stable financial future than most ragtime composers. Stark also provided unusual artistic support, as he believed that the best of ragtime was the equal of classical music.[2]

Eventually, Joplin turned his attention to composing opera, producing *A Guest of Honor* in 1903. The score is lost, but we know that Joplin wrote both music and text and that Joplin's small touring company gave at least eleven performances between August 30 and October 12, 1903.[3] In 1907, Joplin moved to New York City, and in 1911, he self-published his second opera, *Treemonisha,* after it had been turned down by several publishers.[4] An important American opera with English text was apparently unthinkable at the time, and even as late as the 1920s, a serious social commentator such as H. L. Mencken could say, "Opera in English is, in the main, about as sensible as baseball in Italian."[5] A serious ragtime opera by an African American seeming to be an even more complicated idea in 1911, *Treemonisha* lay nearly completely forgotten until the 1970s. Following the publication of Joplin's complete works in 1971, and long after his death in 1917, Joplin's magnum opus reached the stage in 1972 in a joint production of Morehouse College and the Atlanta Symphony Orchestra, although it is best known from the Houston Grand Opera performances of 1975 with stylistically appropriate orchestrations by Gunther Schuller.[6] The 1974 film *The Sting* and the 1976 American bicentennial celebration further encouraged renewed interest in ragtime and its composers.

Scott Joplin's place in American music during his lifetime was primarily determined by the success of his piano rags, particularly "Maple Leaf Rag," in which harmonic surprises and melodic invention revealed Joplin's ability to produce piano works of a sophisticated and artful quality.[7] Given the economic stability and recognition Joplin enjoyed as a ragtime composer, and given the limited prospects for African Americans in the highbrow world of opera at the turn of the century, it is somewhat surprising that Joplin would have pursued serious opera composition further. Moreover, Joplin's early life in Texas and Missouri would seem unlikely to have given him much meaningful exposure to opera. However, American musical life is full of the unexpected, and Joplin's life is a case in point.

While living in Texarkana, Joplin had the good fortune to meet Julius Weiss, a German immigrant music teacher. Observing Joplin's unusual talent, Weiss gave him free lessons and introduced him to European art music. Many years later, Joplin's widow, Lottie, reported that Joplin stayed in touch with Weiss, even sending him money from time to time. It is very likely that Weiss acquainted Joplin with the popular operas of the day, along with other forms of art music. Joplin also knew Alfred Ernst, director of the St. Louis Choral Society, who played parts of Wagner's opera *Tannhäuser* for Joplin.[8] Ernst was so impressed with Joplin's musical ability and potential that after their meeting, he announced his intentions to take copies of Joplin's music to Germany during the summer of 1901 and to tutor Joplin in theory and harmony after returning from Europe.[9] The 1870 *United States Board of Trade* list of published music available for purchase shows opera as a substantial component of late-nineteenth-century popular music, available to both professional musicians and amateurs in an astonishing array of arrangements, ranging from solo piano transcriptions, potpourris, and variations on opera themes to various chamber group and band arrangements.[10] The concept of opera as a large-scale form and the knowledge of the melodic and harmonic content of many great arias may very well have been part of Joplin's musical frame of reference in the formative years of his life.

When Joplin published his opera *Treemonisha,* an eager African American public already awaited its premiere. As early as 1908, the *New York Age* announced, "Music circles have been stirred recently by the announcement that Scott Joplin, known as the apostle of ragtime, is composing scores for grand opera." In 1909, the *Indianapolis Freeman* hailed Joplin's new work: "Mr. Scott Joplin, the composer of the Maple Leaf Rag, has got a new opera. I heard the overture; it is as great as anything written by Mr. Wagner or Gounard [*sic*] or any of the other old masters. It is original Scott Joplin Negro music. Nothing like it ever written in the United States." By 1911, the *New York Age* maintained that Joplin had "hewn an entirely new form of operatic art." However, as noted Joplin scholar Edward Berlin points out, "*Treemonisha* is not a ragtime opera," an opinion shared by Vera Brodsky Lawrence, editor of the complete Joplin works.[11] With three acts of recitatives, arias, ensembles, choruses, and ballet, *Treemonisha* includes all elements considered essential to grand opera in the nineteenth-century European tradition, and its European framework is clear in both libretto and score. Like other European and Euro-American grand operas, all the words are sung. It is worth noting that although contemporary critics and reporters described the opera as a ragtime work, the word *ragtime* does not appear in the title, or in the introductory notes by Joplin, and appears only briefly in the text of the final number of *Treemonisha.* Joplin, however, did create something uniquely and truly American in *Treemonisha,* setting the story in an abandoned post–Civil War plantation and synthesizing current African American political thought with many nineteenth-century African American traditions as well as ragtime rhythms. Unfortunately, the only reading of the opera during Joplin's life, probably in 1911, was unsuccessful.

Some critics blame *Treemonisha*'s early failure on its unusual plot. Ned and Monisha live on a plantation just after the Civil War. They adopt a foundling child as their own, naming her Treemonisha, after her adoptive mother and the "sacred tree" under which she was found. They arrange for her education as well. During an annual corn-husking celebration, Treemonisha, now a young woman, is kidnapped by the local conjuror Zodzetrick, who sees her education, literacy, and disdain for superstition as a threat to his way of life. Rescued by her sweetheart, Remus, whom she has taught to read and write, she is returned to her parents and her community and chosen to be their leader, as they aspire to learn from her and achieve a better way of life.[12]

While Joplin's opera includes a modest love story between Treemonisha and Remus, the focus is really on Treemonisha's education and its benefits to her and the plantation folk, as well as the novel idea of a woman as a community leader. This is a marked contrast to the typical opera plot of the day and most certainly speaks to Joplin's belief in opportunities for women and the transformative power of education.

Musical Signifiers of Black Identity

While much of *Treemonisha*'s music parallels the Euro-American musical style employed by other American opera composers of the early twentieth century, Joplin incorporated nineteenth-century African American musical styles learned during his early years in the South. The call-and-response practice of spirituals and lined-out hymns, quartet singing, and the ring dance (or Ring Play, as Joplin called it) serve as his models.[13] He also made one of the earliest efforts to capture the expressive vocal inflections of nineteenth-century African American shouts, moans, and hollers.

Several numbers in act 1 include two ubiquitous markers of African American music: syncopated rhythm and call-and-response. In number 3, "The Corn-Huskers," a short transitional piece sung by the heroine, Treemonisha, and the chorus of corn huskers, and number 4, "We're Goin' Around," sung by Andy and the chorus, call-and-response appears between individuals and groups, reminiscent of work songs in which a leader sets the pace and the group follows it. The syncopated ragtime rhythm reflects the dance energy commonly associated with ragtime at the turn of the twentieth century. Both these stylistic markers appear within the first four measures of the body of "We're Goin' Around" (example 1).

A more serious example of call-and-response style is found in act 1, number 9, "Good Advice," as sung by Parson Alltalk and the chorus. Parson Alltalk asks his informal congregation a series of questions: "Does yer feel lak you've

Example 1. "We're Goin' Around," measures 1–4, *Treemonisha*. Author's transcription.

been redeemed? Does yer always aim to speak de truth? Does yer love all yo' neighbors too?" After each question, the chorus replies affirmatively, both recognizing the spiritual content of Alltalk's direction and indicating community accord.[14] The dismissal of the pastor and the church implied by the caricature of Parson Alltalk's name is contradicted by the text's powerful message of Christian philosophy and the obvious unity shown by the communal responses.

When Parson Alltalk says, "Listen, friends, do not tell lies an' steal because it ain't right," and asks, "Does yer love all yo' neighbors too?" he is paraphrasing part of the Ten Commandments as found in the Christian Old Testament. And in his refrain, "Does yer feel lak you've been redeemed?"[15] Parson Alltalk connects with a part of Christian doctrine that was very important in the slavery era. While in slave religion the heroic figures in the Old Testament of the Christian Bible such as Abraham, Isaac, Jonah, Joshua, Daniel, and Moses represented deliverance from oppression and God's hand at work to rectify injustice, Jesus was very simply their brother. His human suffering and divine transfiguration signified the opportunity for deliverance and spiritual survival, even in the earthly dimension, for the ordinary person. These ideas are encoded in spirituals now available in printed collections. For many theologians and scholars, the cultural values found in these texts and therefore associated with the melodies are part of the important contributions African Americans have made to American art and culture. Almost certainly, the text, melody, and call-and-response style of "Good Advice" would have conveyed a profound attachment to vibrant Black spiritual life that would have been well understood by Joplin's contemporaries, many of whom had strong southern roots and connections.

An equally important signifier of African American musical style is the expressive use of vocal inflection. Here Joplin shows progressive techniques as he notates some group effects drawn, perhaps, from church or community singing of spirituals or work songs. In answer to Parson Alltalk's sermonizing, the community response is in a moaning style with closed lips. The response takes place over eight beats, with a root position E-minor chord moving to an A minor chord in second inversion and then back to E minor. The effect is somber and dynamic (example 2).

Even more dramatic is Joplin's use of group improvisation in act 1, number 10, "Confusion," where Joplin notates "women crying" and men speaking "in crying tones." His notation symbols are surprisingly modern in appearance in comparison to the nineteenth-century story and atmosphere of the opera, and they effectively elicit the desired effect. He amplifies his symbols with verbal instructions: "Crying should start on a high pitch each time and the sound gradually diminish" and "The crying need not be in strict time, but the accompaniment must be." Interestingly, he leaves pitches up to the performers, thereby incorporating group improvisation.[16] Joplin repeats the closed-lip moan

Example 2. "Good Advice," *Treemonisha*. Author's transcription.

to continued good effect in act 2, number 11, "Superstition," as the community expresses its fear of the conjurors' depiction of the dangers and bad luck at work in their world (example 3).

Similar vocal gestures appear in act 3, number 21, "Treemonisha's Return," where the "Corn-husking boys in distance" give a cry as they return from having rescued Treemonisha from her kidnappers. This cry recalls a field holler, originally meant to help workers communicate across long distances, and it is notated as a downward octave glissando sung in octaves by the men of the chorus.

Although it is not explicitly a reflection of African American expressivity, a final effective use of vocal inflection should be pointed out in act 2, number 13, "Frolic of the Bears," where the roar of the waltzing animals is playfully notated throughout the number (example 4). However, unlike some of the previous examples, these cries are assigned specific pitches.

Twenty-five years later, composers who wanted to capture the unique expressive moans and cries of the black community would still be trying to find notation that could convey vocal inflections adequately. A typical example is Gershwin's *Porgy and Bess*, act 1, scene 2, "Gone, Gone, Gone," in which the community gathers around Robbins's body to mourn his passing, humming together "plaintively" and uttering pitched shouts and chants.[17] Gershwin also employed various

Example 3. "Superstition," *Treemonisha*. Author's transcription.

notated chants and semisung notations at other points in the opera for various characters, including Peter the Honey Man, Serena, and Porgy.

As the call-and-response and unusual vocal inflections in "Good Advice" and "Superstition" recall authentic performances of the African American spiritual, so the Ring Play, act 1, number 4, "We're Goin' Around," sung by Andy and the corn huskers, harks back to ancient traditions that enslaved Africans brought to American soil. Descriptions of ring dances appear in George Washington Cable's 1886 reports of gatherings in New Orleans's Place Congo and also in Allen, Ware, and Garrison's introduction to *Slave Songs of the United States* (1867).[18] Like spiritual singing and ring shouts, these dances were important occasions for community release, entertainment, and social bonding. At a time when many former slaves still survived, the exuberance of the corn huskers and their ring dance in the opera might well have called up memories of community gatherings and already departed family members from earlier decades. As late as the 1930s, when the Federal Writers' Project interviewed more than two thousand former slaves, memories of such gatherings were still vivid. Henry James Trentham, age

Example 4. "Frolic of the Bears," measures 16–26, *Treemonisha*.

ninety-two when interviewed, recalled the welcome arrival of harvest festivities and holidays: "The cornshuckings was a great time. Marster give good liquor to everybody then. When anybody shucked a red ear, he got a extra drink of whiskey. We had big suppers then, and a good time at cornshuckings. After the shucking, at night, there would be a wrestling match to see who was best on the plantation." Other ex-slaves remembered community logrollings, cotton pickings, candy pullings, quiltings, and dances as well.[19] Another musical memory might have been called up by the quartet tradition illustrated by act 2, number 16, "We Will Rest Awhile," whose close harmony was familiar to the many gospel quartets that sang in churches and at social gatherings.

Joplin included the contemporaneous African American styles of the ragtime era in the slow drag dancing and the ragtime rhythms in several of the large choral ensembles: "We're Goin' Around," "Aunt Dinah Has Blowed de Horn," and "A Real Slow Drag." All are permeated with the syncopated rhythm of the overture, described in Joplin's preface to the opera: "This strain of music is the principal strain in the Opera and represents the happiness of the people when they feel free from the conjurors and their spells of superstition." This is not the only time Joplin expressed his feeling about the nature of ragtime. In his programmatic description of the final section of "Wall Street Rag" (1909), he says, "Listening to the strains of genuine negro ragtime, brokers forget their cares." Ragtime historian Edward Berlin maintains that this shows Joplin's thoughts on ragtime: "1) Not all ragtime is 'genuine'; only the African American creation is authentic. 2) Genuine ragtime is a happy music, endowed with the power to alter moods."[20] Joplin's use of this style in the opera is therefore significant. Apart from the overture, ragtime rhythm only appears in the big choruses, which have a jubilant character. "We're Goin' Around" is the first big ensemble piece in the opera and celebrates the community coming together at harvest time to husk the corn crop. "Aunt Dinah Has Blowed de Horn" is the final number in act 2 and occurs as newly rescued Treemonisha and her sweetheart, Remus, are getting directions home from a group of cotton pickers. Again the community is rejoicing, this time for the end of the workday and the prospect of rejoining their families. The third big number is "A Real Slow Drag," the final number of the opera, in which the people exult that Treemonisha has returned to her community and agreed to serve as their leader. They also welcome the conjuror and his henchmen, forgiven for their evil acts and brought back into the community fold. Joplin's specific use of these rhythms is a paean to the resilient spirit of the African American community that survived the slavery era only to face the sharecropping era and the harsh realities of Jim Crow.

Joplin's Use of Language

Along with important musical signifiers of black identity, Joplin employed language to impart cultural and political messages. His use of dialect is carefully chosen to accomplish specific dramaturgical goals. Clearly, he wishes to illuminate characters by assigning certain persons exclusively dialect texts. Zodzetrick and Simon, Parson Alltalk, Andy and Lucy, and the male quartet use dialect in all their pieces. The conjuror Zodzetrick's dialect is seen in his opening speech to Monisha:

I want to sell to you dis bag o' luck,
Yo' enemies it will keep away.
Over yo' front do' you can hang it,
An' good luck will come each day.

This type of plantation nostalgia dialect was very common in early-twentieth-century poetry and song texts by both black and white poets and composers: for example, African American poet Paul Laurence Dunbar (1872–1906), whose lyrics were set by such Broadway composers as Will Marion Cook (as in *Clorindy; or, The Origin of the Cakewalk*, 1898) and songwriter Sidney Homer (1864–1953), who besides being a popular songwriter of the time was husband of the great contralto Louise Homer and uncle to Samuel Barber.

Treemonisha, the only educated person in the community, and Remus, whom Treemonisha has taught to read and write, always speak with perfect English diction. More interesting, there are some characters that move in and out of dialect speech. Monisha uses dialect when she first encounters Zodzetrick, but when she sings her big arias about Treemonisha, her diction is very correct. Similarly with Ned, when he first addresses the slippery Zodzetrick, he uses dialect; for his magisterial act 3 aria, "When Villains Ramble Far and Near," his diction is also impeccable.

It would seem that the "good" or educated characters primarily use proper English, while the "bad" or uneducated characters speak in dialect. However, Joplin also uses dialect to create a sense of time and place, as in Parson Alltalk's sermon. In his "Good Advice," the spiritual style and dialect re-create memories of the old home places in the South. Life there was terribly difficult, but it was the place where families were rooted, childhood memories were created, and ancestors were buried; all those memories incorporated musical experiences. As New Orleans native Sidney Bechet would say later, in the music one could hear there "was something happening all the time to my people, a thing the music had to know for sure. There had to be a memory of it behind the music. . . . It's the remembering song. There's so much to remember."[21]

Joplin may have also been choosing language that indicated his feelings about the benefits of education, or he may have been using the differences between dialect and proper English to remark the differences between conversation and the "message" pieces in the opera. In any case, the chorus uses dialect for most of the opera, but as act 3 draws to a close and important events unfold, he turns completely to proper English. During the last six numbers of the opera, only clear English is used: Remus sings "Wrong Is Never Right," Ned sings "When Villains Ramble Far and Near," the conjurors are forgiven, the community selects Treemonisha as its leader, and the entire company sings the finale, a ragtime piece with proper English text. With the synthesis of ragtime musical figures and proper diction in "A Real Slow Drag," Joplin seems to show the community "marching onward," not only through the dance but metaphorically toward their rightful place in American society.

Treemonisha as Political Statement

Since *Treemonisha* is Joplin's magnum opus, written toward the end of his life when he had matured as a composer, it seems logical that the opera might well be a philosophical as well as an artistic statement. Given the variety of African American musics captured in the score, Joplin most certainly was affirming the artistic value of African American folk and ragtime music. Furthermore, when the plot and characters are considered in historical context, it seems apparent that Joplin was also making a statement about the political, social, and economic status of African Americans in the early twentieth century.

Born in 1868, Joplin would have understood early in life that the hope of opportunities for African Americans during the Reconstruction era faded as federal influence in the South waned beginning in 1877. The *Nation* announced, "The negro will disappear from the field of national politics. Henceforth, the nation, as a nation, will have nothing more to do with him." African Americans generally were unable to hold public office and systematically disenfranchised after 1877, and the failures of the Reconstruction era shaped every part of black life. There was no attempt to enact land reform, which would have helped freedmen support themselves through farming, and there was no guarantee of black suffrage; consequently, political, social, and economic equality was impossible. Although the "autonomous black family and network of religious and social institutions" were still in place at the end of the Reconstruction era, and some progress in education had been made, with the founding of several important historically black colleges and universities, the Supreme Court case of *Plessy v. Ferguson* in 1896, which declared that education in "separate but equal facilities" was legal, showed the true state of affairs for African Americans.[22] Until the later Supreme Court decision of *Brown vs. Board of Education* in 1954 and the beginning of the civil rights movement, education normally was separate, but hardly equal in any sense of the word.

In 1905 an illustrious group of African American leaders met in Buffalo, New York, to form the Niagara Movement. This movement was in part a response to the philosophy of Booker T. Washington, who espoused vocational education as the means to advance African American society. Speaking to the Cotton States Exposition in Atlanta in 1895, Washington calmed the anxieties of many who realized that race relations in America were at a difficult point:

> The wisest among my race understand that the agitation of questions of social equality is the extremest folly, and the progress in the enjoyment of all the privileges that will come to us must be the result of severe and constant struggle,

> rather than of artificial forcing. No race that has anything to contribute to the markets of the world is long in any degree ostracized. It is important that we be prepared for the exercises of these privileges. The opportunity to earn a dollar in a factory just now is worth infinitely more than the opportunity to spend a dollar in an opera house.[23]

This speech eventually came to be known as the "Atlanta Compromise," and while it reassured whites, it rankled many black leaders, including W. E. B. Du Bois and William Monroe Trotter, founder of the *Boston Guardian* newspaper in 1900. Not knowing about many of Washington's quiet but effective efforts on behalf of African Americans nor having experienced life in the South, Trotter called Washington's accommodating attitude a "crime of race ridicule and belittlement." The more radical Du Bois also believed that education was important, saying, "The Negro race, like all races, is going to be saved by its exceptional men." Du Bois advocated concentrating on the "talented tenth" of the population, or the one in ten who was likely to become a leader of their race and who would then advance the cause of general education.[24]

Du Bois had published a fiery manifesto in 1903, *The Souls of Black Folk*, in which he commented on the place of African Americans in American society. "Here," he said, "we brought our three gifts and mingled them with yours: a gift of story and song—soft, stirring melody in an ill-harmonized and unmelodious land; the gift of sweat and brawn to beat back the wilderness, conquer the soil, and lay the foundations of this vast economic empire two hundred years earlier than your weak hands could have done it; the third, a gift of the spirit. . . . Actively we have woven ourselves with the very warp and woof of this nation." At the second meeting of the Niagara Movement, Du Bois hurled another verbal salvo at white political leaders in an inflammatory speech that demanded voting rights, the end of discrimination in public transportation, social equality, equal treatment under the law, and, last, equal education, and he demanded that change occur sooner rather than later. In addressing the needs for education, Du Bois spoke eloquently: "Education is the development of power and ideal. We want our children trained as intelligent human beings should be, and we will fight for all time against any proposal to educate black boys and girls simply as servants and underlings, or simply for the use of other people. They have a right to know, to think, to aspire."[25]

Joplin's incorporation of contemporary thought about progress and education into his opera may seem unusual in comparison to other operas written at that time, where plots based on love stories of a much more sensational, even violent, character are much more typical.[26] However, when the historical and social context of early-twentieth-century America is considered, Joplin's choice of subject matter for his opera indicates his awareness of contemporary political currents. The activities and writings of such luminaries as Booker T. Washington and W. E. B. Du Bois were closely read by the black community and discussed in black newspapers, and intellectual leaders in every field were more than ready to state their opinions of matters so critically important to every African American. It is not surprising that Joplin, remembering the importance of his early education gained through his mother's hard work and the generosity of many, would attend to the debate in the African American community and would comment through his work. In his heroine, Treemonisha, he celebrated Booker T. Washington's often stated credo that education was the answer to many ills and that it was important for everyone to have as much education and apply it in as practical way as possible. In investing this responsibility in a young woman, Joplin responded to Du Bois's call for effective change and openness to new ways of thinking about society, yet affirmed the value of forgiveness and membership in one's community.

As Joplin pursued his artistic dreams and incorporated his worldview into *Treemonisha,* he assembled an array of diverse musical traditions from the American South and Europe, an unusual plot, and characters that set *Treemonisha* apart from nearly all the opera written up to 1911, whether European or American. He commented on women's roles in society, reflecting the suffrage efforts that eventually gave American women the vote in 1921, and confirmed the belief that "education is the road to salvation." In *Treemonisha,* he truly contributed to the goal his widow, Lottie Joplin, claimed for him in 1950: "He wanted to free his people from poverty, ignorance, and superstition, just like the heroine of his ragtime opera, *Treemonisha.*"[27]

Notes

1. *Oxford Dictionary of Quotations,* 3d ed. (New York: Oxford University Press, 1980), quoting from Louis Pasteur's lecture on the inauguration of the Faculty of Science, University of Lille, December 7, 1854.

2. Berlin, *King of Ragtime,* 70.

3. Ibid., 115. According to Berlin, these performances took Joplin through Illinois, Missouri, Kansas, Iowa, and Nebraska.

4. Ibid., 198.

5. Mencken, "The Theatre," 107.

6. During the Joplin revival in the 1970s, Gunther Schuller formed the New England Conservatory Ragtime Ensemble and recorded *The Red Back Book,* a group of ragtime orchestrations published by John Stark around 1909 under the title *Fifteen Standard High Class Rags.* Among the rags in *The Red Back Book* were rags by Joplin and other composers, including James Scott's "Frog Legs Rag" in an orchestration by Joplin. Schuller was therefore uniquely qualified to orchestrate Joplin's *Treemonisha.*

7. Berlin, *King of Ragtime,* 45.

8. Ibid., 7, 94.

9. Monroe Rosenfeld, "The King of Ragtime Composers Is Scott Joplin, a Colored St. Louisan," *St. Louis Globe-Democrat,* June 7, 1903.

10. Epstein, *Complete Catalogue of Sheet Music.*

11. Lawrence, *Joplin's "Treemonisha" Vocal Selections,* 5; Berlin, *King of Ragtime,* 191, 202; Lawrence, *Joplin's "Treemonisha" Vocal Selections,* 8.

12. Joplin's own plot description was published in the original vocal score of *Treemonisha.*

13. Joplin, *Treemonisha,* 35.

14. Ibid., 75–85.

15. Ibid., 35, 38, 76.

16. Ibid., 95–98 (quote on 95).

17. Gershwin, *Porgy and Bess,* 115, 130–31.

18. Floyd, *Power of Black Music,* 35–37.

19. Hurmence, *My Folks,* 7 (quote), 19, 23, 89–90.

20. Joplin, *Treemonisha,* 5; Berlin, *King of Ragtime,* 187.

21. Floyd, *Power of Black Music,* 8–9.

22. Foner, *Short History of Reconstruction,* 245, 255.

23. Meltzer, *Black Americans,* 139–40.

24. Harlan, "Booker T. Washington," 6; Du Bois, "The Talented Tenth," accessed October 8, 2009, at TeachingAmericanHistory.org, Ashbrook Center for Public Affairs at Ashland University.

25. Du Bois, *Souls of Black Folk,* 275; Meltzer, *Black Americans,* 152.

26. For example, in the first decade of the twentieth century, successful opera composers produced the following works: Richard Strauss, *Salome* (1905), *Elektra* (1909), *Der Rosenkavalier* (1911); Giacomo Puccini, *Tosca* (1900), *Madame Butterfly* (1904), *La Fanciulla del West* (1910); and Claude Debussy, *Pelléas et Mélisande* (1902).

27. Lawrence, *Joplin's "Treemonisha" Vocal Selections,* 8; Berlin, *King of Ragtime,* 193.

Bibliography

Berlin, Edward A. *King of Ragtime: Scott Joplin and His Era.* Oxford: Oxford University Press, 1994.

———. "Scott Joplin." In *International Dictionary of Black Composers,* ed. Samuel A. Floyd Jr. Chicago and London: Fitzroy Dearborn, 1999.

Curtis, Susan. *Dancing to a Black Man's Tune: A Life of Scott Joplin.* Columbia: University of Missouri Press, 1994.

Du Bois, W. E. B. *The Souls of Black Folk.* With a new introduction by Randall Kenan. New York: Signet, 1995.

———. "The Talented Tenth." In *The Negro Problem.* New York: James Pott, 1903.

Epstein, Dena J. *Complete Catalogue of Sheet Music and Musical Works, 1870.* New York: Da Capo Press, 1973. Originally published by the Board of Music Trade of the United States of America, 1871.

Floyd, Samuel A., Jr. *The Power of Black Music.* New York: Oxford University Press, 1995.

Foner, Eric. *A Short History of Reconstruction, 1863–1877.* New York: Harper & Row, 1990.

Gershwin, George. *Porgy and Bess.* Vocal score. Secaucus, N.J.: Warner Brothers, 1935.

Harlan, Louis R. "Booker T. Washington and the Politics of Accommodation." In *Black Leaders of the Twentieth Century,* ed. John Hope Franklin and August Meier. Urbana: University of Illinois Press, 1982.

Hurmence, Belinda, ed. *My Folks Don't Want Me to Talk about Slavery.* Winston-Salem, N.C.: John F. Blair, 1984.

Joplin, Scott. *Treemonisha.* Vocal score. 1911. Reprint, New York: Dover, 2001.

———. *"Treemonisha" Vocal Selections.* Milwaukee: Hal Leonard, 1975.

Lawrence, Vera Brodsky. *Scott Joplin Collected Piano Works.* New York: New York Public Library, 1971.

———. *Scott Joplin's "Treemonisha" Vocal Selections.* Milwaukee: Hal Leonard, 1975.

Meltzer, Milton, ed. *The Black Americans: A History in Their Own Words, 1619–1983.* New York: Harper & Row, 1984.

Mencken, H. L. "The Theatre." *American Mercury Magazine* (January–April 1926).

Ping-Robbins, Nancy R. *Scott Joplin: A Guide to Research.* New York: Garland, 1998.

Scott Joplin: The Red Back Book. New England Ragtime Ensemble, Gunther Schuller, conductor. *Elite Syncopations:* The Southland Stingers, George Sponhaltz, conductor. Angel CDC-7 47193 2.

Wright, Kai, ed. *The African-American Archive: The History of the Black Experience through Documents.* New York: Black Dog & Leventhal, 2001.

6

Clarence Cameron White's *Ouanga!* in the World of the Harlem Renaissance

KAREN M. BRYAN

American literature, music, and popular culture of the 1920s are replete with works reflecting the U.S. fascination with the nation of Haiti. In this spirit, Clarence Cameron White (1880–1960), violinist and composer, and John Frederick Matheus (1887–1983), writer and literary scholar, produced the opera *Ouanga!* near the end of the decade, joining other African American artists who worked to counter the more sensationalistic views of Haitian culture. Haiti's role as the first independent black-ruled state in the Western Hemisphere, as well as the prominence of its African heritage and the voudon religion, became a rich source of material for writers and composers interested in basing their works on indigenous themes (or in captivating audiences increasingly interested in non-Western cultures).[1] White and Matheus' approach was realistic and sympathetic, incorporating both the complexities and contrasts of the culture while focusing on the challenges facing a nation whose people belonged to distinct—and frequently unsympathetic—cultural worlds.

American political interests precipitated much of the fascination with Haiti. The U.S. invasion of that country in 1915 was a signal event for African Americans, and the subsequent twenty-year occupation lent impetus to the artistic trends of the 1920s. The official reason for the invasion was to protect American-owned interests on the island from internal political turmoil and from the presence of German naval forces in the area.[2] Long before the actual invasion, the U.S. press reported acts of violence, often indicating that the Haitian people were incapable of forming or maintaining a government without outside (read: American or European) aid.[3]

By 1920, African American writers such as James Weldon Johnson grew critical of the occupation, focusing instead on its implications both for the Haitian people and African Americans. Simultaneously, other African American writers and artists used Haiti and its history as proxies for their own heritage and as a rallying cry for civil rights in the United States. Haiti had long been part of popular culture, but this new and politically charged commentary by African American artists of the 1920s contrasted sharply with the typically romanticized views promoted by white writers and filmmakers.

White and Matheus contributed to this dual view of Haiti. They collaborated on the opera *Ouanga!*, a partnership that began shortly after White's appointment as professor of violin (1924) at the West Virginia Collegiate Institute near Charleston, where Matheus was already on faculty. Matheus had been interested in Haitian history since childhood, reading first Wendell Phillips's account of Toussaint L'Ouverture, then hearing another version of the story from a baseball player named Fleetwood Walker.[4] These accounts spurred him to research the revolution and Haitian culture. He drafted a dramatic work based on L'Ouverture's life but decided instead to persuade White to collaborate on an opera.

They intended the work to conform to the expectations of the Harlem Renaissance. It would be based on themes drawn from the African and African American diaspora, promoting a positive and realistic view of African Americans without resorting to the stereotypes so prominent in popular literature. They also intended to create a performance vehicle for African American artists that would provide a positive outlet for their talents. They achieved these goals in *Ouanga!* but as with most operas written by American composers during that time—particularly those by African American composers requiring an African American cast—there were few performance opportunities. *Ouanga!* was more widely performed than most, but only by smaller companies; it was last performed in 1956.[5]

In this opera, the accurate and sympathetic portrayal of historical events facilitates examining the often conflicting tensions of traditional and contemporary expectations. It can be viewed literally (as a story of Haiti's revolutionary general and his personal struggle to lead a new country with ties to two very different cultures), but it also represents the African American struggle to create and maintain a sense of identity in an atmosphere dominated by racial and cultural conflict. The opera is a study in contrasts, all of which call upon the characters and the audience to reflect on the role of heritage and tradition balanced with emerging social trends. The struggle between European colonialism and local independence strongly relates to the conflicts facing African Americans reaching artistic maturity in the 1920s. Understanding this dichotomy requires a brief synopsis of the impact and legacy of Haiti's revolution on American society in the 1920s.

Haiti's Revolutionary History and the American Occupation: The Foundation for an Opera

The Haitian revolution was a series of uprisings between 1791 and 1803 in the French colony of Saint-Dominigue.[6] As France's wealthiest colony, this portion of the island of Hispaniola produced sugar, coffee, indigo, and cotton, largely through the efforts of a slave labor force. At the time of the French Revolution (1789), the population consisted of approximately forty thousand whites (planters as well as tradesmen and artisans known as *petit blancs*), approximately thirty thousand free blacks, an unknown number of runaway slaves, and a slave population of approximately five hundred thousand. The unrest was inspired by revolution in France, as well as legislation that taxed the colony and limited participation in the government by the *petit blancs* and free blacks. The enslaved population took advantage of the opportunity to overthrow the white planters and gain their freedom.

Toussaint L'Ouverture led the slave revolt beginning in 1791; by 1792, his forces controlled a significant portion of the island. Subsequent violence and a large casualty count led the British, who looked to expand their own influence, to intervene in 1793. They left the island in 1798, having failed to defeat L'Ouverture. In 1802, a new wave of Napoleonic troops arrived to challenge L'Ouverture; he was captured and died in prison in 1803. Jean-Jacques Dessalines, his lieutenant, assumed leadership and succeeded in defeating the French late in 1803. He declared independence on January 1, 1804, changing the name to Haiti and declaring himself emperor. His reign was marked by violence and unrest; his troops assassinated him in 1806. Political instability would continue throughout the nineteenth century, with numerous violent uprisings and frequent changes of leadership.

Haiti and its political situation had long been a topic of interest in the United States. In the early nineteenth century, antislavery advocates cited Haiti as an example of the ability of blacks to rule. However, its political instability, the social and economic differences within the society, and the corruption of the ruling classes undermined its example as a black, independent state, at least in the minds of Anglo-Americans. Leaders within the African American community, concerned about American opinion, regarded the society as irresponsible, uncivilized, and in need of stability.[7]

U.S. policy toward Haiti began to change with the inauguration of Woodrow Wilson in 1913, reflecting a more "authoritative paternalistic" approach to the "Haitian problem."[8] A white diplomat replaced Henry Forniss, the American minister, breaking the tradition of appointing an African American in that post. After the invasion, authority was transferred to military officers, and Haitian officials assumed figurehead roles. The U.S. Marines landed in Port-au-Prince in 1915 to address the violence and instability of the island's government and to protect U.S. interests in the Caribbean against the anticipated expansion of German naval influence. The invasion was precipitated by the assassination of Haiti's president and growing civil unrest. At this point, both the United States and France regarded the black republic as a failed attempt at self-rule.

The harsh treatment of Haitians by occupation forces at first received little public attention due to the continuing focus on the war in Europe. Occupation policies that were unpopular on the island gradually came to be questioned in the United States as well. The marines responded harshly to uprisings, destroying property and shooting anyone suspected of participating in the resistance. Haitian casualties numbered more than three thousand between 1915 and 1919. Forced labor groups were common, as was the relocation and mistreatment of workers. The occupation authority suspended the Haitian constitution, practiced press censorship, imposed unpopular treaties, and instituted inequities in employment mirroring those for which the Haitian government had been criticized prior to the invasion. The attitudes of American government and military officials were in line with typical views of the era and included negative assessments of Haitians' mental ability, lack of civilized behavior, and questionable ancestry; segregationist policies commonly practiced in the United States were also strictly enforced. Ironically, occupation officials became the equivalent of the elitist society and government they had replaced.

Black leaders, even those concerned about the political situation in Haiti prior to 1915, criticized the occupation and its abuses. W. E. B. Du Bois and James Weldon Johnson spoke through the organ of the NAACP, the *Crisis,* maintaining that the government should resolve problems, not amplify them. Pressure intensified through the 1920s to appoint an African American to the governing commission; Napoleon Marshall served as legation clerk (1922 to 1928), though his appointment was largely symbolic. Although they were isolated and experienced discrimination, Marshall and his wife, Harriet Gibbs Marshall, used their time in Haiti to establish relationships with its citizens.[9] Upon their return to America in 1927, they established the Save Haiti Committee, aimed at ending the occupation and supporting educational projects on the island.

The American Reaction to the Haitian Occupation

As the occupation became more politically charged, Haiti assumed a prominent role in defining America's view of its global relationships.[10] It also affected African Americans' view of themselves within the United States and in relation to their African heritage and its influence. Both white and black writers responded to this changing role.

Prior to 1920, many writers supported the occupation. Reports in American newspapers defended the necessity for the invasion and related horrific accounts of the assassination of Haiti's president. Short, factual reports of naval involvement and troop movements coexisted with extended essays on the need for intervention to end the bloodshed. A few African American writers, including James Weldon Johnson, initially supported the invasion, deeming it better to assert control than to ignore the violence.

The tone changed, however, with the American presidential election of 1920. Candidates and commentators debated the American presence and troop actions throughout the election season. James Weldon Johnson traveled to Haiti on a fact-finding mission for the NAACP and his report, "Self-Determining Haiti," was published in installments in the *Nation*. Johnson's essays were a clear indictment of the invasion, claiming that its economic and political justifications were backed, in his view, by significant financial institutions in New York City. He now became a leading critic of the occupation.

As criticism increased, Haiti's culture and history became more popular in American literary and musical circles. Its recent history as a free black state, the social structure that lent itself easily to commentary, and the appeal to the imagination of voudon made it a rich source for creative adaptation. Stories focused on some aspect of Haitian culture or history became staples in literary and popular culture—including novels, travel dialogues, films, radio dramas, and opera—for the next two decades. Such works prominently featured the religion of voudon, an important part of the lives of common people and a practice ready-made for writers seeking to stimulate and titillate readers.

Anglo-American writers contributed works about Haiti to several genres during this period. One of the most popular literary examples was the travel narrative; these in turn contributed descriptive scenes to novels and films. John W. Vandercook's *Black Majesty* (1928) and William Seabrook's *Magic Island* (1929) described local customs and voudon rituals. Popular songs ("Katie Went to Haiti," as performed by Ethel Merman before 1930), novels (Edna Taft's *Puritan in Voodoo Land* [1938]), radio shows (Orson Welles's *Shadow,* which featured Haitian characters and settings), and films (*White Zombie* [1932] and *I Walked with a Zombie* [1943]) portrayed Haiti as a "primitive," passionate, and violent society. Eugene O'Neill's *Emperor Jones* (1920) and Louis Gruenberg's opera of the same name (1933), while not specifically naming Haiti, invoked many of the same images.[11] These works shared a sensationalized view of Haitian history and the "voodoo" religion.[12] Paying little attention to historical or cultural accuracy, they reinforced American perception of the island and its people as primitive, aggressively sexual, violent, and unpredictable, indirectly championing the need for a stabilizing influence that, in the minds of the American public, meant the U.S. government.

African American writers began to contribute to the discourse in the second half of the decade. Artists and writers including Arthur Schomburg, Langston

Hughes, Arna Bontemps, Katherine Dunham, Zora Neale Hurston, John Frederick Matheus, and Clarence Cameron White traveled to the island, exploring the culture firsthand. Their subsequent writings downplayed sensational themes, focusing instead on the proud history and African heritage of the island's inhabitants or on denunciations of the occupation. While voudon often factored into such discussions, authors placed greater emphasis on the accomplishments of the people. They strove for historical accuracy and cultural objectivity, stressing the African heritage and the accomplishments of a government that had been independent for more than a century. Renda claims that James Weldon Johnson's description of the Haitian people in 1920 set the tone for later writers:

> Educated, cultured, and intellectual [Haitians] are not accidental and sporadic offshoots of the Haitian people," Johnson insisted; "they are the Haitian people. Judge Haiti by their accomplishments." Yet, his approach left room for a certain brand of primitivism in his account of the Haitian poor. Johnson acknowledged an opposition between the civilized and the primitive in occupied Haiti, but located it along the axis of class rather than race or nation. "The masses of the Haitian people are . . . industrious and thrifty," wrote Johnson, answering charges that rural peasants sought to avoid labor. "For a woman to walk five to ten miles with a great load of produce on her head, which may barely realize her a dollar is doubtless primitive, and a wasteful expenditure of energy, but it is not a sign of laziness." Similarly, Johnson described the "long rows of wooden shanties, the curious little booths around the market" in the capital city as "no less picturesque and no more primitive . . . than similar quarters in Naples, in Lisbon, in Marseilles." To Johnson the Haitian poor were primitive, to be sure, but no more so than the southern European poor.[13]

The Genesis of *Ouanga!*

When Matheus persuaded White to collaborate on a project concerning Haitian history, their first decision was to determine around which revolutionary figure they would build the work.[14] To Matheus, the story of Dessalines was the larger truth of the Haitian people, not only at the time of the revolution, but also through the intervening century and the American occupation.[15] The ex-slave–turned–military leader and emperor represented the new nation as it left colonial domination and struggled to establish an independent state, one that existed on both political and cultural planes. This conflict and its ramifications were of far greater interest than the revolution itself.[16] White and Matheus pared down the historical record to its essential figures and details, focusing on the implications of the characters' decisions for the new country. These choices, and the decisions of those who follow or reject Dessalines, form the basis of the opera. (A synopsis of the plot may be found in appendix A.)

The plot is simple: Dessalines assumes leadership of the island, naming himself emperor. This act of self-aggrandizement alienates many, including his most loyal officers and soldiers. As he chooses a distinctly European-based form of government, that of absolute rule, he abandons Defilee, his longtime lover, to marry Claire Heureuse, a member of the elite class against whom he had struggled.[17] In the midst of his coronation, a voudon priestess, Mougali, is murdered and Dessalines's fate is sealed: his own men will assassinate him for having forsaken his people and their traditions. Matheus chose not to include the reality of Dessalines's atrocities, the actual motive for his assassination, in order to achieve a more sympathetic portrayal of the leader.

In preparing for this opera, White and Matheus struggled to develop a realistic, though positive, portrait of the country. In particular, they felt it was important to accurately represent Haitian music and dance, a challenge, as both had little direct contact with Haitian culture. An adherent of Harlem Renaissance ideals, White had composed several works in which African American themes and melodies served as component materials (*From the Cotton Fields* and *Bandana Sketches).* While one can reasonably assume he would apply the same sensitivity in representing Haitian culture, he had little experience with those forms and traditions. This same disadvantage applied to religion, for neither man had any experience with voudon as it existed in Haiti itself or as practiced by immigrants in the New York area.

To augment their knowledge, they (along with White's son, William) traveled to Haiti in 1928 as guests of Napoleon and Harriett Gibbs Marshall, with whom White enjoyed a long-standing friendship.[18] The Marshalls introduced him to influential people within Haitian society and helped him gain access to rituals and performances from which he could draw inspiration for his own composition. His plan was only partly successful. Much of the trip was devoted to standard tourist attractions and staged rituals, few of which reflected the daily practice of the religion in the rural regions. We have no indication they were actually able to travel into the countryside or meet people outside of the urban upper classes.

Despite this relatively superficial introduction to the traditions and customs of the country, their trip gave them sufficient insight to construct their opera. They built *Ouanga!* on a foundation of the social contrasts they witnessed and explored how the characters moved between different, yet interconnected worlds. The tension generated by the pressure to choose and conform either to the old or to the new, and the ways in which the characters reacted, provided the dramatic impetus for the entire opera.

As previously noted, the literature of the 1920s demonstrated a growing acknowledgment of Haiti's African heritage and its extension to African Americans. It combined with an increasing emphasis on "race pride" in literature and in news articles and was reflected in the writings of African American authors. Black and white writers used metaphors of familial relationships to describe Haiti's connection to both Africa and Europe. These devices, common throughout literature, were a convenient means not only to describe the island's African heritage, but also to convey the paternalistic attitude held by many Anglo-Americans toward a country they felt needed guidance from a stronger, more stable government—namely, the United States. These relationships became common in the works of both Haitian and American writers.[19]

Matheus and White referenced these themes in *Ouanga!* highlighting the African heritage of individual characters and the Haitian people in general. Haiti became the "daughter of Africa," a common descriptor following the publication of Blair Niles's *Black Haiti: A Biography of Africa's Eldest Daughter* (1926).[20] In act 1, scene 2, when Dessalines turns to Defilee for reassurance and implores her to "sing the songs of Africa," she replies, "Haiti! Haiti! Daughter thou of Africa, and hope of our ancient race, home of the murmuring palm, fold thou thine arms around my love, my warrior bold! Guard him I pray."[21]

The "call" of Africa and an instinctive relationship to that continent become tangible elements in Matheus's libretto. Perhaps coincidentally, he presented many of these references in musical terms: the songs and "drums of Africa." In Matheus's view, these elements speak to all Haitians regardless of class or political sympathies. In the opera, the characters respond to them in various ways, and the conflicts that arise, or the feelings they inspire, become the very foundation of the plot.

Physical Representation and Contrast as a Social and Religious Delimiter

White and Matheus use physical representation and description to heighten the contrast between the concepts of old and new, whether in religion, government, or everyday life. Vivid and explicit descriptions of personal appearance, physical characteristics, and dress polarize individuals, supported in the libretto by narrative explanations and descriptions of scenery and costumes.

Matheus relies on characterizations to strengthen the theme of contrast. Le Boussel (Dessalines's aide) is a participant in the rites of the opening scene. As such, he straddles two worlds: he is a key figure in Dessalines's new government that rejects "voodoo," but still adheres to the old religion in his private life. In act 1, scene 1, Matheus describes the rites as "a hilarious celebration of a primitive African dance" and characterizes Le Boussel as "a gigantic, full-blooded black."[22] Matheus invokes several tropes in these few lines. By identifying Le Boussel's color as well as his race, he establishes his membership in the rural classes, whose status was often identified in contemporary literature in terms of color. Matheus also invokes the image of a wild and uninhibited dance, linking it directly to African influence; he conveys impressions of power and freedom in the use of terms such as *gigantic* and *celebration* (perhaps a subtle allusion to the 1920s occupation and the lack of freedom experienced by contemporary Haitians).[23] Moreover, as leader of the dance, there is no doubt Le Boussel's personal loyalties fall with the traditional religion, placing him in conflict with Dessalines. Ironically, in making these connections, he paints a scene resembling many others in the writings of the 1920s.

Costumes and sets reinforce the trope of cultural contrast. The new, represented by Dessalines and his court, is presented in urban settings, particularly in Cap Haitien. The coronation is set in a great plaza in front of the cathedral, and the music is based in western European traditions, including the liturgical music of the Catholic Church. By contrast, scenes portraying the old ways, including the voudon ceremonies, take place in forested areas and rural villages. They represent a return to tradition and, by extension, the "true" order for the Haitian people. The only characters that move between these worlds with any regularity are Dessalines and Defilee; their transitions are notable. Dessalines always changes attire, abandoning the "fashions of 1804" when he returns to the forest.[24] Defilee, on the other hand, enters the city only in disguise, almost as a protection against the influence of the new ways.

The costumes further emphasize this contrast. Those of the court are the high fashion of 1804, the point at which Haiti gained its freedom. They are modern and expensive, conveying an upper-class rank appropriate for the ruling elite. They are also European, encouraging the audience to make a connection with the power of the departed colonial rulers. By contrast, the costumes of characters associated with the older traditions (for example, Le Boussel, Licite, and Defilee) are more rustic and appropriate to a rural setting.[25] They are described as "ragged" when the characters are caught up in the excitement of the dance; at other times, they are described as "colorful" and include turbans and flowing robes.

Social and Religious Structures Represented in *Ouanga!*

Just as Matheus incorporates themes of African heritage into his libretto, he also uses descriptive language to classify the characters' attitudes and direct the audience's attention to specific characters, issues, or conflicts. He uses silence to isolate entire groups within the story, robbing them of power and influence, regardless of the apparent realities of the situation.

The members of the social elite are either silent or have only limited dialogue in this opera. Matheus thus shifts the balance of expressive power to the rural classes and those characters rooted more firmly in the traditional practices. Members of the rural, peasant class (Licite, Defilee, and the voudon priests and priestesses) use idiomatic language; Matheus borrowed from Creole terms and colloquialisms he heard while in Haiti to shape their dialogue. He uses this dialect for all of their scenes, including religious ceremonies. Ultimately, these characters prevail, and, it is implied, Haitian culture will develop free from the influence of the social elites who allied with their former oppressors.

Only Dessalines functions in both classes. As emperor, he employs formal, more Europeanized forms of address, but as Defilee's former lover, he communicates in the Creole-English mixture of the rural classes. The delineation is clear and becomes more extreme as he is faced with betrayal and assassination at the end of the opera. He is most comfortable and at ease when addressing Defilee, whom he associates most closely with his African heritage and the comfort of the past. He is most cruel when speaking as the ruler who has assumed the colonialists' language. At those times, he assumes not only expressions associated with paternalistic discourse, but also those that are most abusive of the race. In the following example, he addresses a group engaged in religious dances:

> You lazy ones! You will not work!
> All night you dance in the moonlight. All day you sleep in the sun!
> Your fields are empty and barren. You do not see the new day!
> The freedom of Haiti is yours now! Accept the new law and cast away
> your enslaving folly![26]

In this excerpt, Matheus assigns Dessalines the racialized language used by white writers of the 1920s (including members of the occupation forces) who described Haitians, particularly those outside of the cities, as lazy and too closely tied to "voodoo."[27]

As part of their research, White and Matheus tried to gain exposure to voudon rites during their trip to Haiti. Although their experience was limited, they did learn that voudon was associated primarily with rural Haitians and rejected by the ruling elite, regarded as a practice to be expunged from the society as quickly as possible. Reports of its ceremonies enjoyed a mixed reception in both the white and black communities. According to Michael Largey, the attitudes toward the religion (both in Haiti and in the United States) began to change after the publication of Jean Price-Mars's *Ainsi parle l'oncle* in 1928, in which he advocated the acceptance of voudon: "Until the publication of Price-Mars's book, Haitian elites generally saw voudou as a malevolent force that threatened to disrupt the social status quo. As the religion of the majority of rural Haitians, voudou had strong class associations with the poor and illiterate masses. Price-Mars's book helped ease Haitian elites' ideas of voudou as a form of devil worship but in the process made voudou a cultural commodity and turned the music of the voudou ceremony into a product suitable for Haitian middle-class consumption."[28]

Accounts of the 1920s portrayed the religion and its followers in extreme and negative ways. These exaggerations were viewed as reality and complicated the situation for writers who wanted to present a more sympathetic view of the rites and the believers. No matter how firmly they based their accounts on objective facts, audiences expected to see (and hear) what they regarded as the "true" representation of the island and its religion. Yet Matheus and White sought to portray the rites realistically. They included the conflict between believers and nonbelievers, emphasizing the demarcation between the common people and the ruling elites of the island.

Voudon functions as a major dramatic device throughout the opera. It becomes the single most identifying characteristic of the peasant or rural classes, and its contrast with the religion of the elite class, which we are encouraged to believe is European Catholicism, produces much of the dramatic tension. Matheus and White incorporate ritual and music, while the death of the celebrant drives the dramatic motivation for the second half of the opera. White and Matheus also assume Dessalines's complete rejection of voudon, which contributes to his downfall. But they also recognize the pull the religion still exerts on his emotions; in doing so, they illuminate the tangle of relationships that influenced the actions of all Haitians.

The opening scene of the opera, comparable to the music and prayer of the Rada ritual in its invocation of Legba (a serpent deity, "the entity that opens the cosmic gates"), establishes the role of religion as a dividing line between the characters.[29] The masses practice the religion, and the priestess, Mougali, is a powerful and effective figure in their lives. The contrast with Catholic ritual in the coronation scene is powerful and further emphasizes the conflict between the protagonists in the opera.[30] Voudon's status is based in its traditional authority and its association with the island's African heritage. Its influence affects the destiny of both the island and the government.

Dessalines rejects Defilee, his former lover, both physically and emotionally. As she rushes to his side, he pushes her away, and his admonishment of the people is also an accusation of her, since she remains loyal to the faith. He rejects the power of voudon, and thus of superstition, as he refuses to be intimidated by the priestess: "Of idle words, a king is not afraid! If I through words had from my purpose strayed long since would Dessalines have gone to dust. On self and will have I trusted, my breast has fronted the fire. I have defied the fates."[31]

The musical contrast between the prayer and the interruption is clear: the prayers of the crowd are strong and energetic, with all voices in unison, while the text of the priestess is set in a slow and dignified manner. Dessalines interrupts in recitative that lacks the syncopations and dotted rhythms of the chorus. His turn to the new way is thus reinforced by his rejection of the musical style of the people.

Ultimately, the power of voudon prevails. Dessalines is assassinated, ending his influence and that of the elite classes to whom he turned. Although there is no indication of his successor, the opera ends with a triumphal display of the ritual and faith associated with Africa. By extension, this triumph analogously stands for both the occupation of Haiti in the 1920s and the circumstances of African Americans in the United States. The underlying message is clear: remaining faithful to Haitian heritage and culture—that is, resisting the occupation—will lead to triumph; renouncing it will lead to the destruction or dissolution of local culture.

The Musical Representation of Haitian Culture

As White and Matheus prepared this opera, it must have been clear that they had to include three interrelated elements in the work: voudon, drumming, and songs. These three elements were so closely identified with Haitian culture that no works based on it could be complete without them. Despite their seemingly superficial and tourist-level introduction to Haiti, White and Matheus realized their essential importance. Their appropriation of the forms and elements is notable for their attempt to remain as faithful to Haitian practice as possible.

Voudon produces the fundamental tension of the opera. Matheus, in crafting the libretto, relied on elements of the Rada rite, one of Haitian voudon's primary components. White reinforced that association by his choice of dances and musical forms. The Rada rite, like all ceremonies associated with voudon, is intrinsically bound to the use of dance and songs. According to Fleurant, "Drums and Drummers are a significant component of Vodun because it is a danced religion. The term Vodun means 'drum and spirit' in the language of the Fon of Dahomey, West Africa. In Haiti, it is to the powerful beats of the drums that the Rada ceremonies are conducted." Dance and song not only help establish contact with the spiritual world in a visible and participatory way, but are themselves shaped by the influences of these spiritual elements and become a form of communication with the persons performing them.[32]

Drums recur in the libretto and its musical realization, representing both Africa and the African connections with voudon and the "old ways" of the Haitian people.[33] Matheus first uses this trope in his description of act 1, scene 2: "It is growing dusk. Groups of peasants pass, some on foot, others astride donkeys. Goats file by driven by boys. The animals have triangular pieces of wood fastened around their necks. Suddenly a faint rumbling is heard in the distance—the beating of an African drum. Another answers it, seemingly much closer. Several natives asleep under the trees."[34]

In his portrayal of the new nation, Matheus presents the religion as a venerated cultural icon for all but Dessalines who, in reality, fears the consequences of his rejection of it. Matheus also wants the audience to make this connection, for he clearly connects this specific island and culture to the popular associations with voudon and Africa in the 1930s, when the opera was first produced.[35]

As in the libretto, White equates the drums with ancient Africa and uses them in a representational way throughout the music. He relies heavily on the traditional drums of the Haitian voudon rituals, and his attention to their importance demonstrates his awareness of both their function and their importance. Drums used in voudon rites embody a spiritual significance of their own. Ceremonies accompanying the making of these drums imbue them with power and meaning; these ceremonies are repeated at intervals to renew the power of the drums. Offerings of food and prayers are made prior to felling the tree that will be used, ceremonies are conducted to remove any negative spirits or powers, and, once the drum is complete, it is subject to a ritual baptism.[36]

The prominence of the drums in this work is to be expected: they are the most obvious element of the rituals and the most distinctive characteristic of the rite. As a result, their pervasive presence in this work reinforces the power and influence of voudon in the story, underscoring the tension generated by the conflict between the religion's adherents and the nonbelievers.

White used the three important drums of the Rada rite: in descending order of size, they are the *manman*, the *segon*, and the *boula*.[37] All are hollow-log drums, with heads of cowhide or goatskin, and tuned by pegs inserted in the sides. All are separate musical voices, moving independently in a rich polyphonic texture, and form the foundation of the rite's percussive accompaniment and dances. They may be accompanied by the *ogan* (bell), the *ason* (ritual shaker), and the *bas* (a large tambourine), but it is not uncommon for performers to use the drums alone.

White specified the use of authentic Haitian instruments and, when possible (as it was with the relatively large Haitian population in New York), recommended using drummers familiar with the complex rhythms, which were hard to replicate for those who had not undergone the rigorous training required for the rituals and dances. Many of the subtleties would have been lost in an unfamiliar pattern and context, and they were reputedly difficult to reproduce. Although White went to great pains to suggest Haitian drummers to Mary Cardwell Dawson for the National Negro Opera Company performance in 1956, the drums were played by Americans in the majority of the performances. He made substitutions for other instruments, however, such as a shaker and a steel bar that replaced the *ogan*. The musical character of these instruments was maintained, with the steel bar providing the fundamental tempo and rhythmic pattern and the shaker adding complexity to the texture.

Tied closely to the role of the drums, the "songs" of Africa also play an important referential role in the opera. Dessalines and Defilee treat them as important symbols, providing both an anchor to the past and a source of solace in troubled times. When they meet in the forest (act I, scene 2), Dessalines asks Defilee to sing these songs, harking back to a time in which "our people" were safe and established: "Sing to me again o Defilee the songs our people crooned in Africa where palm trees sway beneath a drum-shaped moon. Fain all my life would I forget. My soul is rent in twain! Sing to me! Sing to me the songs our people crooned in Africa! Where palm trees sway beneath the moon."[38]

Matheus uses these songs to underscore another theme of the opera: the past contrasting with the present. In act 2, Dessalines acknowledges his ties to the past and his African heritage; his entire being is shaped by what has gone before. He is further shaped by the "relentless past" that included oppression and domination based on European paternalism. He insists, however, that he cannot cling completely to the outmoded ways. His use of the words *nature* and *barbaric* in negative terms stresses that he is looking to a future in which Haitians are self-determining and independent: "O Priest! I too am linked with Africa. With Africa that claims our minds and fills our blood. I too am moulded by that relentless past. I cannot wholly crush the call, I cannot still the awe. Nature decrees that law . . . No! 'Tis you whose blind misleading lingers on from age barbaric a world that's gone! Mine is the new time, yours the old! Yours is the night! My day the future shall unfold."[39] In these references, we see Matheus's response to rising black nationalism and the "race pride" initiatives of the Harlem Renaissance. His contrast of "old" and "new" and of "night" and "day" leaves no doubt of his underlying sympathies. His acknowledgment of the African cultural heritage in Haiti reflected the growing concern with similar traditions in the United States and would have been recognized by many audience members. His invocation of the past in service of the future (as in the last reference above) mirrored similar themes to come in the writings of James Weldon Johnson, Zora Neale Hurston, and Langston Hughes.

It was clear to both White and Matheus that dance should play an integral part of this drama due to its primacy of place in Haitian rituals. By planning to include at least one merengue, a traditional Haitian dance, it became clear they needed additional exposure to the medium. Their desire to learn more about the style and performance of these dances was one of the overriding reasons for their research trip to Haiti in 1928. According to Matheus, "In our dialogues Mr. White and I knew that an outstanding feature for the success of the opera would be the dances. Choreography must supplement group and solo singing. There would be arias and choruses, drums, rhythmic motion and frenzied dancing. We must catch an authentic local color. It became imperative that we go to Haiti in person. We could hear the songs, see the dances, catch the spirit of the African mood."[40]

White's incorporation of the dance parallels Matheus's use of the drums as the most direct and effective representation of his interpretation of Haitian culture. Their importance is clear, for the dancers and the ability of a conductor to achieve the tempi and rhythms he envisioned dominate the correspondence between White and impresario Mary Cardwell Dawson, founder and director of the National Negro Opera Company, concerning their 1956 performances of the opera.

In the prelude and in the entr'acte between the first and second scenes of act 1, White incorporates dances associated with the peasant classes, specifically those used in voudon ceremonies. In constructing a "tempo di meringue" [*sic*] (prelude, measures 97–141) and a Congo Dance (entr'acte), he interpreted the Rada songs as he had observed them on the island and devised dances he termed "native" to evoke the religious ceremonies.

White's Congo Dance is based on Haitian usage, but with some adaptation to accommodate American drummers who were not familiar with the complex patterns of the tradition. White specified the use of authentic Haitian instruments, but the replication ends there; they play a single line, eliminating the polyphonic texture of the original dance. The drumming accompanies a ritual dance performed in silhouette: the shadows of the dancers were projected on the back of the stage. It was a clever artistic touch that placed them at a remove from the audience, distancing them from Matheus's description of a "wild, uninhibited dance."

White includes another example in act 2, scene 2. Dessalines's coronation marks his rejection of the old ways. He has declared himself a self-made ruler and emperor, establishing himself and his followers as members of the elite. He is crowned in the cathedral, by a priest, and is married to Claire, who ultimately urges him to kill the voudon priestess Mougali. The guests are all members of the upper class, and the music and dance represent the Westernized art and entertainment expected at court. After the coronation ceremony, the celebration moves to the square in front of the cathedral, and the celebration includes a slow, formalized merengue, a minuet, and a second Congo Dance that more closely resembles the minuet than the merengue of the entr'acte. The contrast between the two worlds is sharpest here, for as the finely dressed courtiers perform the formal dances in the foreground, practitioners of voudon, in ceremonial costumes, mimic them in the background. (See appendix B.)

While White was successful in replicating Haitian elements in each of these dances, he achieved his most effective representation of the material at the beginning of the third act in the music for Mougali's funeral. White borrowed material reproduced in Price-Mars's book, reinforcing the anger generated by the execution of the priestess. However, he reverts to the more stereotypical representation of the rituals in the subsequent "Voodoo Death Dance," in which Matheus's text replicates the hissing of snakes accompanying a serpentine dance.

This juxtaposition of the real and imaginary is the direct result of White's needing to conform, to a small extent, to audience expectations by including a more sensational representation of the religious rituals at least once during the opera. (See appendix C.)

Conclusion

Ouanga! is an important example of African American opera in the late 1920s and early 1930s. It represents a mixture of two conceptions of Haiti: a highly romanticized view of Haiti's revolutionary history and an African American response to twentieth-century society and culture. Although the opera is not free of sensationalism, Matheus and White used these elements to illuminate the history, heritage, and complexity of Haitian culture. Their sympathetic portrayal of characters' inner conflicts, and their desire to reconcile their seemingly conflicting goals and desires, made a valuable contribution to the growing awareness of the Haitian condition and of the reality of its history.

Appendix A
Ouanga! Plot Synopsis

Source: Clarence Cameron White, *Ouanga!* (New York: Sam Fox Publishing, 1955, adapted.)

Act I, Scene 1: Midnight on a Mountain Top near Cape Haitian [*sic*]

A Voodoo ceremony is being held to drive the tyrants from Haiti. In the midst of the dancing, Dessalines enters and forbids the sacrifice to continue. Mougali, the High Priestess, attempts to cast the "Ouanga" spell on Dessalines, but she is deterred by Defilee, his sweetheart. Having warned the people that they must forsake the practice of Voodooism, Dessalines leaves angrily with his courtiers.

Act I, Scene 2: The Banana Grove

The insistent, measured beat of the native drums from the mountains ominously strikes the ear as the flamboyant scene with full force flashes upon the eye.

Michele sings of his love for Licite and of the glory of Dessalines whose ambitions have lead [sic] him to take steps to become crowned emperor of Haiti. Michel completes a flowing picture of the course that is to be, thus seeking to swerve Licite from her pagan ways. Defilee tells of her love for Dessalines.

Dessalines tells Defilee of his vision of L'Ouverture's warning about vain glory and tyrannical ambition, to hold steadfast the ancient heritage of the "Ouanga," to beware of the new order and of the bloody strike which will surely follow. But he is convinced that his way is better.

Swayed by her love for Dessalines she is on the point of turning, when the echoes of the drums reverberate down the mountain side. Defilee draws back in fear and, shuddering, refuses.

Dessalines, incensed at Defilee's refusal and panic-stricken by the echoes of the tom-toms, roughly pushes her to the ground. He accuses her that her love is not great enough for complete [ ] to his cause, strides away in great wrath and disappears into the forest.

Act II: The Coronation (Public Square, Cape Haitian)

An expectant throng gathers in the public square, waiting to see the dual festivities of Dessalines' marriage to Claire Hereuse, the daughter of one of the elite, and of his coronation as emperor of Haiti.

Vendors of food and drink wend their way in and out, shouting their wares. Into this hilarious group, striking the first somber note, the sinister figure of Mougali, the Voodoo Priestess, slowly comes. She greets the multitude. The crowd responds with great reverence.

A choir in the distant cathedral chants the "Te Deum." The crowd offstage, hails the Emperor. The same melody, in a more [ ] key, is joyously repeated by the chorus of peasants and the populace gathered in the public square for the festivities.

A joyous fanfare announces the approach of their Majesties. With Father Corneille Brelle, the King and Queen stride joyously to their homes. A host of courtiers follow.

Dessalines, haughtily surveying the people, explains the keynote of the new order, "Liberty and Peace." His hearers cheer vociferously and immediately express their happiness in dancing.

Mougali advances toward the throne as the crowd falls back to let her pass. She assails Dessalines with the warning, "Death to those who desert Legba."

Infuriated, Dessalines orders his soldiers to seize the Priestess. On her knees, Defilee pleads for the life of Mougali. Dessalines refuses, and orders Mougali carried off. The crowds draw back in terror and awe. Defilee continues her distant entreaties for the condemned woman. In vain is her supplication, for the sounds of the execution are heard. The priest steps forward and, making the sign of the cross chants, "Father of Light, receive our Mougali, misguided, but Thy servant."

Act III, Scene I: Ceremonial Hall of the Voodoo Priestess

The curtain slowly rises to the muffled beat of the ceremonial drum, contrasted with the weird wailing of the mourners.

The Papaloi stands before the body of Mougali. Lights flicker upon the corpse, which is wrapped mummy fashion. The mourners invoke "Dambala," the ancient god, to vengeance against Dessalines. They begin a dance around the body of Mougali. There comes a thunderous knocking at the door. A voice cries, "Open in the name of the Emperor."

Amid great consternation, the door is flung open and Dessalines himself strides in majestically. He has come to ask forgiveness. He pleads, cajoles, threatens, but the Papaloi remains unmoved. Dessalines in his fury and frightened rage calls upon his soldiers to destroy the altar. They hesitate and Dessalines, completely beside himself, draws his sword to demolish his enemies.

The Papaloi makes a magic symbol. The dancers sweep into the terrifying incantation of the curse of Ouanga. The "Python of Dambala" has struck.

The hypnotic cry reaches Dessalines. Sword upraised, he trembles, totters, stops, unable to move. The Papaloi holds thumbs pointed at him. His sword falls clattering. With an effort, Dessalines staggers back out of the circle and rushes into the night.

Act III, Scene II: The Red Bridge

It is afternoon of a bright day. Lofty mountains tower in the background. Crossing a stream is the historic Red Bridge of the outskirts of the capital, Port-au-Prince. Defilee awaits Dessalines who has begged for a rendezvous at their old trysting place, beside the Red Bridge. Her reverie is rudely interrupted by Gerin. He attempts to enlist her aid in the betrayal of Dessalines by his soldiers. He ridicules the idea of Dessalines being in love with her. She promises to cooperate if she finds that what he says is true.

The church bells ring in distant Port-au-Prince. Defilee departs in a frantic effort to use her influences with the soldiers to save Dessalines.

Alone, the abandoned Dessalines sings of Haiti, of his love for his beautiful land, and mingled feelings of apprehension for her and her own fate. In the meantime, Gerin and his soldiers stealthily creep over the bridge and quickly surround the Emperor. Too late, he attempts to defend himself. He is overpowered and repeatedly stabbed with the bayonets of the soldiers.

Defilee, rushing back, is seized by Gerin and prevented from reaching Dessalines. She invokes the crew with the cry of "Ouanga." At this word, Gerin and the superstitious soldiers rush back in awe disclosing the dying Dessalines.

Dessalines, recognizing Defilee, begs forgiveness and pleads again for the "songs of Africa" as he expires.

Defilee falls sobbing across his body. The sound of drums beating in the mountains sends forth the message of Dessalines' death.

In the distance, as the curtain descends, is heard again the African chant, ending in a great cry, "Ouanga, Ouanga," and through all, the incessant beating of the drums, signaling the message to all Haiti.

Appendix B

Act 2, scene 1, ballet opening. *Source:* Clarence Cameron White, *Ouanga!* (Chicago: Sam Fox Publishing, n.d.), 98–99.

Example 1. Ballet, excerpts from Dessalines's coronation

Appendix C

Snake Dance, act 3, scene 1. *Source:* Clarence Cameron White, *Ouanga!* (Chicago: Sam Fox Publishing, n.d.), 131.

Example 2. Music for Mougali's funeral

Notes

1. Throughout this article the spelling *voudon* will reference the religion. *Voodoo* will be used to reflect spelling in sources from the 1920s and 1930s.

2. In a report from "Porto Rico" on January 21, 1915, the *New York Times* reported concern over the intermittent activities of the German cruiser *Karlsruhe* in the Caribbean from San Juan to Venezuela, to Haiti. *New York Times,* January 22, 1915, 1.

3. One article, from the *New York Times,* is typical:

> The present Constitution, French in model like the language and most of the customs and institutions of Haiti, dates from 1880. A corrupt and despotic way, dictatorship, won by revolution and punctuated copiously with assassinations, has been the actual form of Government since the declaration of independence in 1804 and the massacres of whites by Governor, afterward, Emperor, Dessalines. A weary list of Presidents, of revolutions, exiles, suicides, slaughters, corruption, a civilization, in spite of the great name of Toussaint L'Ouverture, which has been sinking; brutal, permeated with magical rites. The wife of one President was generally known as the high priestess of voodoo. Her husband in his White House was believed to decide the fate of prisoners by throwing on the floor little clay magical images, naming each with a man. If the image broke the prisoner was shot. If it held together he escaped. ("The Latest Revolution in Haiti," *New York Times,* July 29, 1916, 1)

4. Matheus, "*Ouanga.*"

5. Matheus completed the libretto in 1929, shortly after the Haitian trip. White finished the score in Paris in 1932. *Ouanga!* was performed several times, usually in concert form. These performances include the American Opera Society (Chicago, November 13, 1932, concert scenes), the New School of Social Research (New York City, June 18, 1941, concert performance also broadcast on radio), the Burleigh Music Association (South Bend, Indiana, June 10–11, 1949, staged), the Dra Mu Opera Company (Philadelphia, October 27, 1950, staged), Xavier University (New Orleans, 1955, partially staged), and the National Negro Opera Company (New York City, May 27, 1956, at the Metropolitan Opera House and on September 27, 1956, at Carnegie Hall in New York City, both concert performances). White took great interest in all of these performances, offering advice to the impresarios and conductors concerning performance methods, instruments, and possible singers. He traveled to each one and offered his services in the later rehearsals. His advice helped shape the performances in Indiana, New York, and New Orleans.

6. The following discussion is based on those found in Renda, *Taking Haiti;* Knight, "The Haitian Revolution"; and Ott, *Haitian Revolution.*

7. Plummer, "Afro-American Response," 126–28.

8. Renda, *Taking Haiti,* 100.

9. Harriet Gibbs Marshall (1868–1941) was one of the most influential women in musical circles of the early twentieth century. She founded the Washington Conservatory of Music in 1903 and traveled with her husband to Haiti. There she organized service groups to aid the Haitian poor and rebuild the schools. Upon their return to the United States, the Marshalls were active in several "free Haiti" movements.

10. Renda provides a compelling overview of the cultural impact of the occupation on American society. For further discussions (all of which contributed to this synopsis), see Milde, "Harp and Sword"; Plummer, "Afro-American Response"; Riley, "Imagi-Nations in Black White"; and Twa, "Troubling Island."

11. Renda, *Taking Haiti,* 216–17. While *Emperor Jones* does not specifically reference the Haitian revolution, its tropical setting, the descriptions of the islands, and its themes lead us to consider it part of this trend.

12. The voudon religion often obtained a phonetic spelling in literature through the 1920s, resulting in the familiar *voodoo* that has remained in popular culture through the present day.

13. Ibid., 195.

14. Extensive musical analyses are available in Davidson, "Operas by Afro-American Composers"; and Largey, "*Ouanga!*"

15. Matheus, "*Ouanga,*" 428–29.

16. Ibid., 433. Matheus felt that Dessalines, "who bore on his back the scars of brutal beatings," was the most promising and dramatic protagonist for his opera.

17. Claire is completely anglicized and represents the European focus of the new government. Matheus contrasts her and Defilee with a simple device: Claire does not sing in the opera.

18. Matheus included a brief description of their visit in his personal account of the opera. Ibid., 434ff.

19. Renda, *Taking Haiti,* 242–44.

20. Ibid., 242.

21. John Frederick Matheus, *Ouanga! Music-Drama,* typescript, 1938, 13. From the College of the Music Library, University of North Carolina at Chapel Hill.

22. Ibid., 3.

23. Ibid.

24. Ibid. "A colorful throng is milling about waiting for the ceremonies to being. Peasants, in motley garb, mingle with the elite class, who wear the fashions of 1804."

25. Ibid. "All the dancers wear nondescript clothes and are barefooted."

26. Ibid., 7.

27. Renda summarizes particularly the writings of A. J. Burks, whose descriptions of Haitian traditions and religious practices are filtered through the fears and prejudices of the occupying forces: "For Burks, Christophe was 'the greatest monster in all history' and 'the tale of Toussaint' was 'a tale of beastly lust, brute aggrandizement, freedom from restraint for men with the passions of wild animals, the strength of the savage, and the bloodlust of followers of the green serpent.'" *Taking Haiti,* 216.

28. Largey, "*Ouanga!*" 49.

29. Fleurant, *Dancing Spirits,* 49.

30. The contrast in *Ouanga!* is comparable to the juxtaposition of the "Te Deum" in Puccini's *Tosca,* in which Scarpia's essential malevolence contrasts with his public piety.

31. Matheus, *Ouanga!* typescript, 12.

32. Fleurant, *Dancing Spirits,* 34.

33. According to Daphne Lamothe, "During the 1920s and 1930s, the widespread

desire for the primitive extended beyond a demand for minstrel stereotypes of "happy darkies" into the world of the exotic primitive. These demands dovetailed with Renaissance writers' struggles to define what was unique to African-American culture. One way they did so was by attempting to articulate and define blacks' African heritage. But when imagining African culture's relevance to African-American culture and identity, Hurston and her contemporaries often used stereotypical images of beating drums and the jungle, feeding American society's perceptions of Africa as a savage, primal and uncivilized place." "Vodou Imagery," 160.

34. Matheus, *Ouanga!* typescript, 11.

35. White's audiences were familiar with the details of the occupation, its representation in popular culture, and literary accounts previously referenced.

36. Fleurant, *Dancing Spirits,* 38–39.

37. Averill, "Haiti." The following discussion is based on this article and that in Fleurant, *Dancing Spirits,* 34–48.

38. Matheus, *Ouanga!* typescript, 12.

39. Ibid., 21.

40. Matheus, "*Ouanga!*" 433.

Bibliography

African-American Registry. "Violinist Par Excellent, Clarence Cameron White!" 2005. http://www.aaregistry.com.

Averill, Gage. "Haiti." *Grove Music Online.* http://www.grovemusic.com.

Brooks, Tim. *Lost Sounds: Blacks and the Birth of the Recording Industry, 1890–1919.* Urbana: University of Illinois Press, 2004.

Cheatham, Wallace M. "*Ouanga*! South Bend, Indiana, and the Premiere of a 20th Century American Opera." *Indiana Magazine of History* 100, no. 2 (2004). http://www.historycooperative.org/journals/imh.

Clark, Edgar Rogie. "The Negro Composer: A Mid-Century Review." *Negro History Bulletin* 17, no. 6 (1954): 132–33.

Davidson, Celia Elizabeth. "Operas by Afro-American Composers: A Critical Survey and Analysis of Selected Works." Ph.D. diss., Catholic University of America, 1980.

Fleurant, Gerdès. *Dancing Spirits: Rhythms and Rituals of Haitian Vodun, the Rada Rite.* Contributions to the Study of Music and Dance, no. 42. Westport, Conn.: Greenwood Press, 1996.

Kane, Lynn. "Clarence Cameron White: 1880–1960." In *Encyclopedia of African American Culture and History.* New York: Macmillan, 1996. Reproduced in History Resource Center. Farmington Hills, Mich.: Gale Group. http://galenet.galegroup.com.

Kirk, Elise K. *American Opera.* Urbana: University of Illinois Press, 2001.

Knight, Franklin W. "The Haitian Revolution." *American Historical Review* 105, no. 1 (2000): 103–15.

Lamothe, Daphne. "Vodou Imagery, African-American Tradition, and Cultural Transformation in Zora Neale Hurston's 'Their Eyes Were Watching God.'" *Callaloo* 22, no. 1 (1999): 157–75.

Largey, Michael. "*Ouanga!* An African-American Opera about Haiti." *Lenox Avenue: A Journal of Interartistic Inquiry* 2 (1996): 35–54.

Matheus, John F. "*Ouanga:* My Venture in Libretto Creation." Luncheon address delivered by the Treasurer of the College Language Association at the Thirty-second Annual Convention, Middleton Complex, Morris Brown College, Atlanta, April 13, 1972. Reproduced in *Journal of the College Language Association* 15, no. 4 (1972): 428–40.

Milde, Robert Lyall. "The Harp and the Sword: Rhetorical Depictions of Haiti in Early Twentieth Century U.S. Literature." Ph.D. diss., University of North Carolina at Greensboro, 1999.

"Opera *Ouanga* Composer's Masterpiece." *Negro History Bulletin* 15, no. 9 (1952): 194–95.

Ott, Thomas O. *The Haitian Revolution, 1789–1804.* Knoxville: University of Tennessee Press, 1973.

Plummer, Brenda Gayle. "The Afro-American Response to the Occupation of Haiti, 1915–1934." *Phylon (1960–)* 43, no. 2 (1982): 125–43.

"Pura Belpré." In *Puerto Rican Writers and Migration: Folklore, Autobiography, and History.* 2005. http://www.centropr.org/prwriters.

Renda, Mary A. *Taking Haiti: Military Occupation and the Culture of U.S. Imperialism, 1915–1934.* Chapel Hill: University of North Carolina Press, 2001.

Riis, T. "White, Clarence Cameron." *Grove Music Online.* 2005. http://www.grovemusic.com.

Riley, Shannon Rose. "Imagi-Nations in Black White: Cuba, Haiti, and the Performance of Difference in U.S. National Projects, 1898–1940." Ph.D. diss., University of California at Davis, 1995.

Simms, L. Moody, Jr. "Clarence Cameron White: 1880–1960." In *Dictionary of American Biography,* supp. 6, *1956–1960.* New York: American Council of Learned Societies, 1980.

———. "Clarence Cameron White: Violinist, Composer, Teacher." *Negro History Bulletin* 43, no. 4 (1980): 95–96.

Southern, Eileen. *The Music of Black Americans: A History.* 2nd ed. New York: W. W. Norton, 1983.

———. "White, Clarence Cameron." *Grove Music Online: "Opera."* 2005. http://www.grovemusic.com.

Twa, Lindsay Jean. "Troubling Island: The Imagining and Imaging of Haiti by African-American Artists, 1915–1940." Ph.D. diss., University of North Carolina at Chapel Hill, 2006.

White, Clarence Cameron. "Negro's Gift to American Music." In *Anthology of American Negro Literature,* ed. V. F. Calverton, 267–74. New York: Modern Library, 1929.

White, Clarence Cameron, and John Frederick Matheus. *"Ouanga": A Haitian Opera in Three Acts.* New York: Sam Fox, 1955.

Wright, Josephine R. B. "Art/Classical Music: Chronological Overview." In *African American Music: An Introduction,* ed. Mellonnee V. Burnam and Portia Maultsby, 211–30. New York: Routledge, 2004.

7

New Paradigms in William Grant Still's *Blue Steel*

GAYLE MURCHISON

"My love has always been opera—the theater. This love of operatic music, stimulated in my early youth by listening to operatic records, was the thing that first aroused the desire to compose. All my other work has been a means to this end."[1] So wrote William Grant Still in 1949. By this time he had composed four operas: *Blue Steel* (1934), *Troubled Island* (1938), *A Bayou Legend* (1941), and *A Southern Interlude* (1942), and was progressing on a fifth, *Costaso* (1949–50). He was only two months away from the first full production of any of his operas, *Troubled Island,* which premiered March 31, 1949, at New York's City Center. Enchanted with opera since first hearing recordings in 1912, Still had long desired to compose for the stage. By the time he began work on *Blue Steel,* he had partially realized his dream of composing for the stage with his ballets *La Guiablesse* (1927) and *Sahdji* (1929–30). By 1931, Still was well established as a composer of orchestral music and one of the United States' most promising young composers; he was certainly *the* most prominent African American composer of art music of his generation. His tone poems, symphony, art songs, and ballets had been successfully performed by major orchestras and companies in the United States and in Europe. Yet one goal continued to elude him: a successful opera.

Still's opportunity to devote himself to opera composition full-time finally came in 1934. On March 23, 1934, he received written notice that he had been awarded a Guggenheim Fellowship, which would provide him with twenty-five hundred dollars over the course of one year. A few weeks later, an April 2 *New York Times* headline publicly announced, "Guggenheim Fund Aids 40 in 10th Year."[2] In May 1934, Still left New York for Los Angeles. The fellowship would provide him with sufficient financial support to free him from commercial work so that he could compose his first full-length opera, *Blue Steel.* On May 22, Still arrived in Los Angeles with the scenario of the opera, written by his friend, actor-writer Carlton Moss, in hand.[3] For a libretto, Still turned to one of his most recent collaborators, Harold Bruce Forsythe, a writer and pianist with whom Still had collaborated for his ballet *The Sorcerer* and for the aborted "From the Furnace of the Sun."

When Still began composing *Blue Steel* in the early 1930s, American composers—black and white—were grappling with the challenge of composing American opera. In the 1920s and 1930s, jazz had offered composers such as Louis Gruenberg and John Alden Carpenter (and European composers such as Ernst Krenek and Kurt Weill) an idiom through which they could express a modern, urban, and urbane American identity. For Virgil Thomson, the cubist literary musings of librettist Gertrude Stein coupled with the African American voice and body provided him the means by which to infuse the operatic tradition with something old—the lives of saints—and something new, in this case the conflation of European high modernism with Primitivism. European and white American composers drew freely on Primitivist motifs in order to free themselves from formal restraints of nineteenth-century practices, mining the cultures of peoples from Africa, Asia, and the Pacific—as well as that of African Americans—in search of new techniques that they could appropriate for their own works.

For Europeans and European Americans, such cultures offered them something exotic and fresh, and few concerned themselves with the social or political implications of their aesthetic and artistic choices. With little concern for the "authenticity" of such representations, their practices differed little from composers of previous generations who sought to inject "local color" into their works. African American composers, on the other hand, did not have the same license or aims and found themselves in a perplexing bind as a result. They faced struggles on multiple fronts, from having to fight against racism that questioned the intellectual and artistic capabilities of African Americans and sought to limit them as artists by relegating their participation to jazz, musical theater, or other popular genres. They also had the added burden of having to avoid perpetuating racist stereotypes in their works, which meant that use of their own cultural traditions could be a doubled-edged sword. Such actions could give their works a degree of authenticity and credibility that their white counterparts could not claim, yet, should they falter, they would merely reinforce prevailing beliefs about the capabilities of African Americans.

Thus, a tradition of African American opera emerged in the 1920s that reflected and embraced the aesthetics of the cultural movement known as the Harlem Renaissance (originally referred to as the New Negro Movement).

The movement embraced the use of African American vernacular idioms in cultivated art forms, not merely for aesthetic enjoyment but also for social aims: to combat racial prejudice and to promote interracial understanding. In theory, if African American artists could show the world the beauty of black culture—broadly defined to include Africa, the United States, the Caribbean, and Latin America—this art would disprove those who assumed African Americans intrinsically inferior.[4] Black musical theater had crossed racial barriers and proved successful with audiences at home and abroad. But what of opera? Like musical theater, it was a theatrical genre that could also provide a forum for African American dance. Black opera could be stripped of all traces of minstrelsy and buffoonery and have no traces of the lowbrow comedy and raciness of the Broadway musical. It could conceivably be the perfect art that would bring together the best of all African American arts: drama, music, poetry, stagecraft, and the visual arts with respect to costumes and scenery. But what would constitute a specifically African American opera aesthetic? What would be its subject matter and its music? How could African American composers create an opera tradition?

These were issues Still engaged as he set about composing *Blue Steel.* Still and his peers (including figures such as Shirley Graham Du Bois, Harry Lawrence Freeman, and Clarence Cameron White) apparently realized that if they were to create an African American opera tradition, they would have to find a common dramatic subject with which their targeted audience—largely members of the African American community—would be familiar. In keeping with the goals and aims of the Harlem Renaissance, they sought to embrace the history and culture of the African diaspora. The research of anthropologists such as Melville Herskovits and Zora Neale Hurston had uncovered African cultural traditions that had survived the Middle Passage to thrive in the United States, throughout the Caribbean, and in Latin America. Traditionally, European opera composers and librettists had often drawn on historical subjects or contemporary ones, often those that had veiled social or political overtones. Presumably, African diasporic cultures and their history could prove equally suitable for operatic treatment by African American composers; in so doing, they would further the aesthetic and social goals of the Harlem Renaissance.

In the musicological literature, theorist Johann Mattheson, writing in 1739 on musical affect and rhetoric, borrowed the term *locus topicus* from classical Greek rhetoric to describe composers' technique of treating a musical idea as a subject for exploration and further invention. In preclassical music, in which there was no development section as music scholars have come to understand the concept, applying the rhetorical term provided analysts with a framework for understanding musical processes as found in a given composition or group of works.[5] The term can also be expanded to cover how certain conventions became common practice and, later, tradition. In literary studies, critics can often approach a subject as tropology, following the various uses of a word or phrase in various literary and cultural contexts, looking for parameters, patterns, and repetition of various tropes or themes that remain consistent (or nearly so) or that are reformulated and in what manner.[6] Houston Baker's ideas regarding African American modernism, his concepts of "deformation of mastery" and "and mastery of form," are instructive. Henry Louis Gates's term *signifyin(g)* is also useful in understanding how African American artists put in play a complex system of signs in their literary—and by extension all artistic—work.[7] A conflation of these promises an avenue of inquiry that can serve Still studies and probe *Blue Steel.*

One could ask many questions about Still's *Blue Steel.* Close analytical study of the score would yield discoveries and insights about Still's early opera style and the influence of African American vernacular music. One could also probe how his work in commercial music as a radio arranger and composer aided his development as a composer of drama—how Still made the transition from radio and musical theater to ballet and opera. All these avenues must eventually be explored. One, however, is confronted with the preliminary questions: what did it mean for Still to compose black opera, and what is *Blue Steel*'s genesis? This prolegomenon seeks to address this latter question first, reserving for another juncture close study of the opera's musical style and Still's operatic technique. For now, the focus narrows on aesthetic questions that contextualize *Blue Steel* as a Harlem Renaissance work that engaged with the African past, Still's diasporic present, and then topical issues. Thus, by tailoring their artistic goals to helping fulfill the Pan-Africanist vision of sociologist and political activist W. E. B. Du Bois and the African diasporic cultural autonomy proposed by philosophy professor Alain Locke, Still (and his peers Du Bois, Freeman, and White) found an African *locus topicus,* trope, and signifiers as they mastered the formal challenges of composing opera that would provide a familiar dramatic setting and theme for their audiences. Perhaps they were inspired partly by one of the early-twentieth-century's most famous American plays, Eugene O'Neill's *Emperor Jones,* partly by the scholarly work of Hurston et al., and partly by contemporary political events that appeared in newspaper headlines. These three disparate strands all converge in Still's *Blue Steel.* In *Blue Steel,* Still created an opera that would be clearly identified as African American—one that not only treated an African American subject, but was also rooted in African American and African diasporic culture—namely, its syncretic religion, voodoo or vodun as it is known in Haiti, or hoodoo or conjure, as it is known in the United States.

First Exposure and Early Attempts

Still began working on *Blue Steel* around 1930, but it was not his first opera, nor was he without prior knowledge of the European tradition. His earliest exposure to opera had come via records his stepfather purchased for the family phonograph. In a 1967 speech on his opera *Highway 1, U.S.A.*, Still related:

> My first contact with operatic music is as vivid today as when it happened. The year was 1912 and I, only seventeen, had come home from College for my summer vacation. My stepfather had just bought our Victor phonograph and Red Seal operatic records. The music wove a spell around me. It was like something I had been wanting for a long time without knowing it. I listened to it by the hour, by the day, by the week, playing each record over and over. An entirely new world appeared ahead—especially to a boy who had up to that point known principally the semi-classics of the day, such as Braga's "Angel's Serenade."[8]

He told Eileen Southern just three years before his death the impact these recordings had upon him: "That summer I lay on the floor day after day, all summer long, listening to recordings of operas. I even remember the make—Red Seal records. And the operas? *II Trovatore, Rigoletto, Elixir of Love*, and others. I should say that my deep love of opera dates from that time. I knew then that somehow I had to learn how to compose operatic music."[9] As a student at Wilberforce College (now University) in Xenia, Ohio, Still was able to attend live opera performances in Dayton (thanks to touring opera companies) and Cincinnati where he saw a performance of *I Pagliacci* that left a lasting impression. Over the next few years, Still would avail himself of every opportunity to attend the opera. In 1918, between enlisting in the navy and deploying on the U.S.S. *Kroonland,* he attended the Metropolitan Opera to hear Verdi's *Rigoletto.*[10]

Young Still was ambitious, attempting to compose opera shortly after he had first been exposed to the genre. Although his mother did not permit him to study music at Oberlin as he wished—as Still himself often mentioned, he had entered college to pursue premedical studies, as per his mother's wishes—he became heavily involved in music at Wilberforce, both as a member of and arranger for the student string quartet and as director of the band. Members of the Wilberforce faculty nurtured Still's musical efforts. His earliest compositions date from his college years, including his first opera, *The Golden Legend* (now lost). In preparation for this task, Still undertook a self-directed study of opera, using a portion of his allowance to purchase scores, including Weber's *Oberon* and Wagner's *Flying Dutchman.* His teenage autodidacticism proved fruitful. The Wilberforce College yearbook lists a May 28, 1914, concert featuring Still's compositions that was held on campus. (It is unclear whether this concert took place, as another event conflicted and Still's concert may have been canceled, but Verna Arvey reports that a concert of Still's works did indeed occur while he was in college.) Regardless, the program reveals much about his accomplishments as a young composer. The announced program was quite varied and included works for piano ("Love Song" from *Suite Romantique*—ballet), organ ("Prelude and Spinning Song" from *The Golden Legend*), violin ("Slumber Song," which Still himself performed), *Quartette in A Flat* (string quartet), and three vocal works. The latter were "Who Knows," soprano aria from *The Golden Legend,* and two art songs, a "Song in F Billade" [*sic*] for soprano, and one for baritone, "Why Fades a Dream."[11] Though none of these works survives, the program confirms that Still was accomplished enough to put together a concert of his own compositions and rehearse the musicians. Clearly, by 1914 Still had made his first steps toward becoming an opera composer.

Prior to *Blue Steel,* Still worked on at least two, and perhaps three, other operas. With the lack of self-consciousness often typical of nineteen-year-olds, Still submitted his first "full-length" opera to a national contest during the summer of 1914, as Verna Arvey reports in her memoir of the composer, *In One Lifetime.* "He entered a contest for a three-act opera (and ambitiously mailed out a score totaling twenty pages in length!) and another contest in which the judges wrote to tell him that his music had merit, but that they were afraid they didn't completely understand it!" It was rejected, yet this did not deter him, as it might have discouraged a less confident young composer.[12] Additionally, sometime between 1914 and 1919, Still completed an as-yet-unidentified opera. Its existence is confirmed only by a 1919 letter in the Still-Arvey Papers at the University of Arkansas. While working at Pace & Handy Brothers Music Company in New York, Still wrote to the Metropolitan's Opera's Guilio Gatti-Casazza: "Dear Sir:—I have recently completed an opera based upon Negro life in antebellum days. All of my hopes are centered upon its Production. Will you assist me? I should be happy were you to consent to consider it."[13] Although nothing came of this unknown opera—possibly a revision of one of his college works, which he could have been undertaken after spending two semesters of formal study at Oberlin—Still persevered despite his hectic work schedule pursuing dual careers in art and popular music. In the summer of 1922, Still studied with George W. Chadwick at the New England Conservatory, although little is known about what Still may have learned from Chadwick. Upon returning to New York at the end of the summer, Still continued working for W. C. Handy. In 1923, he began studies with Edgard Varèse, whom Still always credited with having expanded his musical thinking and technique. Before ending his studies with Varèse in 1925, Still completed two more vocal works: *Three Negro Songs* (in which he treats untexted female voices as another timbre in the instrumental ensemble) and *Levee Land,* a suite composed for Broadway sensation Florence Mills that combined dissonant chromaticism with the blues.

Still's next attempt at opera promised to be more fruitful. Realizing that he himself could not write the libretto, Still "begged some of the leading Negro poets, such as Countee Cullen, Arna Bontemps and Langston Hughes for libretti which I could set to music."[14] A turning point came in late 1927 when it seemed as though he would finally fully realize his lifelong dream. Harlem Renaissance poet Countee Cullen—whose work Still admired—agreed to write a libretto for an opera to be called "Roshana,"[15] basing it on sketches that Still apparently made from an unpublished African novel written by his first wife, Grace Bundy Still.[16] Five letters in the Countee Cullen Papers at the Amistad Research Center in New Orleans document part of this collaboration. Sometime early in 1928, Still began writing to Cullen about their planned collaboration. In March, Still wrote to Cullen, informing him that he and his wife were revising the synopsis of *Roshana* and that they would send it as soon as it was finished. The second letter documents that Still sent Cullen a detailed outline of the opera's first scene. By the time Still wrote to Cullen a third time, the opera's name had been changed (to "Rashana"), along with the name of another lead character. Still had already made progress on the music, sending Cullen themes for scene 3.[17]

Still, Bundy, and Cullen were apparently off to a propitious beginning. Still was enthusiastic about the project. He was working with one of the Harlem Renaissance's most acclaimed young poets and believed the project had unlimited potential, clearly evident in the way he devoted much of his time to composing the prelude while he faced a demanding schedule orchestrating a Shubert show, *Americana.* Indeed, he even informed Cullen that he had spoken to Oscar Sonneck, the editor with Schirmer, about publishing the piano-vocal score.[18] This last letter, however, portends the opera's ultimate fate. Still closed it expressing that he was eagerly awaiting more of Cullen's poetry and extended congratulations to Cullen on his marriage to Yolanda Du Bois. In early January, Still had high hopes yet for the opera and continued to pursue publication opportunities. Unfortunately, the Still-Cullen-Bundy collaboration came to an end with Cullen's marriage, as Cullen, supported by a Guggenheim, departed for Paris and lost interest in the project. Ironically, Still's own marital difficulties complicated the project even further. As a staff arranger for Paul Whiteman, in May 1929 Still accompanied his employer to Los Angeles, where he continued to provide arrangements for Whiteman's *Old Gold Hour* while Whiteman filmed *The King of Jazz.* Still's work took him away from his wife and four children for a year, during which he renewed his acquaintance with pianist-composer-writer Harold Bruce Forsythe (whom he had met in New York), completed the orchestral suite *Africa,* and began work on the ballet *Sahdji.* Returning to New York in May 1930, Still completed the *Afro-American Symphony.* In December 1929, Grace wrote to Cullen about her planned trip to Paris the following summer, considering moving there permanently,[19] and in September 1932 she left with their children for Canada. Still had now lost his two principal collaborators; despite valiant efforts to persevere by enlisting Forsythe to complete the libretto, Still was forced to completely abandon "Rashana" by 1930.[20]

Blue Steel: Collaborators and Genesis

Still's first task in composing *Blue Steel* was to find a writer (or writing team) who could fashion both a good, dramatic story and an effective libretto.[21] Still wanted to write *opera,* which meant avoiding anything that might be construed as musical theater, especially of the type of black musicals and revues popular with white audiences. Though he continued his commercial work to support his family, he had expanded beyond musicals and was now working in radio with figures like Paul Whiteman and Willard Robison. His radio work trod the fine line between commercial and concert music, as Still's sophisticated and elegant arrangements and original compositions blurred the line between popular and art music. But as his concert works began regularly appearing on programs of the International Composers' Guild, Georges Barrère's Little Symphony, the League of Composers, and Howard Hanson's Festival of American Composers at Eastman in Rochester, and—thanks to the *Afro-American Symphony*'s critically successful debut performance (1931) in that same city—he had firmly established himself as a "serious" composer. Clearly seeking to establish himself now as a composer of opera and fulfill a lifelong dream, Still would not have seriously considered his old musical theater associates as potential collaborators and probably would have considered instead some of the Harlem Renaissance's leading novelists or poets, such as Langston Hughes (who would later write plays and collaborate with Still on *Troubled Island*), much as he had previously recruited Cullen.

Ultimately, Still enlisted playwright and actor Carlton Moss (ca. 1909 or 1910–97) to write the scenario.[22] Moss was a logical choice. Still had known him when they both lived at the Harlem YMCA and took their dinners together. Born in Newark and raised in North Carolina, Moss had gained familiarity with southern black culture beyond what had come north during the Great Migration (for example, the tradition of conjure, a survival of African religion practiced by some in the Carolinas and Georgia). More importantly, Moss had extensive experience in legitimate theater. While attending Baltimore's Morgan College (now Morgan State University), he formed the group Toward a Black Theater. Moving to New York, he continued to work in theater and began to write for radio. He spent his entire career in theater (and later film) combating racial stereotypes and discrimination and fighting segregation by presenting African Americans as serious actors, rather than perpetuating the old minstrel stereotypes and buffoonish or servant roles typically available to them at the time.[23] In Moss, Still found an experienced dramatist who would not settle for demeaning limitations then placed on African American actors and African American theater.[24]

Additionally, Still turned again to his friend Forsythe to fashion Moss's scenario into a libretto. Forsythe seemed another logical choice. The young writer was also a composer and pianist, having studied at Juilliard before a congenital hearing condition began to progress to deafness, precipitating his return west. He had composed several pieces, including an opera, now lost. By 1930, Forsythe had abandoned performing, turned to writing, and began a biography of Still. His insightful essay "William Grant Still: A Study in Contradictions" proved that he understood the challenges the composer faced in both his personal and his professional life, as well as Still's socially progressive aesthetic vision as a Harlem Renaissance artist.[25] Forsythe was far better suited to collaborate with Still than Cullen would have been: Forsythe was a composer familiar with the opera tradition, held strong convictions about African American art music similar to Still's own, and, perhaps most conveniently, lived in Los Angeles, Still's new home.

Still was bolstered by the new project. As he recalled in his "Autobiographical Manuscript," the composition of *Blue Steel* went rapidly: "This time, I was sure, I'd have an opera that would be worth saving and worth producing. I was enthusiastic, and there was a deep satisfaction in being able to work uninterruptedly at last."[26] Brimming with excitement, Still refused offers to compose musical comedies for the stage and accepted fewer requests for arrangements from Robison. By September 1934, Eastman's Howard Hanson wrote Still that he would be happy to see parts of the new opera as soon as Still completed them. By the beginning of the next year, Still and Forsythe were able to send a completed typescript and a piano-vocal score of the entire first act, most of the second, and a good portion of the third to be deposited for copyright.[27] Still was also assisted by their mutual friend Verna Arvey, a pianist and writer who had taken an interest in Still's music. Arvey primarily worked as Still's assistant, typing parts of the libretto, copying music, and—since Still was not a pianist—playing what he had written on the piano, thus allowing him to hear the work as it progressed. This marked the beginning of a fruitful partnership: after his next opera, *Troubled Island,* Arvey would become his regular librettist, and she later became his second wife.[28]

The sources for *Blue Steel* are copious. The most extensive ones, documenting Still's progress on the opera at its earliest stages, are found in the Library of Congress, where a holograph vocal score of the opera and typescript of the libretto were deposited for copyright. There are additional sources at William Grant Still Music (WGSM; the composer's daughter Judith Still is the proprietor) in Flagstaff, Arizona, which holds both a piano-vocal score and a full orchestral score. The WGSM also has a "December 1926" sketchbook, which contains material for "Rashana" and other materials relating to *Blue Steel,* including a pencil scenario.[29]

Blue Steel: Plot and Characters

Still composed an exceptional opera that was at once accessible yet allegorical. The plot revolves around two lovers, Blue Steel and Neola, and is centered on the conflict between tradition and modernity, the latter of which subtly touches upon the conflict between syncretic African religion and Christianity. The most extensive study of the work—indeed, of Still's operas generally—to date is Beverly Soll's *I Dream a World: The Operas of William Grant Still,*[30] in which she provides a brief summary of the plot, description of the sources, and overview of the opera's structure (presented as a list of recitatives, arias, and choruses). Her summary focuses primarily on the action and general descriptions of the characters. Yet both are more subtly and powerfully drawn than one might assume from Soll's summary. Furthermore, the characters and scenario invite comparison with other African American operas and beg for greater contextualization.

Blue Steel features four main characters: Blue Steel (baritone), an arrogant city dweller from Birmingham; Neola (soprano), daughter of the high priest of a voodoo cult; Doshy (contralto), an aged "conjure woman"; and Venable (tenor), Neola's father and the voodoo cult's high priest. Still described the plot as "a rather fanciful story about a city Negro who finds himself among primitive people and tries to seduce the daughter of the High Priest."[31] Set in a backwoods swamp inhabited by a voodoo cult, the plot revolves around the love between Blue Steel and Neola and the conflict between Neola and Doshy, who seeks to dissuade Neola from abandoning her position in the cult to elope with Blue Steel. Against the backdrop of beating drums, Doshy curses Blue Steel and convinces Neola that she can save him by sacrificing her love and returning to the fold. At the start of the second act, Neola has honored her duties and participates in a voodoo ceremony involving a goat sacrifice, a dance, and the cult (chorus) invoking the *loas* (voudon spirits). Blue Steel bursts in and attempts to convince Neola to come with away him. A fight ensues in which he murders Neola's father, Venable. Witnessing this, the cult members sing a *maledizione*. He exits with Neola as Doshy curses him with death, bringing the second act to a close. The third act returns to the swamp as Neola and Blue Steel flee, pursued by Doshy and members of the cult. Neola is now torn between her love for Blue Steel and her duty, both to her religion and to avenge her father's death. The drums beat incessantly. To Neola, the drums portend death; for Blue Steel, they mark the beginning of a descent into madness. The cult members observe Neola and Blue Steel poling a barge through the swamp in an attempt to escape, but the boat hits a snag. The cult members invoke the gods and continue drumming. Blue

Steel, mocking the drums and the gods, fires his revolver into the crowd, but is perplexed when none of his four shots hits a target. His demeanor changes markedly as madness overtakes him; humbled, he attempts to pray, singing that in scorning the pagans, he has offended God. Neola prays to a voodoo god, begging for mercy, that Blue Steel may have strength to survive and that his love for her be strengthened. Blue Steel finds that his prayers are empty and hollow. Doshy, who has been watching all along, calls for the drums to stop and for all to watch as the "spell is woven." Neola, realizing that Blue Steel is now lost to the madness of the drums, asks him if he would leave her alone and desolate. She then cries out to Damballah. Blue Steel, thinking Neola is a demon witch, pushes her aside. He leaps from the barge and takes three steps before he is caught in quicksand. He struggles to get free. The chorus and Neola watch as he sinks; Neola swoons. The chorus sings its last lines

> The taker of life
> has no longer a life
> The voice of the drum is Damballah.

Working without knowledge of distinctly African American opera traditions, opera composers, or major productions—not even Scott Joplin's seminal *Treemonisha*—Still was largely forging tradition anew. While Soll's study is an important resource for those wishing to pursue further study of Still's operas generally, its primary purpose is to provide a general reference to the more positivistic aspects of works in the genre. To move Still opera studies beyond cataloging, one must place *Blue Steel* in the larger and equally important context of the Harlem Renaissance.

African Awakening

In keeping with aesthetic and political ideas outlined in the writings of W. E. B. Du Bois and the Oxford-educated Howard University philosophy professor Alain Locke, Still did not limit himself to selecting topics related to the history and culture of American blacks. He also embraced the African heritage, Pan-Africanism, and the cultures of those in the African diaspora, particularly those of African descent in South America, the Caribbean, and other parts of what Paul Gilroy refers to as the Black Atlantic (or, in Samuel Floyd Jr.'s term, "circum-Caribbean"). Their call (along with that of Marcus Garvey and his Back to Africa Movement) to embrace the African heritage, which for many early-twentieth-century African Americans was still fraught with conflict, proved powerful. Consciously—sometimes self- and subconsciously—many artists sought to heal the painful wounds of history and correct the contemporary view of Africa and Africans, a formidable challenge in an era when it was not yet seen as problematic or racist for European colonizers and white Americans to view Africans and their culture as products of the "primitive Dark Continent."

The New Negro offers insight into how Africa and the diaspora proved to be a powerful and inspiring trope for Harlem Renaissance artists. Throughout the anthology, African-inspired art motifs headed each chapter and were interspersed among essays, poetry, and fiction. "Sahdji," a short story set in East Africa by Locke's protégé Richard Bruce (Nugent), appeared in the anthology. Locke and Still later worked together to craft this brief story (only two pages) into an eponymous full-length ballet, which included a chorus and a chanter (much like an African griot) who recited *African* proverbs rather than biblical ones (the line the chorus sings at the end of *Blue Steel* also appears at the end of *Sahdji,* Still's "African ballet," as it was called). Two important essays focused not on poetry or fiction, but on the history and culture of Africans. Arthur A. Schomburg (after whom the Harlem research branch of the New York Public Library is named) addressed archaeology in "The Negro Digs Up His Past." Schomburg began, "The American Negro must remake his past in order to make his future." As he went on to write in the introductory paragraph, "History must restore what slavery took away for it is the social damage of slavery that the present generations must repair and offset. So among the rising democratic millions we find the Negro thinking more collectively, more retrospectively than the rest, and apt out of the very pressure of the present to become the most enthusiastic antiquarian of them all."[32] The need to un- and recover the past was particularly pressing and had special import for African Americans.

In "The Legacy of the Ancestral Arts," Locke explicitly linked the African past to contemporary cultures of the African diaspora, emphasizing the diaspora's artistic heritage. The arts, Locke argued, retained a powerful African cultural memory:

> Music and poetry, and to an extent the dance, have been the predominant arts of the American Negro. This is an emphasis quite different from that of the African cultures, where the plastic and craft arts predominate; Africa being one of the great fountain sources of the arts of decoration and design. Except then in his remarkable carry-over of the rhythmic gift, there is little evidence of any direct connection of the American Negro with his ancestral arts. But even with the rude transplanting of slavery, that uprooted the technical elements of his former cultures, the American Negro brought over as an emotional inheritance a deep-seated aesthetic endowment. And with a versatility of a very high order, this offshoot of the African spirit blended itself in with entirely different culture elements and blossomed in strange new forms.[33]

Locke argued that while African American arts and culture were indeed inherently American, African American culture also retained African survivals that had been transformed in the United States by the experience of slavery. He argued further that for the future development of African American arts, artists should reconnect and draw upon their ancestral heritage. Modernist European visual artists (sculptors and painters) had already drawn upon the arts of Africa for inspiration and direct models. By extension, then, if white Americans and Europeans could mine Africa for inspiration and models in their visuals arts, then African American artists could do the same, but with different connections to the source.[34] Arthur Huff Fauset, focusing on a rich variety of story forms, legends, saga cycles, songs, proverbs, and fantastic, almost mythical, material, pointed to Africa as the source of black folklore. Writers who drew upon the African heritage were well represented, supplementing the scholarly essays by Schomburg, Locke, and others.

Du Bois's ideas and activism and the passages in Locke's *New Negro* serve as instructive guides for understanding *Blue Steel,* its music, tropes, and signifiers, in the context of the Harlem Renaissance. Both scholars linked black American history, culture, and contemporary political vision to the African past and present as well as to that of all peoples of African descent in the Americas, the Caribbean, and Europe. This juncture calls for further synthesis. First, if African culture survived in the New World (as per Locke's argument), then surely so did African religion. Similarly, if African Americans could draw upon the visual arts from Africa itself, then they could also draw upon those of other African diasporic cultures that drew from the same cultural wellspring. Syllogistically, then, African Americans could draw upon African diasporic religions found in the New World and recast them for new ends, including artistic ones.

Countee Cullen's poem "Heritage," in which he asks the rhetorical question "What is Africa to me?" expresses both his connection to and his distance from the continent—the land of his ancestors. He thirsts for knowledge of Africa and his ancestral heritage, yet is ambivalent. Cullen, the adopted son of a prominent New York clergyman, articulated his conflict through the metaphor of African Americans' conversion to Christianity, which left him averse to African religion, rejecting it as pagan and primitive. Yet he feels the burden of spiritual loss, and so Cullen begins to embrace the African religious heritage and tries to reconcile the seeming contradiction of being an American of African descent.[35] More systematically, Zora Neale Hurston (and later Katherine Dunham) undertook similar engagement with African diasporic religion as she researched voodoo, hoodoo, and conjure in Haiti, New Orleans, and the Bahamas, as both an anthropologist and a creative writer. Thus, the syncretic African religion of voudon would come to serve as a *locus topicus* and one signifier (among many) of the Africanness of black American religious culture for Harlem Renaissance writers, visual artists, dancers, musicians, and composers—including William Grant Still.

The Topoi of Voodoo

By the time Still completed *Blue Steel* in 1934, voodoo had already long been part of the popular American imagination. Voodoo (or, more accurately, voudon) is fraught with a rich cultural, political, and religious history. As a syncretic religion blending Catholicism and African religion, it has a complex ordering of a Supreme Being, lwas (*loas*), good-evil dichotomy, ancestors, *serviteurs* (believers), houngans and mambos (male priests and female priestesses, respectively), and rituals. In the nineteenth century, white folklorists had written about its Carolina-Georgia cousins, conjure and hoodoo, which the most generous commentators viewed as folk religions (though most treated it simply as superstition). In the early twentieth century, Americans were further confronted with voodoo in fiction, film, popular song, and theater. Arguably the most famous work of the era was Eugene O'Neill's 1920 play, *Emperor Jones*, which also formed the basis for an opera (1931) of the same name by Louis Gruenberg.[36] Historian Mary Renda argues that the subtext of O'Neill's *Emperor Jones* offers political commentary, critiquing race, imperialism, and the U.S. occupation (1919–34) of Haiti inasmuch as it reflects Americans' fascination with this Caribbean nation that resulted.[37] Haiti, voodoo, and zombies further penetrated American popular culture via radio dramas and horror and suspense films such as *Stanley among the Voodoo Worshipers* (1915), *Hoodoo Ann* (1916, written by D. W. Griffith), *Drums o' Voodoo* (1934), *Revolt of the Zombies* (1936), *White Zombie* (1932, starring Bela Lugosi), as well as comedies such as *The Girl Bandit's Hoodoo* (1912) and *The Hoodoo Hat* (1912).[38] Additionally, white authors wrote about Haiti in a variety of contexts, ranging from travelogues to popular fiction, typically depicting it as a place of adventure and "primitive" exoticism, especially in hypersexualized and sensational racial tones, and promoted it as a vacation spot for white Americans.[39]

African Americans, however, viewed Haiti's history and the U. S. occupation differently. Both in its revolution and in the resistance that coalesced around the U.S. occupation, Haiti served as a powerful symbol to African Americans of resistance, anticolonialism, and racial equality;[40] the U.S. occupation served as a *locus topicus* for African American writers, dramatists, and composers in a similar yet significantly different way than it had for white artists like O'Neill. Several African American theater groups of the Federal Theatre Project produced Haitian- and voodoo-themed plays, the most famous of which was the Harlem production *Voodoo Macbeth* (set in nineteenth-century Haiti), directed by Orson Welles, under whom Moss served as an assistant. The Los Angeles section of the Negro Units of the Federal Theatre Project produced *Black Empire*, based on the end of King Henri Christophe's regime, and the political figures of Toussaint L'Ouverture and Jean-Jacques Dessalines also received dramatic treatment. The latter inspired Langston Hughes's play *Drums of Haiti,* which he and Still would later fashion into the libretto for Still's opera *Troubled Island.* African American artists used these Haitian-inspired works to express their racial pride and to challenge prevailing racial stereotypes and demand rights. In short, they undermined the status quo.[41]

Blue Steel and Voodoo: *Locus Topicus*

Like his Harlem Renaissance peers, Still's creative gaze turned to Africa and the Caribbean. By the time Still left Wilberforce, he had already developed a keen interest in Africa and the diaspora. He returned frequently to this topos during the first decade of his concert career, with several African- or Caribbean-themed works (see table 1).

To gain insight into what Africa meant to Still (as well as the African diasporic cultures that inspired *Blue Steel* and other voodoo operas), we turn once again to the writings of Forsythe and an unpublished manuscript, "The Rising Sun (a Biography of the *Sahdji* of William Grant Still)," a supplement to his biographical essay "A Study in Contradictions." "The Rising Sun" provides a brief biography of Still and an analytical study of the ballet's musical, dramatic, and cultural aspects. Though Forsythe's style is rather prosaic, he provides a valuable account of Still's interest in Africa and African music, as well as a revealing glimpse into Still's exploration of spirituality and metaphysics.

For Still, study of Africa and African culture was not merely an artistic exercise. He was only a generation removed from the era of slavery and a culture very close chronologically to its African origin. In fact, Forsythe notes that Still's maternal grandmother, Anne Fambro (who originally came from Georgia), was "an ex-slave who carried in her mind the heritage of the old tunes and tales," and scholars have noted how Fambro sang spirituals to her grandson.[42] In light of the discovery of this early biography, family oral tradition, such as Forsythe relates about the death of Still's father (in which an owl figures as an omen of death),[43] must be more carefully considered (rather than dismissed as colorful), viewing it from the perspective of cultural memory rather than mere superstition. Therefore, Still's grandmother imparted not just the musical tradition of her world to her grandson, but another worldview: metaphysical beliefs with roots in

Table 1. African and African diaspora topology in William Grant Still's early works

Title	Genre	Setting	Date
La Guiablesse	ballet	Martinique (Caribbean)	1927
Sahdji	ballet	Africa	1930
Africa	orchestral suite	Africa	1930

Africa that supplemented her Christian beliefs. While African Americans have traditionally embraced Protestant Christianity, Black religion has many African survivals that were (re)formed during slavery and subsequent generations. This spiritual tradition sometimes coexisted alongside Black Christianity with links to Haitian voudon, Cuban Santería, or Brazilian *Candomblé*. In Georgia and the Carolinas, black folk religious beliefs are called either conjure, working roots, or hoodoo; in New Orleans (which also had a major influx of Haitian and Cuban cultures), it is referred to as voodoo (though Zora Neale Hurston, in her ethnographic study in which she describes her apprenticeship and initiation, refers to it as hoodoo). Though he remained deeply religious throughout his life and inscribed his scores "With humble thanks to God—the source of inspiration," Still was also obviously open to other spiritual and metaphysical practices and traditions, and the inspiration may have been familial in origin. Forsythe makes two early references to Still's spiritual and religious exploration, stating that it had begun while the composer lived in Columbus during the mid-1910s and that Still continued to explore during the early 1930s (and for the remainder of his life), both personally and in his music.[44]

Complementing his interest in non-Christian spirituality, Still also explored African music as best he could during the 1910s and 1920s. Few sound recordings were available to him, so he had to turn to other sources. For example, Still occasionally acted as ethnomusicologist, as revealed in a 1961 speech in which he told of his early exposure to African music at Wilberforce, where four of his fellow classmates from Africa formed a vocal quartet.[45] Years later, Still continued his exploration of African music as he prepared to compose *Sahdji*, a stage work that he and his collaborators (Alain Locke and Richard Nugent) referred to as Still's "African ballet." Still's studies focused on "African rhythm, melody, instruments and dances," as Forsythe writes. Still turned to an African friend again in 1929; he also visited Locke in Washington, consulting with him on matters relating to setting texts spoken by the Chanter and to African custom.[46] Still wanted to avoid imitation and artifice introduced merely for local color or, as Forsythe described, "a mere mechanical transferring of African material" that would result in a "bastard product." Rather, Still drew upon his knowledge of African music for conceptual approaches to *representing* Africa and Africanness through musical signifiers, a practice that also emerges in *Blue Steel*.

For Still, who came to artistic maturity during the U.S. occupation of Haiti, voodoo offered the means to express himself as a Harlem Renaissance artist by functioning as a multifaceted signifier of African identify within the New World. Critical response revolved largely around O'Neill's use of voodoo and the constant drumming throughout the play. As one critic wrote, "The tom-tom stunned us as it stunned the Emperor Jones, and if it had not mercifully stopped when it did I should not have been surprised to see some of my less controlled colleagues climbing on the stage and doing a war dance."[47] Gruenberg's 1931 opera (based on O'Neill's play) also featured the constant beating of the drums. O'Neill and Gruenberg, like other contemporary high modernists in literature, the visual arts, music, and so forth, embraced Africa as part of the Primitivist aesthetic. This *locus topicus* left Still and his librettist considerable room for invention and presented a subject that would resonate with many different audiences, from the highbrow literary set to those more engaged with popular culture. That is not to suggest that Still and his peers pandered to popular taste. On the contrary, assuming that O'Neill's *Emperor Jones* and other popular culture representations of voodoo were fresh in the American's public's memory when Still composed his opera, he had to be particularly careful to avoid making artistic decisions that could be construed as demeaning to or perpetuating negative stereotypes of African Americans. For Still, Forsythe, and Moss, Primitivism was not an aesthetic or musical option.

In *Blue Steel*, Still drew upon the highest models and challenging operatic techniques while offering subject matter and music consistent with the aesthetic and cultural aims of the Harlem Renaissance. Following his European models (and *pace* Houston Baker and his theory of mastery of form), Still drew upon Italian and German operatic traditions and conceived of *Blue Steel* as grand opera, replete with a ballet in the second act, though offered here in the context of a voodoo ritual. Reflecting his study of Wagner, throughout the opera there are leitmotivs associated with specific characters, and voodoo concepts, the most prevalent of which represent Blue Steel, the drum, and Damballah Wedo.

More important, however, Still made musical choices early in the developmental stages that reflect the aesthetics of Du Bois, Locke, and others who embraced African and African diasporic culture. Unlike the locales of the works listed in table 1, *Blue Steel* was set not in an exotic foreign land, but in a swamp in the Deep South. Unlike Hurston or Hughes, Still never traveled to Haiti or any other Caribbean nation—his only known trips outside the United States after he left the Navy were to Mexico. Thus, he had to construct an image of "Africanness" mostly from secondary sources, but he *did* have firsthand knowledge of southern black culture, ranging from his grandmother's accounts to his own experiences of the time he spent in Memphis and traveling through other parts of the South with Handy during the summer of 1916.

Blue Steel reflects Still's interest in African diasporic culture, ultimately manifested in his choice to draw all other prominent motives from one source: the drum. This is the most powerful symbol in the opera—not Forsythe's language, nor the lighting, nor the costume design, nor the scenery. All leitmotivs are put to an African end, as Still used the drum as the master signifier of Africa. All three early sources indicate that Still chose drum motives in the early stages of composition, honing and modifying them over the course of time as the opera took shape. The drum did more than simply add local color; it embodied the concept, history, and culture represented by voodoo and, in so doing, marked a specific locus of African American experience. Thus, Still and his collaborators' choice to have the drum leitmotiv "beating" constantly throughout *Blue Steel* was a sounding strategy that could perhaps signal resistance to the disparaging stereotypes they sought to overturn with such a project—both in terms of how voodoo was popularly perceived and in the way that black composers and musicians were—in much the same way Haitians continued to drum and practice their indigenous African religion. For Still, to drum in his stylized, operatic manner was to invoke the African heritage and allow it to resound for all black Americans.

Notes

This article is dedicated to Dr. Akin Euba, African opera composer, ethnomusicologist, and scholar of Yoruba music. His work on intercultural music is an inspiration and a model.

I would like to acknowledge Naomi André's Cambridge University 2008 conference paper for my thinking about Still's connection to Africa in my use of the opening line of Countee Cullen's "Heritage" ("What is Africa to me?"), table 1, with a list of Still's works based on African themes and the centrality of the drum (especially as it appears in Eugene O'Neill's play *Emperor Jones*).

1. Still, "Composer Needs Determination and Faith."

2. "Guggenheim Fund Aids 40 in 10th Year," *New York Times*, April 2, 1934, 4.

3. Still, "Autobiographical Manuscript," 11, typescript, William Grant Still and Verna Arvey Papers, Special Collections, University of Arkansas, Fayetteville (hereafter cited as Still-Arvey Papers). See also Smith, *Study in Contradictions*, 69, 82; and *William Grant Still*, 46.

4. Laymen generally think of the Harlem Renaissance as focusing solely on African Americans in the United States, but this is a misconception. Although Harlem Renaissance writers, musicians, dancers, and visual artists promoted African American history and culture and drew upon the culture of blacks in the United States, their aesthetic and geopolitical gaze was global. Writers such as Langston Hughes, Zora Neale Hurston, and James Weldon Johnson traveled to nations in the Caribbean (for example, Haiti, Cuba, the Bahamas) and to Europe (Spain, Paris, England). Sociologist and *Crisis* editor Du Bois (who had studied in Germany) was active in leading the Pan-African movement (which gave rise to its own writers such as Léopold Senghor and, later, Aimé Césaire). He linked racism and colonialism and promoted solidarity among black Americans, Africans, and others of the African diaspora.

5. Lenneberg, "Johann Mattheson (I)" and "Johann Mattheson (II)"; Bukofzer, "Allegory in Baroque Music."

6. Morrissette, "French Nouveau Roman"; Guinn and Marder, "Limits of Rhetoric."

7. See Baker, *Blues, Ideology, and Afro-American Literature* and *Modernism and the Harlem Renaissance;* and Gates, *The Signifying Monkey.*

8. William Grant Still, speech on *Highway 1, U.S.A.* for Donald Deschner's book on opera in the United States, typescript, 1, Los Angeles, July 1967, Still-Arvey Papers.

9. Southern and Still, "William Grant Still," 168. See also Still, "Personal Notes," in *Study in Contradictions,* ed. Smith, 217.

10. Arvey, *In One Lifetime,* 39.

11. Smith, "William Grant Still in Ohio."

12. Arvey, *In One Lifetime,* 39 (quote), 50; Still, "Personal Notes," in *Study in Contradictions,* ed. Smith, 217–19; Smith, *Study in Contradictions* and *William Grant Still.*

13. Still to Guilio Gatti-Casazza, Metropolitan Opera, September 26, 1919, Still-Arvey Papers.

14. Still, speech on *Highway 1, U.S.A.,* 2, Still-Arvey Papers.

15. Material for "Rashana," in "December 1926" sketchbook, William Grant Still Music, Flagstaff, Arizona.

16. Edwards, "Life of William Grant Still," 98.

17. Letters 1 and 2, William Grant Still to Countee Cullen, n.d. [1928–30?], Countee Cullen Papers, Amistad Research Center, Tulane University, New Orleans, Louisiana (hereafter cited as Cullen Papers).

18. Letter 5, Still to Cullen, Cullen Papers.

19. Catherine Parsons Smith, email to author, November 30, 1997. Smith references letters from Grace Bundy Still in the Cullen Papers.

20. Still, "Autobiographical Manuscript," 294.

21. Here, the record is not entirely clear, but Smith suggests that Still may have begun work on *Blue Steel* even before he applied for the first Guggenheim in 1931.

22. Carlton Moss was an award-winning African American Harlem Renaissance–era actor, director, and filmmaker who was among the first to work in the film industry in Hollywood, where he fought racial segregation and discrimination. For more on Carlton Moss, see Bond, *Negro and Drama;* Capra, *Name above the Title;* "Carlton Moss, 88, Who Filmed the Black Experience, Dies," *New York Times,* August 15, 1997; Dates and Barlow, *Split Image;* Leab, *From Sambo to Superspade;* Moss, "Negro in American Films"; Noble, *The Negro in Films;* Sampson, *Blacks in Black and White;* Regester, "African-American Writers," 210; Ross, "Role of Blacks"; Herman Wong, "Black Film Maker Still Battling Stereotypes," *Los Angeles Times,* May 30, 1986, OC-E1; Carlton Moss, "The Birth of Los Angeles' Black Film Industry," *Los Angeles Times,* November 27, 1977, P60; "Negro Music Concert to Be Given Sunday," *New York Times,* February 24, 1949, 21; "News of Stage," *New York Times,* August 15, 1936, 6; "Hollywood Four Refuse Replies to Red Inquiry," *Los Angeles Times,* April 14, 1951, 1; Richard L. Coe, "Early Scenes and Acts of the Federal Theater," *Washington Post,* October 30, 1977, 182; and *Notable Black American Men,* Gale Research, 1998, reproduced in Biography Resource Center, Farmington Hills, Mich., Gale Group, 2002 (http://galenet.galegroup.com/servlet/BioRC). For more on the Negro Units of the Federal Theatre Project, see Ross, "Role of Blacks."

23. He wrote for the pioneering NBC radio series *The Negro Hour* during the 1932–33 season. The actors for this series formed the Lafayette Players. Moss later acted, wrote,

and taught theater for the Negro Units of the Federal Theater Project (part of Roosevelt's New Deal Work Projects Administration) and served as director of the WPA's Harlem Federal Theatre. The latter unit performed his play *Prelude to Swing.* He also worked as assistant to Houseman and Orson Welles for the 1935 production of the Negro Theatre's first production, *Macbeth,* set in Haiti, and as John Houseman's assistant at Harlem's Lafayette Theatre. In 1936 an African American board of directors formed, consisting of Moss, along with J. A. "Gus" Smith and Harry V. F. Edwards, then head of New York's WPA Negro Theatre. Moss also had experience with opera: Houseman directed Virgil Thomson's *Four Saints in Three Acts.* A member of Frank Capra's U.S. Army documentary unit during World War II, Moss wrote, directed, and appeared in the pioneering film *The Negro Soldier* (1944) (he had the role of a preacher), a training film for both black and white solders promoting patriotism and racial harmony (Still was originally contracted to provide the music, but his score was later replaced). Moss also worked on other films such as *Team Work* (a 1944 sequel to *The Negro Soldier*) and *Don't Be a Sucker.* He also served as Secretary of War Harold Stimson's consultant and as information specialist for the Information and Education Division. Moss collaborated with director Elia Kazan on the script for the film *Pinky* (1949), though he later resigned. He founded the film program at Fisk University, the first black film program in the United States. His other film credits include *The House on Cedar Hill* (producer and director) and *What about Tomorrow* (producer). His writings include *Negro Music Past and Present.*

24. It is presently unclear why Moss provided Still with only the scenario, but there are several plausible explanations. Moss was busy with numerous other commitments at this time. He wrote for a short-lived NBC radio show, *The Negro Hour* (see Sklaroff, "Variety for the Servicemen"). Furthermore, Still planned to relocate to Los Angeles, and it would have proved exceedingly difficult to work closely on the opera if Moss had served as librettist.

25. For someone like Still, the terms *Race Man* and *Racial Uplift* were not pejoratives but challenges to form a social contract in which educated, middle-class, and upwardly mobile African Americans felt compelled to fight discrimination. Their efforts served as more than individual accomplishments; they were powerful symbols and substantive evidence of the "Genius of the Race."

26. Still, "Autobiographical Manuscript," 155, Still-Arvey Papers.

27. Blue Steel Typescript and Music Manuscript, ML96 S915 Case, Library of Congress. For an overview of manuscript sources pertaining to *Blue Steel,* see Soll, *I Dream a World,* 80–82.

28. Still, "Autobiographical Manuscript," 154, Still-Arvey Papers.

29. The music manuscript bears the same date as the libretto, January 28, 1935 (stamped in ink on the reverse of page 1), suggesting that the libretto and manuscript piano-vocal were deposited at the same time. The score Still submitted is incomplete: he finished only the first act, which is in ink in his neat hand. He made significant progress on the second act, finishing only up to the beginning of the goat sacrifice. From then on, only the melody of the chorus (not all parts) and the basic harmonic progression are sketched out. One of the most complete passages is Blue Steel's aria on page 111,

when he enters the temple. In general, the arias and duets are relatively complete; the chorus is only bare-bones. Act 3 appears to be pretty much complete. The materials at WGSM were inventoried August 30, 31, and September 1, 1997 by Carolyn Quin, Lance Bowling, and Catherine Parsons Smith. I am grateful to Professor Smith for providing me with a copy of this inventory. There is an undated sketchbook archived at William Grant Still Music in Flagstaff that contains sketches Still used in a variety of works: the ballets *Sahdji, The Sorcerer,* and *La Guiablesse;* the aborted opera "Rashana"; various instrumental works including *Deserted Plantation, Miss Malindy, The Black Man Dances,* and *From the Black Belt;* the suite *Africa;* and his first completed mature opera, *Blue Steel.* The sketchbook is unpaginated, but Still numbered all the motives.

30. Soll, *I Dream a World,* 75–85.

31. Still, "Autobiographical Manuscript," Still-Arvey Papers.

32. Arthur A. Schomburg, "The Negro Digs Up His Past," in *The New Negro,* ed. Locke, 231.

33. Alain Locke, "The Legacy of the Ancestral Arts," in ibid., 254.

34. Locke listed several young artists who were doing so (Archibald Motley, Otto Farrill, Albert Smith, John Urquhart, Samuel Blount, Charles Keene, and Aaron Douglas) and included photographs of art from the Bushongo, Soudan-Niger, Yabouba, Ivory Coast, Dahomey, and Congo.

35. Countee Cullen, "Heritage," in ibid., 252–53.

36. The play broke new ground and the race barrier in 1920 by having an African American (Charles Gilpin) rather than a white actor in blackface perform a lead role in a "serious" or "straight" play. The play opened in New York on November 1, 1920, at the Playwright's Theatre (Paul Robeson was chosen for the 1924 revival) and became the Provincetown Players' first Broadway hit. It also established O'Neill's reputation as an experimental, avant-garde American expressionist and the United States' foremost playwright. See Monks, "'Genuine Negroes and Real Bloodhounds,'" 540; Belcher, "Negro Theater," 124; and Steen, "Melancholy Bodies," 343.

37. Following two revolutions (March and July) and mounting foreign debt, Haiti was invaded in July 28, 1915, by the United States. Marines occupied the country until August 1934, though African Americans leaders objected. See Renda, *Taking Haiti,* 82–88, 217–46. See also Heinl, *Written in Blood.*

38. Renda, *Taking Haiti,* 6, 75, 185; Sarris, *The American Cinema;* Internet Movie Database, http://www.imdb.com.

39. The 1936 film *Ouanga,* featuring jazz vocalist Fredi Washington, invites later comparison with Clarence Cameron White's opera.

40. Lawless, *Haiti's Bad Press,* 42.

41. For a more extensive list of U.S. occupation–era plays inspired by Haitian history and produced under the auspices of the Federal Theatre's Negro Units, see Renda, *Taking Haiti,* 188, 285–88.

42. Harold Bruce Forsythe, "The Rising Sun (a Biography of the *Sahdji* of William Grant Still)," 44, 47, typescript, Still-Arvey Papers.

43. Arvey also refers to both these things in her article "My Arkansas Boyhood" and in the memoir *In One Lifetime.*

44. Forsythe, "The Rising Sun," 51ff, Still-Arvey Papers; Oja, "'New Music' and the 'New Negro.'"

45. Edwards, "Life of William Grant Still," 56. Edwards refers to a speech, "'African Music and Its Influence in the New World,' for the Chadwick School, Rolling Hills, California, July 30, 1961."

46. Forsythe, "The Rising Sun," 73 (quote), 76, 82, Still-Arvey Papers.

47. Belcher, "The Negro Theater," 124.

Bibliography

Arvey, Verna. *In One Lifetime.* Fayetteville: University of Arkansas Press, 1984.

Baker, Houston A. *Blues, Ideology, and Afro-American Literature: A Vernacular Theory.* Chicago: University of Chicago Press, 1984.

———. *Modernism and the Harlem Renaissance.* Chicago: University of Chicago Press, 1987.

Belcher, Fannin S. Belcher, Jr. "The Negro Theater: A Glance Backward." *Phylon (1940–1956)* 11 (2nd Quarter 1950): 121–26.

Bond, Frederick W. *The Negro and the Drama.* College Park, Md.: McGrath, 1940.

Bukofzer, Manfred. "Allegory in Baroque Music." *Journal of the Warburg and Courtauld Institutes* (October 1939): 1–21.

Capra, Frank. *The Name above the Title.* New York: Macmillan, 1971.

Dates, Jannette L., and William Barlow, eds. *Split Image.* Washington, D.C.: Howard University Press, 1990.

Edwards, Benjamin Griffin. "The Life of William Grant Still." Ph.D. diss., Harvard University, 1987.

Gates, Henry Louis, Jr. *The Signifying Monkey.* New York: Oxford University Press, 1988.

Guinn, Dorothy Margaret, and Daniel Marder. "Experimenting with the Limits of Rhetoric." *Rhetoric Society Quarterly* 10 (Spring 1980): 83–94.

Heinl, Robert Debs. *Written in Blood: The Story of the Haitian People, 1492–1995.* Rev. ed. Lanham, Md.: University Press of America, 2005.

Lawless, Robert. *Haiti's Bad Press.* Rochester, Vt.: Schenkman Books, 1992.

Leab, Daniel J. *From Sambo to Superspade: The Black Experience in Motion Pictures.* Boston: Houghton Mifflin, 1975.

Lenneberg, Hans. "Johann Mattheson on Affect and Rhetoric in Music (I)." *Journal of Music Theory* 2 (April 1958): 47–84.

———. "Johann Mattheson on Affect and Rhetoric in Music (II)." *Journal of Music Theory* 2 (November 1958): 193–236.

Locke, Alain, ed. *The New Negro.* 1925. Reprint, New York: Atheneum, 1968.

Monks, Aoife. "'Genuine Negroes and Real Bloodhounds': Cross-Dressing, Eugene O'Neill, the Wooster Group, and the Emperor Jones." *Modern Drama* 48 (Fall 2005).

Morrissette, Bruce. "Topology and the French Nouveau Roman." *boundary 2* 1, no. 1 (1972): 45–57.

Moss, Carlton. "The Negro in American Films." *Freedomways* 3 (Spring 1963): 134–42.

Noble, Peter. *The Negro in Films.* Port Washington, N.Y.: Kennikat Press, 1948.

Oja, Carol J. "'New Music' and the 'New Negro': The Background of William Grant Still's 'Afro-American Symphony.'" *Black Music Research Journal* 12 (Autumn 1992): 145–69.

Regester, Charlene. "African-American Writers and Pre-1950 Cinema." *Literature/Film Quarterly* 29, no. 3 (2001): 210.

Renda, Mary A. *Taking Haiti: Military Occupation and the Culture of U.S. Imperialism, 1915–1940.* Chapel Hill: University of North Carolina Press, 2001.

Ross, Ronald. "The Role of Blacks in the Federal Theatre, 1935–1939." *Journal of Negro History* 59 (January 1974): 38–50.

Sampson, Henry T. *Blacks in Black and White.* Metuchen, N.J.: Scarecrow Press, 1977.

Sarris, Andrew. *The American Cinema.* New York: E. P. Dutton, 1968.

Sklaroff, Lauren Rebecca. "Variety for the Servicemen: The Jubilee Show and the Paradox of Racializing Radio during World War II." *American Quarterly* 56, no. 4 (2004): 945–73.

Smith, Catherine Parsons. *William Grant Still.* Urbana: University of Illinois Press, 2008.

———. *William Grant Still: A Study in Contradictions.* Berkeley and Los Angeles: University of California Press, 2000.

———. "William Grant Still in Ohio (1911–1919)." *American Music* 22 (Summer 2004): 203–30.

Soll, Beverley. *I Dream a World: The Operas of William Grant Still.* Fayetteville: University of Arkansas Press, 2005.

Southern, Eileen, and William Grant Still. "William Grant Still: A Birthday Offering to William Grant Still." *Black Perspective in Music* 3 (May 1975).

Steen, Shannon. "Melancholy Bodies: Racial Subjectivity and Whiteness in O'Neill's *The Emperor Jones.*" *Theatre Journal* 52 (2000).

Still, William Grant. "The Composer Needs Determination and Faith." In *William Grant Still: A Study in Contradictions,* by Catherine Parsons Smith. Berkeley and Los Angeles: University of California Press, 2000. Originally published in *Etude* 67 (January 1949): 7–8.

8

Performers in Catfish Row

Porgy and Bess as Collaboration

GWYNNE KUHNER BROWN

> The current revival of the musical "Porgy and Bess" now at the Ziegfeld theater in New York is the most insulting, the most libelous, the most degrading act that could possibly be perpetrated against colored Americans of modern times.
>
> —James Hicks, "We Don't Need *Porgy and Bess*"

In the decades-long debate over *Porgy and Bess,* those offended by its depiction of African Americans have occasionally characterized the opera as a crime against the race. Some have called the work itself harmful, such as playwright Lorraine Hansberry, who noted that African Americans have "had great wounds from great intentions."[1] Others, including Harold Cruse in his oft-quoted book *The Crisis of the Negro Intellectual,* have viewed the opera as problematic because it enables whites to control and profit from black artistry.[2] In some cases, a particular production of *Porgy and Bess* caused offense; this was the position of critic James Hicks who, in the quotation that opens this essay, excoriated the U.S. State Department's plan to support an international tour of the opera in the early 1950s. Each of these arguments casts African Americans as the victims of malevolent or thoughtless white actions.

Despite a broadening consensus that its libretto's depiction of African American life is dated at best, *Porgy and Bess* has been mounted repeatedly over the past fifty years. It could not have survived, let alone established itself as one of the few great American operas, without the willingness of first-rate black artists to bring it to life onstage and support it offstage. The indispensable, active role that African American performers have played in every critically successful production of *Porgy and Bess* challenges the assumption that the work is something done by whites to blacks.

In choosing to perform this opera, singers shoulder a difficult task. *Porgy and Bess* is an extremely challenging work requiring wide vocal ranges, great physical stamina (due to the work's length and the size of its orchestra), and the ability to sing persuasively in musical styles ranging from folk to Broadway to grand opera. Alongside the artistic challenges, performers of *Porgy and Bess* face a unique array of pressures and risks. Even at the time of the first production in 1935, when many black reviewers lauded the new Gershwin opera as a rare and exciting opportunity for its cast members, the performers were privately criticized by fellow African Americans for validating white stereotypes of black life.[3] Anne Brown, the first Bess, recalled, "When my father saw the premiere, the first performance of *Porgy and Bess* in New York, he was very disappointed and very sad that Negroes had been pictured in the usual clichés, as ignorant and dope peddlers and users and criminals and superstitious—all those things. He said, 'We've had enough of that.'" By the 1950s, critics in the black press were saying the same thing publicly, and there was increasing pressure on performers not to take part in the opera. James Hicks, for example, wrote that those who could not find roles less demeaning to African Americans might be better off "shoveling coal" than performing onstage.[4]

Ironically, the reason that the black press initially welcomed *Porgy and Bess*—because it provided a venue for African American performers to demonstrate their operatic abilities and advance their careers—has often proved illusory. Leontyne Price is a rare example of a major opera star whose career was launched by her role in *Porgy and Bess;* for other performers, the opera has been a frustrating dead end. In a 2005 interview conducted by the present author, a dramatic soprano whose résumé is heavy with appearances in *Porgy and Bess* as Serena reported that opera directors do not always view the Gershwin work as a real opera, and thus do not think to cast its performers, however superb, in more traditional operatic roles. She found this remarkable: "I would think just listening to *Porgy* and hearing the music, you can tell someone's voice type, if their voice could sing an Aida or a Turandot, or sing a Tosca. You can tell—the music is very revealing."[5]

Why, then, given the clear risks and dubious benefits, do performers take part in *Porgy and Bess*? The reasons vary, but for most, the draw is the work itself. Despite its flaws, Gershwin's opera offers performers a fascinating and beguiling score, musical and dramatic challenges, uncommonly complex characters, and even, to some performers, a personally resonant story of a black community.[6] *Porgy and Bess* also provides the rare chance to be one African American cast member among many, a situation that many singers find a congenial change from the norm. And although its efficacy as a stepping-stone to roles in canonic European operas is questionable, *Porgy and Bess* does offer black opera singers the opportunity to perform, which no aspiring professional can afford to take lightly.

There are compelling reasons, then, for black performers both to take part in the opera and to keep clear of it. The continuing existence of *Porgy and Bess* onstage is contingent on their willingness to take part despite the risks, since George Gershwin specified that it was to be performed by African Americans, and his brother Ira and the Gershwin estate have enforced this stricture for all American productions following George's death.[7] For the work to succeed critically, however, performers must do far more than merely take part. Because many music critics view Gershwin as a magnificent melodist who was out of his depth as an opera composer, performances of *Porgy and Bess* must be sufficiently compelling to justify the work's length and its stylistic heterogeneity.[8] At the same time, critics' concerns about the libretto's racial issues are eased only if black performers demonstrate an unwavering artistic and personal commitment to the opera.

Several postwar productions of *Porgy and Bess* have managed to bring together performers with the necessary combination of daring, artistry, skill, and enthusiasm to generate critical success. These productions share an important feature: a positive, collaborative relationship between the performers and the director. A director must acknowledge and value the power that performers wield over *Porgy and Bess,* for it is they who determine a production's fate, and ultimately that of the opera itself. If performers do not feel that they have the director's respect, nor that they are empowered to help shape a production, the risks involved in participation can lead them to defend themselves by giving guarded performances or by withholding advocacy for the opera during interviews and in statements to the press. As this essay will demonstrate, this imperative was established in 1935, when *Porgy and Bess* was created via collaboration between the composer and the Theatre Guild cast members. The productive and respectful relationship that developed between them provides a model that directors of subsequent productions have ignored at their peril.

Collaboration and the Theatre Guild Production

Given Gershwin's career as a Tin Pan Alley songwriter and Broadway composer, it is not surprising that *Porgy and Bess,* his most ambitious work for the stage, was created in cooperation with those who would first perform it. His attitudes and working methods had been shaped by the commercial songwriting business, which required flexibility and openness to the ideas of others, including producers, directors, and stars.

When he undertook *Porgy and Bess,* Gershwin brought not only his prodigious talent, skill, and experience as a stage composer to the task, but his willingness and ability to collaborate. From his first letter to DuBose Heyward in 1926 to his participation in cutting the score after the Boston tryout in late 1935, Gershwin created his magnum opus in consultation with others. He knew his own strengths and limitations, and his famously high self-esteem did not prevent him from recognizing and drawing upon other people's strengths as needed. As the opera's longtime choral director Eva Jessye put it, "A man can think about himself or as well of himself all he likes as long as he doesn't think everyone else adds up to a big nothing."[9]

In casting the Theatre Guild production, it is clear that Gershwin sought out performers who had a good deal of presence and confidence—who would, in short, actively help to shape the production. Todd Duncan's description of his initial private audition reveals that he was bold, confident, and even somewhat prickly in his first interaction with the composer:

> [Gershwin] stopped me after twelve measures of "Lungi dal caro bene"—twelve measures! And he said, "Will you go around there? Do you know this by memory?" "Of course I know it by memory, I sing everything by memory," I replied rather indignantly. He said, "Look straight in my eyes. Don't look anywhere else, look straight in my eyes." I sang the same twelve measures and he stopped once again! So I'm thinking, "What is wrong with this man? Why won't he just let me sing this aria?" And he said, "Will you be my Porgy?" Now guess what I had the nerve to say? . . . I said, "Mr. Gershwin, I have to hear your music first." Oh, he loved it! He just loved it![10]

Although the character of Porgy has sometimes been construed as a way for whites to get a black man on his knees (literally as well as figuratively), the fact that Todd Duncan's assertiveness and confidence so appealed to Gershwin demonstrates that he did not conceive of Porgy as a deferential "Uncle Tom."[11] Duncan's willingness to look directly into Gershwin's eyes while singing is particularly noteworthy: this would have required tremendous concentration and unflappability from anyone, given Gershwin's fame, but particularly from an African American raised in a segregated society.

Anne Brown's audition story is similarly revealing:

> I sang a French aria by Massenet, several German lieder, Russian songs in English, even a Gershwin melody. And George Gershwin was full of praise. And then he asked me to sing a Negro spiritual. Well, unless one is nearly as old as I am and has lived in the United States before the Second World War and understood the insidious damage racial prejudice can afflict on both the victim and the racist, it may be difficult to understand my reaction at that moment. I said, "Well, weren't you satisfied with what I sang?" And he said, "Yes, of course, it was lovely—beautiful." "But why do people always ask Negro singers to sing spirituals as if that is the only thing that they should be singing and not German lieder or French

> arias." I was very much on the defensive. George Gershwin simply looked long at me and he said, "Ah huh, I understand." And I realized that he *did* understand and then I wanted more than anything else to sing a spiritual for him.[12]

There can be no doubt that it took an honest effort for Gershwin to win over his desired lead performers: Brown and Duncan were sensitive about not being taken seriously as black opera singers, and Duncan was also skeptical about Gershwin as a serious composer.[13] Gershwin succeeded by showing them respect as people and as artists and by convincing them of the high quality of his opera.

Gershwin had long customized his Broadway songs to suit the styles and talents of celebrities like Fred Astaire and Ethel Merman, and he remained responsive to the individuals who performed his opera, despite their relative obscurity.[14] Duncan recounted, "I loved singing the role of Porgy and after Gershwin had heard me sing, he tailored the part for my voice. Some of the music had already been written but once he knew my sound, everything just seemed to fit so well." The composer also welcomed cast members' contributions and permitted them to take liberties with their parts. According to Anne Brown, Gershwin "never objected to changes in his music. When Ruby Elzy, for example, embroidered [Serena's] prayer with all sorts of ornamentation, he smiled and said, 'That's wonderful, keep it in.'" Helen Dowdy recalled how Gershwin "flipped" over her unique way with the strawberry vendor's cry in act 2, scene 3.[15]

Although Gershwin respected the insights and creativity that the cast members brought to their roles, he did not expect them to have a specific understanding of the characters' Gullah culture simply because they were African Americans. Anne Brown remembered that "at the rehearsals George occasionally complained that many of the people in the cast had unfortunately been born in the north. Everyone laughed at this since many of us had not even *visited* the south. Some of us were college students and didn't know the dialect of the southern Negro."[16]

Because Gershwin had more firsthand experience with Gullah dialect than did most in his cast, he coached them on it from time to time. Some commentators, not aware of Gershwin's extensive contact with Gullah people, have taken this coaching as evidence of arrogance and insensitivity: not only did he have the nerve to appropriate black culture, but he even thought he could teach black people how to "sound black"! Music historian Jeffrey Melnick, for example, characterizes Gershwin's activity this way: "By the time of the 1935 rehearsals for *Porgy and Bess,* as many witnesses have recounted, the idea of a Jewish man teaching an African American how to sing authentically 'Negro' was no longer a joke: George Gershwin spent time tutoring his mostly northern cast in how to capture the proper southern Black dialect he wanted to match to his music."[17]

Although it is true that many whites of Gershwin's time conflated authentic Negritude with southern black culture (often filtered through the lens of blackface minstrelsy), I know of no evidence that Gershwin thought he was teaching his cast "how to sing authentically 'Negro.'"[18] He was, however, aware that his cast members did not share the opera characters' particular background. In my view, his willingness to teach his cast reflects, in addition to an astonishing degree of confidence and unself-consciousness, a rare sensitivity to the diversity of African American culture. Unlike many who would review the opera over the coming decades, Gershwin was fully aware that his performers were engaged in artifice, not a re-creation of their own lives.[19]

The composer's respect for his cast members as individuals can best be seen in his very different working relationships with Anne Brown and John W. Bubbles, who played Sportin' Life. Their professional backgrounds were extremely dissimilar: Brown was a Juilliard-trained but inexperienced young classical singer, Bubbles a musically illiterate star of the vaudeville stage. While completing the score, Gershwin drew regularly on Brown's knowledge of operatic vocal ranges, as well as on her ability to sight-read freshly composed sections of the score. She described her role in the opera's creation:

> I think that no one—other than his family and those strictly connected with the opera—had a closer association and contact with George Gershwin while he was writing *Porgy and Bess* than I did. Maybe Kay Swift did but that was from another point of view. He used me as a guinea pig and he tried everything and he would ask me, "Is this too high for a baritone?" "No, no, not if he doesn't stay up there too long," I would say. "How's this, should I change this note?" "No, no. As a matter of fact, I'd like to do it higher," would be my answer. I even made a few changes in "I Loves You Porgy," notes which fit my voice better and he would say, "That's good, let's use that."[20]

It is clear from Brown's reminiscences that Gershwin relied upon her expertise and also enjoyed her friendship.

He does not seem to have been personally as close to Bubbles, but the two men collaborated productively, albeit in a strikingly different way. The performer recalled how he learned his part:

> Everybody [in the cast] but [my vaudeville partner Ford] Buck and me had finished the conservatory of music. They all had a musical education. But Buck don't read and I don't read. By ear. That's how we did it.
>
> I learned all of the numbers in Gershwin's apartment. He taught me the songs himself. We just sat side by side on the piano bench, and he played and I sang. . . .
>
> I think some of the others in the cast were worried some about how I'd do because I hadn't the fine training they had. But Gershwin was satisfied. He knew I could do it.[21]

The image of Bubbles and Gershwin sharing a piano bench, together with the performer's sense that the composer had faith in his abilities, paints a compelling picture of their relationship. Bubbles may not have felt at ease with his fellow cast members, but he did with Gershwin.

The composer's productive and positive relationships with these performers and others in the cast may be traced to two important factors. First, the unusual path Gershwin's career had taken, from Tin Pan Alley to the operatic stage, enabled him to approach both Anne Brown, who knew more about some aspects of opera than he did, and John Bubbles, whose expertise in "lowbrow" theater mirrored his own, with an understanding of and respect for their different gifts. Second, there is ample evidence that Gershwin was remarkably unconcerned about the racial difference between himself and African Americans—from his eager participation in Gullah music making on Folly Island (noted with astonishment by his white South Carolinian librettist, DuBose Heyward) to his rather remarkable assumption that he could write a perfectly good folk opera about Catfish Row.[22] Once he had demonstrated his lack of prejudice to the Theatre Guild cast, racial difference did not present an insurmountable barrier to their productive collaboration.

Since *Porgy and Bess* came into being as a result of this productive interracial relationship, there is some irony in the opera's racially divisive reception over the past seven decades. The common assumption that the work has consistently been a source of racial contention rather than collaboration (or at least conversation) is a mistaken one, as the relationship between Gershwin and the cast of the Theatre Guild production attests.[23]

That said, it would be no less erroneous to gloss over the negative aspects of that relationship. Gershwin's lack of self-consciousness with regard to race, while enabling him to interact comfortably with African Americans, also made him insensitive at times. *Variety* quoted him offering this blundering praise for the cast: "Colored people are natural actors and natural singers, and they can be assembled for a reasonable salary. Who could afford a cast of white people equal in ability, and could they sing eight times a week?"[24] The power differential between the famous composer and the performers is made very plain by the tendency of white reviewers in 1935 to focus their attention on the achievement of the former and to praise the latter en masse (and often as an afterthought).[25]

Moreover, not every member of the Theatre Guild production staff developed as healthy a relationship with cast members as did Gershwin. Music director Alexander Smallens famously tried to have John Bubbles thrown out in the middle of a dress rehearsal for taking rhythmic liberties with the score, and Anne Brown recalled that while the white staff members regularly socialized with each other, only Gershwin regularly spent time with members of the cast outside of rehearsals, welcoming them into his apartment, dining with them in restaurants, and attending their parties.[26]

Despite the inevitable complications, the performers were, on the whole, enormously fond of Gershwin, as is evident in their reminiscences about him.[27] After his death in 1937, they were eager to take part in the (ultimately flood-truncated) West Coast revival mounted by a friend of the composer, producer Merle Armitage. The latter writes that "Todd Duncan's respect and affection for George made my later invitation to sing Porgy a foregone conclusion, and Todd Duncan was the first to arrive for rehearsals in Los Angeles." Duncan was not alone in his willingness, says Armitage: "Most of the former company [was] so enthused about an opportunity to play Gershwin's music drama again that many members of the cast actually turned down other offers, or took leave from engagements, in order to be with us."[28] Those involved in the production felt a strong commitment to Gershwin, and to the opera that they had had a part in shaping.

Making Performers (Un)comfortable: Five Case Studies

Most productions of *Porgy and Bess* have been affected by some degree of tension in the relationship between white directorial staff and black performers.[29] The inherent power imbalance between these two groups, coupled with the racial controversy about *Porgy and Bess,* makes it essential that each director communicate openly with the cast about his or her intentions for the production. Directors who have provided a compelling artistic vision, and who have reassured cast members that they are both aware of and interested in counteracting the opera's potentially offensive racial content, have typically fostered positive relationships with performers. When a director fails to take these steps, the critical reception tends to suggest that performers have withheld their full artistic and personal engagement from the production, with predictable results.

No production was more hampered by disastrous relations between production staff and cast than the Samuel Goldwyn film of 1959. A number of factors contributed to the film's poor publicity, mediocre finished product, and ultimate withdrawal from public view, not least among them the fact that the height of the civil rights movement was an inauspicious time to make a glorious Technicolor film about Catfish Row.[30] Goldwyn struggled to cast the film, even resorting to arm-twisting in his efforts to get Sidney Poitier to play Porgy.[31] Neither Poitier nor Dorothy Dandridge, who played Bess, talked much to the press before the film's release, leaving it to Sammy Davis Jr. (Sportin' Life) and Pearl Bailey (Maria) to reassure the public that the film was coming together smoothly and that it would not denigrate African Americans.

William Warfield, who turned down the invitation to provide Poitier's singing voice on the soundtrack (for little recognition and "insultingly unacceptable" pay), later described the film as being "conceived in bitterness and hostility—between the original stage producer, Robert Breen, and Samuel Goldwyn; and then between Goldwyn and his director, Otto Preminger; and then between the tyrannical director and his browbeaten cast." Contemporary press accounts of the film's production offer glimpses of dysfunction behind a carefully managed public relations campaign. Cast member Leigh Whipper (also president of the Negro Actors Guild) called Preminger "a man who has no respect for my people" and left the production. Pearl Bailey worked to excise "undignified and unnatural" dialect from the film, taking it upon herself to reprimand lesser-known cast members when they erred, and commenting publicly that Preminger had "said right at the beginning that if there was something we didn't like—just leave it out."[32] This may have been a striking concession of control on Preminger's part, but it also suggests that he did not view Bailey's concern about dialect as requiring *his* attention.

The film displays a similar combination of sensitivity and thoughtlessness. It presents a visually and linguistically sanitized version of the opera, thereby heading off criticism for depicting an African American community as squalid and debased, but there is no evidence that Preminger considered how incongruous the plot (saucer burial, happy dust, and all) would seem in its cleaned-up new surroundings. Wrote the reviewer for one New York newspaper,

> Director Otto Preminger may very well have deliberately shunned any representation of sleaziness inherent in the story. Beggar Porgy, for example, is not once seen crying for a copper. Nor are the slop and debris of the tumbledown locale ever shown. The sets are stark and dramatically impressive, but there are no traces of dirt.
>
> Poitier seems kindly cheerful instead of despondent, and Dorothy Dandridge appears a bit too physically genteel to essay the hard-eyed strumpet Bess. This is not a reflection on either player's performance, however, since both are sincere in the commercial fashion which Preminger has set out for them.[33]

Other critics were less charitable about the performances, with one complaining of "rather flaccid dialogue spoken without much spontaneity or conviction by many of the characters."[34] The most controversial performances came from Dandridge, viewed as touchingly vulnerable by some reviewers but as overly refined by others, and Sammy Davis Jr., who "suggest[ed] too strongly a sophisticated entertainer aping a small-town rascal," according to one critic.[35]

The film's uneasy admixture of impressive scenery, colorful costumes, and gritty plot, of glamorous performers and earthy characters, shows that Goldwyn, Preminger, and the cast never reached any sort of mutual understanding or common goals. (Only Pearl Bailey is a truly warm and relaxed presence in the film, and even negative reviews single her out for praise.) Open discourse and cooperation might have defused the defensiveness and mistrust palpable in the film and its surrounding publicity, resulting in a bolder and more persuasive cinematic version of *Porgy and Bess*. Given the problems inherent in releasing a big-budget film widely viewed as containing badly dated caricatures of African Americans, it is equally plausible that frank dialogue might have revealed to all of the participants just how unwise the project was in the first place.[36]

A decade and a half later, in a very different atmosphere, producer Sherwin M. Goldman's desire to see *Porgy and Bess* given a full operatic staging at the Houston Grand Opera resulted in a tremendously successful production. The sharp contrast between the 1959 film's stilted performances and mixed reception and the enthusiasm with which the Houston production was greeted is a credit to the latter's director, Jack O'Brien, whose open communication with the performers gave them a sense of safety that had clearly been lacking on Preminger's film set. From the beginning, O'Brien was frank about his own anxiety and hopefulness:

> I walked into that rehearsal hall and for a moment I felt very white indeed. There's always a moment of chill at the first rehearsal, even if you've cast the show yourself. I was nervous—I'd never done anything with an all-black cast before—even though I believed that "Porgy" was not a put-down of blacks, written by whites, but a moving story about people who happen to be black. I was determined to tell the truth about the show as I felt it, in terms of how it dealt with love, jealousy, death and adversity. What a revelation! The company went with me all the way.[37]

What resulted was a production that firmly reestablished *Porgy and Bess* as a full-fledged opera, after thirty years of productions that had presented the work as a musical with most of the recitative replaced by spoken dialogue.[38] By taking the work seriously as an opera and as a story with universal resonance, O'Brien earned the trust and commitment of the performers. He also welcomed their input, particularly that of Clamma Dale, who played Bess to ringing critical acclaim. Although Goldman says that he and Dale "argued endlessly" from the very beginning of their professional relationship, it is clear that her personal, feminist approach to the character of Bess ("She has somehow, as most black women always have had, an ability to survive") played an important role in shaping the production and how it was received by the press.[39] She gave numerous interviews in which she spelled out her thoughts about Bess and about the opera, acting very much as a spokesperson.[40] This reflects both her own intense engagement with the opera and the degree to which the cast was empowered to take ownership of the production.[41]

The stories of two subsequent productions drive home the importance of healthy relationships between performers and directors with particular force: the Metropolitan Opera's 1985 mounting and the production at the Glyndebourne Festival less than a year later. Both productions were prestigious and expensive and featured experienced and capable casts and directors. It is clear, however, that the Met's cast had a less harmonious relationship with the production team than did the performers at Glyndebourne. Even the casting was contentious. Simon Estes, who was particularly known for his work in Wagner operas, had played Porgy already in Zurich, and found it satisfying and challenging. He had no qualms about playing the role at the Met, but was concerned about whether the other African American artists who were cast in Gershwin's opera would be seriously considered for future Met roles. In James Standifer's 1999 documentary about *Porgy and Bess,* Estes describes having a conversation with an unnamed administrator who became increasingly angry when he pressed her for more than weak assurances that the male cast members, in particular, would be cast again.[42]

Damon Evans, who played Sportin' Life in the Glyndebourne production, turned down the Met when they offered him the role there, for exactly that reason: "I did say no to the Met's production of *Porgy and Bess.* Yes, I did, and you know something? It's the one decision in my life that I have never regretted. . . . I saw too many brilliantly talented black singers go into the Met doing *Porgy and Bess* and shown the exit sign as soon as it was over, and I knew that would never happen to me. If I never set foot on their stage, that was never going to happen to me."[43]

Grace Bumbry, like Simon Estes, had built an international reputation playing major canonic roles in Europe. Unlike Estes, she had never appeared in *Porgy and Bess* and was unenthusiastic about taking part. She claimed that she ultimately accepted the role of Bess because she did not want the production to go on without her: "It took me about four months to decide. I said to myself, as the Metropolitan Opera didn't ask me could they do 'Porgy and Bess' and they are going to do it with or without me and since I'm often complaining about productions not being done well, I decided it would behoove me to accept so I could put my input into this wonderful piece of music."[44] Although Bumbry said that she had recognized the opera's greatness upon studying its score, and had "gone from reluctance to acceptance to gung-ho," she played a far smaller role in the extensive publicity leading up to opening night than did her costar Simon Estes, who expressed no reservations about playing Porgy. A lengthy *New York Times* article offers extensive quotations from several cast members, but strikingly few words from the famed female lead.[45]

The Met production received mixed reviews, and Bumbry's performance was the most consistently criticized element. Several reviewers said that she was too old for the role, but I strongly suspect that the real problem was that while she may have come to respect the score, she never lost her distaste for the story, and so was unwilling to immerse herself in her role.[46] Instead of playing Bess, she seemed to some to play Grace Bumbry playing Bess, with what more than one reviewer perceived as self-conscious irony. According to the *New York News,* she approached her characterization with "indifference" and "transform[ed] Gershwin's simple, heartfelt melodies into grotesque imitations of Bumbry's mannered Strauss and Verdi princesses." The *Pittsburgh Post-Gazette* praised her singing but said that "her histrionics were nothing short of disastrous. . . . Vamping around like a parody mixture of Tosca and Dalila, she seemed to have walked into the wrong opera, and her final exit, wiggling her hips as she leaves for New York . . . was pure high camp."[47]

These critical comments display a degree of animosity toward Bumbry that do not stem solely from her performance as Bess. She had long been a controversial performer for taking on both soprano and mezzo-soprano roles, and for reputedly being difficult to work with. Bumbry's reflections during a 2001 interview offer some insight into the obstacles she faced in her career:

> Of the challenges of being a black artist, Bumbry says, "That is very private to me, and I have spent my life going back and forth about it. And some people said, 'Oh, she's black and pushy—that's why they're hiring her. And others said, 'Oh, she's black—let's not hire her.' And when I sang Schubert and Liszt and Brahms . . . they said, 'Sing spirituals, don't be so pretentious.' And when I sang spirituals and tried to do it in a way that wasn't slick, they said, 'That's all she can do, and she's crude! A real artist sings Brahms and Liszt!' And when directors and conductors would come along, I would see they were unprepared and didn't care. For my first Eboli, I read the play, all the history, looked at paintings and went over and over the music. I can count on one hand the conductors or directors who knew as much. One said to me, 'You are an overachiever, not a natural talent.' How was I to take that? Act like a cleaning woman and shut up? So maybe I fought, sometimes unwisely."[48]

Bumbry's words shed light on her sometimes contentious relationships with directors and conductors. They also suggest an explanation for her reluctance to appear in *Porgy and Bess* and for her guarded performance: having fought for more than two decades for respect as an African American performer of European operatic roles, she hesitated to commit herself fully to a role commonly seen as a racial stereotype.

If the entire production had been characterized by the kind of deliberately distancing performance given by Bumbry, one might imagine that it resulted from an innovative, ironic directorial concept. Since no one else in the cast took a similar approach, however, this seems unlikely. Instead, Bumbry's metaphorically "off-key" performance indicates a breakdown in communication between her, director Nathaniel Merrill, and music director James Levine. The directors may or may not have been aware of Bumbry's lingering discomfort with the libretto and the character of Bess, but apparently they failed to address its impact on her performance.

A comment made by Merrill before the production opened reveals something about his attitude and suggests why this communication breakdown may have occurred: "The opera has passed into a piece of Americana, where we can look at it objectively, and not feel that we have to apologize for it. I don't think any of the cast feel that they need to be apologized to for the opera anymore."[49] Two points bear underlining. First, the phrase "passed into a piece of Americana" intimates that *Porgy and Bess* has become safe, even quaint, with the passage of time—a directorial perspective unlikely to inspire cast members about the work's artistic value or contemporary relevance, and which seems to have done little to assuage Bumbry's concerns about its libretto. Second, Merrill subtly gives away a critical distinction in his mind between himself and the performers—and, unavoidably, between whites and blacks—because the "we" in his statement is actively engaged in "look[ing] at it objectively" and "not feel[ing] that we have to apologize," while the cast members ("they") are passively (and purportedly) no longer desirous of "be[ing] apologized to." Moreover, Merrill implies that the racial innocuousness of this period piece is demonstrated by blacks no longer expecting whites to apologize for it, a rather simplistic view of the work's racial content and its potential significance for African Americans. If these comments by Merrill accurately reflect his views on the work and the cast, it may help to explain why he did not effectively communicate with Bumbry, and why she gave a guarded and unsympathetic performance.

In contrast to the Met directorship, which seems to have been unaware of the necessity of doing so, Trevor Nunn and Simon Rattle fostered an atmosphere of openness and cooperation in the 1986 Glyndebourne production of the opera. Director Nunn, echoing the sentiments of Houston Grand Opera director Jack O'Brien ten years earlier, relates that he immediately acknowledged to the cast the awkwardness of being a white British director of *Porgy and Bess:* "The first thing that I said [in rehearsal] was, 'I feel like an impostor. You all know much more about this work than I do. I'm going to need your help and guidance constantly.'"[50] This was an invitation to dialogue, not an apology, and it bore fruit.

Music director Simon Rattle shared this approach. Nunn describes an incident that shows Rattle's willingness to engage and empower the chorus, typically the least powerful contingent of an opera's cast:

> There was something about the train spiritual [in act 1, scene 2] that a number of people felt, "We're toppling over, we're rushing, it isn't feeling right." I talked to Simon about the fact that it would be good if people were able to say what they wanted, and at a certain point Simon came up out of the pit and everybody was there, and he said, "Um, talk to me, first of all, about the problem," which lots of people did. And he said, "Okay, what can we do? Okay, look—I'll just give you a downbeat . . . then show me. . . .
>
> This was such an unusual event. I mean, here was an internationally famous conductor saying, "Show me." And he did, and the chorus were completely sensational. It was like, "This we have to prove." Now, unconducted, I mean absolutely nothing dictating what was holding them together, they sang that vast unit of the work, but so movingly and absolutely immaculately, and together, like they were one singer.[51]

In response to the directors' openness, the performers were moved to invest themselves fully in the production and Nunn's concept for it. As Willard White, who played Porgy, put it, "There was tremendous excitement there at the point of rehearsal. Everyone on stage felt a certain commitment about what they were doing, because Trevor Nunn had managed to weave into the whole piece, the whole presentation, a clarity as to who you are." The *New York Times* reported that the first rehearsal ended with the cast in tears, not only (the reporter hypothesized) from being caught up in the music and the story, but also because "they must have known they were part of a rare experience: a production that redeems an artistic vision, rescuing it from doubts, bringing it to life."[52] The attitude that the directors brought to the rehearsal process surely facilitated the performers' openness to the work.

Many reviews of the Glyndebourne production emphasized the uninhibited quality of the performances—a quality that earlier generations of white critics had often perceived as typically characteristic of black people, but was now understood to be the product of individual artistry and courage. Nicholas Kenyon, writing for the *Observer,* noted that *Porgy and Bess* was now being "performed with fantastic commitment and accomplishment by a cast who demonstrate not the slightest qualms about its problems and a conductor with not the slightest doubt about its musical stature." This commitment was reflected in the compelling emotional frankness of the performances, particularly by the leads. *Opera* magazine's Max Loppert wrote that Willard White and Cynthia Haymon "had me in tears throughout 'Bess, you is my woman now': such direct displays of naked tenderness, of painful self-exposure to new, deep emotion, are rare on any stage."[53] This was clearly the work of performers who held nothing back, who did not feel that their personal integrity or professional standing was endangered by full immersion in Gershwin's work.

In 1995, when a production in the United States was at last directed by an African American, the need for the director to bridge the racial divide between herself and the cast was eliminated. Hope Clarke approached a new Houston Grand Opera production as what she called a "joint effort" with the cast: "We all put our recipes into the pot."[54] The communal spirit that she brought to her relationship with the cast seems to have been counterbalanced by a degree of antagonism toward *Porgy and Bess* itself, particularly toward its performance and reception history. Being the first black director of an American production of the work, Clarke was expected to bring a fresh perspective, an expectation founded on the implicit assumption that *Porgy and Bess* was flawed by its white creators' and directors' limited perspective on black life, and that an African American director (however remote her own background from Catfish Row) would be able to remedy this problem.[55]

Clarke's comments to the press frequently emphasized the ways in which her production was different from previous ones. She highlighted the pride and industriousness of Catfish Row's inhabitants, noting that "in my production, everybody works. . . . Just because you are poor doesn't mean you have to be slovenly or ignorant."[56] Even Porgy the beggar carved little African figurines out of wood to give to his "donors."[57] The cultural specificity of the Gullah community was important to Clarke, and she drew on a cast member who had Gullah relatives to assist the other performers with the dialect.[58]

Press accounts portrayed Clarke's approach to the new Houston production as not only correcting decades of misguided decisions by other directors, but improving the opera itself. According to Rebecca Morris of *American Theatre* magazine, Clarke "feels the show's language needs attention. 'I think that's one of the things black people don't like,' she says, referring to the stylized dialect. 'It sounds a little like the speech of totally uneducated, stupid black people. It's supposed to be Gullah. It's not. We will be absolutely Gullah if we can achieve it.'" Clarke's words hint at animosity toward the work, and reporters highlighted this attitude, even though many of her directorial decisions seem to have built on, rather than contradicted, elements of the original opera. For example, her use of African drums onstage during the picnic scene was very much in the spirit of Gershwin's score, but a newspaper account suggested that Clarke was incorporating cultural components that would have been alien to the composer: "Clarke justified her African emphasis on the better understanding we now have of the Gullah community that inhabited the Sea Islands off the coast of the Carolinas and Charleston. . . . Although Gershwin spent time with [librettist DuBose] Heyward in Charleston while he was composing the opera, it is unlikely that two whites could have gained access to the inner circles of the Gullah community."[59] In fact, according to Heyward's own recollection, Gershwin closely listened to, and participated in music making with, the Gullah inhabitants of James Island during his time in South Carolina.[60]

Articles about the production make scant mention of what might have attracted Clarke to *Porgy and Bess* in the first place; she is quoted on more than one occasion calling the work, or at least the music, "great" or "brilliant," but she is not quoted elaborating further.[61] Morris writes that "Clarke candidly admits she hopes *Porgy and Bess* will lead to directing on Broadway and at the Met," indicating that she viewed it as a professional stepping-stone.[62] It is admittedly difficult to glean precisely what Clarke thought or said about *Porgy and Bess* from the way she and the production were written about in the media. It may be that her opposition to certain aspects of the opera made for a better story than did her admiration for it.

Still, Clarke's ambivalence about the opera did not prevent her from inspiring the performers; on the contrary, and unlike many other directors, she seems to have had a far less ambivalent relationship with the cast than with the work. She said in one interview, "I told the cast, 'We're going to laugh all the way to the opening,' and we did." This is curiously incongruous with the serious tone and content that characterize much of the opera, but certainly paints a picture of a pleasant rehearsal process. Clarke went on to tell the interviewer, "We've emphasized the elements of musical theater, and it seems more like a play than an opera."[63] The statement is telling both for her use of the first-person plural—unlike the Met's Nathaniel Merrill, Clarke does not differentiate between herself and the cast—and for her assumption that a non-operatic approach to *Porgy and Bess* is desirable.[64] Clarke's approach implicitly offers a critique of the work on both generic and racial grounds, seeking to make it at once more entertaining (that is, more theatrical, less "operatic") and more culturally accurate. The result was a production that was, by most accounts, compellingly and wholeheartedly performed and likely would have pleased the composer better than a less imaginative production like the Met's in 1985.[65] Despite the antagonistic flavor of some of her comments, the spirit of Clarke's work with her cast was true to Gershwin's own approach in 1935.

There are good reasons to resist viewing *Porgy and Bess* as an opportunity for productive interracial collaboration. Because the racial playing field is not (and has never been) level, *Porgy and Bess* can easily be seen as an example of white profiteers engaging in the degrading commodification of African American culture. As music historian Ray Allen writes of the first production, "Gershwin and Heyward were about the business of transforming white fantasies of black sensuality, spirituality, and violence into a commodity that was marketable as entertainment for primarily white audiences. In spite of the fact that a stellar company of black artists, rather than a band of blackface minstrel buffoons, was recruited to breathe life into the production, the exploitative nature of the white composer/black performer could not be easily dismissed."[66] Allen raises an important point: from its creation by white artists to its profitable perpetuation of "white fantasies" about blackness, *Porgy and Bess* is inherently problematic, regardless of how it is directed and performed. The very fact that directors must try to ameliorate the work's problems by opening the door to dialogue and partnership with cast members is a reflection of its (thus far) inescapable racial baggage. Moreover, it is significant that directors must take the active role in initiating a collaborative relationship; although every successful production relies on performers' creative and personal engagement with the work and its staging, there is an innate power differential between directors and casts, which in the case of *Porgy and Bess* has almost always been compounded by racial difference.

Nonetheless, the history of *Porgy and Bess* is not simply one of white victimizers and black victims. African Americans have actively engaged with the work from the beginning: helping to create and shape it in a variety of ways, taking roles or refusing them, and deepening American society's understanding of its various meanings through analysis, criticism, and commentary. Most fundamentally, *Porgy and Bess* relies on African American performers to accept, inhabit, and essentially complete the work. This completion was begun in direct collaboration with George Gershwin, and continues today.

Notes

I gratefully acknowledge Geoffrey Block, Larry Starr, and Sue Neimoyer for their feedback on drafts of this paper.

1. Pitman, "Lorraine Hansberry Deplores *Porgy.*"

2. "To attack [*Porgy and Bess*], one must see it in terms of something more than mere content. It must be criticized from the Negro point of view as the most perfect symbol of the Negro creative artist's cultural denial, degradation, exclusion, exploitation and acceptance of white paternalism." Cruse, *Crisis of the Negro Intellectual,* 103. Cruse specifically attacks Jewish Americans (such as Gershwin) for their exploitation of African American culture. Recent books that address the role of Jewish musicians as mediators of African American culture for white audiences include Melnick, *A Right to Sing the Blues;* and Most, *Making Americans.*

3. For two examples of the enthusiastic early response in the black press, see Floyd J. Calvin, "Five Broadway Spots Set New High Record for Race Performers," *New York Age,* 7 December 1935; and "*Porgy and Bess,*" *Afro-American,* December 14, 1935, national edition. On the topic of the black press's positive coverage of the cast members, see Allen and Cunningham, "Cultural Uplift and Double-Consciousness," 351–56.

4. Standifer, *"Porgy and Bess"*; James Hicks, "We Don't Need *Porgy and Bess,*" *Afro-American AFRO Magazine,* March 28, 1953. For another example, see the editor's note at the end of Golf Dornseif, "Cab Calloway Overseas," *Afro-American AFRO Magazine,* February 28, 1953.

5. Interview by the author, November 3, 2005. I am grateful to this artist, who preferred to remain anonymous, for allowing me to interview her. For more on the topic of *Porgy and Bess* as a potential dead-end for African American singers, see Oby, "Equity in Operatic Casting," 24.

6. Given the controversy over the libretto, performers publicly make this last point the least often. One of those who has been frank in her admiration for the libretto's depiction of black life, however, is Maya Angelou, who appeared as a chorus member and dancer in the Robert Breen–directed touring production in the early 1950s. She writes, "Who could deny this story? How many Black men had been crippled by the American oppression and had lost the women they loved and who loved them, because they hadn't the strength to fight? How often had the women submitted to loveless arrangements for the sake of bare survival?" *Singin' and Swingin',* 250.

7. Gershwin never publicly detailed his motivations for insisting on an African American cast. He was, of course, an admirer of many black musicians, and the amount of choral music in the opera shows that he particularly prized the sound of African American voices en masse. Additionally, he was doubtless well aware that the positive reception of DuBose and Dorothy Heyward's play *Porgy* (1927) had focused to no small degree

on the fact that it was performed by African Americans; a helpful account of that reception can be found in Allen, "An American Folk Opera?" 246–47. For more on the legal aspects and implications of the Gershwin Trust's control over performances of the opera, see Arewa, "Copyright on Catfish Row," 325–28.

8. A clear example of the ease with which a critic can attribute dissatisfaction with a particular production to the composer's flaws may be found in Porter, "Musical Events." Porter notes that a performance of *Porgy and Bess* at Indiana University had prompted him to write five years earlier that "the more of the score that is done the better," but the Metropolitan Opera production in 1985 led him to conclude that much of the material Gershwin wrote to connect the songs was "feeble."

9. Charles Staff, "Jessye Choir Has Long *Porgy* Experience," *Indianapolis News,* December 29, 1966.

10. Duncan, "Todd Duncan," 221–22.

11. As an example of a critic finding Porgy's posture degrading, see Thompson, "Why Negroes Don't Like *Porgy and Bess*": "We do not want to see six-foot Sidney Poitier on his knees crying for a slit-skirted wench who did him wrong" (54).

12. Brown, "Anne Brown," 229.

13. Recalled Duncan, "I had heard about the new Gershwin opera *Porgy* but had no interest in it at all. My training had been strictly classical and I simply had no interest in any show business stuff." "Todd Duncan," 221.

14. Although Gershwin formed his habit of shaping his music to suit performers on Tin Pan Alley and Broadway, it is worth noting that opera composers had long done the same for singers. The collaborative aspect of *Porgy and Bess*'s genesis is one of several little-noted ways in which it adheres to operatic tradition.

15. Ibid., 224; Brown, "Anne Brown," 231; P. G., "The Unsinkable *Porgy and Bess:* Years Fail to Destroy Its Appeal," *New Pittsburgh Courier,* July 24, 1965.

16. Brown, "Anne Brown," 230.

17. Melnick, *A Right to Sing the Blues,* 49–50. The joke to which Melnick refers is a bit by comedian Phil Silvers, in which Jerome Kern has to teach Paul Robeson to understand and sing "Ol' Man River" properly. In his book, Melnick casts Gershwin as one of several Jewish popular songwriters who advanced in American society and profited professionally by deliberately exploiting African Americans and encroaching on their cultural territory. A compelling response to Melnick's condemnatory perspective can be found in Gottlieb, *Funny, It Doesn't Sound Jewish,* 193–97.

18. The widespread perception in the 1920s and '30s that southern, rural black culture was black culture at its "purest" and most authentic is a recurring theme in Noonan, "*Porgy and Bess* and the American Racial Imaginary."

19. For an example of a critic who praises the performers by denying that they seem to be performing at all, see Peggy Doyle, "*Porgy and Bess* Show in Triumphant Opening," *Boston Evening American,* August 21, 1954. She writes, "These are not actors or singers or actor-singers but actual Catfish dwellers who clam up when the white detective quizzes them about the murder of Robbins." This kind of comment is not uncommon in reviews of *Porgy and Bess,* particularly in the 1950s. While one assumes that the writer is consciously exaggerating for effect, it is noteworthy that similar statements do not appear in reviews of, say, *Oklahoma!*

20. Brown, "Anne Brown," 232. Brown's recollected dialogue leads one to wonder if she may be partially responsible for the opera's formidable demands on singers.

21. Robert Kimball, program notes for Glyndebourne production (1986). Buck played the small role of Mingo.

22. Heyward, "*Porgy and Bess* Return on Wings of Song," 105; George Gershwin, "Rhapsody in Catfish Row," *New York Times,* October 20, 1935, in *George Gershwin in His Time,* ed. Suriano, 112–14, also in *Gershwin Reader,* ed. Wyatt and Johnson, 217–21.

23. Allen and Cunningham's "Culture Uplift and Double-Consciousness" provides a nuanced analysis of the black reception of the Theatre Guild production.

24. Ager, "George Gershwin Thinks You Can Write Opera."

25. There are numerous examples; two particularly clear ones are Elinor Hughes, "A Play Becomes an Opera and the Beholder Wonders," *Boston Herald,* October 6, 1935; and Leonard Liebling, "Gershwin's Music Enthralls Hearers at *Porgy and Bess,*" *New York American,* October 12, 1935.

26. The story of Smallens and Bubbles appears in Kimball, Glyndebourne program notes; a slightly different version can be found in Alpert, *Life and Times of "Porgy and Bess,"* 104–5. Brown's recollection is from "Anne Brown," 235–36.

27. Pollack provides a useful overview of these reminiscences in *George Gershwin,* 595–600.

28. Armitage, *George Gershwin,* 130–31, 133.

29. Irving Barnes (who played Porgy in the 1950s Breen production) was the first African American to direct *Porgy and Bess.* See Dan Morgan, "A Serbian 'Porgy and Bess,'" *Washington Post,* December 13, 1971. Anne Brown and Felicia Weathers also directed the opera in Europe. Since 1995 several African Americans have directed the work in the United States, including Hope Clarke, Tazewell Thompson, Elizabeth Graham, Henry Miller, and Walter Dallas. The production directed by Hope Clarke will be addressed later in the essay.

30. Alpert explains the film's disappearance: "Instead of an outright sale, Goldwyn had bought a fifteen-year lease of the rights. After that time lapse, the film could not be shown without permission of the authors or their estates and, even if permission were given, would have required an additional payment." *Life and Times of "Porgy and Bess,"* 280. Johnson reports that "the film was withdrawn from circulation of any kind in 1987." "Gershwin's 'American Folk Opera,'" 630. To view it today requires a trip to the Library of Congress or a willingness to purchase a bootleg copy on eBay.

31. Poitier later acknowledged that he took part because "there was a threat of my career stopping dead still" if he did not. Joan Barthel, "He Doesn't Want to Be Sexless Sidney," *New York Times,* August 6, 1967. Poitier writes about his experiences with the film in his autobiography, *This Life,* 220–24.

32. Warfield with Miller, *My Music and My Life,* 125–26; Lawrence F. LaMar, "Leigh Whipper Quits *Porgy;* Press Confab Labelled 'Dud,'" *New York Amsterdam News,* August 16, 1958; "Eliminate Dialect in *Porgy,*" *Los Angeles Herald Express,* September 3, 1958.

33. Justin Gilbert, "*Porgy and Bess* Is 21K Gold-wyn," *New York Mirror,* June 25, 1959.

34. Paul V. Beckley, "New Movie by Paul V. Beckley: *Porgy and Bess,*" *New York Herald Tribune,* June 25, 1959.

35. Hatch, "Films."

36. Samuel Goldwyn had expected the film of *Porgy and Bess* to be among his most significant legacies as a producer. He had long admired Gershwin and his opera, and the success he and director Preminger had scored in 1954 with *Carmen Jones,* another prestigious musical with an African American cast including Pearl Bailey and Dorothy Dandridge (the first black woman to be nominated for an Academy Award for Best Actress), seemed to bode well for *Porgy. Carmen Jones* is discussed in Melinda Boyd's essay in the current volume. For more on Goldwyn's expectations for *Porgy and Bess,* see Berg, *Goldwyn: A Biography;* Wainwright, "One-Man Gang"; and Kauffmann, "Two Preminger Premieres."

37. Robert Berkvist, "The Man Who Brought New Life to *Porgy,*" *New York Times,* October 24, 1976.

38. The first production to trim the work of its recitative was producer Cheryl Crawford's revival of 1941–45. That production's enormous critical and box office success doubtless encouraged subsequent directors to follow suit.

39. Goldman is quoted in Alpert, *Life and Times of "Porgy and Bess,"* 305. Dale's comment is from Howard Kissel, "Broadway Black Theater: Goodnatured Politics," *Women's Wear Daily,* August 30, 1976.

40. For examples of Dale's centrality in the press coverage of this production, see Anna Quindlen, "Clamma Dale: The Mouth That Roars," *New York Post,* September 25, 1976; and Mel Gussow, "Clamma Dale Sings Way to Top," *New York Times,* September 29, 1976.

41. Clamma Dale was clearly the most powerful cast member; the production seems to have focused on Bess, and due to Dale's strong personality and charisma she received by far the most media exposure. All the same, the other cast members did not consider themselves less integral to the production. Said Robert Mosley, who played Porgy in some performances, "The secret of this production is that everybody depends on everybody else. We had our problems with Bess in New York, but we got things back together onstage by working things out offstage. This isn't a case, as so many operas or musicals, of just one person in his own little bag doing his own thing." Thomas Willis, "The Black Experience Takes Rich Root in a Hit *Porgy and Bess,*" *Chicago Tribune,* April 10, 1977.

42. Standifer, *"Porgy and Bess."*

43. Ibid.

44. Joseph C. Koennen, "A Grand Entrance for *Porgy and Bess,*" *Newsday,* February 3, 1985.

45. Nan Robertson, "Populating Catfish Row on the Met Opera Stage," *New York Times,* February 5, 1985.

46. Additional evidence of Bumbry's ongoing ambivalence can be found in a televised interview in February 1985, where she claims that the story of *Porgy and Bess* is acceptable insofar as it is a relic of the past and that the Met will do a fine job as they always do (*Channel 4 Today in New York,* transcript from February 8, 1985, Teleclips, Luce Press Clippings, Television News Transcripts).

47. Barton Wimble, "Counterpunch: This Bess, She Ain't My Woman," *New York News,* March 8, 1985, New Jersey edition; Robert Croan, "*Porgy and Bess* Finally Makes It to Met," *Pittsburgh Post-Gazette,* February 14, 1985.

48. Innaurato, "Grace Ann Under Pressure," 45. Bumbry's comments about what kind of music she was expected to sing resonate strikingly with those of Anne Brown, quoted earlier.

49. Koennen, "Grand Entrance for *Porgy and Bess.*"

50. Standifer, "*Porgy and Bess.*"

51. Ibid.

52. Ibid.; Anthony Lewis, "The Music of Life," *New York Times,* August 19, 1986.

53. Nicholas Kenyon, "Summertime Blues," *London Observer,* July 13, 1986; Loppert, "*Porgy and Bess,* August 6," 25.

54. Melinda Bargreen, "Her Version/Vision: First African-American to Stage *Porgy and Bess* Gives It a Different Spin," *Seattle Times,* March 12, 1995.

55. According to David Gockley, the general director of Houston Grand Opera, "From the beginning, 'Porgy and Bess' has been a piece about black people that involved white authors, directors and producers. . . . I was very interested to see a production placed in the hands of a black director." Kenneth Herman, "Performing Arts: *Porgy* Gets a Cultural Makeover," *Los Angeles Times,* March 5, 1995.

56. Story, "Hope Clarke," 14.

57. Since the libretto does not call for Porgy to beg onstage, presumably his exchange of the carvings for money would have been implied.

58. See Charles Ward, "Authentic Touches: Black *Porgy* Director Hones Portrayal of Catfish Row," *Houston Chronicle,* January 22, 1995; R. M. Campbell, "Seattle Shares in a New *Porgy and Bess,*" *Seattle Post-Intelligencer,* March 10, 1995.

59. Morris, "Hope Clarke"; Herman, "*Porgy* Gets a Cultural Makeover."

60. "I shall never forget the night when, at a Negro meeting on a remote sea-island, George started 'shouting' with them. And eventually to their huge delight stole the show from their champion 'shouter.' I think that he is probably the only white man in America who could have done it." Heyward, "*Porgy and Bess* Return on Wings of Song," 105.

61. Campbell, "Seattle Shares in a New *Porgy and Bess.*"

62. Morris, "Hope Clarke," 53.

63. Bargreen, "Her Version/Vision."

64. According to critic Martin Bernheimer, "The score . . . is presented virtually uncut," so the musical theater aspect of the production was apparently more a matter of emphasis and tone than of actual editing of the score. "It Ain't Necessarily Show," *Los Angeles Times,* June 9, 1995.

65. The *Houston Chronicle*'s reviewer reported that the performers "looked at home and portrayed their roles with complete authenticity." Charles Ward, "*Porgy and Bess:* HGO's Third Try Has Measure of Charm," *Houston Chronicle,* January 30, 1995. In spite of generally positive reviews, the production did not please David Gockley, who brought in director Tazewell Thompson to do some midtour "tweaking." See Lewis Segal, "It's Summertime, and the Staging Ain't Easy," *Los Angeles Times,* June 1, 1995.

66. Allen, "An American Folk Opera?" 255.

Bibliography

Ager, Cecelia. "George Gershwin Thinks You Can Write Opera and Make It Tuneful." *Variety,* October 16, 1935.

Allen, Ray. "An American Folk Opera? Triangulating Folkness, Blackness, and Americaness in Gershwin and Heyward's *Porgy and Bess.*" *Journal of American Folklore* 117 (2004): 243–61.

Allen, Ray, and George P. Cunningham. "Cultural Uplift and Double-Consciousness: African American Responses to the 1935 Opera *Porgy and Bess.*" *Musical Quarterly* 88, no. 3 (2005): 342–69.

Alpert, Hollis. *The Life and Times of "Porgy and Bess": The Story of an American Classic.* New York: Alfred A. Knopf, 1999.

Angelou, Maya. *Singin' and Swingin' and Gettin' Merry Like Christmas.* New York: Random House, 1976.

Arewa, Olufunmilayo B. "Copyright on Catfish Row: Musical Borrowing, *Porgy and Bess,* and Unfair Use." *Rutgers Law Journal* 37, no. 2 (2006): 277–354.

Armitage, Merle. *George Gershwin: Man and Legend.* New York: Duell, Sloan, and Pearce, 1958.

Berg, A. Scott. *Goldwyn: A Biography.* New York: Alfred A. Knopf, 1989.

Brown, Anne. "Anne Brown: From an Interview by Robert Wyatt (1995)." In *The George Gershwin Reader,* ed. Robert Wyatt and John Andrew Johnson. New York: Oxford University Press, 2004.

Cruse, Harold. *The Crisis of the Negro Intellectual.* New York: Morrow, 1967.

Duncan, Todd. "Todd Duncan: From an Interview by Robert Wyatt (1990)." In *The George Gershwin Reader,* ed. Robert Wyatt and John Andrew Johnson. New York: Oxford University Press, 2004.

Gottlieb, Jack. *Funny, It Doesn't Sound Jewish: How Yiddish Songs and Synagogue Melodies Influenced Tin Pan Alley, Broadway, and Hollywood.* Albany: State University of New York Press, 2004.

Hatch, Robert. "Films." *Nation,* July 4, 1959, 19.

Heyward, DuBose. "*Porgy and Bess* Return on Wings of Song." In *Gershwin in His Time,* ed. Gregory R. Suriano. New York: Gramercy Books, 1998. Originally published in *Stage* (October 1935).

Innaurato, Albert. "Grace Ann under Pressure." *Opera News,* March 2001.

Johnson, John Andrew. "Gershwin's 'American Folk Opera': The Genesis, Style, and Reputation of *Porgy and Bess* (1935)." Ph.D. diss., Harvard University, 1996.

Kauffmann, Stanley. "Two Preminger Premieres." *New Republic,* July 13, 1959, 22–23.

Loppert, Max. "*Porgy and Bess,* August 6." *Opera* (Autumn 1987).

Melnick, Jeffrey. *A Right to Sing the Blues: African Americans, Jews, and American Popular Song.* Cambridge: Harvard University Press, 1999.

Morris, Rebecca. "Hope Clarke." *American Theatre* (December 1994): 53–54.

Most, Andrea. *Making Americans: Jews and the Broadway Musical.* Cambridge: Harvard University Press, 2004.

Noonan, Marie Ellen. "*Porgy and Bess* and the American Racial Imaginary." Ph.D. diss., New York University, 2002.

Oby, Jason. "Equity in Operatic Casting as Perceived by African American Male Singers." Ph.D. diss., Florida State University School of Music, 1996.

Pitman, Jack. "Lorraine Hansberry Deplores *Porgy.*" *Variety,* May 27, 1959.

Poitier, Sidney. *This Life.* New York: Alfred A. Knopf, 1980.

Pollack, Howard. *George Gershwin: His Life and Work.* Berkeley and Los Angeles: University of California Press, 2006.

Porter, Andrew. "Musical Events: A Long Pull to Get There." *New Yorker,* February 25, 1985.

Standifer, James A., prod. *"Porgy and Bess": An American Voice.* Films for the Humanities and Sciences, 1999.

Story, Rosalyn M. "Hope Clarke, the First African-American to Direct Gershwin's Masterpiece, Casts the Work in a New Light for Houston Grand Opera." *Opera News,* January 21, 1995.

Suriano, Gregory R., ed. *Gershwin in His Time.* New York: Gramercy Books, 1998.

Thompson, Era Bell. "Why Negroes Don't Like *Porgy and Bess.*" *Ebony,* October 1959.

Wainwright, Loudon. "The One-Man Gang Is in Action Again." *Life,* February 16, 1959, 102–16.

Warfield, William, with Alton Miller. *My Music and My Life.* Champaign, Ill.: Sagamore, 1991.

Wyatt, Robert, and John Andrew Johnson, eds. *The George Gershwin Reader.* New York: Oxford University Press, 2004.

9

Searching for "Authenticity" in Paul Bowles's *Denmark Vesey*

MELISSA J. DE GRAAF

In January 1938, Juanita Hall conducted the Negro Melody Singers in an unstaged performance of the first act of *Denmark Vesey* for the New York Composers' Forum. The performance, featuring music by Paul Bowles set to a libretto by Charles Henri Ford, provoked thoughtful and pointed questions from listeners. The work—never completed—was based on the dramatic true story of a slave who purchased his freedom with lottery winnings and organized a violent slave uprising in 1822 against the residents of Charleston, South Carolina. The insurrection was unsuccessful; authorities tried and executed thirty-six leaders and participants, including Vesey and his coconspirator, the African "conjurer" Gullah Jack.

Despite common elements with other "race operas" such as stereotypes of gambling, superstition, voudon, and folk magic, *Denmark Vesey*'s incorporation of racial politics and Marxist allusions was unique, and in some ways superseded all other elements of the work.[1] In the incomplete and unstaged Composers' Forum performance, however, much of this would have been lost. Instead, audiences would most likely have been drawn to the language and music, which overwhelmingly emphasize Africanisms and African American folklore, much of it thoroughly researched and, in the white creators' minds, authentic.

The transcripts from this event, which was part of a series of concerts emphasizing composer-audience dialogue held under the auspices of the Federal Music Project, provide valuable insight into its artistic collaborators' representations of "blackness" and their perception by the public. While the greater part of the opera has been lost, the libretto and recordings of three songs ("You Can't Trust in Love," "You're Right the Day Ain't Mine," and "Think of All the Hairdressing") have survived.[2] These materials, considered in conjunction with the transcripts and other documents at the Harry Ransom Humanities Research Center at the

University of Texas at Austin (including correspondence and copious notes) broaden our context for representations of race in the musical culture of the 1930s generally, while also exposing Bowles's specifically political approach to race in the context of a work that Virgil Thomson once called one of the three best unperformed American operas.

Character and Plot Synopsis

The main characters in the opera are Denmark Vesey, the "conjuror" Gullah Jack, and Clarabelle, Denmark's love interest. The characters in the chorus also play prominent roles throughout. At the beginning of the libretto, Ford describes the main characters in detail: Denmark is "a strong handsome man of 33 . . . Great personal magnetism, strong passion as well as a domineering temper. Intelligent, understands his race—their fervor, faith and superstition." Gullah Jack, the "voodoo man," is "artful, cruel, cunning, and diabolical." The description of Clarabelle is rather one-dimensional: "a beautiful mulatto girl." The chorus members first appear as Rabbit, Bear, Wolf, Fox, Cow, Possum, and Mule, sometimes with masks on, sometimes without. In act 1, scene 2, they have transformed into Peter Owl, Crow, Goose, Mockingbird, Hummingbird, Woodpecker, and Buzzard. In act 2, they appear as a congregation in a revival meeting tent, and in act 3 they dress as buzzards.

The opera opens with Denmark counting his newly won lottery money, his back to the audience. The chorus enters wearing animal masks, forms a semicircle behind him, and warns him that his ill-begotten gains will bring him nothing but trouble. He seems to have won them over when Gullah Jack enters the scene and calls on Samunga, a being associated with the gathering of mud for the creation of "tricks," or amulets. He instructs Denmark in the making of an amulet to ward off evil. As Denmark recites a Bible verse backward (traditionally done to prevent ghosts from entering one's house), Gullah Jack calls out the names of various "conjure" roots, perhaps in the process of making the amulet.[3] Jack leads the chorus in the call-and-response words of an African Calinda dance, then disappears.[4] The chorus attempts to convince Denmark to use his winnings to buy Clarabelle fancy things, but Denmark is resolute: he will buy his freedom. Clarabelle enters and overhears him, and they argue. She exits, and he follows her, sadly counting his money.

In act 1, scene 2, Denmark has purchased his freedom and is working in his shoe shop. The chorus appears in bird masks. They all complain about their lot in life, voicing impatience: "Oh, tell me how long do I have to wait?" (1.2.13).[5] Denmark encourages them instead to believe in their strength and that they deserve better. Fearful, they call instead on their faith in Jesus, but Denmark mocks them and returns to his work. Buzzard enters, dressed as a preacher, encouraging the chorus. Owl changes his tune, saying he is going to kill somebody someday and have his say. Denmark responds by putting his hand on Owl's shoulder and singing, "If everybody felt like you we might get done a thing or two" (1.2.16). Clarabelle, disguised as Sis' Goose, warns them all to stop complaining and voices her contentment with the status quo. Denmark pulls off her mask, she exits, and the chorus comments on her status as a house slave, who won't have "nothin' to do with us field hands" (1.2.17). Denmark, feeling betrayed, sings "You Can't Trust in Love" and throws the goose mask offstage. They all sing about hate, wanting to know what they can do. All but Owl and Denmark exit; they reiterate their hatred of whites and make plans for inciting rebellion. Woodpecker, Hummingbird, and Mockingbird reenter without their masks and tell Denmark of their plan to go back to Africa and start a community of freed slaves. Denmark tells them to come to the revival on Sunday, where he plans to convince them all to revolt with him.

Act 2 begins in a revival meeting tent, the Preacher's words interspersed with responses from the congregation. Sister, recently arrived from Africa, chants an African phrase long associated with insurrection ("Eh! Eh! Bomba, honc, honc!"), which is answered with another one by Gullah Jack. Sister's beliefs and the congregation's come into conflict, and they finally force her into the baptismal font. Denmark enters and goes to the pulpit, where he rouses them with a speech about a Promised Land here on earth. To achieve it, they need to "do like the Hebrews, fight for your race . . . rise and destroy, kill your oppressors, young face and old face, man, woman, girl, and boy!" (2.1.6). Peter Owl warns them to trust only the field slaves—that house slaves like Clarabelle will betray them. The chorus is convinced, but Sassy Singer—Clarabelle, again in disguise—voices concern. Denmark refers to the successful slave uprising in San Domingo, or Haiti, to further encourage them. Gullah Jack enters, selling his tricks and amulets, and Denmark convinces the congregation that they can count on Jack to protect them with his "hoo-doo information" when the time comes to fight. Sassy Singer–Clarabelle continues to voice skepticism but panics and runs out when Gullah Jack throws one of his necklaces around her neck. They begin to plan the uprising in more detail, and Denmark declares they will kill all the whites they encounter. Gunshots are heard offstage, the Preacher runs in, no longer in his Buzzard costume, Gullah Jack disappears under a flap of the tent, and the curtain comes down as the congregation sings "Steal Away to Jesus."[6]

Sassy Singer–Clarabelle and the chorus begin act 3, singing of the curse Gullah Jack has placed on her. Clarabelle describes in detail how she has been "hoodooed" and vows to get revenge on Jack by betraying him to the white authorities. Jessie Hawk, the blacksmith working on all their weapons, meets up with Peter Owl, and they discuss their progress. Denmark enters with his followers, studying the growing list of rebels and anticipating the day that soon will come. Denmark reaffirms that Gullah Jack's charms will protect them. Sassy Singer reenters, warning them all to scatter, as Gullah Jack has been arrested. They plan to meet the following night to free him. The chorus exits, and Denmark and Clarabelle share a sweet duet declaring their love, until she confesses she turned Jack in, to free herself from his curse. Denmark, furious, grabs her by the throat, demanding she tell him everything. The scene shifts to Gullah Jack's interrogation, where he avoids answering their questions about the planned uprising. It is unclear by the end of the scene whether Jack has decided to confess. A brief third scene returns to Clarabelle and Denmark in a passionate embrace. Denmark pulls away, holding a bloody dagger. As Clarabelle collapses, he gathers her body in his arms and exits.

In act 3, scene 4, Denmark questions whether he is strong enough to lead his people without the help of Gullah Jack. Jessie Hawk brings news that Peter Owl has gone to the authorities. They decide to act that night, but then are surprised to hear Gullah Jack's voice from offstage. Jack enters and doles out all manner of "tricks" and amulets and tells them of the "signs" he has seen, confirming that tonight's the night. He swears he did not give them up to the whites. Denmark instructs the chorus to ride through the streets and cut down "white skins, black skins too—if they try to stop you," and then to burn down the city on their way to the arsenal: "Let fire, let blood, run wild!" (3.4.15). A brief fifth scene shows Peter Owl in jail being questioned and tortured. He does not break.

Act 3, scene 6, takes place in the arsenal, which has been captured by Denmark and his followers. Jessie Hawk is immediately shot and staggers from an upstage window, singing one last song before dying. The chorus enters as buzzards, singing off-key. They pick up Jessie Hawk's body and exit singing. The insurgents continue to fight, despite news of white reinforcements. Gullah Jack is heard singing the African "insurrection" chant again, but more violently. Denmark learns that Peter Owl, far from betraying them, is shooting at the whites from a window in the jailhouse. Denmark vows to rescue him. A group of bloody fighters enters, sadly singing the song "Stan,' Boys, Stan.'"[7] Denmark forces his way through them, running out. Shots are heard. The chorus of buzzards enters, carrying Denmark's body. Gunshots grow louder and nearer, and flames appear in the arsenal windows. The fighters sing "The Day Will Come," first heard in act 3, scene 1, as they form a close circle around Denmark's body. The buzzards circle around them and spread their wings until the fighters are completely hidden, and the arsenal goes up in flames as the curtain comes down.

Reactions to the 1938 performance of the first act are recorded in the transcripts of the Composers' Forum. Though it is impossible to determine the race of these listeners, since questions were submitted anonymously, the audience at this Forum session would most likely have been composed mainly of liberal or left-wing whites. In general, audience members criticized Bowles for what they considered unflattering portrayals of Denmark, Gullah Jack, and the other black characters and condemned what they perceived as misrepresentations of black life; in the words of one respondent, "The music and text of the opera are not intelligent or educationally helpful to the Negro race." Another listener wondered at the lack of "the beautiful melodies that are so characteristic [of] early Negro life." The harshest critic stated: "Do you not feel that if composers would stop considering the Negro as an amusing 'it' with queer, incomprehensive traits, they would find in him a subject more inspiring than you have pictured?" (Bowles's somewhat defensive reply: "I do not consider the Negro a mere incomprehensible 'it' at all. I think the question could apply to someone else, not to me.")[8]

Such criticisms are consistent with the commentary typically found in the black musical press in regard to operas that incorporated aspects of African American culture and music. Black critics' ire had flared when confronted with works such as Louis Gruenberg's *Emperor Jones* (1933) and George Gershwin's *Porgy and Bess* (1935). Gruenberg based *The Emperor Jones* on Eugene O'Neill's eponymous play from 1920. At the premiere, white performers in blackface portrayed both Jones, an ex-Pullman porter who declares himself emperor of a West Indian island, and the natives whose beliefs in superstitions he exploits. While the *New York Times* hailed Gruenberg's music as a "sheer emanation . . . of the glimmerings, the shadows, the hallucinations and the strength of the jungle,"[9] it was precisely these exotic elements that had been censured by black critics: "The play is a reflection upon colored people and tends to show the Negro as a degraded people, unfit to govern, incapable of successful competition with the whites."[10]

The denunciation of racial and musical stereotypes reached a critical point with the production of Gershwin's *Porgy and Bess* in 1935. Black critics had already questioned the prominence of beggars, gamblers, dope peddlers, and murderers in Dubose Heyward's *Porgy* eight years earlier,[11] and black critics of the opera decried the stereotypes of gambling and superstition as an updated form of minstrelsy. Hall Johnson, noted composer, conductor, and violist, criticized the depictions of black characters and argued that Gershwin's score lacked an "authentic Negro musical language."[12] Other African American musicians and critics seconded Johnson's views. Duke Ellington wrote, "The times are here to debunk Gershwin's lampblack Negroisms," complaining that "the music does not hitch with the mood and spirit of the story. It does not use the Negro musical idiom," while Ralph Matthews, music critic for the *Afro-American*, agreed that "it most certainly isn't Negro." The music had none of "the deep-sonorous incantations so frequently identified with racial offerings. The singing, even down to the choral and the ensemble numbers, has a conservatory twang. Superimposed on the shoddiness of Catfish Row they seem miscast."[13]

Ford and Bowles's use of African and African American folklore and imagery thus reflects a broader cultural attraction to exoticism at the time, particularly among whites. In the wake of World War I, folk culture in general, and African American culture in particular, seized the imaginations of artists, writers, and musicians on both sides of the Atlantic. New York society abandoned Greenwich Village and turned to Harlem for entertainment, reveling in the heady mixture of bootleg alcohol and exotic spectacle. Black revues appeared throughout the 1920s containing "the same recycled elements—plantation settings, giant watermelons, cotton pickers, and Zulus" as old minstrel stereotypes.[14] In Europe, particularly in Paris, fascination with the primitive manifested itself in connections between African sculpture and cubism, as well as the French obsession with jazz. European visitors to New York flocked to Harlem "eager to mingle with—or at least witness—the exotic world they had constructed in their imaginations."[15] Even some members of the black community viewed the emphasis on African American exoticism as a healthy alternative to commercialization. Alain Locke, prominent leader of the Harlem Renaissance, praised the roots of popular jazz, proclaiming, "There is a vast difference between [jazz's] first healthy and earthy expression in the original peasant paganism out of which it arose and its hectic, artificial and sometimes morally vicious counterpart which was the outcome of the vogue of artificial and commercialized jazz entertainment. The one is primitively erotic; the other, decadently neurotic."[16]

It is small wonder, then, that Bowles and Ford should have been swept along in this tide of the exotic and primitive, expressed for them most prominently in the character of Gullah Jack. The others refer to him and talk about his supernatural abilities, but he does not have a terribly active role in the opera. He throws a necklace around Clarabelle–Sassy Singer's neck, which "hoodoos" her, and passes out all manner of protective amulets to the insurgents. The greater part of his involvement consists of incantations. In short, Jack functions more as an embodiment of African and African American superstitions than a fully developed character, reflecting the sort of primitivist stereotypes about blacks that were already widespread throughout popular culture.

Authenticity in Text, Image, and Music

Gullah Jack notwithstanding, Ford took great pains to emphasize what he believed to be "authentic" representations of blackness in the libretto for *Denmark Vesey*—perhaps because he was aware of the critiques surrounding *Porgy and Bess*. The opera is replete with rhymes, stories, and superstitions, almost all of which can be found in Ford's notes. His handwritten notebook contains copious quotes from a variety of sources, including Benjamin Brawley's *Social History of the American Negro* (1921), W. E. B. Du Bois's *Souls of Black Folk* (1903), Thomas W. Talley's

Negro Folk Rhymes (1922), Martha Young's *Plantation Bird Legends* (1902), and Dorothy Scarborough's *On the Trail of Negro Folk-Songs* (1925).[17]

Most extensive in the libretto are examples from Newbell Niles Puckett's *Folk Beliefs of the Southern Negro* (1926), still regarded as an authoritative source for hoodoo and conjure practices of the American South. Ford includes sixteen examples and references from this source in the first act alone.[18] Some of the most striking are the "African incantations," sung by Gullah Jack and echoed by the chorus, which are prevalent in Ford's notes and in the libretto. These include Gullah Jack's invocation to Samunga from the first act ("Minnie, no, no Samunga / Sangse see sa soh Samunga"), which is quickly followed by a call-and-response between Jack and the chorus:

JACK: Higha!
CHORUS: Malagalujasay!
JACK: Higha!
CHORUS: Lajasay chumba, Um! Um! Um!
JACK: Higha!
CHORUS: Haykeekeedayo, ho! (1.16)

Puckett identifies this text as belonging to a Calinda dance, danced by men and women in a circle accompanied by a barrel drum, a clear vestige of African practice.[19]

One incantation, spoken at times by Gullah Jack, at times by the newly arrived Sister from Africa, is of particular interest:

Eh! Eh! Bomba honc, honc
Canga bafio tay
Canga moon day lay,
Canga do kcc lah,
Canga li!

First identified in 1804 as a "vaudoux" chant used by insurgents in the Haitian revolution, the text was reprinted numerous times. The language of the chant has recently been identified as Kikongo, spoken widely in the western Congo basin. It was not accurately translated until the early 1990s:

Oh! Mbumba, oh!
Render harmless the blacks
Render harmless the European
Render harmless the witch[es]
Render them harmless.[20]

Although untranslated for nearly two hundred years, it carried subversive and violent associations.[21] For Gustave d'Alaux, writing in 1856, it signified the subversive violence that eventually overturned slavery in Haiti. During the U.S. occupation of Haiti between 1915 and 1934, the chant became a recurring theme in the numerous travel books on Haiti, retaining its violent connotations.[22] In 1938, C. L. R. James published a widely circulated mistranslation of the chant: "We swear to destroy the whites and all they possess . . .," which reflected and strengthened its associations with violence.[23]

The associations with race hatred and insurrection were undoubtedly what led Ford to include this text in the opera. For Bowles and Ford, the main theme of the opera—Love versus Hate—had deep political and racial implications. Throughout the work, love is equated with betrayal, and hate (particularly the hatred of whites) with strength and freedom. Denmark refers to hate as a spreading disease, which eventually would ensure the liberty of all blacks: "Hate is the door we'll all go through!" (1.2.21). Denmark and Gullah Jack's hatred of whites is plain to see. Denmark stresses several times the need to kill *all* the white folks in the town, including the children. In act 2 he declares "no use to kill the louse and leave the nit!" (2.1.14), while in act 3, he instructs the insurgents to spare no man, woman, or child (3.4.15). In his wild rage, Jack even slits the throat of a black woman who gets in his way (3.v). In the last act, the insurgents sing "The Day Will Come," calling on all those "whose hate can shed its slumber" to stand up and fight with them.[24] The turbulent relationship between Denmark and Clarabelle also conveys this love-hate duality at a more personal level. Love, personified by Clarabelle, inevitably betrays Vesey in the end; enraged by her actions, he stabs her at precisely the moment that she makes her love manifest to him in the form of a passionate kiss.

Another prominent theme was the use of animal masks. According to Bowles's program notes, the animals represent the "various temptations in Negro animal-mythology. . . . [They] sing sometimes as abstractions; at other times, with masks removed, as characters in the opera. . . . The characters, for the most part, are part of that land of the imagination which the Negro in his folk-lore has peopled, in bird and animal form, [with] his own feelings and weaknesses."[25] While Bowles's analysis was clearly not the most flattering representation, the animal characters he and Ford used had powerful and complex origins and associations.

The chorus first enters wearing masks of the traditional African American characters Br'er Rabbit, Br'er Fox, Big Boy Bear, Willie the Wolf, Mister Mule, Sis Cow, and Old Man Possum. Based on traditional African folktales and adapted by African American slaves, Br'er Rabbit is the classic trickster, deceiving his foes with tricks and clever use of language rather than brute force, in much the same way African American slaves encoded meanings in their music.[26] The other animal characters in this scene also carry positive associations in traditional African and African American cultures. The fox is cunning, a bear seen in a dream augurs happiness, a mule represents general good luck, and carrying the eye of a wolf protects a person from all injuries.[27]

While in scene 1 the animal characters merely taunt Denmark—much in the same way in which members of Yoruba tribes wear masks when playfully insulting and taunting one another—in scene 2 the narrative takes a violent turn. The chorus assumes bird masks: Peter Owl, Goose, Mockingbird, Woodpecker, Hummingbird, Crow, and Br'er Buzzard, all malevolent symbols in African and African American culture. The buzzard is a sign of death, the sight of a crow portends a funeral, the hooting of an owl can mean death, and a woodpecker drilling on the side of a house is a "sure prophecy of death."[28] In this scene, the dialogue turns to murder and death, and the use of bird masks for the chorus underscores this a dramatic narrative shift.

In some places, it is difficult to imagine what Bowles and Ford envisioned in terms of the masks. For the most part, the masked characters are simply real people disguising themselves, though there are some potentially supernatural aspects to the scenes. For instance, the figure of the buzzard held special significance for African American slaves. Katie Sutton, a former slave interviewed in the 1930s for the Slave Narrative Project, recalled, "Ole Missus and Young Missus told the little slave children that stork brought the white babies to their mothers but that the slave children were all hatched out from buzzards' eggs and we believed it was true."[29] The American-created folktale of King Buzzard depicted the African king as a symbol of bad luck, doomed to wander the world alone after betraying his people and selling them into slavery.[30]

In many ways, Ford's use of buzzards verges closer to the symbolic than the realistic. In act 1, scene 2, Buzzard "turns his bald head completely around on his scrawny pink neck" when he intones, "Old Sis Cow's dead." The language is unclear: is the character of Buzzard simply a man wearing a buzzard mask, or has he actually transformed into a buzzard, the personification of death? Similarly, at the end of the opera, Ford notes that the Buzzards convey Vesey's corpse onto the stage—clearly reaffirming the symbolic association between the buzzard and death—before spreading their wings to completely conceal the fighters from view, which once again brings their physical nature into question.

Masks also represent powerful themes of liberation and truth in the opera. Denmark encourages the other slaves to respect themselves, but unmasked Crow nervously says, "Somebody'll hear you!" and snatches his mask back from Denmark, his remasking reflecting his fear. Conversely, Owl is merely a member of the chorus until Denmark rips Owl's mask off. Unmasked, Owl boldly expresses his desires of freedom and killing those who have enslaved him. After Denmark and the chorus discuss the planned revolt, Denmark says to Owl, "Not so fast, where's your mask, be a bird, be a owl, meet me at revival Sunday" (1.2.21). Immediately following this exchange, Hummingbird, Woodpecker, and Mockingbird—without their masks on—reveal their plan to move to Africa and create a community there. The only character not affected by the presence of a mask is Clarabelle. She expresses contempt with Denmark's behavior with and without a mask, then storms out when Denmark reveals her true identity. Her disdainful attitude is so embedded in her character that it is unaffected by the mask.

Ironically, despite Ford's painstaking research and incorporation of numerous examples of folklore and symbols from authoritative sources, the very "authenticity" he tried so hard to achieve in *Denmark Vesey* would likely have played poorly among African American audiences. The "Great Migration" of 1910–30 saw more than a million rural black southerners moving into northern urban areas, bringing them into close contact with whites and more upwardly mobile, elite African Americans.[31] For middle- and upper-class blacks, racial progress required the emulation of white models of economics, education, and religion. Established northern black churches encouraged the surrendering of southern folk practices and superstitions in efforts to assimilate their southern brothers and sisters. Hoodoo practices lingered in the shadows, though white culture pointed to its superstitions as evidence of the ignorance and lack of education in black society.[32] Clearly, Ford's attempts at authenticity often drew on the very stereotypes of primitivist belief and deeply embedded race hatred toward whites that the progressive African American community deplored, even though they also were some of the most prevalent images within popular art forms created by or featuring black performers.

The surviving musical portions of the opera raise similarly complex racial questions. Ford suggested the use of traditional African American musical instruments such as drums, triangles, jawbones, and quills. (Ford would have been familiar with quills from Talley's *Negro Folk Rhymes,* which included illustrations, descriptions, and musical examples; see figures 1 and 2.)[33] Bowles

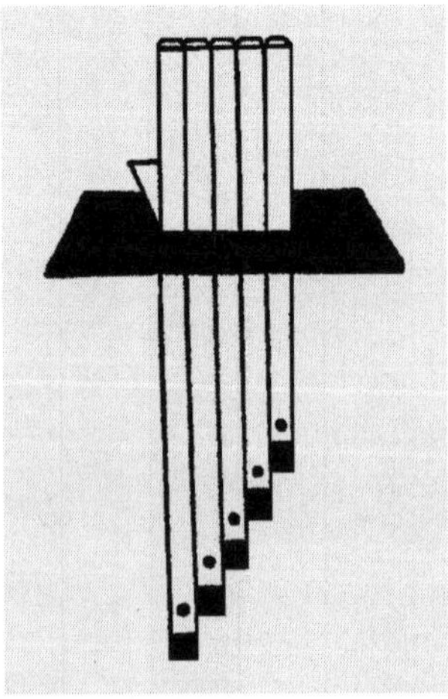

Figure 1. A little set of quills. *Source:* Thomas Washington Talley, *Negro Folk Rhymes* (New York: Macmillan, 1922), title page.

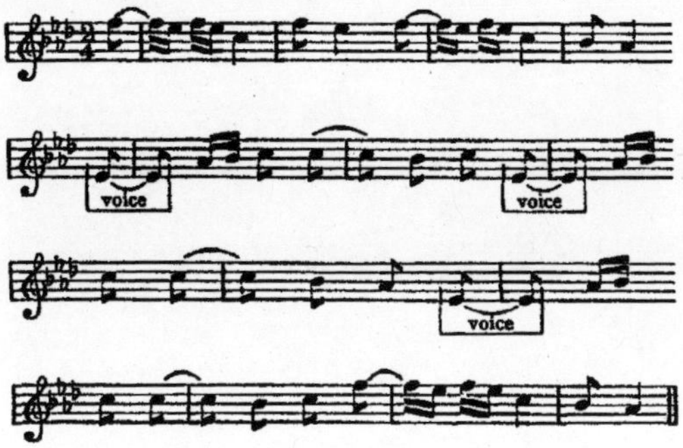

Figure 2. Tune played on a little set of quills. *Source:* Thomas Washington Talley, *Negro Folk Rhymes* (New York: Macmillan, 1922), 306.

adopted Ford's suggestions of instruments, and the Composers' Forum program lists Bowles and Virgil Thomson as percussion players—along with a pianist—accompanying Juanita Hall's Negro Melody Singers.

However, the three songs on the single extant recording are arranged for piano and voice. "You're Right the Day Ain't Mine" and "Think of All the Hairdressing" are different from "You Can't Trust in Love" in tone and character, but share its general musical style.

"You're Right the Day Ain't Mine" is a languorous, lilting melody in major mode sung by Peter Owl, evoking the laziness of a day all to oneself, and features regular phrases and generally diatonic harmonies. "Think of All the Hairdressing" is a fast-paced, humorous song in which Denmark's friends try to dissuade him from purchasing his freedom, tempting him with all the things he could buy for Clarabelle. Though more challenging melodically than "You're Right the Day Ain't Mine," the harmonies of this second tune are again mostly diatonic and in major mode, and the phrasing is regular, consisting of three four-measure sections each plus a two-measure, two-line tag at the end.

The most interesting song of the three is "You Can't Trust in Love," in no small part because it encapsulates the love-hate dichotomy at the heart of the story. Denmark sings this to the mask Clarabelle wore following her betrayal in Act I, Scene 2 (see example 1).[34] The form, melody, and harmony of the song all reflect and accentuate the text's message of distrust and instability. The lyrics perfectly illustrate this, describing love as a "leaky boat full of unexpected holes," slavery as the "ocean," and freedom as a "pond," all of which can drown a person. While the overall form is symmetrical (a four-bar introduction followed by two sixteen-measure sections), the overlapping, often irregular phrases heighten the sense of instability. Four-bar phrases are established as the norm at the opening of the piece but are quickly subverted; in measure 12, for example, the new phrase overlaps with the end of the previous phrase, creating a three-and-a-half-bar phrase plus a five-bar phrase ending in measure 20.

The melody is characterized by prominent seventh intervals, most noticeably

Example 1 (*above and opposite*). "You Can't Trust in Love" from *Denmark Vesey.* Author's transcription.

in the opening motive (a–g), which repeats at measure 9, 21, and 25. In addition, two other important points are marked by sevenths: the first verse closes with the motive in reverse (descending g to a), and the highest note of the piece (measure 30), is approached by ascending leap (g–f). The final melodic motion from f to d is the only important point in the piece lacking a melodic seventh.

Throughout the song, pitches fail to resolve in the correct registers, and most significantly, the tonic is consistently avoided. Though d minor is implied through-

out, it is not until the end that we have the first real resolution to d minor, on the words "trust in hate." However, the apparent stability of this concluding passage is belied by the presence of a major seventh in the final chord. This musical instability reflects Bowles's conception of the story's larger moral: the "failure of blacks to free their race because they were unable to see beyond race hatred."[35] Thus, Bowles, the omniscient composer, appears to possess insight about the eventual failure of the power of hate that Denmark, the protagonist, does not.

Despite their attractiveness and dramatic propriety, Bowles's musical setting of these songs effectively neutralized Ford's goal of authenticity. Though they show signs of the composer's affinity for blues and jazz, the musical language of the three songs is uninfluenced by African American folk songs or spirituals. Indeed, they seem like rather typical Broadway fare with some modern inflections evocative of Marc Blitzstein. If we assume that this stylistic approach was consistent throughout the opera, then Duke Ellington's critique about *Porgy and Bess*—that it was largely devoid of the "Negro musical idiom"—would have applied equally to *Denmark Vesey*.

Communist-Style Insurrection

The similarities between Bowles's *Denmark Vesey* and precursors such as *Porgy and Bess* and *Emperor Jones* are quite clear. All draw on stereotypes of African or African American life such as gambling, superstitions, and folk magic. Each faced intense scrutiny from black critics and audiences for their negative representations of black life as well as for the absence of "authentic" sounds and sentiments. What sets *Denmark Vesey* apart, however, is its evocation of Communist-style revolution. The opera abounds with romanticized Marxist imagery, which would have had powerful resonances in the context of race and labor conflicts in the 1930s.

Denmark and the insurgents in the opera and libretto have been idealized as loyal and courageous brothers-in-arms. Although Denmark speaks briefly several times of the need to kill the entire white population, the audience never sees this taking place. We hear about Jack's murder of a black woman, but another insurgent conveys the tale with shock and disapprobation. Rather than focusing on the intense violence or Gullah Jack's failed charms, the opera emphasizes Peter Owl's loyalty to his compatriots under torture, the fighters' unity in arms, and their courageous, desperate fight to the end.

Most significantly, Bowles and Ford created a romanticized portrait of the fallen hero. While historical events concluded with Denmark's trial and execution by hanging, the opera ends with Denmark running into open fire in a heroic attempt to save Peter Owl from prison. Denmark is shot and killed, and his comrades lift up his body as the arsenal goes up in flames. We never see the trial, the imprisonment, or the execution, all of which seem less heroic than death in battle. The artistic choices Ford and Bowles made transform the opera from a historical event into a heroic, romantic struggle for liberation. Denmark becomes a Soviet-style hero, dying dramatically for the cause.

The depiction of the fallen revolutionary hero held aloft in the arms of his fellow insurgents proliferated in left-wing art, music, and literature. Elie Siegmeister made a musical setting of the poem "Strange Funeral in Braddock," by *New Masses* editor Mike Gold, depicting the cortege of a fallen laborer, victim of the steel industry. Jacob Burck's painting *Death of a Communist* (1934) and Walter Quirt's *Future Belongs to the Workers* (1933) depict the martyrdom of a worker, fallen in the arms of his comrades. Philip Evergood created what are perhaps the most memorable expressions in this genre, with his *Mine Disaster* (1933) and the better-known *American Tragedy* (1937), in which he portrays the Memorial Day Massacre at the South Chicago plant Republic Steel on May 30, 1937.[36]

All of the left-wing portrayals of gunned-down fallen heroes in the arms of their comrades were of white victims. Bowles and Ford's representation of Denmark being carried in the arms of his fellow fighters was utterly distinctive in this respect. Interestingly, the origins of the images and words Ford uses to signify a leftist slant on the events can be found, once again, in sources of African American folklore. Ford includes a long excerpt in his notes of a mournful song sung by the insurgents right before Denmark's death:

> there's no use a-runnin,
> use a runnin.
> Look up yonder hill
> and see them soldiers comin
> soldiers comin
> see em comin.
> Bowie knife in one han,
> pistol in the other,
> stan, boys, stan,
> brother stan by brother,
> stan by brother . . . (3.4.21)

The words are from Scarborough's *On the Trail of Negro Folk-Songs*, from which Ford drew many references and examples. The description of Denmark's body carried aloft in the arms of his fellow soldiers may recall the leftist and Marxist examples mentioned above, yet Ford's specific inspiration may have come from Puckett's account of slaves carrying a fallen comrade in their arms. In his notes, Ford recorded, "In So. Carolina the children march around the father's casket singing a hymn, after which the youngest is passed first over and then under the casket and *the casket is taken out on the run upon the shoulders of two men.*"[37] He was clearly attracted to this image, quite likely for its Communist undertones.

Bowles and Ford's distinctively political conception of *Denmark Vesey* forms a striking contrast with DuBose Heyward's take on the story. His plans for an opera on the subject never materialized, but his wife, Dorothy, wrote a play based on the Vesey account called *Set My People Free*, which premiered in November 1948.[38] Heyward had contributed an essay on Vesey to *The Carolina Low-Country*, put out by the Society for the Preservation of Spirituals in 1932.[39] Heyward was intrigued by the conflict of faiths embodied in Jack, seeing in Jack's last scene a pathetic collapse of faith in African superstitions. Comparing the figures of Vesey and Gullah Jack, Heyward declared, "The one who seizes upon the imagination is not Vesey with his tremendous schemes for revenge and liberation, but Gullah Jack, who looms above the ruins of the evil-starred insurrection a tragic symbol of the failure of the old African Gods. It is not difficult to imagine him going to his death clutching to the last the charmed crab-claw which was supposed to render him invulnerable to the hostile magic of the white man."[40] Bowles and Ford's opera omits this scene, and although it preserves the sense of failure associated with Jack's conjuring abilities, the dramatic emphasis falls elsewhere, with Denmark's heroic death leaving the permanent impression.

Yet tensions and divisions between Ford and Bowles existed over the political representation of race and the implementation of the actual performances. Whereas Bowles was a member of the Communist Party, though an infrequent participant, Ford leaned toward Trotskyism. He quotes Trotsky several times in his notes for the opera, drawing upon his ideas regarding the phases of revolution and challenging authority. Ford opposed Bowles's decision to perform *Vesey* for a *New Masses* benefit concert, fearing a Stalinist trap. Bowles made no secret of his anti-Trotsky position—during a trip to Mexico while Trotsky was in exile there, Bowles allegedly brought with him fifteen thousand "Death to Trotsky" stickers to pass out.[41] Ford, for his part, objected to the apparent influence of the Communist Party in Bowles's request to include the offer of white aid. Bowles replied, "You know quite well there were whites implicated in the story. Why do you pretend to think it the party line when I innocently ask if you will include such mention?"[42]

Bowles assumed Ford had become attracted to the story in the first place because of its relevance to current race conflicts within left-wing labor organizations like the Southern Tenant Farmers' Union (STFU), Committee for Industrial Organization, and National Miners Union (NMU).[43] These unions initially strove for interracial solidarity and broad-based labor rights, but factional battles between Socialist and Communist leadership quashed such aims and created intense dissatisfaction and distrust on the part of the black members. The Southern Tenant Farmers' Union was established during the Depression in response to failed measures of the Agricultural Adjustment Administration and was one of the few unions open to African Americans, who made up a disproportionate number of sharecroppers and tenant farmers. With the moral and financial support of the Socialist Party, the STFU gained nationwide attention by organizing strikes and sending representatives to Washington. In the end, however, they achieved little to ameliorate the dire situation of tenant farmers.[44] The Committee for Industrial Organization, later renamed the Congress of Industrial Organizations, was a federation of unions that grew out of the American Federation of Labor. More militant and aggressive than the AFL, the CIO's young and radical leadership eagerly recruited African American members.[45] The National Miners Union was the only one of the three officially affiliated with the Communist Party. Established in 1928, the NMU, in accordance with Communist Party ideology, attacked white racism and actively sought black participation (although NMU leadership often appeared more concerned with party recruitment than with the plight of striking workers).[46] For a short time, however, the NMU achieved real solidarity between black and white laborers, largely through the efforts of high-ranking black leaders. The Communist Party praised the union, but criticized its failure to politicize "the struggle against

Negro oppression."[47] The logo used by the National Association for the Promotion of Labor Unionism among Negroes illustrates these early attempts at interracial solidarity (see figure 3).

As early as 1933, the Communist Party had made significant strides in establishing enclaves in the African American community. The energetic efforts of the Communist-dominated International Labor Defense on behalf of the "Scottsboro boys" helped establish the party as an increasingly significant voice in Harlem politics. In a significant move toward solidarity, Communists and leftists came together in Chicago with prominent leaders of the black community to convene the Second U.S. Congress of the League against War and Fascism in 1934. The Harlem Workers School, a Marxist study center, began offering courses and lectures, and by 1935, 15 percent of new party members were black.[48]

This intersection of the Communist Party and the African American community was reflected in artistic and literary circles. Plays like Paul Peters and George Sklar's *Stevedore* (1934) and John Wexley's *They Shall Not Die* (1934) underscored the growing determination on the part of white leftists to treat black topics with respect and seriousness.[49] The leftist journal *New Masses* welcomed poetry by Langston Hughes and Richard Wright; the latter expressed racial solidarity with whites in the workers' cause:

> I am black and I have seen black hands
> Raised in fists of revolt, side by side
> with the white fists of white workers.[50]

In his own poetry, Ford took a stand against racial oppression. His 1938 poem "Plaint: Before the Mob of 10,000 at Owensboro, Ky." voices the thoughts of a black man being lynched:

Figure 3. "Black and White Workers Unite." Logo for the National Association for the Promotion of Labor Unionism Among Negroes.

> the minutes like black cherries
> drop from my shady side.
> Oh who is the forester must tend to such a tree, Lord?
> Do angels pick the cherry-blood of folk like me, Lord?[51]

The depiction of the man as a martyr mirrors Ford's sympathetic portrayal of Vesey. In light of this poem, however, it is intriguing that Ford and Bowles removed Denmark's death from the context of lynching, thereby transforming Denmark from victim to martyr-hero.

Both the conflicts and the gradual alliance between blacks and the Left are among the elements that set up the context of *Denmark Vesey.*[52] Bowles and Ford certainly joined in the sympathy leftists felt with the racial cause. Other artists and writers depicted racial solidarity in the labor struggle, yet most failed to perceive or depict the black anger engendered by the failures of labor unions, or by the Communist Party itself. Bowles and Ford were among the few who did. In a letter to Ford, Bowles discussed the bitter refusal of white aid on the part of the insurgents: "It would make the problem, a still unsolved one, more closely related to attempts to solve it today. Which after all is one of the reasons you wrote the play, I suppose. . . . And when I say attempts to solve it today I don't mean the Communist Party; rather the questionable Southern Tenant Farmers' Union, for example, and the C.I.O., and the NMU etc."[53] They discussed the possibility of including the historically accurate offer of aid from several white men but in the end decided against it, fearing black outrage. Bowles wrote: "Of course to me it doesn't matter because the negroes this winter said they would lynch any whites who tried to put the play on. They were quite furious enough about the text without involving white aid."[54] What set apart Ford and Bowles's representations of race in *Vesey* was this reflection of the bitter conflict between the races within left-wing and union politics.

The Demise of *Vesey*

Despite Bowles's intermittent efforts on the opera and another performance for *New Masses* in 1939, he never completed the work. A letter from Bowles to Ford in August 1939 indicates that they were still in the throes of *Vesey*, comparing notes, exchanging ideas, and planning further scenes. This letter is followed by eight years of apparent silence between the two men, broken in 1947 with an excited letter from Ford stating that Lincoln Kirstein wanted to produce their opera and would probably commission its completion. This prompted Bowles's account of the loss of the manuscript in a letter to Peggy Glanville-Hicks.[55] In August 1946, the tenor Romolo de Spirito, accompanied by pianist Carrington Welch, had made a recording for Disc Records (entitled *Night without Sleep*) of a number of Bowles's songs, including three from *Denmark Vesey.* Bowles explained that de Spirito had been given the only copy of the score for this recording, and could Glanville-Hicks please "get it away from him" if she saw him.[56] When Ford sent Bowles the completed libretto in January 1948, Bowles replied, "Of course it's a wonderful scenario, but what good does it do me, when my score appears to have been completely lost by De Spirito? I can't imagine how the hell he could have lost it so easily, or why he didn't phone me to ask me to come and get it if he was going to move. . . . Anyway, I am depressed about it, because it represents two years' work, and naturally I shall never start it again." According to Jeffrey Millers, editor of the Bowles correspondence, the score was actually lost by Carrington Welch, the accompanist. Irene Herrmann, the executor of Bowles's musical estate, stated that Bowles believed de Spirito had lost the score on the IRT subway in New York.[57] The score has never been found.

Clearly, then, *Denmark Vesey* will never be part of the American operatic repertoire. Unless by some miracle the score turns up in somebody's attic or in some dusty archive, we will never know what the bulk of the music sounds like. From the libretto and three extant songs, however, we are able to see a quite different approach to race from other works of the era. While *Vesey* has many elements in common with other "race operas" of the time, including the stereotypes of gambling, superstition, and hoodoo, Bowles and Ford achieved a distinctive result in their integration of race and politics and their bridging of 1820s and 1930s race and labor turmoil. This little-known work is therefore significant in the history of American opera, a "missing link" that enriches our perception and understanding of the intersection of race, politics, and music in the 1930s.

Notes

Work on this project was completed with the support of a fellowship from the American Association of University Women and a Music Library Association Dena Epstein Award for Archival and Library Research in American Music.

1. Though often used interchangeably, the terms *vodun, vodou, voodoo,* and *hoodoo* should be distinguished from one another. *Vodun* is the original form of the religion as found in West Africa, *vodou* is the Haitian form, *voodoo* is found primarily in Louisiana, and *hoodoo*, or "conjure," is not so much a religion as the practice of folk magic, an amalgamation of African, Native American, and European folk traditions. This last practice is most prominent in *Denmark Vesey.* For more information, see Anderson, *Conjure in African American Society.*

2. Several versions of the libretto are housed in the Charles Henri Ford and Paul Bowles collections in the Harry Ransom Humanities Research Center at the University of Texas at Austin (hereafter HRHRC). The libretto to which I will refer is titled *Denmark Vesey: A Lyric Drama,* and can be found in the Paul Bowles Collection, Box

11.3, HRHRC. Three other versions of the libretto, all of different lengths, are located in the Charles Henri Ford Collection, Box 2, Folders 1 and 2, HRHRC. Both Bowles's and Ford's collections contain correspondence between the two men; Ford's also contains his diary and extensive notes for the project. The Composers' Forum transcript of January 12, 1938, can be found in the Federal Music Project Papers, Record Group 69.5.3, National Archives II, College Park, Maryland. Recordings of the three surviving songs may be found on *Night without Sleep,* disc issue #730, 1946. Romolo de Spirito, tenor; Carrington Welch, pianist. For information, see Irene Herrmann's "The Authorized Paul Bowles Website," http://www.paulbowles.org.

3. Most of these roots—which include angel's turnip, devil's shoestring, plant of peace, purpose of the earth, bowels of Christ, and shameweed—are still used today in hoodoo and folk practices. Ford borrowed this, and many other hoodoo practices, from Puckett's *Folk Beliefs of the Southern Negro.*

4. Although no stage directions indicate actions accompanying these words, Ford's source, the Puckett book, includes a detailed description of the Calinda as danced by Africans who came to Alabama after the Civil War. It is quite likely a final production of the opera would have included such a performance.

5. In text, parenthetical citations for the libretto consist of the act, scene, and page number.

6. According to Ford's notes from Talley's *Negro Folk Rhymes,* 300–301, slaves sang "Steal Away to Jesus" as a message to other slaves that a secret religious meeting was taking place that night.

7. Ford most likely picked this up from Dorothy Scarborough's collection, *On the Trail of Negro Folk-Songs,* 232.

8. Composers' Forum Transcripts, January 12, 1938.

9. For a thorough discussion of race and representation in this opera, see Metzer, "'A Wall of Darkness Dividing the World.'" Metzer does not mention the critical reception in the black press.

10. "About That Play *Emperor Jones,*" 1; Ohio Historical Society Web site, 1998, http://dbs.ohiohistory.org/africanam/page1.cfm?ItemID=1557.

11. Floyd Calvin, "Calvin Reviews *Porgy,*" *Pittsburgh Courier,* November 5, 1927, as discussed in Allen, "American Folk Opera?" 247. Another critical review in the black press was E. Johnson, "The Jewel in Ethiope's Ear," 167.

12. H. Johnson, review of *Porgy and Bess,* 25. For more detail on Johnson's opinions about what made for an authentic performance of Negro folk songs, see H. Johnson, "Notes on the Negro Spiritual." For a further discussion of the critical reception of *Porgy and Bess,* see Allen, "American Folk Opera?" 252.

13. Ellington and Matthews quoted with no citation in Alpert, *Life and Times of "Porgy and Bess,"* 121–22.

14. See Watson, *Prepare for Saints,* 201.

15. Ibid., 198. See also Kenney, *Chicago Jazz,* for an analogous example of racial tourism centered in the "Black and Tan" interracial clubs of South Chicago.

16. Locke, *Negro and His Music,* 86–90, as quoted in Walser, *Keeping Time,* 77–78.

17. Some of Ford's other identifiable sources were Boyle, "The Devil's Little Fly"; Puck-

ett, *Folk Beliefs of the Southern Negro;* Brawley, *Social History of the American Negro;* Du Bois, *Souls of Black Folk*; Pendleton, *Negro Folk-lore and Witchcraft;* and Talley, *Negro Folk Rhymes.*

18. These include, among other things, descriptions of burial practices, folk legends, and various types and preparations of charms; a few such examples from the opera that correspond to Puckett's descriptions, sometimes almost verbatim, may be found in Puckett, *Folk Beliefs of the Southern Negro,* 102, 254, 257–58, 275.

19. Ibid., 59. In act 2, scene 1, Jack and the chorus sing another chorus ("Go fay, go fay! / Ingo-ango fay!"). Though uncited in Ford's notes, Scarborough includes a version with this exact spelling in *On the Trail of Negro Folk-Songs,* 26, though she does not translate or explain the contents.

20. Geggus, "Haitian Voodoo in the Eighteenth Century: Language, Culture, and Resistance."

21. Moreau de Saint-Méry, *Description topographique, physique, civile, politique et historique,* 1:67. Moreau de Saint-Méry's version differs slightly in wording and spelling:

> Eh! Eh! Bomba, hen! Hen! Canga bafio té
> Canga moune de lé
> Canga do ki la
> Canga li.

22. Pettinger, "A Decade of Black Atlantic Studies."

23. James, *Black Jacobins,* 11.

24. Act 3, scene 6, repeated from 3.1.4.

25. Composers' Forum Program, January 12, 1938. See also Davis, *Animal Motif in Bamana Art,* 4.

26. Cartwright, *Reading Africa into American Literature,* 111.

27. Puckett, *Folk Beliefs of the Southern Negro,* 315–16. Cartwright observes that the character of Br'er Fox derived from the African *bouki,* or hyena, the trickster's traditional foe.

28. Ibid., 482–90.

29. *Born in Slavery: Slave Narratives from the Federal Writers Project, 1936–38,* WPA Slave Narrative Project, Indiana Narratives, 5:195, http://memory.loc.gov/cgi-bin/ampage?collId=mesn&fileName=050/mesn050.db&recNum=199&itemLink=D?mesnbib:1:./temp/~ammem_MXSG::.

30. Allison, "Origins of African-American Culture."

31. Marks, "Black Workers," 148.

32. For a thorough discussion of the Great Migration and its impact on southern folk practices, see Sernett, *Bound for the Promised Land.*

33. Talley, *Negro Folk Rhymes,* 303–8. Talley also includes a discussion on the triangle.

34. The music example is this author's transcription of the recording. Due to irregularities in the performance, some rhythms and pitches are approximated. For a complete description of the recording, see Miller, *Paul Bowles,* 256–57. Special thanks to Irene Herrmann and "The Authorized Paul Bowles Website," http://www.paulbowles.org, for providing the recording, and to Jacquelyn Sholes for invaluable assistance with the transcription.

35. Unpublished letter from Bowles to Ford, 1116 Woodrow Road, R.F.D. #2, Princes Bay, S.I.N.Y. [Staten Island, New York] July 15 [1938 or 1939], Ford Collection, Box 12, Folder 5, HRHRC.

36. For commentary on these and other paintings influenced by the Communist movement in America, see Hemingway, *Artists on the Left;* and Marquardt, *Art and Journals on the Political Front.*

37. Scarborough, *On the Trail of Negro Folk-Songs,* 232; Puckett, *Folk Beliefs of the Southern Negro,* 99 (emphasis added; Ford marked the emphasized phrase in the margin).

38. The critic Brooks Atkinson called *Set My People Free* one of the season's "best theater experiences." See Caponi, *Paul Bowles: Romantic Savage,* 80. In 1939 Bowles complained to Ford that Heyward had stolen his idea for an opera about Vesey, titling it *Don't You Want to Be Free?* He was determined not to give the score to any more "Broadway people." Bowles to Ford, August 1939, Bowles Collection, HRHRC. That the Heywards got the initial idea from Bowles seems unlikely.

39. Heyward, "The Negro in the Low-Country," in *The Carolina Low-Country.*

40. Heyward, "The Negro in the Low-Country," in *A Dubose Heyward Reader,* 42; see also 39–40.

41. Gary Pulsifer, "Paul Bowles, Obituary," *Manchester Guardian,* November 19, 1999.

42. Unpublished letter from Bowles to Ford, 1116 Woodrow Road, R.F.D. #2, Princes Bay, S.I.N.Y. [Staten Island, New York] July 15 [1938 or 1939], Ford Collection, Box 12, Folder 5, HRHRC.

43. Unpublished letter from Bowles to Ford, undated [1939], Ford Collection, HRHRC.

44. For a detailed account of the internecine political struggles within the STFU between Socialist and Communist affiliations, see Dyson, "Southern Tenant Farmers Union."

45. In its later years, before merging with the AFL, the CIO experienced debilitating internal struggles with Communist factions among the leadership, resulting in the purging of several prominent leaders. For a thorough discussion of the CIO and its engagement with racial and Communist politics, see Zieger, *The CIO, 1935–1955.*

46. Romalis, *Pistol Packin' Mama,* 35.

47. See Solomon, *The Cry Was Unity,* 104–5.

48. For the most thorough account of the intersections of the Communist Party and the African American community, see Solomon, *The Cry Was Unity.*

49. That is not to suggest that such efforts met with unanimous approbation; see Garvey, "Paul Robeson as an Actor," 3–6, 8–9, as quoted in *Garvey and Universal Negro Improvement Association Papers,* ed. Hill, 627. John Wexley's *They Shall Not Die* engaged audiences with the plight of the Scottsboro boys. For further information, see Solomon, *The Cry Was Unity,* 279.

50. From "I Have Seen Black Hands," quoted in Solomon, *The Cry Was Unity,* 277.

51. Ford, *Garden of Disorder.* In his introduction to Ford's collection, poet William Carlos Williams pointed out the crucifixion associations as well as allusion to the cherry-tree legend. Also that year, another image coupled lynchings and fruit trees: Billie Holi-

day's "Strange Fruit," with a text by a Communist schoolteacher, became the rallying cry for the antilynching movement in America.

52. In New York, and across the country, there sprang up production companies led and staffed by blacks and intended for black audiences. The Negro People's Theater, under the direction of the noted black actors Rose McLendon and Chick McKinney, kicked off its string of accomplishments with Clifford Odets's scathing play about the New York taxi drivers' strike, *Waiting for Lefty* (1935).

53. Unpublished letter from Bowles to Ford, undated, Ford Collection, HRHRC.

54. Unpublished letter from Bowles to Ford, July 15 [1938 or 1939], Ford Collection, HRHRC. Though this letter is not dated by year, it is clear from the contents of the letter that Bowles wrote it in 1938 or '39. Regarding the angry comments by African American critics and audiences, Bowles could be referring to the Composers' Forum performance of January 1938, though the transcripts of the postconcert discussion do not record any violent threats from listeners, or to the *New Masses* benefit concert one month later. A postcard from Bowles to Ford—probably from 1939—mentions another performance of act 1 and part of act 2 by Juanita Hall's Negro Melody Singers at Tony's Nightclub on Fifty-second Street. Ford also had plans to publish their project as either a play or a libretto, perhaps intending a production. It is unknown whether he organized nonmusical readings of his work. Another possibility is that the threats concerned an operatic production of *Denmark* by Dubose Heyward that never materialized. Dorothy Heyward's play on the subject, *Set My People Free,* premiered in 1948.

55. Bowles mentions Ford's news in a letter to Peggy Glanville-Hicks, December 1947, in *In Touch,* ed. Miller, 182. Miller's edition of the letters does not include any correspondence between the two from 1939 to 1946, although it is possible that further correspondence does, in fact, exist. Furthermore, the edition only includes letters written by Bowles and does not cite the specific collections housing individual letters. Ten letters from Ford to Bowles are included in the Bowles Collection at the HRHRC.

56. Bowles to Glanville-Hicks, December 1947, in ibid. In a second letter to Glanville-Hicks, he further explained that de Spirito "went South" the day after they made the recordings, saying, "I dislike to say what I think has become of it." Bowles to Glanville-Hicks, January 16, 1948, in ibid., 187–88.

57. Bowles to Ford, January 25, 1948, in ibid., 191; Miller, *In Touch,* 576n187; Irene Herrmann, personal email communication, November 18, 2003.

Bibliography

"About That Play *Emperor Jones.*" *Union* 17, no. 6 (1922).

Allen, Ray. "An American Folk Opera? Triangulating Folkness, Blackness, and Americaness in Gershwin and Heyward's *Porgy and Bess.*" *Journal of American Folklore* 117 (Summer 2004).

Allison, Robert J. "The Origins of African-American Culture." *Journal of Interdisciplinary History* 30, no. 3 (1999): 475–81.

Alpert, Hollis. *The Life and Times of "Porgy and Bess": The Story of an American Classic.* New York: Alfred A. Knopf, 1990.

Anderson, Jeffrey E. *Conjure in African American Society.* Baton Rouge: Louisiana State University Press, 2005.

Boyle, Virginia Frazer. "The Devil's Little Fly." In *Devil Tales.* New York: Harper and Brothers, 1900.

Brawley, Benjamin. *Social History of the American Negro.* New York: Macmillan, 1921.

Caponi, Gena. *Paul Bowles: Romantic Savage.* Carbondale: Southern Illinois University Press, 1994.

Cartwright, Keith. *Reading Africa into American Literature: Epics, Fables, and Gothic Tales.* Lexington: University Press of Kentucky, 2002.

Davis, Charles B. *The Animal Motif in Bamana Art.* New Orleans: Davis Gallery, 1981.

Du Bois, W. E. B. *The Souls of Black Folk.* 1903. Reprint, New York: Signet, 1995.

Dyson, Lowell K. "The Southern Tenant Farmers Union and Depression Politics." *Political Science Quarterly* 88, no. 2 (June 1973): 230–52.

Ford, Charles Henri. *The Garden of Disorder, and Other Poems.* London: Europa Press; Norfolk, Conn.: New Directions, 1938.

Garvey, Marcus. "Paul Robeson as an Actor." *Blackman* 1, no. 7 (June 1935).

Geggus, David. "Haitian Voodoo in the Eighteenth Century: Language, Culture, and Resistance." *Jahrbuch für Geschichte von Staat, Wirtschaft und Gesellschaft Latein Amerikas* 28 (1991): 21–51.

Hemingway, Andrew. *Artists on the Left: American Artists and the Communist Movement, 1926–1956.* New Haven: Yale University Press, 2002.

Heyward, DuBose. "The Negro in the Low-Country." In *The Carolina Low-Country.* New York: Macmillan, 1931.

———. "The Negro in the Low-Country." In *A Dubose Heyward Reader,* ed. James M. Hutchinson. Athens: University of Georgia Press, 2003.

Hill, Robert A., ed. *The Marcus Garvey and Universal Negro Improvement Association Papers.* Berkeley and Los Angeles: University of California Press, 1983.

James, C. L. R. *The Black Jacobins: Toussaint L'Ouverture and the San Domingo Revolution.* New York: Dial Press, 1938.

Johnson, Edwin D. "The Jewel in Ethiope's Ear." *Opportunity* (June 1928).

Johnson, Hall. "Notes on the Negro Spiritual." In *Readings in Black American Music,* ed. Eileen Southern, 273–80. Rev. ed. New York: W. W. Norton, 1983.

———. Review of *Porgy and Bess. Opportunity* (January 1936).

Kenney, William. *Chicago Jazz: A Cultural History, 1904–1930.* New York: Oxford University Press, 1993.

Locke, Alain. *The Negro and His Music.* Washington, D.C.: Associates in Negro Folk Education, 1936.

Marks, Carole. "Black Workers and the Great Migration North." *Phylon* 46, no. 2 (1985).

Marquardt, Virginia Hagelstein, ed. *Art and Journals on the Political Front, 1910–1940.* Gainesville: University Press of Florida, 1997.

Metzer, David. "'A Wall of Darkness Dividing the World': Blackness and Whiteness in Louis Gruenberg's *The Emperor Jones.*" *Cambridge Opera Journal* 7, no. 1 (March 1995): 55–72.

Miller, Jeffrey, ed. *In Touch: The Letters of Paul Bowles.* New York: Farrar, Straus, and Giroux, 1994.

———. *Paul Bowles: A Descriptive Bibliography.* Santa Barbara: Black Sparrow Press, 1986.

Moreau de Saint-Méry, M. L. E. *Description topographique, physique, civile, politique et historique de la partie française de l'isle Saint-Domingue* [1797]. Ed. Blanche Maurel and Étienne Taillemite. Paris: Société de l'histoire des Colonies Françaises et Librairie Larose, 1958.

Pendleton, Louis. "Notes on Negro Folk-Lore and Witchcraft in the South." *The Journal of American Folklore,* 3, no. 10 (July–September 1890): 201–7.

Pettinger, Alisdair. "A Decade of Black Atlantic Studies." January 26, 2005. http://www.uclan.ac.uk/amatas/english/05november12.htm.

Puckett, Newbell Niles. *Folk Beliefs of the Southern Negro.* Chapel Hill: University of North Carolina Press, 1926.

Romalis, Shelley. *Pistol Packin' Mama: Aunt Molly Jackson and the Politics of Folksong.* Urbana: University of Illinois Press, 1999.

Scarborough, Dorothy. *On the Trail of Negro Folk-Songs.* Cambridge: Harvard University Press, 1925.

Sernett, Milton C. *Bound for the Promised Land: African American Religion and the Great Migration.* Durham: Duke University Press, 1997.

Solomon, Mark. *The Cry Was Unity: Communists and African Americans, 1917–36.* Jackson: University Press of Mississippi, 1998.

Talley, Thomas Washington. *Negro Folk Rhymes.* New York: Macmillan, 1922.

Walser, Robert. *Keeping Time: Readings in Jazz History.* New York: Oxford University Press, 1998.

Watson, Steven. *Prepare for Saints: Gertrude Stein, Virgil Thomson, and the Mainstreaming of American Modernism.* New York: Random House, 1998.

Zieger, Robert H. *The CIO, 1935–1955.* Chapel Hill: University of North Carolina Press, 1995.

10

The Politics of Color in Oscar Hammerstein's *Carmen Jones*

MELINDA BOYD

I first met "Miss Jones" (Carmen Jones, that is), a few years ago when I was searching for a suitable video of Bizet's *Carmen* for my opera history class, and it immediately struck me as a work that begged to be examined through the lens of feminist and cultural theory. Susan McClary, Catherine Clément, and many others have shown (with respect to operatic subjects like *Carmen*) that scholars need to ask who creates representations of whom, with what imagery, and toward what ends. For example, on stage and on film, *Carmen Jones* must be considered a box-office hit.[1] The Broadway stage version of *Carmen Jones* enjoyed an original New York run of 502 performances and numerous tours and revivals, and was adapted for film by Otto Preminger in 1954 (a feint for mass accessibility that has continued with the film's rerelease on DVD).[2] Yet the work sits uneasily on the margins of musical theater. Since it was adapted from opera, it necessarily bears the cultural baggage of another time, place, and genre. Moreover, as neither Bizet nor Hammerstein were ethnographers, Hammerstein's *Carmen Jones* is about as authentic a representation of African American culture as Bizet's *Carmen* was of Spanish culture—that is to say, not very. Oscar Hammerstein II may have been striving for a sensitive translation of the libretto, but his lyrics adopt common clichés of Negro speech. This oversight contributes to noxious stereotypes of the racial Other that are heightened by the residue of vicarious exoticism in Bizet's score.

At the time, critics raved that Hammerstein rejuvenated Bizet's opera by providing lyrics that not only captured the subtleties of the plot and nuances of characterization, but often surpassed the original in both respects. Until James Baldwin's scathing commentary on the film was published in 1954, few seemed to notice that Hammerstein equated Bizet's sexually liberated gypsy with a lower-class African American woman.[3] In the following discussion, I will peel away the various layers of representation in the stage and film versions of *Carmen Jones.* I will begin by examining the circumstances, precedents, and models that inspired Hammerstein's conception of the work. Next, I will look at Hammerstein's transformation of the plot and his text-translation practice, and examine how these factors are by-products of an opera history aesthetic best described as "anti-operatic." Along the way, I will investigate the critical reception of *Carmen Jones* in light of the socioeconomic status and race of the work's 1943 audience. Finally, I will turn to Otto Preminger's 1954 film version, described by Baldwin as "one of the first and most explicit—and far and away the most self-conscious—weddings of sex and color which Hollywood has yet turned out," and show how Preminger's film brought the story of Carmen to a new and broader audience.[4] Hammerstein's dream of liberating opera from the elitist confines of the opera house was finally and completely realized, immortalized in CinemaScope for future generations.

Background, Precedents, and Models

Carmen Jones was not the first Broadway show to have an all-black cast, nor was it the first instance of an opera to be transplanted onto the Broadway stage. Hammerstein had already set a racial precedent collaborating with Jerome Kern on the smash hit *Show Boat* in 1927, but even *Show Boat*'s integrated cast was hardly a new phenomenon: as early as 1904 there were multiracial cast productions, notably *The Southerners.* Yet as Frank Rich has argued, "without *Show Boat,* there would have been no *Porgy and Bess,* no *Oklahoma!,* no *West Side Story.*" What made *Show Boat* different, according to John Graziano, was that "instead of the caricatures that populated most black musicals of the Harlem Renaissance, Hammerstein offered a serious and sympathetic portrayal of African Americans." *Show Boat* provided Hammerstein with a template for depicting "the black experience," even though the black characters were minimally developed and black roles were performed by white actors in blackface. Still, the work was not without controversy in terms of its racial stereotypes. When Paul Robeson played the minor role of Joe in a 1928 London production, the European correspondent for the *New York Amsterdam News* criticized Robeson's onstage character as "simply another instance of the 'lazy, good-natured, lolling darky' stereotype." A 1993 revival of the musical in Toronto elicited an equally strong response from the black community, who picketed in front of the box office and formed the "Coalition to Stop *Show Boat*" because it "contained scenes that perpetuate racial stereotypes demeaning to black life and culture."[5] Despite its superficial diversity, *Show Boat* perpetuated racial stereotypes that continued in *Carmen Jones.*

If *Show Boat* established a personal working model for Hammerstein, two unusual versions of Gilbert and Sullivan's *Mikado* from the late 1930s may have shown him how operas could be adapted both to all-black casts and the Broadway stage. The first of these, *The Swing Mikado,* opened at Chicago's Great Northern Theater on September 25, 1938, its cast composed of the Negro Unit from the Works Progress Administration (WPA) Federal Theatre.[6] Because several of the actors in the Negro Unit had previously performed *The Mikado,* the story seemed a natural choice. The success of *The Swing Mikado* attracted Broadway producer Michael Todd, who offered to take over the show. When the Federal Theatre rejected Todd's offer, he responded by mounting his own production in New York. Todd's *Hot Mikado* was directed by Hassard Short, who would later be in charge of stage lighting and color schemes in *Carmen Jones.*[7] Before Todd's production opened at the Broadhurst Theater on March 23, 1939, the WPA moved *The Swing Mikado* to the New Yorker Theatre on Fifty-fourth Street, ten blocks north of the Broadhurst, where it opened on March 1. Todd protested that the WPA's government-subsidized production constituted unfair competition for commercial enterprises, but the WPA production went ahead. While *The Swing Mikado* and *The Hot Mikado* fought to attract audiences, both productions became important showcases for black talent when there were few opportunities for steady employment elsewhere.[8]

The black *Mikado*s transformed Gilbert and Sullivan's operetta in ways that would have implications for *Carmen Jones.* Both productions kept the original (ridiculous) character names—Nanki-Poo, Pish-Tush, Pooh-Bah, and so on—but adjusted the locale, the text, and especially the music. In preparation for the WPA's production, director Henry Minturn expressed concern over whether "black actors could play Japanese characters in an English operetta." Minturn and his production team transferred the setting from Japan to a generic South Seas island, which allowed for "barbaric scenery and 'savage' costumes." Some of the lyrics were updated, but most of the original dialogue was retained. More important, five of the songs received a jazz arrangement from Gentry Warden. By contrast, the producers of *The Hot Mikado* had no reservations about black actors playing Japanese characters; the first act of their show takes place on a Japanese street. Todd and Short's production aimed for a more contemporary, sophisticated image, with costumes ranging from "beanies and bobby socks for the dancers to pseudo-oriental robes for the ladies and a gold-and-white suit for the Mikado."[9] While *The Swing Mikado* jazzed up only five numbers, almost every number in *The Hot Mikado* was "swung": the first verse was sung in straight time, but the chorus and remaining verses were increasingly syncopated.

Certainly, the visual and musical elements of the black *Mikado*s contributed to the racialization of the story, yet the textual treatment is equally pertinent (in terms of both these productions and the development of *Carmen Jones*). Some of Gilbert's song lyrics were updated in order to appeal to contemporary audiences. In *The Swing Mikado,* for example, Ko-Ko's "I've Got a Little List" (act 1) makes reference to movies and radio:

> There's the pretty Movie Hero,
> Looking too sweet to be kissed
> . . . There's the Radio Comedian
> Whose jokes are thick with mold.[10]

Compared to Gilbert's original lyrics, the revision brings the subject into 1930s America by incorporating contemporary tropes. Although Short and Todd refrained from employing dialect (at least in this particular number), much of the dialogue was rewritten in what was assumed to be an "authentic" representation of black vernacular. For the most part, these textual revisions simply meant replacing diphthongs with a single letter and dropping the final consonants. For example, Gilbert's Ko-Ko asks Nanki-Poo, "What are you going to do with that rope?" but in *The Swing Mikado* the same line is delivered as "What you-all fixin' to do wid dat rope?" Disrupting proper English grammar and syntax, as in the opening chorus from *The Hot Mikado* ("Does you want to know who we are? / We is the gentlemen of Japan"), was another common technique. Generally speaking, opera libretti written in a language other than that of the source material from which they are drawn may erase elements of racial difference. Puccini's *Madama Butterfly* (1904) is a case in point: Cio-Cio San's pidgin English, marking her as the racial Other, was prominent in John Luther Long's short story and in David Belasco's play, which were used as the source texts for the opera. Librettists Illica and Giocosa transformed this pidgin English into eloquent Italian.[11] Although Gilbert's Japanese characters speak a sophisticated, upper-class English—in keeping with his propensity for depicting English cultural mores beneath a thin veneer of exoticism—the characters in the black *Mikado*s are reracialized as lower-class and uneducated. Minturn's concern about the believability of black actors playing Japanese characters was thus circumvented by heightening the racial and class differences of the cast rather than glossing over them.

Was Oscar Hammerstein familiar with the two black *Mikados*? *The Swing Mikado* had a combined New York run of eighty-six performances, while *The Hot Mikado* lasted for eighty-five.[12] Both productions were widely reviewed in the New York press, so much so that one can safely assume that Hammerstein would have at least been aware of them. But even before either of these productions appeared on Broadway, Hammerstein had toyed with the subject of *Carmen* and the idea of converting an opera into a musical. In 1934, he pitched the concept to MGM musical supervisor Sam Katz. According to Hammerstein biographer Hugh Fordin, Hammerstein considered *Carmen* to be an appropriate subject, but he also saw "possibilities in *Faust, Boheme, Butterfly, Tosca, Pagliacci,* and *Louise.*"[13] In a follow-up letter to Katz, Hammerstein made it clear that he felt *Carmen* was the best choice, but the project with Katz and MGM never materialized.

We may, however, be able to trace Hammerstein's interest in *Carmen* back to a more direct model than the *Mikados*. According to Annegret Fauser, Hammerstein wanted to do "a version of 'Lula Belle' [*sic*], which was the Carmen story . . . and I had invited Duke Ellington to do the score with me."[14] A four-act play by Edward Sheldon and Charles MacArthur, *Lulu Belle* premiered less than two years before *Show Boat.* Set in New York (Harlem) and Paris, this adaptation of the *Carmen* story preserved the plot but "only a very small amount of Bizet's music." *Lulu Belle*'s integrated cast, setting, and unseemly plot evoked strong reactions from the press—both for and against the production—but the viability of the project in terms of its box-office success was what mattered. Although the collaboration with Ellington fell through, Fauser argues that traces of *Lulu Belle* can be found in the earliest version of *Carmen Jones.* If *Lulu Belle* was a "memorable model because of its historical and thematic proximity to *Show Boat,*" as Fauser claims, it seems odd that Hammerstein did not acknowledge it until 1959.[15]

Even though *Carmen Jones* may belong to "a longer genealogy of *Carmen* adaptations involving African American performers," it is an anomaly in Oscar Hammerstein's oeuvre, separate from both his earlier successful collaborations with Jerome Kern and his later work with Richard Rodgers.[16] Perhaps for that reason, Hammerstein's biographers tend to pass rather quickly over *Carmen Jones* in order to move on to the more fertile ground of works such as *Oklahoma!, Carousel,* and *South Pacific.* For example, Fordin reminds us—in a way that becomes an implicit apologia—that *Carmen Jones* was conceived and written at a low point in Hammerstein's career, when much bigger and better things were just around the corner. Hammerstein had not had a hit, either on stage or on film, for nearly a decade; he was "out of touch with what the public wanted, with what was considered good by current standards." Hammerstein may have been out of touch, yet Fordin contends that he also "had had many lucky accidents in his life, and he had made the most of them."[17] With this statement Fordin encourages us to perceive *Carmen Jones* as just another "lucky accident," a trifle from an unproductive period, and, consequently, we should not take Hammerstein's efforts too seriously, and latter-day viewers should also excuse any racial insensitivities they might perceive.

Carmen Jones may have been conceived during a fallow period in Hammerstein's career; however, if Fordin is to be believed, it was also a somewhat clandestine project. As Fordin tells it, "Sitting alone on the farm one day in January 1942, Oscar listened to a recording of Bizet's *Carmen.* He played it over and over as he studied the libretto with an English translation of the original French and the complete piano score. Without saying a word to anyone outside his family, he set to work modernizing the opera. . . . Oscar worked without deadlines or pressures, not even certain that the work would ever be produced. He enjoyed this project more than any other he had ever done." Work on *Carmen* may have given Hammerstein a new lease on life, but Fordin's account is not entirely accurate. Fauser has proved conclusively that by February 1942, Hammerstein had already gone outside the family, enlisting the help of producer Richard Berger and arranger Robert Russell Bennett. Although it is true that there was no deadline, Hammerstein clearly "worked toward realizing the production before even the first act of his new musical play was completed."[18] Hammerstein's new libretto was finally completed in July 1942, just days before he was offered an opportunity to work with Richard Rodgers on an adaptation of *Green Grow the Lilacs,* later renamed *Oklahoma!*[19] This new collaboration with Rodgers, not *Carmen Jones,* ultimately rejuvenated Hammerstein's sagging career.

Although the thought of Hammerstein working alone and in secret is intriguing (and untrue), his gravitation toward opera generally (and *Carmen* specifically) is even more so. Hammerstein's unsympathetic attitude toward opera, and his subsequent aesthetic approach to *Carmen Jones,* was deeply rooted in his family history. His grandfather Oscar Hammerstein I founded the Manhattan Opera Company in 1906 (later selling his interest to the Metropolitan Opera),[20] while his father, William, and his uncle Arthur were producers and theater managers. Strangely, however, young Oscar II developed an aversion to opera early in life. His objections to the genre were twofold: first, Hammerstein explained, "When I was a small boy, 'opera' was a bad word in my home. Opera was a way people lost money, especially Grandpa." His second objection, according to Fordin, was that "a small musical clique had turned [opera] into a pretentious elitist form." The problem was not so much that opera was sung in foreign languages—in the days before the projection of supertitles above the stage—but rather that even when opera was sung in English, there was little regard for the words. Poor diction that obscured the text was one issue, but Hammerstein was more concerned with translations "written by scholarly gentlemen who know nothing about the science of writing singable lyrics. . . . [T]heir concern with a literal translation that slavishly followed the text diminished the richness of the characters and the emotional power of the plot."[21] With that challenge in mind, Hammerstein the wordsmith set out to attack the problem.

But why choose *Carmen*? In his original proposal to Sam Katz, Hammerstein argued that "as a popular opera subject, *Carmen* stands alone. It has a universally interesting story, fine characterizations and as melodic a score as was ever written." Later, Hammerstein also declared that "the story of the good boy in love with the good girl and the bad girl who comes between them to cause tragedy for all is as old as time itself. Its locale has been Egypt, Africa, China, Japan, the United States or any corner of the globe where three or more people live."[22] The universality of the story and the accessibility of the music were clearly important considerations: *Carmen* had all of the elements of a successful Broadway show, except a happy ending. Obviously, this cannot be said for all operas; it would be difficult, if not impossible, to imagine such a project based on, for example, *Tristan und Isolde.* But in the case of *Carmen,* a simple translation was not enough. Hammerstein wanted to bring the story into the twentieth century, and into a familiar American setting.

Transforming *Carmen:* Hammerstein's Procedure

In transforming *Carmen* into *Carmen Jones,* Hammerstein avoided the issue of black actors playing Spanish gypsies by moving the location from a cigarette factory in nineteenth-century Seville to a parachute factory in South Carolina during World War II.[23] In order to fit into their new American surroundings, most of the characters underwent a change of name and job description. Bizet's Don José became GI Joe, a corporal in the United States Army. Cindy Lou took Micaëla's place as Joe's fiancée, while the toreador, Escamillo, was replaced first by a swing band leader named Hepcat Miller, who was to become a prizefighter named Husky Miller in the final version (see table 1).[24]

Only the title character, Carmen, retained her original name, but with the newly minted surname of "Jones." Although she is no longer a gypsy, Hammerstein's Carmen remains a factory worker. Some minor details of the plot were also adjusted to fit the new setting, yet perhaps the most striking feature Hammerstein kept from the original was the tragic ending, as unusual in the opéra comique genre as it was on the Broadway stage.

Table 1. Character names and cast lists for *Carmen* and *Carmen Jones*

Carmen	*Carmen Jones* (stage)[a]	*Carmen Jones* (film)
Carmen	Carmen Jones: Muriel Smith / Muriel Rahn	Dorothy Dandridge (voice of Marilyn Horne)
Don José	Joe: Luther Saxon / Napoleon Reed	Harry Belafonte (voice of LeVern Hutcherson)
Micäela	Cindy Lou: Carlotta Franzell / Elton J. Warren	Olga James (not voiced over)
Escamillo	Husky Miller: Glenn Bryant	Joe Adams (voice of Marvin Hayes)
Frasquita	Frankie: June Hawkins	Pearl Bailey
Mercedes	Myrt: Jessica Russell	Diahann Carroll (voice of Bernice Peterson)

[a]The three main roles were double-cast for the original Broadway production. For a complete cast list, see Lewis Nichols, "The Play," *New York Times,* December 3, 1943, 26.

Experience had taught Hammerstein that traditional opera was a money-losing enterprise, so he went about dressing the new *Carmen* in nontraditional clothing. The black *Mikado* productions had enjoyed tremendous box-office success, yet Hammerstein tried to distance himself from the commercial aspects of those earlier productions, declaring that "my choice of Negroes as the principal figures in the story was not motivated by any desire to pull an eccentric theatrical stunt." Instead, he rationalized his casting choice as "the logical result of my decision to write a modern American version of *Carmen*." After all, he argued, "the nearest thing in our modern American life to an equivalent of the gypsies in Spain is the Negro. Like the gypsy, he expresses his feelings simply, honestly, and graphically. Also like the gypsy there is rhythm in his body and music in his heart." Hammerstein recognized in the opera a set of cultural stereotypes that could be readily transferred from one ethnic group to another, including graphic expression of feelings and a natural rhythm in the body and the music. These stereotypes are precisely those that Donald Bogle identified in his interpretive history of blacks in American film: the "tragic mulatto" (Carmen), the "good black boy gone bad" (Joe), the "black buck" (Husky Miller), and so on.[25] (I will return to these issues later in conjunction with discussion of the film.)

The most pressing issue for Hammerstein was the translation of the libretto. He acknowledged *Carmen*'s roots in opéra comique while at the same time adhering to the musical theater convention of having scenes of spoken dialogue between the sung numbers. "In our elimination of the recitatif passages," Hammerstein argued, "we are not taking as great a liberty as may be supposed. Bizet and his collaborators originally wrote *Carmen* with spoken dialogue scenes between the airs that were sung."[26] It is also possible that Hammerstein was wary of using recitative in light of the adverse criticism it generated in George Gershwin's *Porgy and Bess* (1935).[27] Fauser suggests that there were additional motivating factors involving contemporary debates surrounding "a national (that is, American) theater, its genres, and languages" in the wartime United States. She explains that a heightened sense of nationalism clashed with an apparent "dependence on imported cultural objects. . . . With opera in particular, dependence on the canonic European repertoire remained unavoidable." Translating a libretto into idiomatically American English served two purposes: it "Americanized" the genre by providing a sense of distance from its European models, and it "democratized" it for a broader audience beyond the elitist environment of the opera house.[28]

To that end, instead of a literal, scholarly translation, Hammerstein endeavored to produce his "singable lyrics" in the black vernacular. Fauser maintains that the action "placed Hammerstein's book in a long tradition of linguistic regionalism in the American theater."[29] Hammerstein may have engaged with tradition, but nothing in the current literature suggests that he made any ethnographic studies, formal or otherwise. His technique, like that of the producers of the two black *Mikados*, relied on replacing diphthongs, dropping final consonants, and disrupting grammar and syntax.

Hammerstein's reworking of the familiar "Habañera" from act 1 serves as an example of his methodology. Table 2 provides Bizet's original French lyrics in the left column and the lyrics for *Carmen Jones* in the right column.[30]

Hammerstein does more than just tinker with the grammar: he also plays somewhat fast and loose with the content and meaning of the song. In verse 2, Carmen Jones is tied to her operatic namesake through the reference to "cigarette," but in the following verse, the reference to the gypsy (Bohême) is dropped altogether. Hammerstein takes the most extreme poetic license at the end of this verse. Whereas the original French text reiterates the verb *love* ("je t'*aime*"—I love you), Hammerstein's new words revise the concept of love (in the first couplet, "you go for me / I go for you"), portraying Carmen Jones as even more independent, if not predatory. This aspect of her character is further emphasized in verse 4, where the lovebird "pecks" and "flicks de salt from her tail."[31] The "peck" is a brief kiss good-bye, but the bird's beak can also be sharp; the salt on the tail prevents the bird from flying away. In the final verse, Hammerstein alters

Table 2. "Habañera" texts and translations

BIZET'S "HABAÑERA"	HAMMERSTEIN'S "DAT'S LOVE"
L'amour est un oiseau rebelle Que nul ne peut apprivoiser, Et c'est bien en vain qu'on l'appelle S'il lui convient de refuser.	Love's a baby dat grows up wild An' he don't do what you want him to, Love ain' nobody's angel child An' he won't pay any mind to you.
Rien n'y fait, menace ou prière, L'un parle bien, l'autre se tait: Et c'est l'autre que je préfère, Il n'a rien dit, mais il me plaît.	One man gives me his diamon' stud An' I won't give him a cigarette. One man treats me like I was mud An' what I got dat man c'n get.
L'amour, l'amour . . .	Dat's love, dat's love . . .
L'amour est enfant de Bohême. Il n'a jamais, jamais connu de loi; Si tu ne m'aimes pas, je t'aime, Si je t'aime, prends garde â toi!	You go for me an' I'm taboo, But if yo're hard to get, I go for you, An' if I do, den you are through, boy My baby, dat's de end of you.
L'oiseau que tu croyais surprendre Battit de l'aile et s'envola; L'amour est loin, tu peux l'attendre, Tu ne l'attends plus, il est là.	When your love-bird decides to fly Dere ain' no door dat you c'n close. She jus' pecks you a quick good-bye An' flicks de salt from her tail an' goes!
Tout autour de toi vite, vite, Il vient, s'en va, puis il revient, Tu crois le tenir, il t'évite, Tu crois l'éviter, il te tient!	If you listen, den you' get taught, An' here's your lesson for today: If I chase you, den you'll get caught, But once I got you, I go my way!

the personal pronouns. *You* (tu) and *it* (il) become *I* and *you,* so that instead of the song's addressee (Joe) catching and holding love, it is Carmen Jones who is once again the pursuer.

All of the other characters in *Carmen Jones* come in for similar linguistic treatment. When Cindy Lou sings "My Joe" in act 2, the vernacular that Hammerstein supplies ("I is skeered, oh Lawd! I is skeered!") reminds us not only of her naïveté, but also of her humble working-class background. The act 1 duet between Cindy Lou and Joe ("You Walk Just Like My Maw") is reminiscent of "Bess, You Is My Woman Now" from *Porgy and Bess,* in its formal scheme, dramatic theme, and deployment of black vernacular. Although the language portrays his characters as lower-class and uneducated, Hammerstein argued that they were not caricatures but "simple, everyday, honest, American Negro war workers, soldiers, and human beings. There isn't a tap dancer in the entire company."[32]

The authenticity of Hammerstein's black vernacular was problematic. On the one hand, according to a white reviewer for *Time,* Hammerstein had "dipped his big toe in the Mississippi mud and wrote some lyrics that should be thrown back to the catfish." On the other hand, African American music critic Nora Holt described Hammerstein's "Negro idiom" in the stage version as "so quaint and piquant it is a great joy to read it and everyone should have a copy to follow the play." In the postwar years, on the heels of Preminger's film version, criticism was less than favorable. James Baldwin offered the following critique from the black perspective: "Negro speech is parodied out of its charm and liberalized, if one may so put it, out of its force and precision. The result is not that the characters are like everybody else, which would be bad enough; the result is that they sound ludicrously false and affected, like ante bellum Negroes imitating their masters. . . . They could easily have been dreamed up by someone determined to prove that Negroes are as 'clean' and as 'modern' as white people, and, I suppose, in one way or another, that is exactly how they *were* dreamed up."[33] The foreign language of opera can and does eliminate differences of class and race, as noted earlier. We know that Hammerstein was deeply concerned with human rights,[34] but the "ders," "deses," and "dats" of *Carmen Jones* mark all of the characters as lower-class citizens. Viewed in the light of the post–civil rights era, Hammerstein's lyrics are squirm inducing.

The Politics of Color: Words and Music

Perhaps responding to negative publicity surrounding the musical treatment of the black *Mikado* productions, Hammerstein swore that "swing will not be part of the music, unless it is the natural swing contained in the Bizet score, and Bizet wrote good modern dance music which the all-Negro cast will find to their liking." Hammerstein perceived a certain "hotness" in Bizet's score that he associated with Afro-Cuban spirituals and blues. It is tempting to assume that he was familiar with Nietzsche's view of *Carmen:* in *The Case of Wagner,* Nietzsche wrote, "This music is cheerful, but not in a French or German way. Its cheerfulness is *African.* . . . I envy Bizet for having had the courage for this sensibility which had hitherto had no language in the cultivated music of Europe—for this more southern, *brown, burnt sensibility.*" Although Nietzsche is mentioned in some of the publicity material for *Carmen Jones,* Hammerstein was unaware of the connection until after the fact, when "our publicity man dug up a fascinating story. He found a critique of Carmen by Nietsche [*sic*]."[35] The Afro-Cuban nature of the score reflects the extent of Bizet's ethnographic "fieldwork," which took place largely in Paris cafés. For example, the tune for "Habañera" originated not in an authentic Spanish dance but in a pseudofolk (Creole) composition, "El Arreglito" by Sebastián Yradier, that was popular on the Paris café scene in the 1870s.[36]

Whereas Gershwin spent some time during the summer of 1934 in South Carolina listening to regional dialects and music as part of his preparation for *Porgy and Bess,* Hammerstein was a wordsmith, not a composer or ethnographer. Robert Russell Bennett was brought in to arrange the score for the smaller Broadway pit orchestra, but with the exception of two excised arias and the elimination of the Spanish-sounding castanets, Bizet's original music was left more or less intact. The only number that was truly jazzed up was Bizet's "Gypsy Song" that opens the second act. In the opera, Carmen and her friends Frasquita and Mercedes dance to the rhythms of castanets at Lillas Pastia's tavern. McClary notes that "Bizet's music during this scene resembles Spanish music perhaps more closely than any of his other exotic numbers." For the Broadway stage, the Spanish influence was toned down; a set of trap drums became the contemporary equivalent of castanets. Renamed "Beat Out Dat Rhythm on a Drum," the number became a virtuosic showpiece, a "full three-chorus interlude" for drummer Cozy Cole on Broadway and for Max Roach on film.[37]

More compelling is what happens when Hammerstein's words meet Bizet's music. McClary has shown how Bizet's exotic music was composed "by means of this well-developed set of signs that he and his audiences shared, as do most contemporary listeners."[38] The laundry list of standard western European exotic effects may be summarized as pitch deviations (augmented seconds and fourths), extensive melodic chromaticism, bass drones, ostinatos, and incessant dance rhythms. In the opera, Bizet uses such effects to mark Carmen as Other. Her music is in stark contrast to the diatonic, high-art music that Bizet provided for Don José,[39] but in this case musical exoticism is more than a mere signifier of racial and class difference. McClary argues that Bizet had a second, more nefarious, goal in mind: to "enact musically one of the central events in the opera—Carmen's seduction of Don José." Carmen's slippery chromaticism and taboo intervals are combined with the dance rhythms of the "Habañera" and "Seguidilla," rhythms "calculated to engage the body in a very particular set of physical responses."[40] Carmen is aware of and celebrates her own body; her swaying hips attract Don José and the audience. Consequently, the "Habañera" and "Seguidilla" are Carmen's—and thus by extension Carmen Jones's—*ars erotica:* it is the dance that seduces Don José, not her singing or her words. More than illicit pitches and modal inflections, the "rhythm + body = race" equation is a crucial issue in both the opera and the musical. With all the baggage of perceived seductiveness and animalistic sexuality that African Americans carried at the time, it is this equation that binds the amoral gypsy to the lower-class African American woman. Hammerstein may have changed the words, but the music's psychological effect on the listener remains the same. In that respect, *Carmen Jones* can hardly be considered a revisionist reading of Bizet's opera.

Carmen Jones, CinemaScope, and the Technicolor Body

In *Carmen Jones,* the visual element of dance is as important as the music. Although I do not intend to conflate the live performance on stage of *Carmen Jones* with the film version, the camera's lens offers a convenient, and much different, means of capturing specific moments. In Preminger's conception of *Carmen Jones,* the emphasis is on the visual image, not the music. The film was shot in CinemaScope, a relatively new wide-screen technology that provided wide horizontal vistas, which facilitated capturing the spectacle of the Technicolor bodies on film. Preminger's handling of the three dance scenes, in particular, seems to value image over musical quality, thereby undermining the seductive power of Bizet's score in favor of the exotic (and erotic) black body. What is more, issues of casting and voice-over techniques further exacerbate racial stereotypes.

During the 1950s, social-political tensions and competition from the emerging medium of television pushed the film industry in new directions. As television sets and network broadcasting became more accessible, the major motion picture studios found their box-office receipts diminishing rapidly and consequently employed new technologies, such as CinemaScope and 3-D, combined with bold new themes, in order to draw audiences back into the theaters. According to Donald Bogle, this era of "silent change" in the film industry was important and provided a platform for a number of black actors in American motion pictures. One of the most significant films that contributed to this breakthrough was *Bright Road* (1953), starring Dorothy Dandridge and Harry Belafonte as schoolteachers in the "first ever nonstereotypical, nonmusical Hollywood film centering on middle-class Blacks in the north." Although *Carmen Jones* could be seen as a throwback to the black musicals of the early 1940s, Preminger's 1954 film still contributed to this breakthrough. Its cast list presented a veritable "who's who" of the decade's most prominent and most promising black actors, including Dandridge, Belafonte, Pearl Bailey, and Diahann Carroll (see table 1). Not surprisingly, the film was the 1950s' "most lavish, most publicized, and most successful all-black spectacle."[41]

In addition to *Bright Road,* Dorothy Dandridge appeared in two other low-budget films before her breakthrough role in *Carmen Jones*: *Tarzan's Peril* (1951) and *The Harlem Globetrotters* (1951). With the exception of *Tarzan's Peril,* Dandridge played "good girl" roles. When Dandridge attended the initial casting call for the title role in *Carmen Jones,* Preminger thought her "too sleek and sophisticated for the role of a whore." He suggested that she was better suited to play Cindy Lou. In order to win the part of Carmen, Dandridge underwent an extreme image makeover. Bogle's account of the legend is worth examining closely: "Dorothy Dandridge completely redid her appearance and style. *She taught herself a Southern dialect. She mastered wildly uninhibited body movements.* She shrewdly exploited her own nervous tension. With her new image perfected, she tossed her hair about her head, made up her eyes darkly, dressed herself in a sheer low-cut blouse and a long, tight skirt, and then audaciously strutted into Preminger's office. Vivacious, sportive, alluring yet somehow haunted and vulnerable, Dorothy Dandridge was the living embodiment of the director's Carmen. The role was given to her."[42] By teaching herself a southern dialect and uninhibited body movements, Dandridge learned to conform to the stereotype of the lower-class African American woman: Preminger's "whore."

Dandridge earned an Oscar nomination for Best Actress (she lost to Grace Kelly), but the film did more than just make her a star; Bogle asserts that the movie "established her as the definitive tragic mulatto."[43] The latter is one of several stereotypes that Bogle identifies in his work on blacks in American film. He describes the tragic mulatto as a "moviemaker's darling," a woman who is exotic, self-destructive, unfulfilled, and doomed because of her color.[44] Yet if we substitute *gypsy* for *mulatto* and *race* for *color,* we also have the stereotypical description of Carmen.

While Dandridge portrayed the definitive tragic mulatto, Harry Belafonte, cast as Joe, presents a more ambiguous (and less successful) commingling of two other black film stereotypes. In the 1950s Belafonte was considered "so handsome and slick a black dude . . . that he seemed a born movie star, a natural new-style romantic hero. Hollywood capitalized on his looks and his sexuality." Due to Belafonte's obvious sex appeal, Bogle argues that he "fell into the black buck category"; however, black bucks were "always big, baadddd [*sic*] niggers, oversexed and savage, violent and frenzied as they lust for white flesh." Despite his good looks and (potential) sexuality, Belafonte's acting skills were minimal at best; he was usually cast in good-guy roles more suited to his polite and naive demeanor. In *Carmen Jones,* he plays another variation on the "good colored boy" stereotype, the one who is led astray by the seductive Carmen. The black-buck type, even if it had been within Belafonte's range, would not have made a suitable foil for Carmen. Instead, the black-buck stereotype was safely, and more appropriately in terms of the plot, assigned to the prizefighter Husky Miller, played by Joe Adams. Bogle contends that in this role, Adams was "such an overtly sexual performer that audiences could understand why he never went far in films. White audiences still found sexually aggressive black males hard to accept."[45]

The film may have put the black faces and bodies of Dandridge, Belafonte, and the rest of the cast on full Technicolor display, but black voices were another matter. Even though Dandridge and Belafonte had already established successful careers as singers, both of their singing parts were voiced over by other singers. Recording the soundtrack separate from the film and the dubbing of actors' singing voices was a common practice in Hollywood film musicals, but in *Carmen Jones,* the issue of vocal quality goes deeper than Hollywood convention or the question of the actors' abilities: it is inextricably bound to and informed by race, representation, and ideologies of high art steeped in nineteenth-century culture. In order to disentangle the messy web of threads that make up the multiple layers of race, representation, and culture, we need to go back to the casting process for the original stage version of *Carmen Jones.*

When Hammerstein decided to swap one ethnic group for another, there was one problem that he may not have anticipated. While the Broadway production was being prepared, producer Billy Rose "ran afoul" of Bizet's estate, who "had no problem with African American performers or with Hammerstein's approximation of a Negro folk dialect as long as the performers did not sound like African American singers but adhered to the more 'universal' standards of classical vocal performance." In 1943, meeting the vocal standard set forth by Bizet's estate posed significant challenges. With the assistance of John Henry Hammond Jr., an "expert on Negro singers and players," Rose assembled a largely amateur cast with little or no previous stage experience or formal vocal training.[46] Reviewers made much of the fact that Luther Saxon (Joe) was a checker in the Philadelphia navy shipyard, Glenn Bryant (Husky Miller) had taken a leave of absence from the New York Police Department, while the rest of the cast was made up of a "Detroit social worker, a Cleveland housewife, [and] a Los Angeles chauffeur." Saxon's voice was described as "good" but "small," his acting ability "stiff and rather inarticulate."[47] If Saxon—or any other members of the original cast—had any formal vocal training, that fact was not publicized. A case in point is Muriel Smith, who, along with Muriel Rahn, was cast as Carmen Jones. Before she got the part, Smith had a day job cleaning film for a Philadelphia photographer.[48] As Carmen Jones, Smith "looked sultry, had a fine swagger and a dangerous smile and a voice that matched the part." However, reviewers neglected to mention that Smith had also trained at the Curtis Institute; after her successful run in *Carmen Jones* on Broadway and on tour, she moved to England in 1949 and later became the first African American woman to perform the role of Bizet's Carmen at Covent Garden.[49]

Rather than exploiting Smith's credentials—and thus upholding the Bizet estate's standards of classical vocal performance—Rose and his publicity machine seemed content to let the reviewers and the theatergoing public believe that these were ordinary, untrained, working-class African Americans. Fauser argues that the issue of casting was exploited with a specific agenda in mind. "In this story," she writes, "*Carmen Jones* became an embodiment of the 'American dream' through the Pygmalion plot of its cast, awkwardly combining the notion of racial and social uplift and 'all-American' inclusiveness with one of white patronage and control." The fact that most of the cast were plucked from mundane day jobs and were not working in the theater speaks more to the lack of opportunities for African American performers than to their supposed lack of abilities. Moreover, when *Carmen Jones* hit the stage, despite its pedigree as an adapted opera, it joined the ranks of a long line of musical theater works with all-black casts. As reviewer Olin Downes noted, audiences expected a certain kind of performance: "But we were considerably disappointed in one thing of which *we had expected a great deal.* This was the prevailing self-consciousness and a degree of restraint in much of the acting and nearly all of the dancing. A performance by Negroes—yes—and they do a highly creditable job! *But it was not a Negro performance* in the natural creative way of that race of born actors and musicians *that we had expected to see*. There was evidence of *too much white man's training* in it all."[50] *Carmen Jones* was clearly trapped between two aesthetic worlds, unable to escape the deeply entrenched stereotypes of African American performance.

The aesthetic double bind of conflicting visual and aural representations lurks beneath the film's glossy surface as well. Marilyn Horne and LeVern Hutcherson—both trained opera singers—were brought in to dub the singing voices of Dandridge and Belafonte. Horne was in her early twenties, a college music major who had dropped out to pursue a professional singing career. When Twentieth Century–Fox put out the casting call for the soundtrack, Horne attended, expecting to earn a little money for singing in the chorus. As she notes in her autobiography, "There was no color barrier either—whites could apply."[51] Her audition process was a near inversion of Dandridge's initial meetings with Preminger. Horne sang Micaëla's aria "Je dis que rien ne m'épouvante" in the original French, but quickly realized that this was not the effect the producers were striving for.[52] Given a second attempt, she sang "Habañera" with Hammerstein's lyrics, admitting later that "I was embarrassed to say I tore into those lyrics with the most blatant imitation of darky dialogue this side of Catfish Row."[53] Horne was called back the next day to test for the singing role of Carmen.

Although Horne was not yet an established opera star, there is something unsettling about the vocal quality in the dubbing. Her Carmen Jones voice is thin and reedy, her execution of the runs and roulades in "Der's a Café on de Corner" (the "Seguidilla") sound "suspiciously sloppy, again as though the producers assumed that since 'Carmen Jones' could not be expected to negotiate such ornaments, Horne would need to smear them."[54] Likewise, Hutcherson's voice for Joe is thin, halting, and breathy. McClary argues that the producers were striving for the illusion of "authenticity" rather than any European operatic ideal, which is partially true. Horne was white, but LeVern Hutcherson was African American, a trained lyrical spinto tenor who had pushed his voice down to the baritone range to sing Porgy.[55] One can speculate that his vocal problems on the film resulted from the higher vocal range demanded for Joe. Such was not the case for Horne. She explained that she "worked closely with Dorothy Dandridge, listening carefully to her speaking and singing voice in order to *match the timbre and accent* so that when I recorded the songs, I had a little bit of Dandridge in my throat. She sang in a register comfortable for her; then *I mimicked her voice* in the proper key."[56] The statement "in the proper key" implies that Dandridge did not have the vocal range to sing the part, but more unsettling is Horne's concept of mimicking timbre and accent, disguising whiteness in "blatant imitation of darky dialogue."

Horne's limpid vocalization, combined with the setting for Carmen Jones's two main seduction scenes, undermines the character's powerful sexuality and physicality, both crucial elements if the audience is to accept what appears to be an all-too-easy seduction of Joe. In the opera, on stage, and on screen, Carmen–Carmen Jones makes her much-anticipated hip-swaying entrance to the tango rhythm of "Habañera" (Hammerstein's "Dat's Love"). In the film, however, the scene is set in a cafeteria, where the soldiers and parachute factory workers eat lunch. Despite the wide angle of the camera's lens, Carmen Jones is forced to work her magic by weaving her way between the rows of tables, while the cafeteria's patrons look on. Her restrained physicality in this scene is even more pronounced in the "Seguidilla" ("Der's a Café on de Corner"). As in the opera, Carmen Jones has been arrested, and Joe has been ordered to take her to jail, but in a town more than fifty miles away. Enclosed within the confines of an army jeep, Carmen Jones is already imprisoned: she is not free to dance. Nonetheless, it is her body that seduces Joe. As he drives, she invades his personal space, stretching her legs across the seats, leaning over the front seat, touching him, caressing him, and teasing, while singing (albeit badly) the sinuous roulades, flourishes, and chromatic excesses of the song. Joe brushes her off but does not respond musically; a substantial, and very important part, of Bizet's original music has been cut from this scene. In the opera and in the 1991 London cast recording of the musical, Don José–Joe is pulled into Carmen–Carmen Jones's musical world.[57] He falls victim here to what McClary describes as Carmen's "discursive perversity," which argues that Carmen can "converse fluently in José's musical tongue and seduces him in the 'Seguidilla' by dictating to him in his own histrionic style the terms of his passion."[58] In the film, the moment when Carmen Jones slips from her rather lowbrow, cabaret-style dance tune into high-art operatic song was cut, as was Joe's capitulation. Both musically and in terms of the plot, the seduction of the "Seguidilla"—its whole raison d'être—has been eliminated. At the end of the song, Joe is unconvinced. Carmen Jones momentarily escapes, but he chases her down and restrains her, first tying her feet with his belt(!), then her hands with his handkerchief. In a near flashback to *Tarzan's Peril,* Dandridge once again became the "jungle queen tied to the stakes."[59]

If the dance is restrained or subdued in the two previous scenes, such is not the case later in the film. The party at Billy Pastor's begins with an ensemble dance number, "Beat Out Dat Rhythm on a Drum," an extensive rearrangement of Bizet's "Gypsy Song." Using soft mallets, the drummer seems intent on imitating the sound of primitive jungle drums, with the rhythm engaging the collective body of the ensemble in a wild, impassioned jitterbug.[60] The panoramic view of CinemaScope technology heightens the impact of the scene, capturing every frenzied gesture. The drumbeat as signifier of blackness is made explicit when Pearl Bailey—as Carmen's friend Frankie—belts out the lyrics to the second verse, "testifying to the innate relationship between drums and black bodies":[61]

> I feel it beatin' in my bones
> It feel like twenty millyun tom-toms,
> I know dere's twenty millyun tom-toms
> Beatin' 'way down deep inside my bones!
> I feel it beatin' in my heart
> An' den I get a kin' o' dream
> An' in my dream it kin' o' seem
> Dere's jus' one heart in all de worl.'

Bailey sings in her own voice, not in a quasi-operatic style, and at one point in the song borrows a phrase from an earlier black musical film, *Stormy Weather* (1943). Musically and visually, the scene is the most unequivocal fusion of Spanish gypsies with southern blacks. The scene is also a significant departure from Bizet in one other respect: in the opera, this number is sung by Carmen herself. The music was transposed down nearly an octave to accommodate Bailey's alto voice, raising the question as to why no such accommodation was made for either Dandridge or Belafonte. Jeff Smith asserts that "Bailey sings her own part because she, more than any other character, must bear the burden of *Carmen Jones*'s construction of racial identity."[62] If Dandridge and Belafonte "mime" the voices of white European culture, Bailey is the "authentic" voice of blackness as it was understood in 1950s American culture.

Although the stage version of *Carmen Jones* drew overwhelmingly favorable reviews, Preminger's film provoked a mixed response from the critics, especially from members of the African American community. Donald Bogle demonstrated the historical lineage of the various stereotypes in *Carmen Jones*, but he provided little in the way of a critique or deconstruction of those stereotypes. For Bogle, the film's box-office success and Dandridge's subsequent launch into motion-picture stardom seems to have negated any need for such a critique. James Baldwin, on the other hand, offered a far more caustic commentary on the plot incongruities and the exoticized and erotic representation of blackness in this film. Baldwin asserts, "The only reason, finally, that the eroticism of *Carmen Jones* is more potent than, say, the eroticism of a Lana Turner vehicle is that *Carmen Jones* has Negro bodies before the camera and Negroes are associated in the public mind with sex. Since darker races always seem to have for lighter races an aura of sexuality, this fact is not distressing in itself. What is distressing is the conjecture this movie leaves one with as to what Americans take sex to be." He reminds us that the film has nothing to do with the realities of Negro life and that the cast are "*exceptional* Negroes, as American, that is, as you and me, interpreting lower class Negroes." Nevertheless, Baldwin argues that "Negroes . . . have until now survived public images even more appalling" and would likely continue to do so. White critics, too, finally had something to say other than over-the-top superlatives, acknowledging that there was an element of commercial exploitation behind the all-black cast. *Carmen Jones* was "a pretty obvious device for converting color into coin," one that Hollywood shrewdly packaged and promoted to appeal to the taste of white audiences.[63]

Conclusion

Whether on stage or on screen, in sound or in image, representations of blackness in *Carmen Jones* are problematic. Although the Technicolor bodies were used to maximum effect, providing an important vehicle for black talent when little other opportunity was available, that talent—Baldwin's "exceptional Negroes"—was confined to a version of African American culture that was not of their own making. As sociologist John Bush Jones has noted, "Like segregated black military units commanded by white officers, most black-performed musicals were white-created and directed; in both, whites were in the position of power, with blacks executing their ideas and orders." Music historian Rudi Blesh, writing about *Porgy and Bess* in 1946, lamented the ramifications of such white control. "By enlisting actual Negroes for the public performance of Tin Pan Alley potpourri," Blesh contended, "a new stereotype—this time a cultural one—is being fitted to the Negro in which he is set forth as an able entertainer singing a music that the white public finds to be just like *its own.*"[64] For some time, whites effectively blocked the institutional space and financial backing that would allow black creative control over black cultural productions.[65] In terms of the *Carmen* story, even when black creative control is manifest, representations of blackness are still embroiled in nineteenth-century bourgeois cultural values. Despite whatever Hammerstein may have intended, *Carmen Jones* is a construction of the racial Other, just like the original *Carmen:* a spectacle written and staged by white producers, directors, and managers, for consumption by primarily white audiences. *Carmen Jones* may have brought the story of *Carmen* to a wider audience, but when we ask who is creating images of whom, and toward what ends, we find that the politics of color on the Broadway stage are not so different from those of the opera house.

Notes

1. Green, *Rodgers and Hammerstein Fact Book,* 498–507.

2. Preminger, *Carmen Jones.*

3. Baldwin, "*Carmen Jones,*" 35–41.

4. Ibid., 38.

5. Frank Rich, "*Show Boat:* The Musical Classic, Is New Again," *New York Times,* October 25, 1993, B1; Graziano, "Images of African Americans," 99; Breon, "*Show Boat,*" 94, 86. According to Breon, the *Amsterdam News* was the largest black circulation newspaper in the United States.

6. In addition to *The Swing Mikado,* the Negro Units "had been active in adapting [other] European works for African American performers"—for example, *Macbeth* (1936) and *Fra Diavolo* (1937). See Fauser, "*Dixie Carmen,*" 129.

7. Vallillo, "Battle of the Black Mikados," 153, 154–55.

8. Actors in the WPA production were paid $44.50 weekly, slightly more than the minimum $40.00 for actors on the road with commercial productions. In addition, the WPA actors were not required to belong to Equity, thereby avoiding the union's $50.00 initiation fee and dues. Even with the higher wages for its cast, the top ticket price for *The Swing Mikado* was $1.10, while *The Hot Mikado* topped out at $3.30. See "WPA 'Swing Mikado' to Go Commercial," *New York Times,* April 11, 1939, 25.

9. Vallillo, "Battle of the Black Mikados," 153, 155.

10. Ibid., 155.

11. For more on this issue, see Boyd, "Re-Orienting the Vision."

12. Vallillo, "Battle of the Black Mikados," 157.

13. Fordin, *Getting to Know Him,* 180.

14. Evidence of Hammerstein's interest in *Lulu Belle* dates from a remark made in 1959. See Fauser, "*Dixie Carmen,*" 131, esp. nn. 10 and 12.

15. Ibid., 131, 133.

16. Ibid., 131.

17. Fordin, *Getting to Know Him,* 178.

18. Ibid., 179, 182; Fauser, "*Dixie Carmen,*" 134.

19. Hammerstein was not the first choice for this project. According to Ann Sears, Richard Rodgers's longtime lyricist Lorenz Hart had refused to work on it, even though Rodgers threatened to find another lyricist. See Sears, "Coming of the Musical Play," 148.

20. Oscar Hammerstein I spearheaded a number of projects aimed at producing grand opera in English. His most audacious undertaking, the Manhattan Opera Company, ran from 1906 to 1910 in direct competition with the Metropolitan Opera. Oscar I was first and foremost a showman; he offered lucrative contracts to the leading singers and conductors of the time. According to Irving Kolodin, the Manhattan Opera Company was "the most worrisome competition that the Metropolitan Opera had ever known—artistically, without question, even though the social luster was silver and rhinestones, rather than gold and diamonds." Cone, *Hammerstein's Manhattan Opera Company,* vii.

21. Hammerstein quoted in Mordden, *Beautiful Mornin',* 79; Fordin, *Getting to Know Him,* 180.

22. Fordin, *Getting to Know Him,* 180; Hammerstein quoted in Irving Spiegel, "Negro Cast Will Sing *Carmen,*" *New York Times,* August 24, 1942, X1.

23. It is worth noting that George Gershwin's *Porgy and Bess* (1935) was also set in South Carolina. Oscar Hammerstein II and Jerome Kern had considered setting DuBose Heyward's *Porgy* (the play) to music for Al Jolson, but "ultimately dropped their option, allowing Gershwin to begin developing the Heywards' work." Woll, *Black Musical Theatre,* 164–65. Fauser notes that the original version of *Carmen Jones* was set in a cigarette factory (like Bizet's opera), not a parachute factory. Hammerstein's extensive revisions, including the change in locale, were part of a larger effort on Hammerstein's part to focus on "World War II and modern U.S. life as a framework for the *Carmen* story." "*Dixie Carmen,*" 142.

24. Spiegel noted that "a ban on toreadors and the transformation of Toreador Escamillo into Hepcat Miller represented the only conspicuous liberty Oscar 2d has taken with the music-drama personnel." "Negro Cast Will Sing *Carmen,*" X1.

25. McClary, *Georges Bizet: Carmen,* 132; Bogle, *Toms, Coons, Mulattoes, Mammies, and Bucks,* esp. chap. 1.

26. Green, *Rodgers and Hammerstein Fact Book,* 501. Bizet's *Carmen* was commissioned by the Paris Opéra-Comique, which required spoken dialogue between musical numbers. Following Bizet's death in 1875, only a few months after the premiere of *Carmen,* the dialogue was set as recitative by Ernest Guiraud in time for the Vienna premiere in October 1875. See McClary, *Georges Bizet: Carmen,* 18.

27. Brooks Atkinson, drama critic for the *New York Times,* lamented, "Turning *Porgy* into an opera has resulted in a deluge of casual remarks that have to be thoughtfully intoned and that amazingly impede the action. . . . Now, why in heaven's name must two characters in an opera clear their throats before they can exchange that sort of information?" Woll, *Black Musical Theatre,* 171.

28. Fauser, "*Dixie Carmen,*" 148, 149.

29. Ibid., 150.

30. Fordin provides a brief example of the type of "stiff" scholarly translation that Hammerstein abhorred:

> Ah! Love thou art a willful wild bird,
> And none may hope thy wings to tame,
> If it please thee to be a rebel,
> Say, who can try and thee reclaim?
> Threat and prayers alike unheeding;
> Oft ardent homage thou'lt refuse,
> Whilst he who doth coldly slight thee
> Thou for my master oft thou'lt choose.

(*Getting to Know Him,* 181; lyrics for "Dat's Love" from Hammerstein, *Carmen Jones: Vocal Selections*)

31. According to the old wives' tale, putting salt on a bird's tail is supposed to prevent the bird from flying away.

32. Richard Maney, "Billy Rose and *Carmen Jones,*" *New York Times,* November 28, 1943, X1.

33. Henry Bradford Darrach Jr., *Time,* November 1, 1954, quoted in Green, *Rodgers and Hammerstein Fact Book,* 506; Nora Holt, "*Carman* [*sic*] *Jones* Magnificent with Quips, Says Nora Holt," *New York Amsterdam News,* January 8, 1944, cited in Fauser, "*Dixie Carmen,*" 153; Baldwin, "*Carmen Jones,*" 37 (emphasis in the original).

34. Julian Wollford, liner notes to *Carmen Jones,* original London cast recording (EMI Classics, CDC 7 54351 2, 1991), 10.

35. Spiegel, "Negro Cast Will Sing *Carmen,*" X1; Nietzsche, *The Case of Wagner,* 158 (emphasis added). In a private communication to his son Bill (October 1943), Hammerstein also noted, "I am not as original as I thought and Nietsche was ahead of his time. Furthermore, I am pretty sure I am misspelling his name." Fauser, "*Dixie Carmen,*" 155.

36. McClary, *Georges Bizet: Carmen,* 51–52.

37. Ibid., 90; Bill Doll, "Beating the Drums for *Carmen Jones,*" *New York Times,* January 30, 1944, X1.

38. McClary, *Georges Bizet: Carmen,* 54.

39. It is worth noting, as McClary reminds us, that "Bizet gives the other potentially exotic characters besides Carmen (the cigarette girls, the male gypsies) relatively normative discourses not marked by the 'Orient.'" Ibid., 56.

40. Ibid., 56, 55.

41. Bogle, *Toms, Coons, Mulattoes, Mammies, and Bucks,* 160; Rhines, *Black Film/White Money,* 40; Bogle, *Toms, Coons, Mulattoes, Mammies, and Bucks,* 169.

42. Ibid., 168, 169 (emphasis added). The contrast of Dandridge's image makeover is vividly depicted in HBO's 1999 biopic *Introducing Dorothy Dandridge.* In this film, Dandridge (portrayed by Halle Berry), dressed in a stylish yet demure skirt suit, hat, and gloves, attends a private reading with Otto Preminger, hoping to be cast in the title role in *Carmen Jones.* When Preminger offers her the minor role of Cindy Lou, Dandridge

returns for a second reading, transformed in dress and demeanor, into Carmen Jones. Coolidge, *Introducing Dorothy Dandridge.*

43. Bogle, *Toms, Coons, Mulattoes, Mammies, and Bucks,* 168. Dandridge's mother, an actress-comedienne, was black, and her father, a minister, was white.

44. Ibid., 9.

45. Ibid., 190, 13, 169.

46. Smith, "Black Face, White Voices," 32; Lewis Nichols, "The Play," *New York Times,* December 3, 1943, 26.

47. Richard Maney, "Billy Rose and *Carmen Jones,*" *New York Times,* November 28, 1943, X1; Olin Downes, "*Carmen Jones:* New Treatment, though Brilliant, Not Equal to the Original in Many Ways," *New York Times,* December 19, 1943, X9.

48. Maney, "Billy Rose and *Carmen Jones,*" X1.

49. Nichols, "The Play," 26; "Muriel Smith," 244–45.

50. Fauser, "*Dixie Carmen,*" 141; Downes, "*Carmen Jones,*" X9 (emphasis added).

51. Horne with Scovell, *Marilyn Horne,* 64–65.

52. Olga James, who was trained at Juilliard, was cast as the film's Cindy Lou (Micaëla) and sang in her own voice.

53. Ibid., 65.

54. McClary, *Georges Bizet: Carmen,* 133.

55. Hutcherson sang Porgy in the 1953 revival and on the 1956 European tour. See http://www.soundfountain.com/gershwin/porgybess.html.

56. Horne with Scovell, *Marilyn Horne,* 67 (emphasis added).

57. Oscar Hammerstein, *Carmen Jones,* original London cast recording, Wilhelmenia Fernandez (Carmen Jones), Damon Evans (Joe), and musical director and conductor Henry Lewis (EMI Classics CDC 7 54351 2, 1991).

58. McClary, *Georges Bizet: Carmen,* 57.

59. Donald Bogle has noted the resemblance between this scene and the one in Dandridge's earlier film *Tarzan's Peril* (1951), where Dandridge, "as a kidnapped African princess, was tied to the stakes by a warlike tribal leader. As she lay with legs sprawled apart, heaving and turning to break loose, it was apparent that never before had the black woman been so erotically and obviously used as a sex object." See *Toms, Coons, Mulattoes, Mammies, and Bucks,* 168–69.

60. The scene is reminiscent of a similar scene in *Cabin in the Sky* (1943), where the music is provided by Duke Ellington and his orchestra.

61. McClary, *Georges Bizet: Carmen,* 134.

62. Smith, "Black Faces, White Voices," 36.

63. Baldwin, "*Carmen Jones,*" 40, 37–38 (emphasis in the original), 40; Darrach quoted in Green, *Rodgers and Hammerstein Fact Book,* 506.

64. Jones, "World War II and the Rodgers and Hammerstein Years," 130; Blesh quoted in Melnick, "Harold Cruse's Worst Nightmare," 96 (emphasis in the original).

65. The issue of white control over cultural productions, especially with respect to Jewish artistic identity and expression, is explored in several recent studies. John Bush Jones's *Our Musicals, Ourselves* and Jeffrey Melnick's critique of Harold Cruse are but two examples.

Bibliography

Baldwin, James. "*Carmen Jones:* The Dark Is Light Enough." In *Collected Essays.* New York: Literary Classics of the United States, 1998.

Bogle, Donald. *Toms, Coons, Mulattoes, Mammies, and Bucks: An Interpretive History of Blacks in American Film.* 3rd ed. New York: Continuum, 1994.

Boyd, Melinda. "Re-Orienting the Vision: Ethnicity and Authenticity from Suzuki to Comrade Chin." In *A Vision of the Orient: Texts, Intertexts, and Contexts of Madame Butterfly,* ed. Jonathan Wisenthal, Sherrill Grace, Melinda Boyd, Brian McIlroy, and Vera Micznik, 59–71. Toronto: University of Toronto Press, 2006.

Breon, Robin. "*Show Boat:* The Revival, the Racism." *Drama Review* 39, no. 2 (1995).

Cone, Frederick. *Oscar Hammerstein's Manhattan Opera Company.* Norman: University of Oklahoma Press, 1966.

Coolidge, Martha, dir. *Introducing Dorothy Dandridge.* HBO Home Video, DVD 0783116788, 1999.

Fauser, Annegret. "*Dixie Carmen:* War, Race, and Identity in Oscar Hammerstein's *Carmen Jones* (1943)." *Journal of the Society for American Music* 4, no. 2 (2010).

Fordin, Hugh. *Getting to Know Him: A Biography of Oscar Hammerstein.* Introduction by Stephen Sondheim. 1977. Reprint, New York: Ungar, 1986.

Graziano, John. "Images of African Americans: African-American Musical Theatre, *Show Boat,* and *Porgy and Bess.*" In *The Cambridge Companion to the Musical,* ed. William A. Everett and Paul R. Laird. 2nd ed. Cambridge: Cambridge University Press, 2008.

Green, Stanley, ed. *Rodgers and Hammerstein Fact Book.* New York: Lynn Farnol Group, 1980.

Hammerstein, Oscar, II. *Carmen Jones: Vocal Selections.* New York: Williamson Music, 1943.

Horne, Marilyn, with Jane Scovell. *Marilyn Horne: The Song Continues.* Fort Worth: Baskerville, 2004.

Jones, John Bush. "World War II and the Rodgers and Hammerstein Years." In *Our Musicals, Ourselves: A Social History of the American Musical Theatre.* Hanover, N.H.: Brandeis University Press, 2003.

McClary, Susan. *Georges Bizet: Carmen.* Cambridge Opera Handbook. Cambridge: Cambridge University Press, 1992.

Melnick, Jeffrey. "Harold Cruse's Worst Nightmare: Rethinking *Porgy and Bess.*" In *Harold Cruse's "The Crisis of the Negro Intellectual" Reconsidered,* ed. Jerry Watts. New York and London: Routledge, 2004.

Mordden, Ethan. *Beautiful Mornin': The Broadway Musical in the 1940s.* Oxford: Oxford University Press, 1999.

"Muriel Smith." *Black Perspective in Music* 13, no. 2 (Autumn 1985).

Nietzsche, Friedrich. *The Case of Wagner.* Trans. Walter Kaufmann. New York: Random House, 1967.

Preminger, Otto. *Carmen Jones.* Twentieth Century-Fox, DVD, 2001.

Rhines, Jesse Algernon. *Black Film/White Money.* New Brunswick: Rutgers University Press, 1996.

Sears, Ann. "The Coming of the Musical Play." In *The Cambridge Companion to the Musical,* ed. William A. Everett and Paul R. Laird. 2nd ed. Cambridge: Cambridge University Press, 2009.

Smith, Jeff. "Black Face, White Voices: The Politics of Dubbing in *Carmen Jones.*" *Velvet Light Trap* 51 (Spring 2003).

Vallillo, Stephen M. "The Battle of the Black Mikados." *Black American Literature Forum* 16, no. 4 (1982).

Woll, Allan. *Black Musical Theatre: From Coontown to Dreamgirls.* Baton Rouge: Louisiana State University Press, 1989.

11

Performing Race in Ernst Krenek's *Jonny spielt auf*

JONATHAN O. WIPPLINGER

Though by far his most well-known work, Ernst Krenek had an ambiguous relationship toward his fourth opera, *Jonny spielt auf*, or "Jonny Strikes Up" (1927). This work is an ambitious combination of European modernism, American popular music, and what Krenek took to be jazz. Its plot pits a central European composer, Max, against an African American jazz musician, Jonny, popular and vital "jazz" against an icy and intellectual modernism. In the end, Jonny wins out over his European counterpart, and the opera concludes with a panegyric to Jonny, jazz, and America.[1] Despite the daring of the experiment, audiences generally responded enthusiastically. First in Germany and then from Paris to Moscow, Belgrade to Antwerp and beyond,[2] audiences swarmed to the opera's more than four hundred performances in the late 1920s.[3] Indeed, its fame was such that it was possible for a brand of Jonny cigarettes to be marketed in Austria.[4] Such unparalleled success brought the twenty-seven-year-old Krenek financial security and international recognition, but the opera's inclusion of jazz, modern technology, and interracial relations brought him controversy as well. Conservatives lambasted the work as a travesty of the Western tradition, while some quarters of the avant-garde, the Schoenberg circle in particular, criticized Krenek for forsaking their revolution in music for mere monetary gain.[5] All this, the success and the critique, came as a shock to the young Krenek, who would insist in later writings that his intentions behind *Jonny spielt auf* had been misunderstood, both by its admirers and by its critics.

Above all else, Krenek resisted the notion that *Jonny spielt auf* was a "jazz opera," a term often applied to the opera during the Weimar Republic.[6] Krenek was by no means unaware of the friction between the nomenclature of the "jazz opera" and his actual sparing use of jazz music in the opera; indeed, as many contemporary critics have pointed out, there is very little resembling authentic jazz in the opera, even as it was practiced in the 1920s.[7] As early as 1928 and as late as 1980, Krenek made clear that jazz did not constitute the musical foundation of this work. By the same token, however, jazz and African American culture are important points of reference for the opera: Jonny is the black band leader of the jazz band heard throughout the opera, and it is his music, rhythmic, tonal, and melodious, that contrasts most sharply to that of the other characters. So although *Jonny spielt auf* cannot be said to be a "jazz opera"—its "jazz" remains all too European and serves more as a point of contrast than as a foundational principle—it is a work deeply concerned with jazz, African Americans, and their image within European culture.

I will explore this idea through an analysis of the role of race and racial representation within Krenek's work. This will mean paying particular attention to how Jonny's musical, cultural, and racial identities are constructed in the opera. Beginning with a discussion of race and racial stereotypes within the score and libretto, also authored by Krenek, I suggest that Jonny is an amalgam of contradictory and competing ideas about African Americans and their music, drawing equally from the world of blackface minstrelsy, "jazz age" images of African Americans, and European ideas about African American spirituals and folk music. These multiple strands of Jonny's identity, between blackface and blackness, are never entirely reconciled in the opera. As a result, Jonny's true origin, the home to which he sings of returning toward the end of the opera, remains undefined. Unsurprisingly, the complexity of Jonny's character has had important consequences for the performance history of the opera. As I show in the second half, productions of the opera from the 1920s to the present have more often than not eschewed the ambiguity of the figure in favor of one element over another. From the Nazi appropriation of the image of Jonny as an essentialized black musician to the New York Metropolitan Opera's staging of Jonny as a white blackface minstrel, Jonny's identity has been the most consistently inconsistent aspect of the opera's production history. Yet these inconsistencies have not been forced on Krenek's work from the outside; rather, they form the core of the opera itself. So before looking to how others interpreted Jonny, we must first examine Krenek's own indeterminate construction of Jonny's identity.

"Saxophone in his hand and a comical hat on his head": Racial Stereotype in *Jonny spielt auf*

Though Jonny is first introduced in the third scene of the opera, a racial subtext is present in the work from almost the very beginning. At the opening of the second scene—before a single note of Jonny's "jazz" has sounded—we are given a visual clue as to the importance of African American music to the opera. In the hotel room of the opera singer Anita, there lies a banjo on top of a grand piano. This banjo will later play a pivotal role in the plot, but its presence here is significant insofar as it is the first material connection between European (the piano) and African American (the banjo) music. Directly following this visual foreshadowing, we hear, for the first time, the jazz music with which the opera has long been associated. An isolated woodblock strikes out a rhythmic figure consisting of two eighth notes followed by three quarter notes in an upbeat cut-time tempo. This "shimmy figure," as J. Bradford Robinson has convincingly argued, was a standardized means of Weimar-era composers to indicate a jazz milieu. "As inconspicuous as it may seem," Robinson argues, the shimmy figure "was in fact central to the musical thought of those Weimar composers who adapted what they considered to be jazz for their stage works. It was set aside for crucial moments in the drama, heralding the entrance of a jazz backdrop, precipitating a turning point in the hero's fortunes, or standing out by being placed in the spotlight of an onstage jazz combo."[8] Krenek uses the shimmy figure in *Jonny spielt auf* to signal the shift within the musical world of the opera from the neo-romantic, tonally ambiguous introduction to that of Jonny—tonally centered and dominated by a succinct yet powerful rhythm.

The jazz world intimated by this turn, however, is complicated through the imagery that accompanies this music. Though the audience may have the jazzy shimmy figure in its ears when Jonny enters, what it sees is an amalgam of blackface minstrelsy and jazz-age iconography.[9] Krenek's initial description of his "jazz" protagonist is as follows: "Jonny comes after ending his song with a saxophone in his hand and a comical hat on his head."[10] It is of course important that his entrance is accompanied by a saxophone, which by the mid-1920s was replacing the drums as the primary symbol for jazz in Germany. As can be gathered from publicity photographs from the period, the saxophone, though seen only for a moment, was crucial to the marketing of the opera (figure 1).

The meticulousness of Jonny's half-tuxedo, as well, places him within the contemporary nightclub milieu of jazz performers.[11] At the same time, other elements of Jonny's costume, including his tattered checkered pants and blackface makeup, clearly reference minstrelsy and its racist lampooning of African Americans. Furthermore, the comic quality ascribed to his bowler hat acts to distance Jonny from the seriousness and brooding of his high-culture counterpart, Max. Through the visual keys of Jonny's costume, then, the shimmy figure's unequivocal expression of jazz-age symbolism becomes alloyed with elements of minstrelsy. Like much in the opera, this introduction straddles two modes of representation, without ever reconciling them.

Krenek's treatment of Jonny's language further undercuts the jazziness of Jonny's introduction. Throughout the opera, Jonny's speech is peppered with numerous supposed Americanisms, which serve to constantly reinforce the foreignness of the character to the German setting. And though Jonny does at

Figure 1. Alfred Jerger as Jonny (Vienna, 1928).

times speak fluent German, Krenek's repeated interruptions of his speech with obvious and jarring grammatical errors outweigh any temporary fluency.[12] For instance, the first words uttered by Jonny, "Oh, ma bell,'" derive from German stereotypes about African American speech. As Michael von der Linn shows, this phrase is directly indebted to the German reception of ragtime and "coon" songs from the early 1900s.[13] By infusing Jonny's speech with such minstrel argot, Krenek maintains Jonny's distance from the audience, which may laugh at Jonny, but seldom with him.

More important to Krenek's stereotypical presentation of his opera's namesake than this linguistic or visual coding is the positioning of Jonny in relation to the other main figures of the opera, particularly white women. The subject of Jonny's desire for and power over white women first becomes apparent through his relationship with the chambermaid, Yvonne. In their ensuing duet after his shimmy introduction, Jonny and Yvonne exchange kisses and proclamations of love.[14] Jonny's sexual conquest of a white woman obviously plays on longstanding tropes of the minstrel stage. German audiences at the time, however, would also have seen such behavior as an allusion to the so-called Black Horror on the Rhine (*Schwarze Schmach am Rhein*). The "horror" consisted of the French stationing of African troops, mostly from Senegal, in postwar Germany in order to exact reparations from the Germans. An international campaign resisting this occupation grew during the early 1920s, centering on the purported sexual savagery of the Africans toward German women.[15] Though most of the troops were removed after 1925, fears surrounding black male sexuality remained. In Jonny's relationships with the opera's white females, German and American racial politics mix as Krenek exploits this theme of the minstrel stage to excite the fears of the German populace.[16]

Jonny's hypersexuality is coupled with his extreme materialism. The full force of this characteristic emerges through the introduction of a third male figure, Daniello, who is the owner of an Amati violin desired by Jonny.[17] Daniello is essential to any understanding of the function of race within the opera: a southern European violin virtuoso and sexually ravenous Don Juan figure, he provides Krenek with a third model of musical and sexual relationships. He is in many ways identical to Jonny, their shared obsession with the Amati violin the most obvious sign of their connection. As Krenek described in a 1928 lecture delivered on the occasion of the Vienna premiere of *Jonny spielt auf,* Daniello represents "the European version of the Negro, who combines the close proximity to life and vitality of Jonny with a cultivated and dapper exterior agreeable to the civilized white person [*weißer Zivilisationsmensch*]."[18] Daniello, for example, also demands and receives sexual attention from the two female leads of the opera, Anita and Yvonne. Further, like Jonny (and importantly unlike Max), Daniello possesses a large, adoring audience, one that clamors for his autograph when he makes his first entrance.[19] Yet whereas Jonny seduces his audience through the sounds of the New World, Daniello's seduction occurs through his misuse of European tradition for material rather than spiritual purposes. Krenek summarized his view of Daniello, saying, it is this "conceited, empty headed, yet instinctual smooth operator who greedily profits from the precious, yet abandoned inheritance of our artistic culture and, . . . unworthy of the noble Amati violin in his possession, hands over the heritage of a better past to an empty age."[20]

The symbolic rivalry between Jonny and Daniello peaks in their simultaneous attempt to woo Anita. As suggested earlier, the "threat" to Anita by Jonny is present from the beginning through the presence of the banjo in her room. This instrument now appears in her hands as she carries it up to her room toward the middle of the third scene.[21] Encountering Anita and the banjo, Jonny proclaims his unmediated desire, saying, "Oh, by jove, the white woman is beautiful."[22]

Krenek simultaneously plays into and off of fears surrounding the "Black Horror" and "miscegenation" in the following scene in which Jonny attempts to seduce Anita. Anita parries his initial advance, but only with difficulty. Jonny responds, "I know you whites: First you resist. Then you are overjoyed, and then adieu! It's like this that you make savage beasts out of us."[23] Daniello confronts Jonny at this point, saying: "*Ôte toi négrillon!*"[24] Though Jonny assumes a threatening posture in response, Daniello is able to deflate his rage by giving him one thousand francs. Krenek describes the change in Jonny's demeanor that results from this exchange as the transformation from an "animalistic, sensuous, raging grimace" to a broad grin.[25] As Kevin Amidon has argued, this transfer of money instigates a fundamental shift in the opera's (and Jonny's) gravitational center. Amidon suggests that through this exchange, "Jonny . . . separates himself from the body of the human female, and his desires are concentrated on the violin from this point on."[26] What this moment highlights is not only the reinforcement of Jonny's materialism, but also a shift away from black-white sexual relations toward the theme of black-white musical and cultural relations. Beginning with Jonny's acceptance of the money, the racial threat and difference of Jonny are transferred from the sexual to the cultural realm. This conflict is allegorized in Jonny's desire for and eventual possession of Daniello's violin. With this transference of desire, then, music becomes the battleground on which Krenek stages the confrontation between African American and European culture.

Jonny's Music

Though Jonny's music becomes a central theme of the opera after his exchange with Daniello, my focus in elaborating Krenek's conception of African American music will be on Jonny's solo pieces, rather than on performances of his jazz band or his jazzy duets. Jazz does not constitute a true reflection of Jonny's music—not because Krenek had a limited understanding of this art form, but because Krenek purposefully separates his title character from jazz. For an opera so long associated with the music played by Jonny's jazz band, Krenek's score repeatedly instructs that the jazz band is not to be visible to the audience when it plays, and, more important, we never actually see Jonny playing jazz.[27] In *Jonny spielt auf*, the audience has only a mediated encounter with jazz music, which is heard as an echo from a nearby ballroom or over the ether on a radio. One might go so far as to say that jazz is not necessarily Jonny's music, but the music he plays for others. Instead of through jazz, Krenek seeks to distinguish Jonny's music through other forms of what he took to be African American music: the minstrel song, the spiritual, and African American folk music.

Entering Daniello's room, Jonny comes to steal the Amati violin. Here Krenek again invokes the world of minstrelsy in his stage directions. Jonny is to "sneer bestially" as he passes the room with Anita and Daniello, who is apparently enjoying the night for which he paid Jonny.[28] Rather than immediately taking the violin, however, Jonny places it into the felt case of the banjo, which Anita has left hanging outside of her room, putting his bowler hat on top to make it appear as if a banjo were inside. To the accompaniment of the banjo, he now sings to the sleeping violin in a polyglot of English and imperfect German. It is significant that he does so with the aid of this instrument, neither part of Krenek's instrumentation for the orchestra nor that for Jonny's jazz band.[29] Indeed, Jonny is the only character to play the banjo, and though it is in Anita's possession at the beginning, culturally and musically it belongs to him. In addition to being the only time he sings with the banjo, it is also his only solo to be sung in a minor key.[30] In keeping with his caricatured presentation throughout the first act, this piece is designated in the score as to be played "in the manner of a Nigger-song," but this scene also marks the first moment in the opera in which Jonny is heard and seen performing for himself, rather than with or for others.[31] So although it remains constricted by the stereotypical presentation of Jonny in the first act, it is our first hint at Jonny's unique musical identity that emerges fully once he has taken possession of the violin.

Jonny's next solo moment occurs during the second act after the setting has shifted to an anonymous central European city. Jonny has followed Anita and Yvonne to reacquire the violin, which he left with them for safekeeping. He grabs the banjo case at the beginning of the scene and, to Yvonne's surprise, reveals the stolen violin. Jonny now enters into his song of triumph, or "Triumphlied," as this song was later marketed to the public through recordings and sheet music.[32] The stage directions continue with the minstrel setting of the earlier piece. As he unpacks the violin, he removes his hat, places it on his head, and turns with a "triumphal circus attitude" toward the audience to sing:[33]

> JONNY: Now the violin is mine and I want to play it like *old* David once struck the harp, and praise Jehovah, who created black mankind.
> YVONNE: Yes, but does it belong to you?
> JONNY: I possess everything that is good in the world. The old world created it, but no longer knows what to do with it. Now the new world comes from across the sea with splendor and inherits old Europe through dance.[34]

This piece represents the first time Jonny expresses an idea that goes beyond the base materialism and hypersexuality he shares with Daniello. Krenek explicitly states that Jonny "experiences a great moment, a vision of his destiny," in singing these words.[35] The music is major and tonal, strikingly so in the context of the generally dissonant idiom of the opera. Further, and like his other solos, the "Triumphlied" lacks the rhythmic pulse of the jazzier duets and background music supplied by the jazz band. In fact, Krenek's instructions indicate that this song is to be performed "in the manner of a Negro Spiritual."[36]

It is important that one take seriously the distinction between this "spiritual" and the jazz and minstrel music of the opera, which can be seen as belonging to Krenek's attempt to differentiate Jonny's solo music from the latter. Contrary to later statements by Krenek, in the 1920s he appears to have had clear and precise ideas about African American music and how it was misunderstood by European audiences.[37] In his 1928 lecture, Krenek explained the reasoning for inserting African American music into the opera. Comparing his use of jazz to the presence of technology in the opera, he asserts that an opera that takes place in the current age cannot avoid jazz, as it is the "world-dominating artistic force of our time."[38] However, he also rejects the idea that he set out to create a jazz opera. He does so not because this would be a denigration of European tradition, but because he feels that *Jonny spielt auf* does not achieve a full integration of jazz:

> The true jazz opera . . . will only be written when we rid ourselves of the idea that jazz music is something that is in essence entertaining and grotesque. . . . Whoever knows the unheard of power of expression that lies in the spirituals and folk songs [*Heimatgesänge*] of the American Negro, in which with an almost crushing intensity the entire naïve and unbroken emotional strength of a strong and tragic people are expressed in all possible shades of human feeling, will see jazz music as more than a comic form of entertainment. And the world conquering force of jazz lies above all in this side of its being, even if the other, viz. its tremendous usefulness and timeliness for the interests of modern man, initially received prominence.[39]

Here and elsewhere in the lecture, Krenek displays a patronizing attitude toward African Americans as natural and naive.[40] Yet just as importantly, Krenek distances himself from the view of jazz as comic and grotesque, an aspect of European jazz reception he references in the initial presentation of Jonny with a comical hat. Jonny's divine insight, his expression of something beyond the entertaining and grotesque, is, however, short-lived. Both before and after Jonny's profession of faith, Krenek surrounds him with stereotypes from the first act. As we saw, Jonny retrieves his comical hat and returns it to his head before he proceeds, and then, after his "Triumphlied" ends, the very same shimmy figure from the beginning returns.[41] Even performances of unmistakably "authentic" African American music—at least for Krenek—thus remain caught up between stereotypes of blackface and blackness.

In the third solo, the important matter of Jonny's home, both culturally and aesthetically, is addressed. It is here that we learn of his desire to leave Europe and return to America. While similar issues of displacement plague other figures, as a rural African American living in the European metropolis, Jonny represents an extreme case of dislocation and exile within modern society.[42] Indeed, whereas the first two solos engage with the indeterminate nature of Jonny's musical home between minstrelesque caricature, jazz, and African American spiritual, Krenek turns to African American folk music for his third solo. In the eighth scene of the second act, Jonny is on the run from the police for his theft of the violin and concludes that he must bid farewell to Europe and travel across the Atlantic.[43] As Jonny approaches the climax of his final solo, he sings, "I bought a ticket to Amsterdam and I'm going back home. I will see Alabama once more and never again leave my Swanee River."[44] What makes this passage so singular within the opera is not only what is sung, but what Krenek has inserted into the score: a seemingly innocuous footnote indicating that the source of Jonny's music is an "Old American Negro song" (example 1).[45] This is the sole explanatory note in a score littered with musical allusions, and Krenek's need to add this strange reference begs explanation.[46]

First, the quotation is not from an African American folk song, but Stephen Foster's "Old Folks at Home." Not only one of Foster's most well-known songs, this piece was an important part of the repertoire of blackface minstrel troupes after first being performed by Christy's Minstrels in 1854. Krenek's mistake may have stemmed from a performance he attended of the *Chocolate Kiddies,* the first African American revue to perform in Germany after World War I. In the program to this revue, the song "Swanee River" is listed as a "famous old Negro song."[47] Krenek might also have feared that the reference would fall on deaf ears, that is, that it would not be recognized as a quotation of (what he took to be) authentic African American music. In addition to Foster's "Old Folks at Home" and the *Chocolate Kiddies,* one can add two further precedents for the tune that would have made it recognizable to German audiences of the 1920s. These are Irving Berlin's 1914 ragtime song "Alexander's Ragtime Band," which quotes almost the same passage from Foster as Krenek, and the massive hit "Swanee" (1920), recorded by the blackface minstrel par excellence Al Jolson, a figure who will literally cross paths with Jonny two years later in New York.[48]

As we have seen, Krenek placed great emphasis on distinguishing Jonny's solo music from the jazz and "comedy" of other sections, and Jonny's "Swanee River" song is no exception. It is written in C-sharp major, which, as Amidon points out, is seldom used in this opera; tonal music in *Jonny spielt auf* is associated not with C-sharp major, but with its enharmonic equivalent, D-flat major.[49] The shift here to C-sharp highlights the fact that while Jonny's music may be tonal, its content is not identical to its European version—for example, Daniello. Like the "Triumphlied," Jonny's performance of the "Swanee River" song exists beyond the banality of the jazz band, and, although he does not experience a moment of transcendence, singing this piece does act to displace

Example 1. Jonny's "Old American Negro Song."

him from his immediate European context. After the last note has dissipated and the dissonance that frames his song returns, Jonny "looks around in order to orient himself somewhat."[50] The music surrounding him, clearly foreign for him, has brought Jonny back from the otherworldly home his folk song had taken him to.

Here as elsewhere, Jonny's music is unable to extricate itself from the strictures of the European setting, but the strange footnote and this song as a whole can be seen as belonging to Krenek's desire to draw a distinction between Jonny's music and the jazz he plays for others. The solo pieces make of Jonny a more rounded figure and elevate him, even if only for brief moments, above the mundane, commodified jazz of Europe as well as blackface stereotypes. Yet as Krenek's mistaken attribution of "Old Folks at Home" to the African American idiom demonstrates, the opera's realization of this ideal is imperfect and fraught with contradiction. The balance struck by the triangulation of Jonny's identity, between jazz, minstrelsy, and African American music, remains precarious. Not entirely successful in the original, productions of the opera have struggled, mostly unsuccessfully, to do justice to these overlapping identities. It is to these attempts that we now turn.

Performing Jonny's Identities

In the 1920s, the opera received the greatest number of productions in the German-speaking world, highlighted by its premiere in Leipzig (1927), as well as performances in Berlin (1927) and Vienna (1927–28). Reviewers across Germany had a mixed response. Along with the expected critique from conservative corners regarding the opera's depiction of "the triumph of black over white culture" came equally vociferous support for Krenek's attempt to place opera in conversation with contemporary society. Critic Adolf Aber went so far as to thank Krenek: "We owe a great deal to the young Ernst Krenek for an opera . . . that almost entirely corresponds to the sensibility and events of our day." The presence of jazz was especially valued as a sign of the opera's contemporaneity. Alfred Baresel, himself the author of a handbook on jazz, began his review, "Ernst Krenek has brought forth the *first jazz opera* . . . by using as a *means* what the world wishes to have as an end in itself. Jazz is here for him just like the racing cars, locomotives, loud speakers and physically uninhibited women—a means and prop for designating the world of Jonny." The world of Jonny referred to by Baresel is indicative of a trend in German productions to focus on jazz and the technological wonders of the opera to the detriment of Krenek's composer alter ego, Max. As Andreas Eichhorn demonstrates in his analysis of the German reception of the opera, the tremendous popularity enjoyed by *Jonny spielt auf* was not due to Krenek's score alone. Its success resulted, at least in part, from directors paring down those scenes involving Max, which audiences found to be static and boring, while emphasizing those involving Jonny and jazz, technology and tempo.[51] The increased attention placed on these elements may have made the opera more palatable to audiences, but without the counterweight of Max, Jonny's music becomes dislodged from the constellation of issues at work in the opera. No longer in dialogue with questions surrounding the commodification of culture, contemporary aesthetics, race, and gender, *Jonny spielt auf* became more and more just about "jazz," comedy, and entertainment.

In the rush to proclaim (or reject) the new operatic genre of the "jazz opera," critics not only missed Krenek's sparing use of jazz; they also failed to question whether his portrayal of African Americans was all that sympathetic, let alone realistic.[52] And no reviewer in Germany took note that in all of the performances, the role of Jonny was played by a white singer in blackface makeup, raising the question of whether Jonny's blackface mask was even visible to its German audience. That is to say, did German audiences view the blackfaced white performer as a caricature or as an "authentic" portrayal of African Americans? One particularly telling event occurred in Munich, where *Jonny spielt auf* was performed in 1928. In this conservative region and stronghold of the Nazi movement, resistance to the opera was great, as described by Susan C. Cook:

> Reports in the Munich press, prior to the opera's opening night, misrepresented the opera's theme and stated that a black singer would perform the title role. Protesters gathered outside the theater before the start of the sold-out premier. A full-fledged riot broke out when Alfred Jerger [a white singer in blackface] . . . began "Jetzt ist die Geige mein." Stink bombs went off, fights broke out, the manager stopped the performance, and the police were required to restore order. Jerger claimed a large crowd then assembled outside his dressing room and threatened to lynch the supposedly black performer. However, they quieted down upon realizing their mistake, and some carried Jerger upon their shoulders back to his hotel.[53]

This moment of misrecognition carries profound implications in terms of the role of race in the opera's reception. While at first sight, it suggests that German audiences unreflexively saw Jonny as a black character, a much deeper significance to the event emerges when it is considered in relation to the history of blackface minstrelsy in America. In *Love and Theft,* Eric Lott argues that early minstrel performances involved audience and performer in an unending oscillation of identities between blackface and blackness. "There was in minstrelsy," he maintains, "an unsteady but structured fluctuation between fascination with (or dread of) 'blackness' and fearful ridicule of it, underscored . . . by a fluctuation between sympathetic belief in the authenticity of blackface and ironic distance from its counterfeit representations."[54] In other words, the reaction of the audience to the blackface performer alternated between the suspension of disbelief regarding his identity and recognition of the counterfeit. Following Lott, one might suggest that in perceiving Jonny as a black person, the Nazis unwittingly disrupted the very racial hierarchies they intended to uphold. Their hatred for the black figure turned into adoration when the "true" whiteness of

Jonny was revealed. This oscillation between authenticity and fakery, fear and adulation means that even in his German reception, Jonny remained entangled in the indeterminacy that marked him in the original.

If European Jonnys faced the unintended consequences of performing an implicitly blackface role, entirely new dynamics arose when the opera came to New York's Metropolitan Opera in 1929. Though the New York staging took place almost two years after the premiere in Germany, it is one of the most important in the opera's history: not only did it present the European image of America to an American audience, but it was also the first production to substantially alter the character of Jonny. Due to segregation and fears of a negative reaction to the opera's many scenes and intimations of interracial sexual relations, the Metropolitan Opera explicitly staged Jonny as a white blackface minstrel and labeled him as such in the program.[55] Further, the libretto (though still in German) was sanitized and scenes upsetting racial hierarchies removed.[56] According to Olin Downes, who reviewed the opera for the *New York Times,* the scenes between Jonny and Anita were almost entirely eliminated from the American production, transforming her conflicted rejection of Jonny's advances into pure indigination.[57] In the finale, staged as an explosion of patriotic regalia, the male chorus performed in blackface and a "patriotic" costume of striped red pants and blue tailcoats.[58] Such changes transformed Krenek's opera into little more than a lighthearted, garish farce. Downes, who had attended the Leipzig premiere, criticized the New York take on *Jonny spielt auf,* writing, "Krenek did not dream of American flags or the Statues of Liberty, or pickaninny dancers, or any of the effects gratuitously wished upon him in the final scene at the Metropolitan."[59]

Though the matter is hardly as simple as Downes implies, the American production should be seen as being qualitatively different from its European counterparts. Although certainly not a true reflection of Krenek's piece, the Met's minstrelization of *Jonny spielt auf* is by the same token no bowdlerization: instead, it should be seen as concentrating the minstrel elements already present within the opera. This is nowhere more the case than with Jonny himself. No longer split between identities, the American Jonny, first played by Michael Bohnen and later succeeded by Lawrence Tibbett, could further emphasize the minstrelsy of the character. In one review, Tibbett's dress and makeup, black tuxedo with checkered yellow pants, are described in detail, as well as the audience's response to "laugh at and with" Tibbett. The linkage of the role to blackface minstrelsy in the minds of the audience was cemented through the presence of Al Jolson at the premiere, where Jolson reportedly gave Bohnen tips on his blackface makeup. Downes went so far as to suggest that Bohnen had "modeled his impersonation after the style of Al Jolson."[60]

The swing toward minstrelsy witnessed in the New York production radically affects how race functions within the opera. In its avowal of Jonny's minstrel heritage, it reinforces rather than upsets established racial hierarchies. The indeterminacy of the original gives way to a static representation of Otherness, and Jonny becomes nothing more than what he is supposed to be: a vicious caricature of African Americans. There are, therefore, no redeeming moments for America's minstrel Jonny; reduced to nothing more than a racial stereotype, the humanity of Jonny, tenuous in the original, is wholly forsaken here.

It is unsurprising that while New York audiences politely applauded Jonny's antics, critics found little of note in Krenek's work, and the European success of *Jonny spielt auf* failed to translate to America. With the disappointing response to the New York production and the descent of Germany into the abyss of National Socialism, *Jonny spielt auf* also went silent. Though Krenek was himself Catholic, the Nazis branded him and his music as primary examples of "cultural bolshevism" and "degenerate art," forcing the composer to flee, first from Germany to his native Austria and then to America, where he would live for the remainder of his life.[61] Yet while Krenek left the European scene for the American one, his creation remained. In 1938, Jonny once again took center stage within European cultural politics, this time as part of the Nazi exhibition of *Entartete Musik* (Degenerate Music). In this aural corollary to the more famous visual exhibition of a year earlier, the Nazis resuscitated the image of Jonny as a saxophone player with a comical hat. On the cover for the pamphlet that accompanied the exhibition, one finds the well-known, horrific caricature of a black saxophone player portrayed as more simian than human. This image of "Jonny," created by Ludwig Tersch, added yet another layer to the Jonny figure. It substitutes the flower on Jonny's lapel for a Star of David as part of the Nazi's ideological project of linking atonal, that is, "Jewish," music with African American jazz.[62] Inverting the Metropolitan Opera's admission of Jonny's fakery, the Nazis essentialize Jonny's blackness as an animalistic and corporeal primitivity, thereby seeking to exclude Africans and African Americans from the human race.

The genocidal racial politics employed against this work and its Gentile composer lent *Jonny spielt auf* an impeccable antifascist provenance, theoretically creating the chance for an unproblematic revival of the work after 1945. Even so, it took more than twenty years for the opera to be performed in Germany again.[63] It was in 1968 that Jonny received two new productions, one in Regensburg, Germany, and another in Salzburg, Austria. In these new productions, however, Jonny was for the first time performed by an African American. Juilliard graduate Allan Evans, then a student at Salzburg's Mozarteum, took the title role in both productions that year.[64] Though he was singled out for praise in reviews, no mention is made of the fact that he was the first African American to perform the role.[65] Yet if reviewers missed the momentousness of Evans's 1968 performances, there was one spectator for whom this event would have had more significance: Ernst Krenek, who was personally present in Salzburg as well as twelve years later when Evans performed the role for a third time as part of the *Wiener Festwochen* under the direction of Axel Corti. Evans once again received praise for his portrayal of Jonny, reviewer Walter Szmolyan calling him the highlight of the production.[66]

Before this 1980 production, Krenek authored a short piece recalling his opera's origins and performance history, which he titled "Jonny erinnert sich" (Jonny reminisces).[67] Particularly interesting about this article is that while the title brings Krenek closer to Jonny (rather than Max), Krenek uses the opportunity to distance his work from the genre of the jazz opera. Though this argument is not new, the reasoning behind it has changed. He seeks not to distance his work from the "true jazz opera," as had been the case in the 1928 lecture, but to distance the music of *Jonny spielt auf* from authentic African American jazz. By this time in his life, Krenek had lived longer in the United States than in Germany or Austria, and he found his lack of knowledge about jazz and African American music striking. "At the time," he writes, "we had only very vague conceptions about real jazz, which were primarily influenced by the touring 'jazz orchestras' of Paul Whiteman and other groups."[68] And in a move reflecting greater sensitivity toward the problematic stereotypes employed within his opera, Krenek spoke about the minstrel overtones in the New York production:

> When the Metropolitan Opera in New York released the piece, they prepared a special nuance for it. As it was "intolerable" according to the American mentality of the time that a white chambermaid have a relationship with a Negro, Jonny was described as "blackface" in the theater program, i.e. as a "minstrel." . . . So there was a white man (Michael Bohnen), who admitted to being a white man masked as a Negro so that he could play one. This is a logic only a schooled American can understand. Added to this, the opera was performed in German. I wasn't involved in the production as I had no desire to travel to the land of gangsters and prohibition.[69]

In rejecting the 1929 New York production and accepting the more recent versions with Evans, Krenek obviously sought to salvage the work's integrity as a racially progressive work, while avoiding the trickier question of Jonny's relatively seamless transformation into a blackface minstrel. As for Evans, he is keen to refer to the 1968 staging, remarking that this was the first time that his Jonny was performed by a "real black American."[70] The presence of an African American opera singer thus enabled Krenek to insist on the fidelity of the overall representation of African Americans in the opera, if not on the specifics of his rendering of jazz.

The tradition of casting African Americans and singers of African descent in the lead role of *Jonny spielt auf* continued throughout the 1980s and 1990s through productions in Leeds (1984) and Palermo (1987),[71] and through the 1993 Decca recording with Afro-European Krister St. Hill.[72] When white singers performed the role during this time, as was the case in Karlsruhe (1997) and Osnabrück (1998), the racial politics of this work were increasingly called into question. Reading reviews of these productions, one senses a growing discomfort among critics with the problematic minstrel components of the opera's main character.[73]

In 2002, the uncomfortable subtext of Jonny's blackface minstrelsy was confronted head-on in the lavish production by the Wiener Staatsoper. The Viennese staging, marking the eighty-fifth anniversary of the premiere, was less a new version of *Jonny spielt auf* than an attempt at coming to terms with the opera's history, origins, and "jazz" protagonist. To a large extent, the model appears not to have been the German original, but the minstrelized version presented in New York. Jonny, played by the white Bo Skovhus, is outfitted in a red-sequined jumpsuit, white gloves, a wig, and blackface makeup clearly reminiscent of Al Jolson.[74] The minstrel thrust behind director Günter Krämer's production is also evident in its treatment of jazz. It will be remembered that during the original productions, the jazz band was never to be seen onstage, but rather heard from a distance or over the radio. The 2002 production reverses this and prominently displays an all-white jazz band throughout the opera. The viewer now repeatedly sees Jonny's white jazz band mechanically strolling on and off the stage, playing without emotion or connection to the music. Another significant difference is that Jonny is not the only character in blackface; the French chambermaid Yvonne is similarly blackfaced and costumed.[75]

Such changes were motivated by Krämer's innovative directorial perspective: the "secret" of this production is that the opera's plot and music are being written and rewritten on the spot by the Max character. Max is seen at various moments during the performance either reading from music he has "just" written, following the action in the score, or even conducting the orchestra from stage. Thus, when the blackfaced Jonny and Yvonne later remove their makeup onstage to reveal themselves as white, we are to understand that Max-Krenek had originally misrecognized them as black. He has now rewritten them "correctly" as blackface (or white) characters.[76]

This act of transformation from blackness to blackface takes place at a central moment in the opera, where Jonny sings of returning home to Alabama, quoting Foster's "Old Folks at Home." As he sings this "old American Negro song" now rewritten as minstrel parody, Skovhus lends his performance a strongly Jolsonesque quality by stretching his neck and lifting his eyebrows as his voice rises and falls. His removal of blackface makeup might also be seen as in conversation with the scene from the *Jazz Singer* where Jolson applies burnt cork to his face in front of a mirror, thereby transforming his identity. In the 2002 version of *Jonny spielt auf*, the removal of Jonny's blackface signals a retrospective whitening of the opera. The viewer can now see the work's engagement with African Americans as having been but an insular affair of European high-modernist dabbling. Krämer's production suggests that Jonny's home, the place to which he sings of returning, has been right in front us all along. It is located in the mistaken perception of the European composer Krenek.

The gulf between Jonny's true music and Europe grows within this production, and the connection between America, African Americans, and Europe in the 1920s is limited to the European cultural imagination. For the moment, the minstrelsy of Vienna's production appears to be Jonny's resting place. Yet it is clear from the opera's history that he will not rest in any one place for long.[77] Jonny, as the homeless artist of modernity, is always on the move, always simultaneously leaving and returning. He has repeatedly returned "home" throughout the opera's history: in the 1920s to New York, then after the war back to Germany and Austria when African Americans first took hold of the role, and finally to Vienna, Krenek's home, where the minstrelsy of the work has again taken predominance. These multiple contradictory myths of Jonny's origins are neither extraneous nor tangential to the original, but are inextricably part of it. And the opera's montage of ideas and styles, its ambiguous, often adversarial, and clearly racialized appraisal of jazz music and African American music mean that Jonny must continue to remain a deeply problematic figure.

Appendix
Jonny spielt auf, Opera in Two Acts

Premiere: Neues Theater, Leipzig, Germany, February 10, 1927. Music and Libretto by Ernst Krenek

Cast:
Composer Max
Singer Anita
Negro Jonny, jazz band violinist
Violin virtuoso Daniello
Chambermaid Yvonne
Manager
Hotel director
Train station agent
First policeman
Second policeman
Third policeman

The first act opens on a mountain glacier to a view of the central European composer Max, who has sought refuge there. He meets Anita, an opera singer, staying at a nearby hotel. The two jointly return to the hotel, while she prepares to leave for Paris and her next role. Max, having fallen in love, tries to convince her not to leave him, which, however, she does. The next scene opens in a hotel in Paris. We meet the chambermaid Yvonne, the momentary love interest of jazz band violinist Jonny, as she listens to his jazz band from a hotel corridor. Next, Daniello, a violin virtuoso, returns to the hotel from a concert, and a throng of autograph seekers greets him. Seeing this, Jonny decides to steal Daniello's Amati violin. Anita, on her way back to her room, meets Jonny, who makes sexual advances toward her. Jonny is finally rebuffed when Daniello intercedes and pays him off to leave. Anita and Daniello then spend the night together. While these two are together, Jonny sneaks into Daniello's room and steals the violin. Knowing that he will be suspected by the police, Jonny hides the violin in Anita's room in the banjo case she has been carrying around for her new role. At this point, the hotel manager informs Anita that she has received a lucrative contract for an American tour. When Daniello discovers his violin missing, he accuses Yvonne, who is summarily fired, but then immediately hired by Anita, who is off for an unnamed central European city that same day. After losing both the violin and Anita, Daniello conspires to avenge himself by destroying Anita's relationship with Max. He gives Yvonne Anita's ring, which she had given to him after their evening together, and tells her to deliver it to Max. Leaving the hotel to follow the violin, Jonny, along with the rest of the cast, departs from Paris to end the first act.

The second act begins with Max alone in his room, where he awaits Anita's arrival in taut anticipation. As day passes into night, Max becomes more and more anxious, finally falling asleep sometime in the middle of the night. Anita appears the next morning, and, though Max is upset with her at first, she is able to reassure him. Yvonne waits until Anita has left and then hands the ring to Max with a note that it is from Daniello. Max leaves in an angry rush to return to his glacier. Jonny enters the room to retrieve the violin and, after speaking with the surprised Yvonne, leaves through the window. Anita comes into the room and learns from Yvonne what has happened. Back at his glacier, Max is at first inconsolable. The glacier admonishes him to return to the world of the living. Returning from his glacier, Max is greeted by Anita's voice over the hotel's loudspeaker. After this, we hear Jonny's jazz band from the radio. The hotel guests dance to the music as a stunned Daniello emerges from the hotel to recognize the sound of his Amati violin. Daniello next enlists the police to track down Jonny, who in turn goes immediately into hiding and plans to leave Europe for good. Daniello and the police track Jonny to the train station, where Max is already waiting for Anita before her departure for America. Still in fear of the police, Jonny places the violin with Max's luggage, and Max is mistakenly charged with pilfering the instrument. Anita convinces Yvonne to go to the police and inform them of Max's innocence but is held up by Daniello, who, after a shoving match with Yvonne, is pushed toward the oncoming train and dies. Through a clever ruse of Jonny, Max (and the violin) is liberated from the police, and all three return to the train station. At this point, Jonny strikes up the band and plays for the crowd. The opera closes as the station clock upon which Jonny is standing transforms into a globe, signaling Jonny's triumph over the world.

Notes

1. For a plot synopsis, see appendix.

2. For a list of the more than fifty cities in which *Jonny spielt auf* was performed in 1927 and 1928, see Rogge, *Ernst Kreneks Opern,* 63.

3. During the 1927–28 performance season, Krenek's *Jonny* was performed on forty-five stages and enjoyed 421 performances, making the opera almost omnipresent on the German opera scene. See Dietrich, "Auf den Spuren zu Jonnys Erfolg," 119.

4. Drexel, "American Jazz in Krenek's *Jonny spielt auf,*" 109.

5. Krenek was by no means entirely innocent in their fleeting dispute, having obliquely criticized Schoenberg in a publication in the mid-1920s. On Krenek and Schoenberg, see Stewart, *Ernst Krenek: The Man and His Music,* 97.

6. For example, Krenek, "Self-Analysis," 17; and Krenek, *Horizons Circled,* 26.

7. See above all Robinson, "Jazz Reception in Weimar Germany," 108–13.

8. Ibid., 112.

9. The subject of blackface minstrelsy in Germany and in *Jonny spielt auf* is discussed in Alan Lareau, "Jonny's Jazz"; Von der Linn, "*Jonny, Mahagonny,* and Tin Pan Alley"; Ritzel, "Synkopen-Tänze."

10. Krenek, *Jonny spielt auf,* m680, 29 ("Jonny kommt nach beendetem Spiel, mit einem Saxophon in der Hand, komischen, steifen Hut auf dem Kopf"). All translations from the German are my own.

11. Sam Wooding's jazz band, which Krenek saw in 1926, was dressed impeccably in tuxedos and comported themselves accordingly, that is, without the minstrelesque mannerisms performed by Jonny.

12. Most common are errors of declination, but errors in verb conjugation are also present. For example, Jonny consistently uses the nominative feminine ending for masculine nouns of all cases. As in "Gib' mir eine kiss," or in "sleep well in deine Sack" (Krenek, *Jonny spielt auf,* 1954, m687, 29, and m1293, 59). Other examples of Krenek's deformation of Jonny's speech include "Ich müssen die Geige haben" (mm728–30, 32) and "Ich worden verrückt" (mm734–35, 32).

13. Ibid., m685, 29; Von der Linn, "*Jonny, Mahagonny,* and Tin Pan Alley," 170.

14. See Krenek, *Jonny spielt auf,* 29–33.

15. On the "Black Horror," see Lebzelter, "Die 'Schwarze Schmach'"; and Marks, "Black Watch on the Rhine."

16. For a more extended analysis of the opera's sexual and gender politics in the context of the Weimar Republic, see Auner, "'Soulless Machines' and Steppenwolves."

17. On Jonny's materialism and fetishistic relationship to the Amati violin, see Amidon, *Nirgends brennen wir genauer,* 100–101.

18. Krenek, "*Jonny spielt auf,*" 20.

19. Krenek, *Jonny spielt auf,* mm754–59, 33–34.

20. Krenek, "*Jonny spielt auf,*" 19.

21. Krenek, *Jonny spielt auf,* mm805–9, 37.

22. Ibid., m847, 39 ("Oh, by Jove, die weiße Frau ist schön").

23. Ibid., mm914–24, 42–43 ("Ich kenne ja euch Weißen: erst wehrt ihr euch. Dann seid ihr beglück, und dann, adieu! So macht ihr wilde Tiere aus uns").

24. Ibid., mm931–33, 43.

25. Ibid. ("Jonnys tierisch—sinnlich-wütende Fratze verwandelt sich in ein breites Grinsen").

26. Amidon, *Nirgends brennen wir genauer,* 101.

27. With one possible exception occurring immediately after he is introduced with the saxophone and he plays a few notes with the instrument. Krenek, *Jonny spielt auf,* 31.

28. Ibid., m1201, 57 ("mit brutalen Grinsen").

29. The score gives instrumentation for the opera's orchestra and, separately, for "Percussion and Jazz instruments," which included a number of exotic instruments like the tam-tam, a siren, and a "Swanee whistle." Ibid., 2.

30. On this piece, as well as others in *Jonny spielt auf* referencing African American music, see Cook, *Opera for a New Republic,* 97.

31. Krenek, *Jonny spielt auf,* m1289, 59 ("im Ton eines Niggerliedes").

32. On the marketing of this song through recordings, see Rogge, *Ernst Kreneks Opern,* 64.

33. Krenek, *Jonny spielt auf,* m883, 128 ("triumphiernde Zirkusattitüde").

34. Ibid., mm885–912, 129–30:

JONNY: Jetzt ist die Geige mein, und ich will drauf spielen, wie old David einst die Harfe schlug, und preisen Jehova, der die Menschen schwarz erschuf.

YVONNE: Ja, gehört sie denn dir?

JONNY: Mir gehört alles, was gut ist in der Welt. Die alte Welt hat es erzeugt, sie weiß damit nichts mehr zu tun. Da kommt die neue Welt übers Meer gefahren mit Glanz und erbt das alte Europa durch Tanz.

35. Ibid. ("Er erlebt den großen Moment, die Vision seiner Bestimmung").

36. Ibid. ("im Ton eines Neger-Spirituals").

37. According to his biographer John L. Stewart, Krenek had been introduced to American popular music and ragtime through Arthur Schnabel in the early 1920s. *Ernst Krenek,* 31. Krenek had also attended a performance of the African American revue *Chocolate Kiddies* in 1926 and later wrote a glowing review of James Weldon Johnson's *Autobiography of an Ex-Colored Man* when it appeared in German translation in 1928. Ernst Krenek, "Der weisse Neger," review, *Frankfurter Zeitung,* November 25, 1928.

38. Krenek, "*Jonny spielt auf,*" 22.

39. Ibid., 30.

40. See ibid., 20.

41. Krenek, *Jonny spielt auf,* mm853–60, 882–83, 128; mm913–14, 130.

42. Jonny both is "homeless" as an African American in Europe and, as we learn in the following solo, has left the rural country for the modern metropolis.

43. Krenek, *Jonny spielt auf,* m1628, 160.

44. Ibid., mm1632–42, 160 ("Ich kaufte mir ein Billett nach Amsterdam und kehr' in meine Heimat wieder zurück. Ich werde Alabama wieder schauen und meinen lieben Swanee River nie mehr verlassen"). Interestingly, even as Jonny sings this supposedly heartfelt lament, Krenek has already undercut the possibility of his return. In a move resembling a Freudian slip, Jonny has dropped his ticket to Amsterdam and thus to America.

45. Ibid.

46. At the end of the first act, for example, Krenek unmistakably quotes from Gershwin's *Rhapsody in Blue* yet gives no comment. Instead, Krenek offers up this and other allusions without any further note as part of the overall montage effect of the opera's music.

47. *Program of Chocolate Kiddies Revue,* n.p.

48. On Krenek's use of Foster and the relationship to minstrelsy within the piece, see Amidon, *Nirgends brennen wir genauer,* 105–14.

49. Ibid., 114.

50. Krenek, *Jonny spielt auf,* mm1642–43, 160 ("er sieht sich um, um sich gewissermaßen zu orientieren").

51. Chop, "Ernst Krenek," 1479; Aber, "Ernst Krenek," 127; Alfred Baresel, "*Jonny spielt auf,*" 43 (emphasis in the original) (his was one of the earliest book-length studies of jazz in Europe, *Das Jazzbuch*); Eichhorn, "'Amerika als Wunschbild zukünftiger Gesellschaft'?" 179.

52. One American critic, Herbert Peyser, later wrote, he had told his German friends that African Americans "did not act or talk" the way Jonny does. "Jonny Over There," 34.

53. Cook, *Opera for a New Republic,* 105.

54. Lott, *Love and Theft,* 124.

55. There was at least one voice in the African American community who resisted this move. James Weldon Johnson publicly protested the role of Jonny being played by a white actor in blackface, writing, "We have in this country colored singers who could masterfully sing that role. I need only name Jules Bledsoe and Paul Robeson." Duberman, *Paul Robeson,* 111. Johnson's protest was originally published in the *New York Graphic,* January 19, 1929. My thanks to Bob Shingleton for alerting me to this reference.

56. See Cook, *Opera for a New Republic,* 108–9, for further examples of changes made by the Met.

57. See Olin Downes, "*Jonny spielt auf:* Opera of This Age," *New York Times,* January 20, 1929.

58. An image of the finale as staged in New York is reproduced in *New York Times,* January 27, 1929, RP33.

59. Quoted in Cook, *Opera for a New Republic,* 109.

60. "Tibbett as Jazz Leader," *New York Times,* February 28, 1929; "Al Jolson Greets Jonny," *New York Times,* January 20, 1929; Downes, "*Jonny spielt auf.*"

61. On Krenek's early life in America, see Stewart, *Ernst Krenek,* 211–36.

62. On the history of the Nazi image of Jonny, see Mungen, "Music Iconography of Modernism," 260–62.

63. It should, however, be pointed out that the opera's first rebirth after the Second World War was in Italy, where it was performed twice, in 1963 and 1965, as part of Florence's Maggio Musicale festival. The opera then returned to the home of the composer, Austria, in 1964, not in a full stage production, but in a recording made by the Vienna Volksoper and released on Amadeo records, with a white singer, Gerd Feldhoff, playing the role of Jonny. *Jonny spielt auf* (Amadeo AVRS 5038, 1964).

64. Evans resides in Germany and is still performing to this day. In 1996 he was additionally granted the prestigious title of *Kammersänger* by the federal state of Baden-Württemberg. Currently, he is an instructor in voice at the Internationale Theater-Akademie in Göttingen.

65. See Kutschera, "Kreneks *Jonny spielt auf*," 286.

66. Szmolyan, "Kreneks *Jonny spielt auf*." Stewart provides more details on the production in his biography. *Ernst Krenek*, 89.

67. Krenek, "Jonny erinnert sich."

68. Ibid., 187–88.

69. Ibid., 189.

70. Ibid.

71. Cf. Cook, *Opera for a New Republic*, 235n33.

72. *Ernst Krenek: Jonny spielt auf*, Gewandhausorchester Leipzig, conductor Lothar Zagrossek (Decca 1993).

73. See "Flucht ins ewige Eis: Ernst Kreneks Jazz-Oper *Jonny spielt auf* am Staatstheater Karlsruhe," *Süddeutsche Zeitung*, December 6, 1997; and "Der Neger auf der Zimmerpalme: Kreneks *Jonny spielt auf* in Osnabrück," *Frankfurter Allgemeine Zeitung*, June 19, 1998.

74. Unlike the New York production, however, Jonny's sexual potency and proclivities are ramped up throughout the production, and, in direct contrast to the New York version, they are at their most explicit in scenes with Anita.

75. On the questionable move to dress Yvonne in blackface, see James R. Oestreich, "Jazz Age *Jonny* Fiddles While Sensibilities Burn," *New York Times*, January 6, 2003, E5.

76. For a more detailed description of Krämer's production and its innovative use of the Max character, see Knessl, "Jazzer Jonny Heute," 49–50.

77. For example, a 2008 production at the Pfalztheater in Kaiserlautern puts Jonny into the virtual world of computer gaming! See Herkommer, "Welcome Back."

Bibliography

Aber, Adolf. "Ernst Krenek: *Jonny spielt auf*." *Anbruch* 9 (March 1927): 127–32.

Amidon, Kevin. *Nirgends brennen wir genauer: Institution, Experiment, and Crisis in the Germany Zeitoper, 1924–1931*. Ann Arbor: UMI Press, 2001.

Auner, Joseph. "'Soulless Machines' and Steppenwolves: Renegotiating Masculinity in Krenek's *Jonny spielt auf*." *Critical Matrix* 10, nos. 1–2 (1996): 58–72.

Baresel, Alfred. *Das Jazzbuch*. Leipzig: Zimmermann, 1926.

———. "*Jonny spielt auf*: Leipziger Uraufführung der neuen Krenek-Oper." *Auftakt* 7 (1927): 43–44.

Chop, Max. "Ernst Krenek: *Jonny spielt auf* (An der Städtischen Oper in Berlin-Charlottenburg)." *Signale für die musikalische Welt* 85, no. 43 (1927): 1477–80.

Cook, Susan C. *Opera for a New Republic: The Zeitopern of Ernst Krenek, Kurt Weill, and Paul Hindemith*. Ann Arbor: UMI Press, 1988.

Dietrich, Eva. "Auf den Spuren zu Jonnys Erfolg." In *Ernst Krenek*, ed. Otto Kolleritsch, 119–23. Vienna: Universal Edition, 1982.

Drexel, Kurt. "American Jazz in Ernst Krenek's Opera *Jonny spielt auf*." In *The Americanization/Westernization of Austria*, ed. Günter Bischof and Anton Pelinka, 102–11. New Brunswick: Transaction, 2004.

Duberman, Martin. *Paul Robeson*. New York: Alfred A. Knopf, 1989.

Eichhorn, Andreas. "'Amerika als Wunschbild zukünftiger Gesellschaft'? Zur Rezeption von Ernst Kreneks Oper *Jonny spielt auf*." In *Amerikanismus, Americanism, Weill: Die Suche nach kultureller Identität in der Moderne*, ed. Hermann Danuser and Hermann Gottschewski, 171–83. Schliengen: Edition Argus, 2003.

Ernst Krenek: Jonny spielt auf. Gewandhausorchester Leipzig. Conductor Lothar Zagrossek. Decca 436 631-2, 1993.

Herkommer, Frank. "Welcome Back." February 2008. http://www.opernnetz.de///seiten/rezensionen/kais_john.htm.

Jonny spielt auf. Amadeo AVRS 5038, 1964.

Knessl, Lothar. "Jazzer Jonny Heute: Kein Heilsbringer." *Österreichische Musikzeitschrift* 58 (February 2003): 47–50.

Krenek, Ernst. *Horizons Circled: Reflections on My Music*. Berkeley and Los Angeles: University of California Press, 1974.

———. "Jonny erinnert sich." *Österreichische Musikzeitschrift* 35 (April–May 1980): 187–89.

———. "*Jonny spielt auf*." In *Im Zweifelsfalle: Aufsätze über Musik*, 13–32. Vienna: Europa Verlag, 1984.

———. *Jonny spielt auf. Oper in 2 Teilen. Klavierauszug mit Text vom Komponisten*. Vienna: Universal Edition, 1954.

———. "Self-Analysis." *New Mexico Quarterly* 23 (Spring 1953): 5–57.

Kutschera, Hans. "Krenek's *Jonny spielt auf* im Salzburger Landestheater." *Österreichische Musikzeitschrift* 23 (January 1968): 286–87.

Lareau, Alan. "Jonny's Jazz." In *Jazz and the Germans: Essays on the Influence of "Hot" American Idioms on 20th-Century Music*, ed. Michael J. Budds, 19–60. Hillsdale, N.Y.: Pendragon Press, 2002.

Lebzelter, Gisela. "Die 'Schwarze Schmach': Vorurteile, Propaganda, Mythos." *Geschichte und Gesellschaft* 11, no. 1 (1985): 37–58.

Lott, Eric. *Love and Theft: Blackface Minstrelsy and the American Working Class*. Oxford: Oxford University Press, 1993.

Marks, Sally. "Black Watch on the Rhine: A Study in Propaganda, Prejudice, and Prurience." *European Studies Review* 13 (1983): 297–334.

Mungen, Anno. "Music Iconography of Modernism from the Weimar Republic to Nazi Germany and Beyond." *Music in Art: International Journal for Music Iconography* 29, nos. 1–2 (2004): 257–64.

Peyser, Herbert. "Jonny Over There." *Modern Music* 6 (January–February 1929): 32–35.

Program of Chocolate Kiddies Revue. Berlin: n.p., 1925.

Ritzel, Fred. "Synkopen-Tänze: Über Importe populärer Musik aus Amerika in der Zeit vor dem Ersten Weltkrieg." In *Schund und Schönheit: Populäre Kultur um 1900*, ed. Kaspar Maase and Wolfgang Kaschuba, 161–83. Cologne: Böhlau, 2001.

Robinson, J. Bradford. "Jazz Reception in Weimar Germany: In Search of a Shimmy Figure." *Music and Performance during the Weimar Republic,* ed. Bryan Gilliam, 107–34. New York: Cambridge University Press, 1994.

Rogge, Wolfgang. *Ernst Kreneks Opern.* Wolfenbüttel: Möseler, 1970.

Stewart, John. *Ernst Krenek: The Man and His Music.* Berkeley and Los Angeles: University of California Press, 1991.

Szmolyan, Walter. "Kreneks *Jonny spielt auf* im Theater an der Wien." *Österreichische Musikzeitschrift* 35 (September 1980): 476–77.

Von der Linn, Michael. "*Jonny, Mahagonny,* and the Songs of Tin Pan Alley." In *Amerikanismus, Americanism, Weill: Die Suche nach kultureller Identität in der Moderne,* ed. Hermann Danuser and Hermann Gottschewski, 160–70. Schliengen: Edition Argus, 2003.

12

Il Rodolfo Nero, or The Masque of Blackness

GEORGE SHIRLEY

In the fall of 1960, I made my European operatic debut at the Teatro Nuovo in Milan, Italy, singing the role of Rodolfo in Giacomo Puccini's perennial favorite, *La Bohème.* One of the headlines in the news the following day proclaimed, "Il Rodolfo nero ha superato l'esame!" In translation: "The black Rodolfo has exceeded (passed) the examination!"

I did not take this as an insult, for in Italy fifteen years after the end of World War II Blacks were still considered exotica, evoking a mix of emotions ranging from fascination to derisiveness. At that time, Otello and Haile Selassie were likely the best-known individuals of color in the land! When my wife and I walked down a street, little children would grab their mothers' skirts and say in utter amazement, "Mamma, guarda il moro!" (Mama, look at the Moor!). On one occasion as we stood on the platform of the train station in the hamlet of Vercelli, I had the feeling we were being watched. I turned to look behind us, and there was a file of natives lined up along the wall, staring in silent wonder at the backs of the aliens who had miraculously appeared in their midst. At no time in these encounters with the public did I feel the unbidden attention to be negative, but, rather, an honest, wonder-struck reaction to the phenomena standing before them; hence my mild response to the reporter's focus upon my racial heritage. Ironically, his headline, as well as numerous references to "il Rodolfo nero" in practically all the Italian newspaper accounts of our *Bohème* performances, constituted the first journalistic commentary on my race that I had encountered following my entry into the singing profession. The reviews from my debut season and minitour in America with the Turnau Opera Players in 1959 generated no such racial observations.

In truth, I knew of a certainty before I launched my career that my blackness would play a role covertly or overtly wherever and whenever I appeared onstage

Figure 1. Rodolfo, Puccini's *La Bohème*. Metropolitan Opera, 1964. Photo by Louis Mélancon.

in an operatic role. I, like every performer, wished to be assessed, accepted, or rejected on my artistic merits alone. Given the fact that I had gained cachet as a desirable racial token due to the groundswell of social change that was beginning to erupt across the Continent when I set out upon my career path, it was subsequently impossible to discern the role my artistic virtues played upon my successes and failures. Were critics being especially kind in writing good reviews of my performances? Were they incapable of subduing their racial biases when their reviews were harsh? Were opera managers on the lookout for black singers because they truly wanted to embrace their artistry or because they wanted to keep the NAACP off their backs by being able to point to a token or two in order to prove they were not racially biased? Was I paranoid to entertain such thoughts? Would I have been naive not to entertain such thoughts?

Black American singers of opera have always been relatively few in number for reasons external to the race as well as internal. We remain minorities in the profession numerically and racially, which should certainly come as no surprise in an art form that appeals only to a minority of the majority in America! Opera draws a minority of white and black aficionados to its fold in comparison to, say, musical theater, rock, R&B, country western, and rap. Large numbers of young Whites and an increasing number of youths of color are focusing their studies and dreams of success on musical theater, arguably America's distinctive form of opera, as well as on other popular musico-dramatic performance media. It appears those craving stardom in native modes of music drama now exceed the numbers matriculating in traditional European opera studies.

When I began my career in 1959, there were but a handful of African Americans finding work in opera around the globe, and most of those were women. However, since the very beginning of operatic history in America, black singers have been drawn to the art for reasons that, once explored and understood, are not arcane.

Traditional sub-Saharan African tribal life centers upon ritual that embodies music, drama, and dance, the stuff of operatic performance. Making the step from one passionate heart-on-the-sleeve outpouring of emotion to the other is, at bottom, organic. Tribal ritual, sacred and secular, is arguably never divorced from a spiritual *raison d'être*; operatic performance, on the other hand, is an entertainment that can reach the level of spiritual experience when the work performed and the quality of its performance combine to transcend the level of mere entertainment. The best black popular singers transfer their spiritual commitment from hymns and gospel songs sung in the black church to the R&B, jazz, and blues shouts and wails that express the secular experience of black life in America. Black opera singers make the same spiritual commitment to "Vissi d'arte" (from Puccini's *Tosca*) as they do to "Done Made My Vow to the Lord" or "Amazing Grace." The soul expressed in an aria is fairly easy to identify with; what remain to be mastered are the spoken and musical languages that form the corpus of the work. Gaining ownership of these demanding skills lies well within the possibility of any singer gifted with voice and musical ear appropriate to the task.

One of the first Blacks to be accorded approbation as a singer possessing a voice of operatic proportions was Elizabeth Taylor Greenfield, dubbed "The Black Swan" in the early nineteenth century, a time when sobriquets were in fashion. She was followed by one of her students, tenor Thomas Bowers, hailed by the press as "The Black Mario" after a renowned Italian tenor of the era. Numerous other black singers of art songs and operatic arias followed, performing in solo concerts or with troupes, but never with an established opera company featuring white performers. Although black audiences witnessed these singers in performance, classical concert music and opera remained as foreign to the larger black community as it did to its white counterpart. Such is the case today.

An early incidence of Blacks and Whites performing an opera together in the United States came in 1933 in New York City at the Hippodrome Theater. Soprano Caterina Jarboro, a.k.a. Catherine Yarborough, and baritone Jules Bledsoe interpreted the roles of Aida and Amonasro in a production of Verdi's masterpiece mounted by the Chicago Opera Company; the impresario who headed this company was Alfredo Salmaggi, a tenor of Italian heritage. This performance opportunity was intended to provide Madame Jarboro with a forum for her outstanding talents.

Texas-born Bledsoe had sung Amonasro with the Cleveland Stadium Opera in 1932 before joining Madame Jarboro at the Hippodrome in 1933; in 1934, he repeated his role with the Cosmopolitan Opera, again at the Hippodrome. Although Jarboro is often credited as being the first black singer to perform with an established opera company in the United States, it would appear this honor was earned by Bledsoe, whose Amonasro in 1932 marked the first critically appraised performance of the role by an African American bass-baritone to be recorded in the historical annals of operatic performance in America. In researching an article I wrote for *Opera News* in 1971, I found no evidence of black singers performing opera in other than their own troupes before Bledsoe's debut with the Cleveland Stadium Opera. The Cleveland critic's ecstatic review of Bledsoe's performance, reprinted in the *New York World Telegram* of July 11, 1932, lavished his artistry with praise: "If the Metropolitan does not have him singing that role . . . and whatever other Negro roles there be, next year, it will be asininity downright criminal. . . . Higgins and Lert [the producers of Cleveland's summer opera] feared casting him as Amonasro, forecasting criticism of his wrestling a white Aida around. Last night's volunteer cast permitted of his American Amonasro debut. . . . Bledsoe's singing left the Stadium resounding with applause—16 curtain calls." Thus recognized as a singer of stature, Bledsoe became the first black male to achieve operatic renown in this country as well as in Europe. Ironically, the great Paul Robeson's career and charisma overshadowed that of his confrere, even though Robeson never performed an operatic role.

Mary Cardwell Dawson created the National Negro Opera Company in 1941, providing performance opportunities for black singers, some of whom had already established reputations as performers of merit outside the circuit of white professional companies. One of her stars, Lillian Evanti, a.k.a. Lillian Evans-Tibbs, is recognized as the first black singer to perform with an established opera company in Europe. Her debut as Lakmé took place in 1925 in Nice, France. It is said that part of Dawson's motivation for founding her company was to give Evanti a stage on which to perform, since a Met audition allegedly granted following the singer's return from abroad had borne no fruit.

A promising young baritone named Robert McFerrin Sr., destined to become the first African American male to sing leading roles with the Metropolitan Opera, gained crucial performance experience with Dawson's company. As the result of winning the Metropolitan Opera Auditions in 1953, McFerrin was being groomed to become the first black singer to debut with the company, but it was decided in the eleventh hour to bestow that honor upon contralto Marian Anderson. Although at age fifty-eight no longer in her vocal prime, Anderson's immense stature as a superstar and symbol of dignified defiance to racial injustice no doubt played a role in granting her the contract she arguably would have won at least a decade before, had social justice ruled in American society. McFerrin enjoyed his evening in the spotlight three weeks after Anderson's debut.

The advent of Rudolf Bing as general manager of the Metropolitan marked the beginning of an era of change in that venerable house. However, a full decade before Bing opened the Met's doors to black singers, the upstart New York City Center Opera trumped its big sister by inviting baritone Todd Duncan of *Porgy and Bess* fame to break the operatic color barrier that had stubbornly remained intact following the Jarboro-Bledsoe success of twelve years earlier. Duncan's 1945 debut as Tonio in Leoncavallo's *I Pagliacci* opened the New York City Center's operatic door to sopranos Camilla Williams, Adele Addison, and Billie Lynne Daniels; baritones Lawrence Winters and Andrew Frierson; contralto Carol Brice; and tenor William DuPree. Although tardy upon the scene, the Met played catch-up in notable fashion during Sir Rudolf's tenure, following Anderson and McFerrin with coloratura soprano Mattiwilda Dobbs, the first black singer signed to a long-term contract with the Met, and spinto sopranos Gloria Davy, Martina Arroyo, and Leontyne Price.

My entry into the company as the second black male and first black tenor came as a result of my winning the Metropolitan Opera Auditions in 1961. By this time the African American female presence in opera in the United States was dominant. Lawrence Winters had long since departed for Europe where he subsequently became a star in Hamburg, Germany, in the early 1950s, singing Wagner's Wotan and other leading bass-baritone roles. This was no mean feat, given the racist horrors perpetrated by that country a scant decade before. Charles Holland and Arthur Herndon, tenors, were enjoying success in Europe as well, but I was not aware of their careers. When I made my debut in Italy—the result of my winning a Cincinnati-based competition called the American Opera Auditions—I met another black tenor, Nat Boyd, who was pursuing a career there. I heard him sing two years later in a portion of a radio broadcast of a live performance of *Otello,* and I recently found reference on the Internet to a North American tenor, Nathan Boyd, having been engaged for the 1962–63 season at Barcelona's Gran Teatre del Liceu to sing the role of Radames in *Aida*. I assume this to be the same man and have no idea what happened with his career beyond that point.

During that initial visit to Italy, I met and sang for one of the most important artists' managers in Milan who, following my audition, promised he could put

Figure 2. Lord Percy, Donizetti's *Anna Bolena*. Glyndebourne Festival, 1968. Photo by Guy Gravett.

me to work if I remained in Italy. I decided against it, rather certain of the fact that, if I were to accept his offer, I, like Boyd, would probably be engaged only for roles like Otello and Radames, roles that were unsuitable for my voice. This perception was borne out when, after my debut as Herod in Strauss's *Salome* at the 1961 Spoleto Festival in Italy, I was approached by Gian-Carlo Menotti, founder and artistic director of the festival, and Luchino Visconti, the famed movie director who had staged *Salome,* and asked if I would sing Otello in the following season. When I protested that the role was too heavy for me, Gian-Carlo said, "But you would *look* wonderful!"

One week later Menotti approached me in the hall of the elegant Caio Melisso Theater in Spoleto and asked if I would consider singing the role of Tristan. I politely declined the offer, but subsequently agreed to return the following season to sing Don José in Bizet's *Carmen.*

A truly great African American lyric tenor named Charles Holland came to New York City in 1969 to perform Blitzstein's *Airborne Symphony* with the New York Philharmonic conducted by the noted black maestro Dean Dixon. At age sixty, Holland sang with beauty and purity of tone and a pristine clarity of diction that were astounding. I came to know him better when we met a few years later in the Netherlands, where I performed in the Amsterdam Festival. He shared with me his history and his experience in Europe, to which continent he and Dixon had removed in 1949 in search of opportunities worthy of their respective talents.

Charles found employment in Paris nightclubs, utilizing talents honed as a jazz singer with the Fletcher Henderson Band back in the States. He gained further recognition through performances on French radio and was encouraged to audition for L'Opéra de Paris, where a new production of *Die Zauberflöte* was to be mounted in the coming season. The *répétiteur* for whom he auditioned suggested Charles speak with an associate conductor about the role of Monostatos, to which Charles replied, "I don't sing Monostatos; I sing Tamino!" The *répétiteur* replied, "But Monsieur Holland, Monsieur Gedda is singing Tamino." Unmoved, the Virginia-born Holland refused to contemplate a role he considered an embarrassment to the race. Monostatos is the overseer of black slaves like himself who are in the power of Sarastro, High Priest and Keeper of the Mysteries of Isis. In his lone aria, Monostatos lusts after the heroine of the opera, the pure and virtuous Princess Pamina, and bemoans his own blackness. Holland rightly determined this role unsuitable for his persona and talents, and, thus, inappropriate for his operatic debut.

Charles's wife informed him of plans for a new production of Bizet's *Pecheurs de Perles* planned for L'Opéra Comique. She suggested he consider striking a deal with the staff at L'Opéra de Paris, who evidently exercised artistic control of the Comique as well. The proposal: if they would give him the role of Nadir—a person of color, but also of dignity—in the premiere of the Bizet, he would consider performing Monostatos. Charles swallowed hard and returned to L'Opéra with his proposal. The opera administration accepted it, and Holland became the first African American, to my knowledge, to be engaged by L'Opéra de Paris *and,* a year later, by L'Opéra Comique. His historic accomplishment was considerable, but it came at a personal sacrifice he never forgot. His *New York Times* obituary (November 10, 1987) and other media sources make mention of his 1954 debut at L'Opéra de Paris in *Die Zauberflöte,* but do not identify the role he sang. In stark contrast, all references to his debut at L'Opéra Comique highlight his appearance as Nadir and identify him as the first black singer to be offered a contract by that house.

Holland performed successfully in Germany, France, and the Netherlands, singing the title role in Gounod's *Faust* and, in the following operas by Verdi, the roles of Don Alvaro in *La Forza del Destino,* Radames in *Aida,* and the title role in *Otello,* the latter two even though his voice was not dramatic in size or weight. He performed *Otello* in a televised production for the BBC in London in the early 1950s and informed me that, on one occasion in Hildesheim, Germany, he sang both the matinee and evening performances of that role on the same day! Of the roles referenced in this paragraph, only the first two were suitable for Charles's lyrical vocal endowment; in this regard, Verdi's Alfredo (*La Traviata*) and the Duke of Mantua (*Rigoletto*) would have proved choices more fitting than the stentorian—and swarthier—Egyptian soldier Radames (*Aida*) and ill-fated Moorish general Otello. Even Don Alvaro, also a character "of color," was a somewhat risky vocal choice because it is a spinto (literally, "pushed") role, lying between the lyric and dramatic categories of vocal codification.

Holland survived the typecasting that relegated him to roles inappropriate for his excellent lyric voice. He returned to New York City in the early 1980s for two recitals, the first in Carnegie Recital Hall and the second in Carnegie Hall proper. I heard the first performance only and was moved to tears at the beauty of his pure tone and limpid, expressive singing, both especially telling in Duparc's magical setting of Jean Lahor's *Extase.*

Mention must be made of yet another pioneering operatic tenor, the late Arthur Herndon, who was the first African American to graduate from the University of Cincinnati College-Conservatory of Music. In the early 1960s, this Korean War veteran was awarded a Fulbright Scholarship to study in Italy with the renowned Luigi Ricci. While there, he performed in *Der Rosenkavalier* at the Spoleto Festival and subsequently became the first black tenor to be offered a *fest* (fixed, or permanent) contract with a state opera house in Germany, in this case the ensemble of the Stadtstheater in Kassel, where he performed leading roles.

When I stepped onstage at the Byrdcliffe Theater in Woodstock, New York, in the summer of 1959 to make my professional debut with the Turnau Opera Players, my assignments consisted of five roles that covered a wide range of characterizations, three of which could conceivably be characterized as roles of color—Haroun in Bizet's first opera, *Djamileh;* Belmonte in Mozart's *Die Entfürung aus dem Serail;* and Torquemada in Ravel's *L'Heure Espagnole.*[1] The remaining roles were Rodolfo in *La Bohème* and my debut role, Eisenstein in J. Strauss's *Die Fledermaus.* The other tenor in our small (eight singers total) company sang Pedrillo in the Mozart, Ernesto in Donizetti's *Don Pasquale,* and the tenor role in Bernstein's *Trouble in Tahiti.* Thus, my entry into the profession was not constrained by casting decisions having to do with the color of my skin. For whatever reason, I was fortunate, for my career was never limited by typecasting, and, as in Spoleto, I avoided any possibility of it whenever it arose.

In the mid-1960s, I was offered an opportunity to sing the role of Sportin' Life in what I am sure would have been an excellent production of *Porgy and Bess,* for the offer came from Nathaniel Merrill, the resident stage director at the Metropolitan Opera with whom I had by then worked numerous times and for whom I had the greatest respect. This production of Gershwin's masterpiece was not a Metropolitan Opera project, for the Met had not yet seen fit to declare *Porgy* worthy of its stage. The performances were to take place in another venue, the whereabouts of which I cannot recall. I declined the offer because I was aware of the difficulty that plagued black male singers who, following successful performances of their roles in this fiendishly difficult opera, were rarely to never successful in gaining contracts for other roles with the companies that had hired them for *Porgy.* Even though I was enjoying success at the Met and in other houses globally, I was reluctant to take the chance of being typecast as Sportin' Life, a role I knew I could perform with flair. I did not want to do anything that might make opera houses look at me as other than a Pinkerton, Don Ottavio, or Tamino. I did not want to give them ideas or reasons to rethink my utility to them.

Eventually, I did perform Sportin' Life in Götz Friedrich's controversial production of *Porgy* at the Bregenz Festival in 1998, and it proved to be one of the most satisfying experiences of my career.[2] I figured that by that time, at age sixty-four, I didn't have anything to lose!

In 1959, the Turnau Opera Players accepted me solely on the basis of my vocal audition, and the patient resident stage director was the perfect soul to usher me gently into my first encounter with the full range of dramatic demands required of a *primo tenore.* I relied on my helpful colleagues at Turnau to give me guidance in many aspects of theatrical life, including use of stage makeup. We had no official makeup artist on staff, so everyone was on their own. Wigs were not in the budget. Before the season began, I purchased some pancake makeup and soft greaselike colors in tubes, plus eyeliner, rouge, and grease pencils. The results of my initial efforts at transformation were decidedly amateurish, but not disastrous. I had dabbled in visual art over the years of my youth, so I owned some sense of form, color, and shading that on opening night saved me from looking

Figure 3. Sportin' Life, Gershwin's *Porgy and Bess*. Bregenz Festival, Austria, 1998. Photo by Karl Foster.

as though I had dipped myself in an ash pile in my attempt to approximate the physical features of a Viennese gentleman named Gabriel von Eisenstein.

Following that initial season and my subsequent move to New York City, I joined the Hunter College Opera Workshop in search of badly needed additional stage training. My university degree was in music education, and I had not been exposed to opera workshop during my baccalaureate studies. Indeed, my sole music drama experience before Turnau had taken place in my senior year when I was asked by Dr. Harry Langsford, the conductor of the Wayne (State) University Men's Glee Club, to sing the title role in a stage production of Stravinsky's opera-oratorio *Oedipus Rex*. This proved to be a thrilling foray into the realm of drama-cum-music, but the statuesque poses dictated by the composer and closely adhered to by the director allowed for a minimum of physical gestures and zero perambulation. With a student from the Theatre Department assigned to apply our stylized makeup, my sole responsibility was to stand in one place (atop a seven-foot tower), make a few slow-motion gestures, and sing Stravinsky's challenging masterpiece.

At Hunter College, I had the good fortune of participating in a performance of Jan Meyerowitz's opera *Esther* in which I sang the role of Mordecai, an elderly Jew. The professional makeup artist Michael Arshansky was on staff at the New York City Center Opera. A professional dancer before becoming a makeup specialist, he worked with greasepaint exclusively and did such an expert job on me, including a false nose, that members of the cast did not recognize me when I exited the makeup room!

Completely taken by his expertise, I decided to hone my skills using greasepaint rather than pancake or soft makeup. My trip to Italy further convinced me that doing my own makeup was imperative. The makeup "artist" for the *Bohème* performances in Milan was a former tenor who was also the voice teacher of Nat Boyd. I can only hope he was a better teacher than he was makeup artist, for in this latter category he was simply incompetent. I had achieved far better results with my fledgling attempts in Woodstock, so for our subsequent performances, which took place at the Teatro La Pergola in Florence, I did my own makeup with markedly improved results. Save for Arshansky, there were precious few makeup specialists in those days that knew how to work with dark skin, thus my budding expertise worked to my benefit in this crucial area of theater art. I continued to do my own makeup even after I went to the Met, for I found it a perfect method of getting myself in the zone I needed to occupy for interpreting whatever role I was preparing to perform.

During performances of *Pelléas et Mélisande* with the Scottish Opera in the 1970s, I met a fan who was also a political activist; a native Scot, her marriage to a Nigerian had ended tragically when he came up missing in the 1960s during the Biafra civil war. She challenged my use of makeup onstage, arguing that I should appear basically as myself in whatever role I played.

A case can certainly be made for Rodolfo as well as any number of characters from, say, the Spanish cohort—for example, Alvaro or Belmonte—being interpreted as gentlemen of color. Dumas *fils et père,* Blacks by American standards, graced Paris in the nineteenth century. Why not, then, a black Rodolfo? A black Don Ottavio or Ferrando? Maybe. A black Pelléas in the Symbolist land of *Allemonde* (from Debussy's *Pelléas et Mélisande*)? *C'est possible* if the artistic concept woven throughout the production supports it; all manner of fascinating symbolism could obtain from such an approach, and I could see it as a legitimate artistic venture, but not as a political one.

I have sung Rodolfo with wig and au naturel depending on the desires of the director or circumstances governing the production, but never without makeup. My 1967 debut with the Scottish Opera in Glasgow was as a bewigged Rodolfo; no critical notice was taken of my race. Nine years later, I repeated the role with that company without a wig, and, although I was not trying to make a point, one critic chose to mention Rodolfo's racial heritage, in not particularly endearing terms.

Whereas my debut in Scotland in 1967 was, to my recollection, free of critical reference to my race, such was not the case here at home in 1963, for my blackness penetrated wig and greasepaint in the mind of a major New York critic when I appeared as Des Grieux in a new Metropolitan Opera production of Massenet's *Manon.* I entered the cast as an eleventh-hour substitute for Nicolai Gedda when, following the opening performance, he departed for the funeral of his father in Sweden. I donned my usual makeup, plus a periwig (photos show I looked pretty authentic), and joined Anna Moffo for the second and third performances.

The critic in question's review of my performance made reference to my race as being inappropriate for the character, a French nobleman. Evidently, the critic was not aware of the fact that the Chevalier de Saint George (1745–99), a contemporary of Mozart and a man of many parts—soldier, champion swordsman, and noted composer—was a nobleman of color, thus providing historical precedent for the existence of at least *one* black eighteenth-century French nobleman. I decided not to let the critic's comment, which I deemed unwarranted and out of place, go unchallenged—a dangerous decision for a performer to make, as you will see.

I penned a personal letter meant only for the eyes of the critic; the public was not made privy to this private communiqué, as it was not reprinted in the "Letters to the Editor" section of his publication. In my letter, I asked whether he felt it inappropriate for Mario Del Monaco, an Italian, to sing the role of Otello, a Moor, or whether, in his view, Zinka Milanov was racially incorrect for the role of Aida. His response, read by the public at large, took the form of negative reviews for the next three years! He never communicated directly with me, but made it clear in his reviews that, whatever I performed, it was not good enough to garner *his* approval. Needless to say, I was astounded when he finally wrote a positive report of one of my performances, Tamino in Mozart's *Die Zauberflöte.*

Figure 4. Tamino, Mozart's *Magic Flute*. Glyndebourne Festival, 1966. Photo by Guy Gravett.

There had, as a result of an article that appeared in *Time* in 1965, been a huge flap over my use of makeup. I sang the title role in the American Premiere of Hans Werner Henze's opera *The Stag King* at Santa Fe and was interviewed by a local "stringer" for *Time* who lived in the city. She took my comments about makeup and made it appear as though I was forced by the powers that be to use a "pink" cream to alter my appearance onstage. The article was picked up by the critic for London's *Evening Standard* and made into something of an "issue" that I had subsequently to refute in conversations with the critic and with others who, like he, had been misled. The fallout from this article followed me for a number of years and was likely the catalyst for the Scottish opera fan's reaction to my physical appearance as Pelléas.

My professional stance has always been to play by the rules everyone else observes. I have claimed it my right as an artist to portray white characters as Whites, in the same manner as white singers have portrayed black characters as Blacks. I have always reserved the right to look as foolish as everyone else onstage, sporting makeup and wig in order to give the appearance of the character as it has traditionally been played. As I would not appreciate seeing a white performer interpret Aida or Otello in "white" makeup, or not make some attempt to appear Asian when singing Cio-Cio San, I can see no valid artistic reason to interpret Pinkerton, Tamino, Nemorino, Faust, or Alfredo, for example, as Black for black's sake. I see no gain in making a political statement during a performance that says, "Look at *me; I'm* here, like it or not!" I would rather make a political statement that says, "If I stand out on this stage, it will be because of my *artistry* . . . like it or not!" The other stuff is incidental.

Do I use a "pink cream" on my face solely to hide my race? No. I build the externals of my character using greasepaint and at times a wig. I highlight my face with color to prevent my dark skin from absorbing the stage lighting and becoming darker, thus robbing my features of definition. A white singer uses makeup for the same reasons, but in his case the stage lighting washes out his facial features by draining color from his skin; color must then be added in order to prevent obliteration of facial definition. Ergo, makeup serves practical purposes that have nothing to do with hiding one's race for social reasons. The technical demands of the theater must be obeyed. The conventions of theater demand fealty.

Black singers are rarely, if ever, selected to interpret white roles in operas that focus on life in contemporary white society. In order to maintain an aura of "believability," there is reluctance to cast a person of color as a white protagonist in a drama that centers on ethnic community life in the twentieth or twenty-first century. Until we attain a color-blind society that will not flinch when, say, Simon Estes portrays George Washington, or Denyce Graves Marilyn Monroe, or when Blacks are given serious consideration for and are hired to sing leads in productions of contemporary works like Bolcom's *View from the Bridge* and Picker's *American Tragedy,* I would argue in favor of continuing—for the sake of "believability"—the practice of reserving the leading roles in Gershwin's *Porgy and Bess* for black singers, as mandated by the Gershwin estate. I mention this here because of sentiments expressed of late by certain leading white singers who would dearly love to perform these great roles now that *Porgy* has finally been granted status as a genuine opera, a designation unjustly withheld from it for decades.

For those who deem it of utmost importance, one surefire way of creating heightened theatrical believability in opera on these shores is for poets and composers to mine the rich resources of American history for material that will bring our gripping story to the operatic arena in all its loving, poignant, violent, and bloody veracity. We do not need more operas based on medieval themes or fairy tales of yore. We *do* need music dramas like Danielpour's *Margaret Garner* that reflect the realities of black life in the New World, operas that will, because of their story lines, enable Blacks and other singers of color to play *themselves,* and Whites to play Whites, thereby highlighting in dramatic fashion the troubled symbiosis that inextricably fetters us and makes for thrilling theater.

Opera has never been about believability in the shallowest sense of that word. Theater requires suspension of disbelief, opera, arguably, demanding it to the highest degree. Once the music begins, the audience plays its role by embracing the convention that human beings actually sing to one another rather than speak and that the scenery is really a mountain town in Sicily, a forest grove in Bohemia, or a boulevard in Paris. The patrons accept the fact that the hero may be a tad shorter than the heroine, who may also be rather large in girth. In such moments, opera accurately mirrors reality wherein true love trumps physique, class, and race. The singing, if great, validates the whole process and lifts the event to heights that transcend the fantasy world where only blonde sylphs and tall, handsome matinee idols have the right to fall in love.

In truth, opera has from the beginning been about *great singing.* Today, as a result of increasing interest in the visual component of the art form, that priority is under fire. Movies and television have linked forces with the fashion, exercise, and cosmetics industries to shape the aesthetic desires and expectations of society to the point where a physique deemed unglamorous is less liable to be welcomed upon the operatic stage. The art of the makeup specialist, wig maker, and costumer is no longer trusted to suffice in slenderizing and *beautifying* the less aesthetically endowed physique that may well house the spectacular voice and artistry requisite for fulfilling the demands of a particular role. In the name of believability, the unacceptable physical specimen—for example, the soprano deemed too *tall* for Mimì or too *dark* for Sophie, or the baritone ruled too *old* for Onegin or *rotund* for Don Giovanni—is locked out of contention for reasons that are at once shallow and inane. We cannot afford to allow the present focus on "looking the part" to institute new forms of exclusion that lock the door on worthy talent. We cannot afford to waste the riches that constitute the allness of this nation.

I will not discourage young black singers from following their dreams of singing the great roles if their vocal gifts and artistic sensibilities are of proper merit. If the vocal technique is inadequate, I will encourage pursuit of technical perfection. If musicality is weak, I will encourage its reinforcement. If a singer is unhealthy, I will encourage the pursuit of health both spiritual and physical. If stage deportment is wanting, I will encourage acquisition of physical poise and grace of movement. If languages are faulty, I will insist upon perfection of pronunciation.

When the singer is ready for career entry, I will expect the profession to have remained sagacious enough to respect what the artist brings to the operatic banquet vocally, musically, and dramatically and respect as well the voracious appetite of the opera-loving public for great singing, a hunger that can never be sated by the froth of pulchritude.

Notes

1. The company, founded in 1955 by Josef Turnau from a core of students in his opera workshop at Hunter College in New York City, occupied a small theater on the famed Byrdcliffe Artists Colony grounds in Woodstock, New York. I was not the first black singer to be hired by the company; thus, audiences were accustomed to integrated casting. As there were few minorities resident in the area, few, if any, attended our performances; there were certainly no restrictions forbidding their presence. The company expanded its reach in 1960 when it inaugurated a season of opera at the Asolo Theatre in Sarasota, Florida. I was not invited to join them in 1960, due, I believe, to the atmosphere that still prevailed in much of the South. In 1974 the Turnau became the Asolo Opera Company and, in 1979, was christened the Sarasota Opera.

2. This production of *Porgy* was set under an earthquake-ruined bridge in Los Angeles, not in anything resembling the usual setting for Catfish Row! The characters lived in trailers, and the director of the festival, Alfred Wopmann, was quoted in the August 6, 1997, issue of the *New York Times,* "The idea was to show a social earthquake, a place where communication has been broken." Götz Friedrich was nothing if not political, and the productions in which I performed (Offenbach's *Orpheus in der Unterwelt,* Wagner's *Das Rheingold,* and *Porgy*) were well clothed in sociopolitical garb.

Contributors

NAOMI ANDRÉ is Associate Professor of Women's Studies and the Residential College at the University of Michigan. She received her Ph.D. in musicology from Harvard University. Her research focuses on nineteenth-century opera and issues surrounding women, gender, and voice as well as race, ethnicity, and identity in opera. She has published articles on Italian opera, Schoenberg, and women and black composers, and her book *Voicing Gender: Castrati, Travesti, and the Second Woman in Early Nineteenth-Century Italian Opera* was published in 2006. Her current work explores blackness in opera since 1985 in the United States and in postapartheid South Africa.

MELINDA BOYD is Assistant Professor of Music History and Chair of the Music History Division in the School of Music at the University of Northern Iowa. She received her Ph.D. from the University of British Columbia and is coeditor and contributing author of the interdisciplinary volume *A Vision of the Orient: Texts, Intertexts, and Contexts of Madame Butterfly* (2006). With Karin Pendle, she is coeditor of the second edition of *Women and Music: A Research and Information Guide* (2010). Her research interests include nineteenth- and twentieth-century opera, aesthetics, popular music and culture, and women composers. Boyd is currently completing a monograph on women opera composers.

GWYNNE KUHNER BROWN is Assistant Professor of Music History and Theory at the University of Puget Sound. She received her Ph.D. in music history from the University of Washington in 2006, with a dissertation titled "Problems of Race and Genre in the Critical Reception of *Porgy and Bess.*" She has presented her research at national meetings of the American Musicological Society and the Society for American Music. Her current research focuses on arrangements of Negro spirituals by African Americans and on the life and work of composer and choral director William Levi Dawson.

KAREN M. BRYAN is Director of the School of Music at the University of South Florida. She received her Ph.D. in musicology from Indiana University. Her areas of research include *primo ottocento* Italian opera and African American operatic performance. She is completing work on the history of the National Negro Opera Company and is engaged in research on regional opera companies represented by the American Guild of Musical Artists from 1936 to the present.

MELISSA J. DE GRAAF is Assistant Professor of Musicology at the Frost School of Music at the University of Miami, where she teaches courses in twentieth-century music, American music, and music and gender. She received her Ph.D. in musicology from Brandeis University. Her articles have appeared in *MLA Notes* and *American Music*. De Graaf contributed to *Aaron Copland and His World*, edited by Judith Tick and Carol Oja, and *Ruth Crawford Seeger's Worlds*, edited by Ellie Hisama and Ray Allen. She is currently writing a book about music in the New Deal and the New York Composers' Forum concerts, 1935–40, in which she discusses issues of modernism, national identity, politics, race, and gender.

CHRISTOPHER R. GAUTHIER is a Ph.D. candidate in the Department of Sociology at the University of Michigan. His research focuses on analyzing how race is constructed, performed, and contested in the United States in the post–civil rights era. He is currently collecting ethnographic data at a voluntarily desegregated suburban high school for a dissertation on the formation and expression of white racial identities. As a musician, he is also interested in bringing sociological theory and inquiry to the study of Western art music. In 2005 he published a paper with Jennifer McFarlane-Harris that examined discipline, control, and representations of the colonized subject in Verdi's *Aida*. His general interests within sociology include the sociology of education, race and culture, twentieth-century metropolitan history, and identity.

JENNIFER MCFARLANE-HARRIS received her Ph.D. in English and Women's Studies from the University of Michigan in 2010. Her dissertation, "Autobiographical Theologies: Subjectivity and Religious Language in Spiritual Narratives, Poetry, and Hymnody by African-American Women, 1830–1900," explores the function of divinity in these texts and theology making as self-constitutive. She is also coauthor with Christopher Gauthier of the article "Verdi's Disciplined Subjects: Radames, Amneris, and the Power of the Panopticon," published in the *Discourse of Sociological Practice*. In the fall of 2011, McFarlane-Harris joined the faculty at Messiah College in Grantham, Pennsylvania, as Assistant Professor of English.

GAYLE MURCHISON is Associate Professor in the Department of Music and Program in Africana Studies at the College of William and Mary. She received her Ph.D. in musicology from Yale University. Her research interests include William Grant Still, Aaron Copland, Mary Lou Williams, music of the Harlem Renaissance, and post–World War II African American popular music. Her book *The American Stravinsky: The Early Works of Aaron Copland, 1921–1938* is forthcoming. She is currently researching a biography of William Grant Still and a book on black popular music and civil rights.

GUTHRIE P. RAMSEY JR. is the Edmund J. and Louise W. Kahn Term Professor of Music at the University of Pennsylvania. He specializes in American music, jazz, African American music, cultural studies, popular music, film studies, and historiography. After receiving his Ph.D. from the University of Michigan, Ramsey has had the distinction of being a Thurgood Marshall Dissertation Fellow at Dartmouth and a DuBois Institute Fellow at Harvard and has taught at Tufts University, Princeton University, and Harvard University. He has also been recognized for his published work as the recipient of the Lowens Award, from the Society for American Music for best article on an American music topic. His book *Race Music: Black Cultures from Bebop to Hip-Hop* (2003) was named Outstanding Book of the Year by the International Association for the Study of Popular Music. His book on jazz pianist Bud Powell, titled *In Walked Bud: Earl Bud Powell and the Modern Jazz Challenge*, is forthcoming. Along with his academic work, Ramsey is also active as a pianist, composer, and leader of jazz sextet Dr. Guy's MusiQology.

ERIC SAYLOR is Associate Professor of Music History at Drake University, specializing in British music of the nineteenth and twentieth centuries. He completed his graduate studies in musicology at Arizona State University and the University of Michigan, where he completed his doctoral dissertation on the significance of nation in the music of Ralph Vaughan Williams. His research has been published in the *Journal of the Royal Musical Association, Musical Quarterly, Nineteenth-Century Music Review,* and *Musik-Konzepte*, and he has presented at national conferences of the American Musicological Society, the Society for American Music, and the North American British Music Studies Association. He is also the author of the Vaughan Williams entry in *Oxford Bibliographies Online* and is a contributor to the second edition of the *New Grove Dictionary of American Music.* His other areas of interest include pastoralism, historiography, intersections of music and politics, and shape-note hymnody.

SARAH SCHMALENBERGER is Associate Professor of Music History, teaching music history and horn at the University of St. Thomas in St. Paul, Minnesota. She earned her Ph.D. in musicology from the University of Minnesota. Her research on black women in the concert tradition includes extensive study of the Washington Conservatory of Music (featured in the new anthology *Black Women in Music: More than the Blues*) and the discovery of an opera manuscript of Shirley Graham Du Bois (which appears in *Black Music Research Journal*). She is the Principal Investigator of the Life and Livelihood Study, a qualitative inquiry into the occupational and medical well-being of musicians surviving breast cancer. Schmalenberger is an active freelance musician on both modern and Baroque horns.

ANN SEARS is Professor of Music and Director of Performance at Wheaton College in Norton, Massachusetts, where she teaches piano and courses in American music and holds the Mary Heuser Endowed Chair for the Arts. She has degrees from the New England Conservatory of Music, Arizona State University, and the Catholic University of America, where her doctoral dissertation was about American art song in turn-of-the-century Boston. She has presented papers and lecture-recitals at national meetings of the Society for American Music, the College Music Society, and the American Matthay Association, while her research has been published in the *Journal for Black Music Research, Feel the Spirit: Studies in Nineteenth-Century Afro-American Music,* and the *International Dictionary of Black Composers.* Her research interests include American art song, the concert tradition in African American music, and American opera and musical theater.

GEORGE SHIRLEY is the Joseph Edgar Maddy Distinguished University Professor Emeritus of Music and former Director of the Vocal Arts Division of the University of Michigan School of Music, Theatre, and Dance. He has won international acclaim for his performances with the Metropolitan Opera and with major opera houses and festivals in Europe, Asia, and South America. Shirley received a Grammy Award in 1968 for his role as Ferrando in the RCA recording of Mozart's *Così fan Tutte.* He has performed more than eighty operatic roles as well as oratorio and recital literature over the span of his fifty-two-year career.

JONATHAN O. WIPPLINGER is Assistant Professor of German at North Carolina State University. He received his Ph.D. in German languages and literatures from the University of Michigan. His work explores the intersection of music, culture, and literature in Germany, with particular focus on the early twentieth century. He has published on jazz during the Weimar Republic and African American music and culture in journals such as *Germanic Review* and *German Quarterly.*

Index

Note: Page numbers in *italics* indicate illustrations. The letter *t* following a page number indicates a table.

Aber, Adolf, 246
Addison, Adele, 264
Africa (Still, orchestral suite), 147
African American opera tradition, 142–44, 262–64
African heritage, 122–23, 125–28, 150–53, 155–56, 193. *See also* drums and drumming; *specific works*
"African incantations," 193
"Africanist" presence, ix, 1, 4, 7, 7n3, 144
Afro-American Folksongs (Krehbiel), 81
Afro-American Symphony (Still), 147, 148, 162
Afro-Cuban spirituals and blues, 221–22
Agate, Edward, 83, 96n17
Aida (Verdi): 12, 31, 80, 85, 88, 96n8, 165, 263, 265, 267, 271, 272; "blacking up," 2; blackness, 5; Egyptian nationalism, 58, 59; European domination, 57, 58–59; exoticism, 64–66, 74n48; Orientalism, 56–58, 71n12, 72n14, 72n17; political and social context, 69–70, 75n64; power, 67–68, 74n55; premieres, 55, 58, 70n3; race/class distinctions and contradictions, 88; race relations, 55–56; racial difference portrayed by music, 60–61, 63–64, 66, 67, 74n39; racial Other, 58, 69; racial politics, 59–61; women and nationalism, 67, 74n55; woodwinds, 60–61, 66. *See also* Verdi, Giuseppe
Ainsi parle l'oncle (Price-Mars), 125
Airborne Symphony (Blitzstein), 266
"Alexander's Ragtime Band" (Berlin), 244
alienation and violence, 18–19, 23–25
Allen, Ray, 178
American popular music, 236
American Theatre (magazine), 178
American Tragedy (Evergood), 200
American Tragedy (Picker), 273
Amistad (Davis), 7
Anderson, Albert, 87
Anderson, Benedict, 60
Anderson, Marian, 264
Angelou, Maya, 180n6
animal masks: *Denmark Vesey* (Bowles), 188–89, 194–96
Anne of Denmark. *See* Queen Anne (wife of James I)
Armitage, Merle, 171
Arroyo, Martina, 264
Arshansky, Michael, 269–70
artificiality, 223–29
Arvey, Verna, 146, 149
"Atlanta Compromise" (Booker T. Washington), 111–12
Atlanta Symphony Orchestra, 102
authentic/authenticity: 4, 84, 88, 109, 129, 142, 168–69, 181n18, 187, 192, 196, 199, 200, 212, 227, 229, 243, 248; and blackface, 247; in dance, 222; instruments, 128, 130; jazz, 250; in language, 191, 215, 221; make-up, 271; in music, 243, 244; in performance, 107, 168, 185n65, 206n12; visual, 97
ayres, 38

Bailey, Pearl, 171, 172, 218t
Baker, Houston, 144
Baldwin, James, 212, 221
ballet, 141, 142, 157
banjo, 20–22, 28n24, 87, 88, 240, 242, 253
banjo music, 237–38
Bantock, Granville, 91
Baresel, Alfred, 246
Barnes, Irving, 182n29
Barthelemy, Anthony Gerard, 40–41, 42
Bayou Legend, A (Still), 141
Bechet, Sidney, 110
Beecham, Thomas, 80, 83, 96n7, 96n17, 97n21
Belafonte, Harry, 218t, 223–25, 226, 228, 229
Bell, Jutta, 79, 81, 82, 96n16
Bennett, Robert Russell, 217, 222
Berg, Alban, 12, 18, 27n3
Berger, Richard, 217
Berlin, Edward, 103, 109
Berlin, Irving, 244
Bess (character), 22–23, 171–76, 183n41
Bing, Rudolf, 264
Bishop, Tom, 38–39
"blackamoors," 32, 35. *See also* blackface
Black Atlantic, 151
"black buck" stereotype, 224–25
blackface: 2, 7n3, 28n21, 191, 237, 238, 243, 246, 250, 251, 254n9, 256n55, 257n75; *Carmen Jones* (Hammerstein), 213; *Jonny spielt auf* (Krenek), 20, 244, 247, 248; *Koanga* (Delius), 88, 94, 97n26; *The Masque of Blackness* (Ferrabosco), 33, 40–42, 43–45, 47–48; *Show Boat* (Kern, Hammerstein), 213; significance, 47–48. *See also* minstrelsy
Black Haiti: A Biography of Africa's Eldest Daughter (Niles), 123
"blacking up," 2–4, 5. *See also* blackface
Black Majesty (Vandercook), 120
blackness: ix–x, 19–20, 39, 47–48, 61, 79; of Africans, 41–42, 63–64, 69; *Denmark Vesey* (Bowles), 187–92; in English nomenclature, 41; *Jonny spielt auf* (Krenek), 2, 237, 243, 247, 249, 251; *Koanga* (Delius), 90–94; Monostatos (character), 266; Othello (character), 23; George Shirley, 260
black Other: 3, 4; *Aida* (Verdi), 56, 58, 61–64, 65, 67, 69; *Carmen Jones* (Hammerstein), 222–23; *Carmen Jones* (Preminger), 212–13; *Jonny spielt auf* (Krenek), 249; *Koanga* (Delius), 79, 84, 85, 88, 91–92; *Madama Butterfly* (Puccini), 215; *The Masque of Beauty* (Ferrabosco), 43–45; *The Masque of Blackness* (Ferrabosco), 33, 36, 39, 40–42, 47–48; *Otello* (Verdi), 14, 16, 23; Otherness, 5, 33; *Porgy and Bess* (Gershwin), 11; varieties, 5; white vs., 47–48
Bledsoe, Jules, 263, 264
Blitzstein, Marc, 199, 266
Bloechel, Olivia, 46
Blue Steel (Still): African American opera tradition, 144; ballet, 157; characters, 149–50; collaborators, 148–50; composition, 141; creative process, 141–43, 148–50; diasporic black cultures, 153; drums and drumming, 149–50, 156–57; Haiti, 153–54; Harlem Renaissance, 144, 151–53; incomplete nature, 160–61n29; plot, 149; primitivism, 157; setting, 149, 156; sources, 149–50; vernacular music influence, 144; voudon, 150, 153–54, 155–57. *See also* Still, William Grant
Bogle, Donald, 219, 223–25, 229, 233n59
Bohlman, Philip, 1
Bontemps, Arna, 121, 147
"Borough, The" (Crabbe), 18–19
Bowers, Thomas, 262–63
Bowles, Paul, 4, 6, 187, 202, 204–5. See also *Denmark Vesey* (Bowles)
Boyd, Nathan, 264–65
Brawley, Benjamin, 192
Brice, Carol, 264
Britten, Benjamin, 12, 18–19, 28n20. See also *Peter Grimes* (Britten)
Broadway, 110, 143, 146, 161n36, 165, 166, 168, 178, 181n14, 199, 208n38, 212, 213–14, 215, 218, 222, 225–26, 230
Brown, Anne, 165, 167–68, 169, 170, 182n29, 184n48
Bryant, Glenn, 218t, 225
Bubbles, John W., 169–70, 182n48
Büchner, Georg, 18. See also *Woyzeck* (Büchner); *Wozzeck* (Berg)
Bumbry, Grace, 174, 176, 183n46, 184n48
Burck, Jacob, 200
Busch, Hans, 58

Cable, George Washington, 78, 80–81, 82, 84, 86, 87, 88, 96nn9–12, 97n20, 97n26, 98n35, 107
Calinda, 98n35, 188, 193, 206n4
call-and-response, 104, 106, 107, 193
Candomblé, 5, 156
Caribbean: 5, 6, 11; African diaspora, 149,

151, 153, 155, 157, 158n4; U. S. interests, 119
Carleton, Dudley, 32–33, 50n41, 51n48. *See also* diaspora, African
Carley, Lionel, 91
Carmen (Bizet), 212–13, 216–17, 218, 219, 220t, 221–23, 228, 231n23, 231n26, 232n39, 266
Carmen Jones (film). See *Carmen Jones* (Preminger)
Carmen Jones (Hammerstein): artificiality, 223–29; background, 213–18; blackness representations, 229–30; black Other, 222–23; black vernacular translation, 220–21, 220t, 222; as box-office hit, 212; criticism, 221; ending, 218; exoticism, 222–23; as Hammerstein anomaly, 216; music and lyrics, 221–23; overviews, 212–13, 229–30; reviews, 226; setting, 218, 231n23; singing, 225–26; stereotypes, 213, 219, 226. *See also* Hammerstein, Oscar
Carmen Jones (Preminger): cast, 224; criticism, 212; dance, 223; drums and drumming, 228; dubbing, 226–28; filmmaking technology, 223; sexuality, 222, 227–28; singing, 226–29; stereotypes, 223, 224–25; voiceovers, 225, 226–29. *See also* Hammerstein, Oscar; Preminger, Otto
Carolina Low-Country, The (Society for the Preservation of Spirituals, 1932), 201
Carpenter, John Alden, 142
Carroll, Diahann, 218t
Catfish Row, 22, 25, 170, 171, 177, 180n7, 181n19, 191, 227. See also *Porgy and Bess* (Gershwin)
Catholic religion/church: 124; Catholicism, 126, 154; ritual, 126
Chadwick, George, 146
chant(s), 106, 107, 189, 190, 193, 194
charismatic black leader stereotype, 85–86
"chocolate" descriptor, 12–13
Chocolate Kiddies, 244, 255n37
Christianity: and African religion, 150; black, 156; conversion to/from, 82, 153
Christian Old Testament, 105, 107–8
Civil War (United States), 6, 75n64, 101, 103
Clarke, Hope (director), 177–79
classical music: 6–7; classical training, 169, 181n13, 263; compared to ragtime, 101, 143; *Jonny spielt auf* (Krenek), 19–20, 21
Code Noir, 80, 81, 96n12
Coleridge-Taylor, Samuel, 27n4, 95n3
colonialism, 23, 61–64, 73n35, 154
Colonising Egypt (Mitchell), 58–59
colonization/colonizing: 41, 62; of Africa, 2, 13, 62; from within, 59
"Come Away" (Ferrabasco), 36–37, *37*, 38–39
commedia dell'arte, 40
Committee For Industrial Organization, 202
Communist: 208nn44–45, 208–9n51; insurrection/revolution, 200; Party, 202–3, 204
Composers' Forum (New York), 187, 190–91, 197, 205n2, 209n54
Congress of Industrial Organizations (CIO), 202, 208n45
"conjure," 5, 144, 148, 150, 153, 154, 188, 193, 205n1. *See also* voudon
Cook, Susan C., 247
Cook, Will Marion, 110
Crabbe, George, 18
Craig, Douglas, 83–84, 97n21, 98n43, 99n48
Creole: language, 125; music and culture, 80–81, 88, 222; stories, 81
Crisis of the Negro Intellectual, The (Cruse), 164, 180n1
Cruse, Harold, 164, 180n1
Cullen, Countee, 147, 148, 149, 153, 158
Cyprus, 14, 27–28n13

d'Alaux, Gustave, 193–94
Dale, Clamma, 173, 183nn39–41
dance: 26; African American, 143; *Aida* (Verdi), 65–66, 74n48; *Blue Steel* (Still), 150, 152, 156, 157; calinda, 188, 193, 206n4; *Carmen Jones* (Preminger), 222–23; *Denmark Vesey* (Bowles), 193, 206n4; jazz, 19; *Jonny spielt auf* (Krenek), 242; *Koanga* (Delius), 81, 88, 98n35; *The Masque of Blackness* (Ferrabosco), 34–38, 39, 45, 46, 47, 49n21, 50n30, 51n48; *Ouanga!* (White, Matheus), 122, 123–24, 125, 127, 128, 129–30; *Treemonisha* (Joplin), 104, 107, 109
Dandridge, Dorothy, 171, 172, 223–24, 225, 226, 227–29, 232–33n42, 233n59
Daniello (character), 20–21, 29n28, 240–42, 244, 252, 253
Daniels, Billie, 264
darkness. *See* blackness
"daughter of Africa," 123
Davis, Anthony, 7
Davis, Sammy Jr., 171, 172
Davy, Gloria, 264
Dawson, Mary Cardwell, 128, 130, 263–64
Death of a Communist (Burck), 200

Delius, Frederick, 78–80, 87–94, 88, *89*, *90*, *93*
Denmark Vesey (Bowles): 200–204; African American folklore, 200, 201; African American musical instruments, 196–97, *196*, *197*; "African incantations," 193; animal masks, 188–89, 194–96; authenticity, 192–99, 194–95, 206n3; blackness in libretto, 192–94; call-and-response, 193; chant, 193; characters, 188; Communist-style revolution, 200, 201; criticism, 190–91, 209n54; exoticism, 192; fallen hero, 201; first performance, 187, 209n54; Haiti, 194; incomplete nature, 204–5; leftist imagery and elements, 202–4; love vs. hate, 194; Marxist imagery, 200, 201; overview, 187; plot, 188–90; as "race opera," 205; recording, 204–5; songs, 197–99, *197*, *198*, *199*; stereotypes, 200; themes, 194–95; voudon, 192, 205n1, 206n3. *See also* Bowles, Paul; Ford, Charles Henri
Der Rosenkavalier (Strauss), 267
Description de l'Égypte (Mariette), 57
Dessalines, Jean-Jacques (character), 118, 121, 138n16. See also *Ouanga!* (White, Matheus); White, Clarence Cameron
dialect: 109–11; African, 125; *Carmen Jones* (Hammerstein), 215, 222, 224, 225; *Porgy and Bess* (Gershwin), 168, 173, 178
diaspora, African, ix, 1, 5, 117, 143, 151, 152, 155, 158n4
diasporic black cultures, 4, 142, 156
Die Entfürung aus dem Serail (Mozart), 271
Die Fledermaus (Strauss), 271
Die Meistersinger von Nürnberg (Wagner), 79, 85
Die Zauberflöte (Mozart), 266, 267, 271, *271*
Different Shade of Colonialism, A (Powell), 61–63
disposizione scenica, 15, 16
Dixon, Dean, 266
Djamileh (Bizet), 271
Dobbs, Mattiwilda, 264
Don Pasquale (Donizetti), 271
Dowdy, Helen, 168
Downes, Olin, 226, 248
Dragonetti, Domenico, 15
drums and drumming: 127, 128; *Blue Steel* (Still), 150–51, 156–58; *Carmen Jones* (Preminger), 228; *Denmark Vesey* (Bowles), 193, 196; *Emperor Jones* (O'Neill), 156–57; *Jonny spielt auf* (Krenek), 238; *Ouanga!* (White, Matheus), 127–30, 138–39n33; *Porgy and Bess* (Gershwin), 178; as signifiers of Africa, 157–58
Drums of Haiti (Hughes), 154
Du Bois, Shirley Graham, 143, 144
Du Bois, W. E. B., 101, 112–13, 119, 143, 144, 147, 151, 153, 157, 158n4, 192
Du Locle, Camille, 61
Dunbar, Paul Laurence, 110
Duncan, Todd, 167, 168, 171, 181n13, 264
Dunham, Katherine, 121, 153
DuPree, William, 264

echoing, 39
Edward VI, 41
Eichhorn, Andreas, 246
Elixir of Love (Donizetti), 145
Elizabeth I, 41, 42
Ellington, Duke, 191, 199, 216, 233n60
Elzy, Ruby, 168
Emperor Jones (Gruenberg), 191. *See also* Gruenberg, Louis
Emperor Jones (O'Neill), 120, 138n11, 144, 154, 156–57, 158, 161n36, 191, 200. *See also* O'Neill, Eugene
Entartete Musik, 249
Ernst, Alfred, 102
essentialism, x
Estes, Simon, 173–74
Esther (Meyerowitz), 269
Ethiopia/Ethiopians, 7n3, 42, *44*, 56, 58 61, 63–64, 66, 67, 69, 70, 72n17, 72n19, 73n34, 88
Europeanization, 58–59
Evans, Allen, 249–50, 257n64
Evans, Damon, 174
Evanti, Lillian (Evans-Tibbs), 263–64
Evening Standard (newspaper), 272
Evergood, Philip, 200
exoticism: *Aida* (Verdi), 64–66, 74n48; blackness as exotic or Other, 4; *Carmen (Bizet)*, 212; *Carmen Jones* (Hammerstein), 215, 222–23; *Denmark Vesey* (Bowles), 192; *Koanga* (Delius), 78, 79, 80, 82, 84, 89, 91–92, 94, 98n37; masculinity, 11–18; *The Masque of Blackness* (Ferrabosco), 44–45, 47–48; music, 44–45, 64–66; Otello (character), 12–13. *See also* Orientalism
Extase (Duparc), 267

Fahmy, Khaled, 59
fallen hero stereotype, 200, 201
Falstaff (Verdi), 80, 96n7

Fate (leitmotif), 92–93, *93*
Fauser, Annegret, 216, 217, 219, 226, 231n23
Fauset, Arthur Huff, 153
Faust (Gounod), 216, 267
Federal Music Project, 187, 205–6n2
Federal Theatre Project, 214
Federal Writers' Project, 107
Fenby, Eric, 83–84, 87, 91
Ferrabosco, Alfonso, 32, 36, 37–40, 45, 47, 49n21, 49n25, 50nn30–31. See also *The Masque of Beauty* (Ferrabosco); *The Masque of Blackness* (Ferrabosco)
Fétis, François-Joseph, 57
Fleurant, Gerdes, 127
Floyd, Samuel A., ix–x, 1, 151
Flying Dutchman (Wagner), 145
folk: 103; dialect, 225; folklore, 154, 192, 194, 195, 196, 201, 205n1, 206n3, 207n18, 207n32; magic, 187, 200; opera, 20, 170; religions, 154, 156; tunes and music, 78, 81, 87–89, 94, 96n11, 111, 166, 199, 206n12, 222, 237, 241, 243, 244, 245
Folk Beliefs of the Southern Negro (Puckett), 193
Ford, Charles Henri, 4, 187,188, 192–97, 199, 200–202, 203–4, 205–6n2, 206nn3–4, 206n6, 206–7n17, 207n19, 208n38, 209nn54–55. See also *Denmark Vesey* (Bowles)
Fordin, Hugh, 215–17
former slaves' memories, 107–9
Forsythe, Harold Bruce, 142, 147, 148, 149, 155–57
Foster, Stephen, 244, 251, 256n48
Foucault, Michel, 59, 71n6, 72n22
Four Saints in Three Acts (Thomson), 7, 88, 159–60n23
Freeman, Harry Lawrence, 143, 144
French Grand Opera, 80, 82, 97n21
French Revolution, 118
Frierson, Andrew, 264
Future Belongs to the Workers (Quirt), 200

Gates, Henry Louis, 144
Gershwin, George: 4, 6, 12, 19–20, 22, 24, 27n3, 28n25, 106, 165–71, 174, 177–80, 180–81n7, 181n8, 181nn13–14, 181n17, 183n36, 184n60, 191, 219, 222, 231n23, 256n46, 268, 273. See also *Porgy and Bess* (Gershwin)
Gershwin, Ira, 165
Gilbert and Sullivan, 214–15
Glanville-Hicks, Peggy, 204–5, 209nn55–56
Glyndebourne Festival *Porgy and Bess* production (1986), 173–77
Goldman, Sherwin M., 173
Goldwyn, Samuel, 171–72, 182n30
Goldwyn film production of *Porgy and Bess*. See *Porgy and Bess* (Preminger)
"good colored boy" stereotype, 224–25
grand opera tradition, 11, 27n1
Graziano, John, 213
Great American Opera, 20, 28n24
"Great Migration," 148, 196, 207n32
Greenfield, Elizabeth Taylor, 262
group improvisation, 106
Gruenberg, Louis, 120, 142, 154, 157, 191. See also *Emperor Jones* (Gruenberg)
Guest of Honor, A (Joplin), 101
Gullah: dialect, 168, 178; music, 170
gypsy, 212, 218, 219, 220, 222, 223, 224

Haiti: *Denmark Vesey* (Bowles): 194; dual view, 116–17; Harlem Renaissance writers and artists, 121, 158n4; history and American occupation, 6, 116–17, 118–21, 125–28, 137n3, 156, 161n41, 189, 194; Matheus research, 122; musical instruments, 128; opera, 159–60n23; *Ouanga!* (White, Matheus), 116–17, 128; Save Haiti Committee, 119; as subject for popular media, 120–21; voudon, 120, 144, 153, 154–55, 156, 158, 193, 205n1
Hall, Juanita, 187, 197, 209n54
Hammerstein, Oscar, 212–13, 215–23, 231nn19–20. See also *Carmen Jones* (Hammerstein)
Handy, W. C., 146
Haney López, Ian F., 56
Hansberry, Lorraine, 164
Harlem, 192
Harlem Renaissance: African American opera tradition, 142–43; African heritage, 150–53; *Blue Steel* (Still), 144, 151–53; *Denmark Vesey* (Bowles), 192; Haiti treatment by writers and artists, 121; John Frederick Matheus, 122; multiple African diaspora nation focus, 158n4; *Ouanga!* (White, Matheus), 129, 138–39n33; William Grant Still, 156–58; symbols in antidiscrimination battle, 160n25; writers and composers, 6, 117. *See also specific writers and composers*
Harlem Workers School, 203
Harry Ransom Humanities Research Center, 187–88

Haymon, Cynthia, 177
Henry VIII, 41
"Heritage" (Cullen), 153
Herndon, Arthur, 264, 267
Herskovits, Melville, 143
Heyward, Dorothy, 180–81n7, 201, 209n54
Heyward, DuBose, 20, 28n25, 167, 170, 178, 179, 180–81n7, 191, 201, 208n38, 209n54. See also *Porgy and Bess* (Gershwin)
Hiawatha's Wedding Feast (Coleridge-Taylor), 95n3
Hicks, James, 164, 165
Highway 1, U.S.A. (Still), 145. *See also* Still, William Grant
Holiday, Billie, 208–9n51
Holland, Charles, 264, 266–67
Holt, Nora, 221
Homer, Sidney, 110
hoodoo, 5, 205n1. *See also* voudon
Horne, Marilyn, 218t, 226–28
Hot Mikado, 214–15, 221–24, 230n8
Houston Grand Opera's *Porgy and Bess* productions, 173, 177–79, 184n55
Hughes, Langston, 10, 120–21, 129, 147, 148, 154, 155, 157, 158n4, 203
Hunter College Opera Workshop, 270–71, 274n1
Hurston, Zora Neale, 121, 129, 138–39n33, 143, 144, 153, 156, 157, 158n4
Hutcherson, LeVern, 218t, 226–28, 233n55

I Dream a World: The Operas of William Grant Still (Soll), 149
Il Trovatore (Verdi), 145
Imagined Communities (Anderson), 60
imperialism, 58–59, 61–64, 70, 71n35, 75n64, 154
Indianapolis Freeman (newspaper), 102–3
In One Lifetime (Arvey), 146
International Labor Defense, 203
Isolde (character): 92, 94, 95; analogous character, 92, 93–94
I Walked with a Zombie (film), 120

James I (of England), 32, 34, 36, 41–42, 45–47, 48, 48nn5–6, 46n8, 50–51n42, 52n53
James VI (of Scotland). *See* James I (of England)
Jarboro, Caterina, 263, 264
jazz opera, 236–37, 243, 246, 247
Jazz Singer, The, 251–52
Jessye, Eva, 165, 181n9
Johnson, Hall, 191
Johnson, James Weldon, 116–17, 119, 120, 121, 129, 256n55
Jolson, Al, 20, 244, 248, 251–52
Jones, Inigo, 32, 39, 42, *43*
Jones, John Bush, 229
Jonny (character), 12, 18–22, 25–26, 28n26, 29n28, 237–46, *239*
Jonny spielt auf (Krenek): 19–22; blackface, 20, 244, 247, 248; black Other, 249; cast, 250–51, 252; criticism, 256n55; German revivals, 249–50; influences, 256n46; jazz, 236–37, 246; later performances and recordings, 250–51; Metropolitan Opera production, 248–49; minstrelsy, 238–39, 241–42, 248, 249, 250, 251–52; modernism, 21, 236; music, 241–46; Nazism, 247–48, 249; new vs. old, 19, 20; overviews, 236–37; plot, 252–53; post World War II productions, 256n53; problematic nature, 252; reviews, 246–47, 248, 250; sexuality, 21, 239–41, 242; spirituals, 243; stereotypes, 237–41, *239*, 243–46; transcendence of stereotype, 20. *See also* Krenek, Ernst
Jonson, Ben, 32, 34–36, 37, 38, 39, 40–41, 45–46, 48n9, 49nn20–21, 50n34, 50–51n42. See also *The Masque of Blackness* (Ferrabosco)
Joplin, Scott, 6, 101–3, 104, 109–11, 112–13, 133n6, 151. See also *Treemonisha* (Joplin)

Katz, Sam, 215–16, 217
Keary, Charles, 78–79, 81–86, 91–92, 94, 95, 96n17, 97n20, 97nn27–28
Kenyon, Nicholas, 177
Kern, Jerome, 213, 216, 231n23
Kirstein, Lincoln, 204
Koanga (Delius): African American music, 79, 81, 87, 88, 94; blackness model, 90–94; characterization, 96n16; charismatic black leader stereotype, 86; complexity and instability, 97n23; creative intent, 78–79; dichotomies, 79; exoticism, 78, 79, 82, 91–92, 98n37; flashback frame, 82, 85; French Grand Opera influence, 80, 82; Italian opera influence, 80; libretto, 81–86, 90, 91–92, 96nn16–17; "noble savage," 86, 89–90, 97n23, 98n41; Orientalism, 85, 91–92, 98n37; overview, 92–94; power and race, 84–85; powerlessness and punishment, 85–86, 92–94, 99n48; premiere, 78, 95nn1–3; problematic nature, 94; protagonists, 78, 84; race/class distinctions and contradictions, 5, 88–89, 90–91, 98n43;

racial Other, 79, 84, 91–92; racism codified, 80–81; Romantic influence, 78–79, 85, 91–92; slave chorus, 88–89, 97n23; source, 78; supernatural plot devices, 85, 97n27, 97n28; textual variations, 81, 83–85, 84t; tone, 82; voudon spirits, 86, 97n27; influence of Wagner, 79, 80–81, 82, 92, 94. *See also* Delius, Frederick
Krehbiel, Henry, 81, 96n11
Krenek, Ernst, 19, 142, 236–37, 238, 241, 243, 250, 254n11, 255n37. See also *Jonny spielt auf* (Krenek)

La Bohème (Puccini), 216, 260, *261*, 267
La Forza del Destino (Verdi), 85, 267
La Guiablesse (Still), 141
Largey, Michael, 125
leftist imagery and elements, 200–204
"Legacy of Ancestral Arts, The" (Locke), 152
Levee Land (Still), 146
Levine, James, 175
L'Heure Espagnole (Ravel), 268
lined-out hymns, 104
Linn, Michael von der, 238
Locke, Alain, 144, 151, 152–53, 156, 157, 161n34, 192
Locke, Ralph, 70, 98n37
locus topicus: 143–44, 153, 154; voudon, 155–57
Lohengrin (Wagner), 79
Loppert, Max, 177
Lorde, Audre, 67–68
Lott, Eric, 247
Louise (Charpentier), 216
L'Ouverture, Toussaint, 6, 117, 118, 131, 137n3
Love and Theft (Lott), 247
Lulu Belle (Sheldon, MacArthur), 216

MacArthur, Charles, 216
Madama Butterfly (Puccini), 215, 216
madrigalism, 39
Magic Island (Seabrook), 120
makeup, 2–3, 33, 43, 44–45, 52n55, 83, 87, 238, 247, 248, 251, 268–72, 273
Manhattan Opera Company, 217, 231n20
Manon (Massenet), 271
"Maple Leaf Rag" (Joplin), 101, 102
Margaret Garner (Danielpour), 7, 273
Mariette, Auguste, 57
Marshall, Harriet Gibbs, 119, 137n9
Marshall, Napoleon, 119
Marx/Marxist, 187, 200, 201, 203
masculinity, 11–18
mask(s), 40, 43, 47, 52n55, 247, 250. *See also* animal masks; *Denmark Vesey* (Bowles)
Masque of Beauty, The (Ferrabosco), 34–36, 35t
Masque of Blackness, The (Ferrabosco): 43; blackface, 33, 40–42, 44–45, 47–48; blackness devalued, 42, 50n38–51n42; compositional conventions, 38–39; dance, 51n48; definition of black only in relation to white races, 47–48; dramatic elements clarified by music, 39–40; emblems and impresa, 34–35, 35t; English music, 45–46; exoticism, 44–45, 47–48; music, 36–45, 49n21; political content, 34, 36, 40, 41–42, 47–48; sovereign power, 42–43; spectacle, 44–45; values implied by music, 46–48. *See also* Ferrabosco, Alfonso
masques, 33–34, 36, *44*
Matheus, John Frederick, 116, 121, 122, 129, 137n5. See also *Ouanga!* (White, Matheus); White, Clarence Cameron
Mattheson, Johann, 143
Matthews, Ralph, 191
Max (character), 19, 21, 236, 238, 240, 244, 246, 250, 251, 252, 253, 257n76
McClary, Susan, 212, 222, 227–28, 232n39
McFerrin, Robert Sr., 264
Mencken, H. L., 101
Menotti, Gian-Carlo, 266
merengue, 129, 130
Merrill, Nathaniel, 175–76, 179, 268
Metropolitan Opera, 145, 146, 173, 174, 181n8, 217, 231n20, 237, 248, 249, 250, *261*, 263, 264, 268, 271
Metropolitan Opera's *Porgy and Bess* (1985), 173–76
Meyerowitz, Jan, 269
Middle Passage, 4, 5–6, 143
Mikado, The (Gilbert & Sullivan), adaptations, 213–15
Mine Disaster (Evergood), 200
minstrelsy: 8n4; blackface, 2, 169, 237; as "black opera" for black performers, 3, 143; as British as well as American, 52n54; *Jonny spielt auf* (Krenek), 20, 28n24, 238–39, 241–42, 248–52; minstrel show, 2, 3, 20, 47, 52; *Porgy and Bess* (Gershwin), 20, 191; portraying blackness, 6; stereotypes providing norm for "African" presence, 2
Minturn, Henry, 214
miscegenation, 239–41
Mitchell, Timothy, 58–59

modernism, 142, 144, 236
Moor: 7n3, 16, 23, 40–41, 266, 271
Morehouse College, 102
Morris, Rebecca, 178
Morrison, Toni, 1, 7
Moss, Carlton, 142, 148–49, 159–60nn22–23, 160n24
Mubârak, Alî, 62, 63
music: characterization via association, 59–61; as clarifying text or narrative, 38–40; as conveyer of meaning, 36; Delius, Frederick, 87–94; echoing, 39; implication of values, 46–48; *Jonny spielt auf* (Krenek), 241–46; *Koanga* (Delius), 79, 81, 87, 88, *89*, *90*, 91–92, *93*, 94; *Masque of Blackness* (Ferrabosco), 36–45, 49n21; new compositional conventions, 38–39; Orientalism, 71nn11–12; *Ouanga!* (White, Matheus), 127–31, *134–35*; as portraying racial difference, 63–64, 66, 67, 74n39; race/class distinctions and contradictions, 88–89; as racial and value differentiator, 46–47, 52n54; racial difference portrayal, 60–61; racial implication via association, 59–61; social meaning and context factor, 56
Mussolini, Benito, 13

NAACP (National Association for the Advancement of Colored People), 119, 120
National Association for the Promotion of Labor Unionism among Negroes, 203, *203*
nationalism, 67–68
National Miners' Union (NMU), 202
National Negro Opera Company, 128, 130, 137n5, 263–64
Nazi Party, 19, 237, 247, 249, 256n62
Negritude, 168
Negro Actors' Guild, 172
Negro Folk Rhymes (Talley), 192–93
Negro Melody Singers, 187, 197, 209n54
Negro People's Theater, 209n52
New Masses (magazine), 203
Newman, Ernest, 92
New Negro, The (Locke), 150–53
New Negro Movement, 6, 142
New York Age (newspaper), 102
New York Amsterdam News (newspaper), 213
New York News (newspaper), 174
New York Times (newspaper), 174, 177, 191, 248
Niagara Movement, 111–12
Nietzsche, Friedrich, 82, 222
Niles, Blair, 123
"noble savage" stereotype, 86, 89–90, 97n23, 98n41
Nugent, Richard, 156
Nunn, Trevor, 176

Oberon (Weber), 145
O'Brien, Jack, 173
Observer (newspaper), 177
Oedipus Rex (Stravinsky), 269
"Old Folks at Home" (Foster), 244, *245*
O'Neill, Eugene, 120, 144, 154. See also *Emperor Jones* (O'Neill)
On the Trail of Negro Folk-Songs (Scarborough), 193
Opera (magazine), 177
Orgel, Stephen, 34
Orientalism: *Aida* (Verdi), 56–58, 71n11, 72n14, 72n17; *Koanga* (Delius), 85, 91–92, 98n37. *See also* exoticism
Orientalism (Said), 1, 57, 85
Orientalist, 56–58, 81, 75n64
Otello (character), 13, 14–15, 23, 88, 260, 266. See also *Otello* (Verdi); Verdi, Giuseppe
Otello (Verdi): aural cues, 15, 16, 17; character description, 14; as "chocolate project," 12–13; darkness expressed sonically, 16, *17*; double bass, 15–16; exoticism, 14; masculinity image reinforced in other operas, 18; performance of, 264; race/class distinctions and contradictions, 88; setting, 14. *See also* Verdi, Giuseppe
Ouanga! (White, Matheus): African heritage, 122–23, 127–28; characterization and contrast representation, 123–24; contrast and conflict, 138n17; costumes, 124; dance, 129; dichotomies, 117, 126, 128–29, 131; drums and drumming, 127, 128, 129–30; Haitian events and popular interest, 116–17; Haitian instruments, 128; Harlem Renaissance, 129, 138–39n33; historical foundation, 118–19; language and dialect, 124–25; music, 127–31, *134–35*; plot, 122, 131–33; purposes, 117; race pride, 122–23; religious structures, 125–27; sets, 124; social structures, 124–25; songs, 128–29; U.S. political and military action, 116–17; voudon, 125–28. *See also* Matheus, John Frederick; White, Clarence Cameron
Outlines of Primitive Belief among the Indo-European Races (Keary), 85

Page, Andrew, 83–84, 97n21, 98n43, 99n48
Pagliacci (Leoncavallo), 145, 216, 264
Palmer, Christopher, 87
Palumbo, Patrizia, 13
Parsifal (Wagner), 79
Pecheurs de Perles (Bizet), 266
Pelléas et Mélisande (Debussy), 270
Peter Grimes (Britten), 18–19, 23–24. *See also* Britten, Benjamin
Peters, Paul, 203
Phillips, Wendell, 117
Pittsburgh Post-Gazette (newspaper), 174
"Plaint: Before the Mob of 10,000 at Owensboro, Ky." (Ford), 203–4
plantation: 3, 192; *Koanga* (Delius), 82, 86, 87, 89, 91, 92; *Treemonisha* (Joplin), 103, 108, 110
Plantation Bird Legends (Young), 193
plantation nostalgia dialect vs. proper English, 109–11
Playing in the Dark: Whiteness and the Literary Imagination (Morrison), 1
Poitier, Sidney, 171, 172, 181n11, 182n31
popular music. *See* American popular music
Porgy (character), 20, 22–23, 25, 26, 167, 172, 178, 181n11
Porgy and Bess (Gershwin): 95n3, *269*; African American involvement in creation and shaping, 179–80; as African American story, 19; alienation and violence, 22–23; Angelou on, 180n6; Bregenz Festival production, 268, *269*; challenges to performers, 164; collaborative failures, 173–76; collaborative successes, 173, 176–79; critical reviews, 172, 174–75, 177, 181n17, 181n19, 184n65; criticism, 191, 229–30; as dead end for performers, 164, 268; directors, 182n29; draw for performers, 164–65; as exclusively for black performers, 164–65, 180–81n7, 273; failures of collaboration, 171–72; Glyndebourne Festival production (1986), 173–77; Gullah dialect, 168–69; Houston Grand Opera productions, 173, 177–79, 184n55; as interracial collaboration opportunity, 170, 178; irony inherent in critics' assumptions and comments, 170; minstrelsy, 20; operatic tradition of collaboration, 181n14; sociopolitical interpretations, 274n2; stereotype transcendence, 20; successful collaborations, 173, 176–79; Theatre Guild production of 1935, 165; as validation of black stereotypes, 164; vocal inflection, 106–7. *See also* Gershwin, George
Porgy and Bess (Preminger), 171–72, 182nn29–30, 183n36
power and race, 25, 26, 42–43, 64–68, 74n38, 84–85
power and sexuality, 67–68, 84, 222, 229–31, 242
powerlessness and punishment, 26, 85–86, 92–94, 99n48
Preminger, Otto, 171–72, 212
Price, Leontyne, 164, 264
Price-Mars, Jean, 125
primitivism, 121, 142, 157, 192
progress and education theme, 110–11
Puckett, Newbell Niles, 193
Puritan in Voodoo Land (Taft), 120

quartet singing, 104
Queen Anne (wife of James I), 32–33, 34, 35, 40, 42–44, 46, 48, 48n6, 49n14, 50–51n42, 51n48
Quirt, Walter, 200

race and power, 25, 26, 42–43, 64–68, 74n38, 84–85
race and sexuality, 2, 67–68, 222, 239–41, 242
race/class distinctions and contradictions, 4, 88–89, 90–91, 98n43
"race operas," 187, 205
racial categorization, 56, 71n6
racial difference portrayed by music, 60–61, 63–64, 66, 67, 74n39
"racial fabrication," 56
racial insensitivity, 87–88
racial Other. *See* black Other
racial politics: xi, 59–61; *Carmen Jones* (Hammerstein), 230; *Denmark Vesey* (Bowles), 187; *Jonny spielt auf* (Krenek), 240, 249, 251; in Louisiana, 80; race and politics, 203–4, 205, 208n45
Radano, Ronald M., x, 1
Rada rite, 127, 128, 130
ragtime, 101, 102, 110–11, 113, 239; musical style, 109; rhythms, 103, 104, 109
Rahn, Muriel, 218t, 225
Ramsey, Guthrie, 1
Rattle, Simon, 176
Reconstruction, 3, 111
Renda, Mary A., 121, 154
Rich, Frank, 213

Ricordi, Giulio, 28n15, 65
Rigoletto (Verdi), 85, 145, 267
Ring cycle (Wagner): 79, 85; "Fate" motif from, 92–93
ring dance, 104, 107
"Rising Sun (a Biography of the *Sahdji* of William Grant Still), The" (Forsythe), 155
Robeson, Paul, 213
Robinson, Bradford, 238
Robinson, Paul, 58
Romanticism, 91–92
"Roshana" (Still opera concept), 147

"Sahdji" (Nugent short story), 152
Sahdji (Still), 141, 156
Said, Edward, 1, 56–58, 85
Salome (Strauss), 266
Santería, 5, 156
savage: 14, 16, 48, 63, 85, 86, 91, 241; ennobled/noble savage, 23, 89; *Jonny spielt auf* (Krenek), 21; Romantic Savage, 6; savage nature, 26; savagery, 62, 63, 240
Saxon, Luther, 225
Scarborough, Dorothy, 193
Schlegel, August Wilhelm, 13–14
Schomburg, Arthur, 120, 152
Schuller, Gunther, 102
Seabrook, William, 120
"Self-Determining Haiti" (Johnson), 120
Set My People Free (Heyward), 201
sexuality and power, 67–68, 222, 239–41, 242
Shadow (radio show), 120
Shakespeare, William, 8n6, 13–14, 18, 23, 27n4, 40
sharecropping, 109
Sheldon, Edward, 216
"shimmy figure," 238
Shirley, George: *261*, *265*, *269*, *271*; American debut, 268; on believability, 272–73; as black man and opera singer, 260–62; on critical references to race, 271–72; European operatic debut, 260; makeup techniques, 270; on operatic characters as gentlemen of color, 270–71; professional stance, 272–73; on purpose of opera, 273–74; as racial token, 261–62; on rules of opera and theater, 272–73; stage makeup techniques, 268–69
Short, Hassard, 214
Show Boat (Kern, Hammerstein), 213
Siegmeister, Ellen, 200
signifyin(g), 144
Sklar, George, 203
Skovhus, Bo, 251–52
Slater, Montagu, 18–19
slave: 5, 7n3, 46, 63, 64, 107, 108, 187, 194, 195, 201; *Aida* (Verdi), 58, 60–61, 65, 66, 67, 69, 75n64; *Denmark Vesey* (Bowles), 189; *Koanga* (Delius), 81, 82, 83, 84, 86, 88–91, 95, 97n28, 98n39; in Mozart, 266; *Ouanga!* (White, Matheus), 121; and slaveholders, 3; slavery, 2, 4, 42, 80, 101, 105, 109, 152–53, 155, 156, 194, 197; trade, 23, 62; uprisings, 6, 118
slave chorus, 88–89
Slave Narrative Project, 194
slave narratives, 107–9
Slave Songs of the United States, 107
Smallens, Alexander, 170
Smith, Catherine Parsons, 12
Smith, Muriel, 218t, 225–26
Social History of the American Negro (Brawley), 192
Soll, Beverly, 149
songs, 128–29. *See also* music
Souls of Black Folk, The (Du Bois), 101, 112, 192
Southern, Eileen, 145
Southerners, The, 213
Southern Interlude, A (Still), 141
Southern Tenant Farmers' Union (STFU), 202
Spirito, Romolo de, 204–5, 209n56
spirituals, 84, 87, 88, 104, 107–8, 167, 175, 199, 237, 243, 245; Afro-Cuban, 222
Stag King, The (Henze), 272
Standifer, James, 174
stereotypes: "black buck," 224; *Carmen Jones* (Hammerstein), 213, 226; *Carmen Jones* (Preminger), 222, 223, 224–25, 227–28; charismatic black leader, 86; *Denmark Vesey* (Bowles), 200, 201; fallen hero, 201; good colored boy, 224–25; *Jonny spielt auf* (Krenek), 237–41, 242; *Koanga* (Delius), 86; minstrelsy, 2; "noble savage," 98n41; *Porgy and Bess* (Gershwin), 164; sexuality, 222, 227–28; "shimmy figure," 238; tragic mulatto, 164
Stevedore (Peters and Sklar), 203
Still, William Grant, 141, 144, 145–47, 155–58. See also *Blue Steel* (Still)
"Strange Funeral in Braddock" (Gold), 200
Study in Contradictions, A (Forsythe), 155

Sutton, Katie, 194
Swing Mikado, The, 214, 215, 216, 219–22, 230n6, 230n8
Szmolyn, Walter, 250

Taft, Edna, 120
Tahtawi, Rifa'ah Rafi' al, 62, 63
Talley, Thomas W., 192–93
Tannhäuser (Wagner), 79, 102
Theatre Guild production of *Porgy and Bess*, 166–71
themes. *See* power and race; power and sexuality; powerlessness and punishment; *specific operas*
They Shall Not Die (Wexley), 203
Thomson, Virgil, 142, 197, 197–98
Three Negro Songs (Still), 146
Tibbett, Lawrence, 248
Time (magazine), 221, 272
Todd, Michael, 214
Tosca (character), 11, 174, 185
Tosca (Puccini), 11, 114n26, 216, 262
tragic mulatto type, 224
Treemonisha (Joplin): 95n3, *104*, *105*, *107*, *108*; African American musical elements, 103–9; language, 109–11; plantation nostalgia dialect vs. proper English, 109–11; plot, 103; political content, 111–13; pre-performance reviews, 102; productions of 1970s, 101–2; progress and education theme, 112–13; self-publication and neglect, 101–2; western traditions and focus, 103. *See also* Joplin, Scott
trickster, 194, 207n27
Tristan: analogous character, 92, 93; character, 92, 93, 94–95, 266; chord, 92–93, *93*
Tristan und Isolde (Wagner), 79, 92, 94, 218; *Liebestod* from, 82, 86, 92
"Triumphlied," 242
Trotter, William Monroe, 112
Troubled Island (Still), 141, 148, 149
Trouble in Tahiti (Bernstein), 268
Troutt Powell, Eve M., 61–63
Turnau Opera Players, 260, 267–68, 269–70

"Uncle Tom," 167

Vandercook, John W., 120
Varèse, Edgard, 146
Vaughan, Virginia Mason, 41
Vecellio, Cesare, 42, *44*
Verdi, Giuseppe, 12–13, 15, 55, 70n2. See also *Aida* (Verdi); *Otello* (Verdi)
View from the Bridge (Bolcom), 272
violin (Amati), 20–22, 25, 240–42, 244, 253, 254n17
vocal inflection, 106
vodou. *See* voudon
voodoo. *See* voudon
voudon: 5, 78; African heritage, 116; *Blue Steel* (Still), 150, 153–54, 155–57; *Denmark Vesey* (Bowles), 192, 205n1, 206n3; *Emperor Jones* (O'Neill), 156–57; Haiti, 6, 125–28, 156; *Koanga* (Delius), 82, 84, 86, 90, 92, 96n8, 97n27; *Ouanga!* (White, Matheus), 120, 125–28; in popular media, 154; spelling variations, 5, 138n12

Ward, Thomas, 87
Warfield, William, 171
Washington, Booker T., 110–12
Weill, Kurt, 7, 142
Weiss, Julius, 102
Welles, Orson, 120
Wexley, John, 203
Whipper, Leigh, 172
White, Clarence Cameron, 116, 121, 122, 143, 144. *See also* Matheus, John Frederick; *Ouanga!* (White, Matheus)
White, Willard, 176–77, 177
Whitehill, Clarence, 87
White Zombie (film), 120
Wiener Staatsoper, 251–52
"William Grant Still: A Study in Contradictions" (Forsythe), 149
Williams, Camilla, 264
Williams, William Carlos, 208n51
Winters, Lawrence, 264
Works Progress Administration (WPA), 214, 230n8
Woyzeck (Büchner), 18
Wozzeck (Berg), 18, 19
Wozzeck (character), 19, 20, 23–24
Wright, Richard, 203

X: The Life and Times of Malcolm X (Davis), 7

Yarborough, Catherine. *See* Jarboro, Caterina
Young, Martha, 193

The University of Illinois Press
is a founding member of the
Association of American University Presses.

University of Illinois Press
1325 South Oak Street
Champaign, IL 61820-6903
www.press.uillinois.edu